The Age Distribution
of the Indian Population

The Age Distribution of the Indian Population

A reconstruction for the states and territories, 1881–1961

Sudhansu Bhusan Mukherjee

East-West Center
East-West Population Institute
Honolulu

Library of Congress Cataloging in Publication Data

Mukherjee, Sudhansu Bhusan, 1923-
 The age distribution of the Indian population.

 Bibliography: p. 243–257.
 1. Age distribution (Demography)–India.
2. India–Statistics, Vital. I. Title.
HB1679.M84   312'.92'0954   76-28367
ISBN 0-8248-0518-6

To my father

Sri Jyotish Chandra Mukherjee
(1883–1967)

and my mother

Srimati Umasashi Devi
(1894–1963)

Contents

Tables

Text tables

Basic tables

Figures

Maps, worksheets, exhibit

Foreword

The unbroken series of the decennial population censuses of India, now spanning a century, provide an extraordinarily valuable storehouse of information for students of demography. The present monograph by S.B. Mukherjee represents an important entry in the long list of demographic studies, marked by numerous notable achievements, that seek to analyze and interpret that record. The outstanding significance of Indian census statistics for demographers is easily understood if one considers the scarcity of comparable data sets. Of other large countries, only the United States and a number of European states possess census records that match the length and consistency of those available for India; and in Europe, and to a lesser extent in the United States, the existence of birth and death statistics makes the census a less important source of information for reconstructing demographic history. In what is called nowadays "the developing world," the Indian record is quite without parallel. The contrast to that other Asian giant, China, is of course particularly striking; and even among the countries of the Subcontinent, only India succeeded fully in preserving the decennial regularity of its census in the post-Independence period.

The synergistic possibilities for demographic analysis inherent in successive census descriptions of the state of a population are truly remarkable. In the hands of the skilled analyst, cross-sectional observations can be transformed into reliable estimates of indices characterizing demographic dynamics. In particular, since the age distribution of a population is a reflection of past mortality, fertility, and migration processes, information on these phenomena can be distilled from census data alone, provided that censuses supply consistent records on the size and age composition of the population at successive dates. For India as a whole, such analyses have been performed with signal success by several investigators. Work on the subnational level has been hampered, however, by a multiplicity of problems affecting the availability and comparability of data on age distribution for smaller areas. Boundary changes, lack of uniformity in the methods of collecting and publishing age information, and errors in reporting age are the main sources of the difficulty encountered by the analyst.

By successfully constructing a uniform and consistent series of age and sex distributions covering the period 1881–1961 for the main territorial subdivisions of contemporary India, Mukherjee has eliminated most of these problems and, as a result, provides the basis for deepened understanding of Indian demographic history. His results, obtained through painstaking and ingenious adjustment of data gathered from virtually hundreds of publications of nine successive censuses, not only will be accepted as an authoritative description of a phenomenon that is of interest in its own right, but will also be utilized in future demographic analyses that require such data as raw material. Mukherjee's study itself provides the best illustration of how productive the mining of such data can be by developing a variety of new estimates of population dynamics for subnational units of India. While the bulk of his study treats phenomena that lie in the domain of demographic history, this hardly diminishes the timeliness of his contribution. Understanding the past is an indispensable first step toward understanding the present and the unfolding future. Mukherjee's work will not lose significance as modern India reaches and passes a demographic watershed, the historic significance of which will be fully visible only after the 1981 census results will have been collected and made available.

Readers and users of this book will be mostly demographers. This makes it unnecessary to dwell on what will be obvious to any practitioner of the trade: the truly monumental labor and the analytical virtuosity that went into this study. To persevere in the kind of task Mr. Mukherjee set for himself would have been impossible without his special mixture of professional skills and seemingly unlimited capacity for meticulous work. During the preparation of this volume, he cheerfully coped with difficulties that would have deterred lesser souls and carried the work to conclusion with a stubborn singleness of purpose. It gives me great pleasure to register here my admiration and appreciation for his accomplishment.

Paul Demeny

Acknowledgments

I wish to express my grateful thanks to the East-West Population Institute for the fellowship offered to me in 1970 which enabled me to complete this research by March 1972. The director of the Institute, Professor Paul Demeny, provided help, inspiration, and guidance at every stage of the work. He also very kindly contributed a foreword to this volume. I cannot thank him adequately for all this.

The high-level academic atmosphere in the Institute, the scholarly exchange among researchers, the superbly managed library, the un-stinted cooperation of the secretarial staff, the all-pervading Yes attitude to the manifold problems faced by a foreign scholar doing research in the Institute—all were extremely helpful in my day-to-day progress of work. It is difficult to select names from among a large number of colleagues and friends. Any list would have to include Professors Lee-Jay Cho, James Palmore, Bradley Wells, and Johannes Overbeek, Executive Officer Keith Adamson, Librarian Alice Harris, and Administrative Assistant Virginia Dolan. My student assistants James O'Heron, Enamul Huq Chudhury, Steven Honda, Tan Chun Ling, and James Modecki helped in the collection and collation of the data, and I put on record my appreciation for their hard work.

While in Honolulu I received great encouragement and inspiration from eminent demographers who visited the Institute from time to time. Special thanks are due for this to Professors C. Chandrasekharan, Philip Hauser, Nathan Keyfitz, Charles Westoff, and the late lamented Irene Taeuber. Thanks are due also to the government of West Bengal and to the commissioner, Development and Planning (Town and Country Planning) Department, for kindly granting me study leave and enabling me to take up research at the East-West Population Institute.

When the question of publishing this book came up, I received invaluable help and cooperation from two persons—Sandra Ward of the East-West Population Institute and Professor Karol Krotki of the University of Alberta, who read the manuscript and suggested a number of modifications for improving the presentation as well as the content of the various chapters. Thanks are also due to Griffith Feeney and Robert Gardner of the East-West Population Institute for their helpful comments on the manuscript, and to copyeditor Don Yoder, cartographer and graphic artist Gregory Chu, and compositor Lois Bender for their assistance in bringing the volume to press.

Last but most important, I would like to acknowledge my deep sense of gratitude to Professor Ansley J. Coale, who initiated me into the study of age distribution and has frequently provided guidance through personal correspondence. With regard to my training in demography, I consider the Office of Population Research (Princeton University) to be my Alma Mater and regard Professor Coale as my *guru* in the truest traditional sense of the term.

S.B. Mukherjee

1

Introduction

There are two outstanding features of the Indian population: its massive growth and its static structure. During the 80-year period 1881 through 1961 the population of India* increased from 190 million to 440 million—revealing a growth of 130 percent. The period can be divided into two halves. During the first 40 years the population increased from 190 million to 250 million—at an approximate average annual rate of 0.6 percent. During the second 40 years it increased from 250 million to 440 million—at an average annual rate of about 1.6 percent. The preliminary results of the 1971 census indicate that the annual rate of increase has since shot up to 2.2 percent.

All these phenomena are fairly well known. What is not so well known is the fact that a nearly static age structure has been coexisting with such a vast growth in the size of the population. An unchanging age composition accompanied by a rapid increase in the total population has important and interesting implications from the standpoint of future population increase and economic development in the country.

This treatise aims at a longitudinal study of the age distribution in India: its five zones, eighteen states, and eleven territories as defined

---

* Indian Union as defined since independence in 1947.

for the purpose of the 1971 census [32].* It attempts to compile the age-sex data from the nine decennial censuses of 1881 through 1961, to regroup the age data for the changes that occurred in the political divisions of the country from one census to another, and to recast these age data into a uniform set of quinquennial age intervals for a uniformly defined set of states and territories. It is only after such a reconstruction that the age compositions for the different years and for different zones and territories can be compared.

Age composition as a demographic variable

As a basic demographic variable, age composition is intertwined with all other demographic variables. Age composition affects and is affected by fertility, mortality, and migration. Births occur to women aged 15 to 50. Within this range the rate of childbearing usually rises slowly between ages 15 and 20, then sharply between ages 20 and 30, and thereafter declines first slowly and then rapidly [4, 35, 80].

Deaths occur to men and women of all ages. But here again there are typical age patterns in the incidence of mortality. Starting high during infancy, the incidence of mortality decreases in childhood years until ages 10 to 15 and then continues at a low level until about age 30. Thereafter it starts increasing, first gradually and then sharply [90, 105].

So far as migration is concerned, the effect of age is not so much a biological phenomenon as a sociological one. While people of all ages and both sexes can migrate, in many societies including the developing ones the incidence of migration is particularly high among men of early working age (15—29) and women around the age of marriage or birth of the first or second child (15—35).

So much for the effect of age composition on fertility, mortality, and migration. The cause-effect relationship could be viewed from the reverse side also. Age composition itself is determined by fertility, mortality, and migration. When a child is born, its age is invariably zero years. Hence an increase in the birth rate tends to increase the proportion of children in the population and make the population younger. The effects of a change in death rate depend on the age incidence of the change in the risks of dying. To the extent that the age composition of migrants differs from that of the general population, the age composition of a community undergoes changes because of migration.

---

* Throughout this study, numbers in brackets refer to the bibliographic references presented at the end of the book.

The intricacies of these interrelationships may be further exemplified if one recalls that even with a moderate gross reproduction rate a high proportion of women in the age group 15–49 makes for a high birth rate. The high birth rate in turn results in a high proportion of children and consequently helps to keep the future birth rate high. A young age composition working via a high birth rate thus tends to perpetuate itself. When fertility-depressing factors are operating in such a population, the young age composition puts up a resistance against their effectiveness. If postponement of marriage, increasing practice of contraception, and legalization of abortion lead to a decrease in the number of live births per married woman, the high proportion of women in the reproductive ages tends to slow down the rate of decline in the resultant birth rate.*

Age composition as an economic variable

Age composition and per capita income are interdependent variables. Per capita income and the standard of living affect the level of fertility, mortality, and migration and through them the age composition of a population. A high per capita income is usually associated with a low birth rate, which leads to an aging of the population, and a low death rate, which has a slight rejuvenating effect on the age composition. A low per capita income is usually associated with a high birth rate, which generates a young age distribution, and a high death rate, which reduces the proportion of children in the population. Migration is usually age-selective and sex-selective and hence affects the age-sex composition of both the donor community and the receiving community.

Age distribution affects people both as producers and as consumers of wealth. Manpower is the most valuable economic resource in all societies,† and the share of the population belonging to the working ages is its only source. Definition of the working ages varies from country to country, but whatever the definition may be, the important element in manpower supply is the size of the population and its distribution by age and sex. It has been estimated that 89 percent of the net change in the world labor supply during the decade 1950–1960 was due to

---

* As Notestein [82:275] has observed, "the size and age composition of a population are heavily influenced by the size and age composition a quarter century earlier."

† Okazaki [83:94] has argued that "too little attention to the importance of human resources, and too much attention to physical capital, has been one of the mistakes made in discussions of development policies for developing countries."

changes in the population size and age-sex structure—the remaining 11 percent being due to socioeconomic, cultural, and other factors [1].

The size of the labor force in proportion to the total population is measured by the crude activity rate, which is determined by the age-specific activity rates of males and females together with the sex-age composition of the population [51]. It is worthwhile mentioning here that the proportion of population in the working age groups (15–59) is generally smaller in developing countries than in developed ones—a consequence of a lower level of fertility in the developed countries generally.

To measure the changes that occur in the labor force over time, it is not sufficient to compare the total figures at two different times. A meaningful picture of such changes emerges only when we know the number of new entrants into the labor force belonging to early adult ages and the number of withdrawals from the labor force belonging to ages 60 and above. If fertility declines, the number of new entrants will start declining 15 or 20 years after the onset of fertility decline. But the immediate effect may be a little increase in the number of job-seeking women—released from the burden of childbearing owing to the decline in fertility.

It has been observed that the average age of entry into the labor force rises under the impact of urbanization, industrialization, and growth of education. On the other hand, if mortality declines or the age of retirement is postponed, there are fewer withdrawals from employment by older people and the average age of workers tends to increase.

Young workers are more responsive than older ones to the introduction of new methods of work, new technology, and new products, and they are more adaptable to work in new places. Modern economic development is characterized by rapid structural change, shifts in the relative importance of industries, and shifts in their location within the country. Sluggish response of the labor force to such changes can be a serious obstacle to economic growth and greater per capita product. A young or otherwise mobile group within the labor force is therefore strategically important [72]. A country with a high proportion of persons in early adult ages (like India or Pakistan) enjoys an advantage over a country with a high proportion of persons in late working ages (like France or Japan).

Looking at people as savers of wealth, we may, following Meade, introduce the concept of the dependency ratio: other things remaining the same, a high dependency ratio reduces the capacity to save, while a low dependency ratio releases a portion of the immediately consumable goods and services for investment purposes. Meade [79:121] has defined the dependency ratio as

$$\frac{\text{The population measured in consuming units}}{\text{The population measured in producing units}}$$

where the population measured in consuming units is the sum of the populations in the different age and sex groups in the population, each weighed by its relevant specific need rate, and the population measured in working units is the sum of the numbers in the different age-sex groups in the population each weighed by its relevant specific work rate. If we assumed that the specific need rates and the specific work rates are fixed, regardless of the level of the standard of living, the dependency ratio will depend solely upon the age and sex composition of the population.

Because of the younger age distribution in India than in Japan, the dependency ratio in India (1.9) is higher than that in Japan (1.5). If the per earner income were the same in India and Japan, the per capita income would be 26 percent higher in Japan than in India. As facts stand, the per earner income is much lower in India than in Japan. The adverse effect of a low per earner income is severely accentuated by a higher dependency ratio in India.

A high dependency ratio erodes the saving potential of the three sources of saving in a country: private household saving, the public sector's surplus on current accounts, and corporate saving. The link between a high dependency ratio and low household savings is direct. As taxes are supposed to be paid at least partly out of potential household savings, the connection between government revenues and surplus on the one hand and the rate of saving on the other is well established. A young age distribution compels the state to spend more for schools and hospitals, leaving less for the creation of the material base for the development of the economy in the state sector.

Taking people as consumers of wealth, one has to recall that the consumption of goods and services is related to age and hence the disaggregated components of the consumption function are correlated with changes in the age structure. If the proportion of children in a population decreases and that of old people increases, the nature and composition of the consumption needs in the society will undergo significant shifts, leading in their turn to changes in the pattern of expenditure and investments both in the private and in the public sectors.

In a subsistence economy with low income and low level of living, the differentiated production for different age groups may not always be visible. The whole economy may have been geared to the production of essential food items like grains and cereals and a minimum of clothes and shelter. Even in such a state of the economy, a careful observer discerns some differences in the product mix if children constitute 35 percent of the population instead of 45 percent. When the economy starts developing and the per capita income and per capita consumption go up, the differentiation in the product mix will be more and more visible. In a developed economy every change in the age structure is carefully taken into account by industrialists and entrepreneurs in making investment decisions for producing goods and services for babies, children, schoolchildren, college students, housewives, working people, old people, and so forth.

Age composition in development planning

Development planning involves first a statement of goals and objectives, then the formulation of a strategy to achieve the objectives, and finally the preparation of programs and projects in the light of the strategy. The age composition enters into the decision-making process at each stage and with regard to each of these elements.

A declared goal of planning in developing countries like India is an expansion of employment opportunities, both for the purpose of wiping off the backlog of unemployment and also to provide employment to new entrants into the labor force [58]. Knowledge of the age distribution of the population is essential for making estimates of existing unemployment and the present and future size of the labor force. The rightful weight of the age composition has started to assert itself in the enunciation of plan objectives in recent years [98]. Maximization of productivity and maximization of employment per unit of capital are often incompatible and conflicting goals. The size of the labor force, depending on the age distribution of the population, is one of the criteria with which to judge the relative merits of the two goals.

Investment in physical capital and investment in human capital are often alternative strategies in developmental planning [61, 62]. Expenditures on education and health are regarded as investments made to improve the quality and adaptability of men as workers, to make them more productive, and in some cases to lengthen their working lives. Education is both an end itself as a component of the level of living and also a means to achieving higher domestic product through higher productivity. The developing countries lag behind in general education as well as vocational education. The objectives in the planning of education are twofold: to increase enrollment in primary and secondary levels of education and to increase facilities for vocational training. Current estimates and future projection of the number of persons aged 6–11, 12–14, 15–17, and so forth are needed for setting up programs for educational development. The spread of education keeps people in school and thus diminishes labor force participation at younger ages [46]. The age at entry into the labor force is deferred with education, and studies on the deferment effect are relevant to employment planning. This calls for joint planning of education, employment, and manpower—all based upon the data on age composition of the national, regional, and local populations [108].

Health planning is an essential component of welfare planning and is now recognized as an aspect of economic planning also, because health is a factor of high productivity. The causes and pattern of morbidity, the conditions of health, and the kind of health services needed vary from age to age. Therefore the current and projected estimates of population by age and sex are essential ingredients also for efficient health planning [107].

Forecasting of consumer demand is an essential prerequisite for planning of agriculture and industries producing consumer goods and intermediate goods. The practice in most countries is to forecast demand with the help of a projected growth rate of the total population. But demand forecasts can be much more sophisticated and realistic, if changes in the age distribution of the population are taken into account along with the overall growth rate of the population. To estimate the marketable surplus or exportable surplus of food from a region, analysts need cross-tabulated data on farm size, family size, and age distribution.

Regional planning introduces a new dimension in the planning process—the dimension of space. While sectoral planning is involved in questions like what to plan and how much to plan for, regional planning tries to find answers to questions like where to plan and where to locate specific investment projects. Data on the age distribution of the population are an essential ingredient for program planning and project planning at the regional level. The knowledge of the number of males and females in various age groups intercorrelated with household headship rates is necessary for the assessment of the need for housing and hence the planning of housing projects [101]. The priorities for employment-oriented projects or productivity-oriented projects in particular regions are determined according to the relative magnitudes of unemployed manpower and locally mobilizable resources both real and financial.

Urban planning is an important aspect of regional planning. The age composition of the urban population is often different from that of the rural population. As the working people belong to a particular age segment of the population, the planning of the spatial distribution of economic activities as well as the planning of traffic and transportation for carrying people to their places of work depend on information about age composition. Cultural needs, recreational habits, leisure-time pursuits—all are different for people belonging to different age groups. Hence the social planner, involved in planning a fuller life for citizens, must be well apprised of the age composition of the urban people who are the customers and recipients of these amenities.

Underutilization of age data from census tables

India is one of the few developing countries in which eleven consecutive decennial censuses have been undertaken. The census reports contain a vast amount of information on the sex and age composition of the population at both the national and the subnational levels. It is somewhat surprising that this information has been inadequately utilized up till now. A crucial inhibiting element must have been that the data were not available in convenient form to the intended users—because of frequent changes in the boundaries of administrative divisions and because the number and definition of age intervals vary from one census to the next.

The primary objective of this study is to make available to demographers, economists, and other social scientists a part of the census data on age and sex in a convenient and usable form. A secondary objective is to demonstrate how these reconstructed data can be used to derive estimates of the basic demographic parameters—birth rate, death rate, gross reproduction rate, and expectation of life at birth.

$$2$$

Regrouping age data
from census tables

Changes in administrative divisions

The task of reconstructing the age data in a common series of quinquennial age intervals for a set of uniformly defined states and territories in India over a period of 80 years involves three operations.
First, the age data collected from census reports have to be recast and
regrouped for changes in the political boundaries of these states and
territories that occurred between 1881 and 1971. Second, interpola-
tions have to be made for changes in the boundaries of age intervals
and also for those in the formats of the age tables from year to year.
Third, adjustments have to be made for the special nature of the census age data for the years 1931, 1941, and 1951 so that the resultant
age distributions may be comparable with those for other years.

To regroup the data to match the currently (1971) defined administrative divisions, we need to know how their definition changed from
census to census. Then we must collect the age data for the lowest-
level administrative units for which such data are available and recast
these data for the states and territories according to their 1971 definition.

The political map of India and its administrative divisions has been
undergoing continual change over the last hundred years. Exhibit 2.1
lists the constituent units of India in the 11 censuses during the period

Exhibit 2.1   Administrative units of the Indian subcontinent: 1872–1971

1872	1881	1891	1901
1. Bengal	1. Ajmer	1. Ajmer-Merwara	1. Ajmer-Merwara
2. Assam	2. Assam	2. Assam	2. Andaman and
3. North-West	3. Bengal	3. Bengal	Nicobar
Provinces	4. Berar	4. Berar	3. Assam
4. Ajmer	5. Bombay	5. Bombay	4. Baluchistan
5. Oudh	British Territory	(Presidency)	(districts and
6. Central	Feudatory States	6. Burma	administered
Provinces	6. Burma	7. Central Provinces	territories)
7. Berar	7. Central Provinces	8. Coorg	5. Bengal
8. Mysore	British Territory	9. Madras	6. Berar
9. Coorg	Feudatory States	10. North-West	7. Bombay
10. British	8. Coorg	Provinces	8. Burma
Burma	9. Madras	11. Punjab	9. Central Provinces
11. Bombay	10. North-West Provinces	12. Quettah	10. Coorg
	British Territory	13. Andamans	11. Madras
	Feudatory States	14. Hyderabad	12. North-West
	11. Punjab	15. Baroda	Frontier Province
	British Territory	16. Mysore	13. Punjab
	Feudatory States	17. Kashmir	14. United Provinces
	12. Baroda	18. Rajputana	of Agra and Oudh
	13. Central India	19. Central India	15. Baluchistan States
	14. Cochin	20. Bombay States	16. Baroda
	15. Hyderabad	21. Madras States	17. Bengal States
	16. Mysore	22. Central Provinces	18. Bombay States
	17. Rajputana	States	19. Central India
	18. Travancore	23. Bengal States	Agency
		24. Punjab States	20. Central Provinces
		25. Shan States	States
			21. Hyderabad State
			22. Kashmir State
			23. Madras States
			24. Mysore State
			25. Punjab States
			26. Rajputana Agency
			27. United Provinces
			States

1911	1921	1931	1941
1. Ajmer-Merwara	1. Ajmer-Merwara	1. Ajmer-Merwara	1. Ajmer-Merwara
2. Andaman and Nicobar	2. Andaman and Nicobar	2. Andaman and Nicobar Islands	2. Andaman and Nicobar Islands
3. Assam	3. Assam	3. Assam	3. Assam
4. Baluchistan	4. Baluchistan	4. Baluchistan	4. Baluchistan
5. Bengal	5. Bengal	5. Bengal	5. Bengal
6. Bihar and Orissa	6. Bihar and Orissa	6. Bihar and Orissa	6. Bihar
7. Bombay	7. Bombay	7. Bombay	7. Bombay
8. Burma	8. Burma	8. Burma	8. Central Provinces and Berar
9. Central Provinces and Berar	9. Central Provinces and Berar	9. Central Provinces and Berar	9. Coorg
10. Coorg	10. Coorg	10. Coorg	10. Delhi
11. Madras	11. Delhi	11. Delhi	11. Madras
12. North-West Province	12. Madras	12. Madras	12. North-West Frontier Provinces
13. Punjab	13. North-West Frontier Province	13. North-West Frontier Province	13. Orissa
14. United Provinces of Agra and Oudh	14. Punjab	14. Punjab	14. Punjab
15. Assam States (Manipur)	15. United Provinces of Agra and Oudh	15. United Provinces of Agra and Orissa	15. Sind
16. Baluchistan States	16. Assam States	16. Assam States	16. United Provinces
17. Baroda	17. Baluchistan States	17. Baluchistan States	17. Baroda
18. Bengal States	18. Baroda States	18. Baroda State	18. Central India
19. Bihar and Orissa States	19. Bengal States	19. Bengal States	19. Cochin
20. Bombay States	20. Bihar and Orissa States	20. Bihar and Orissa States	20. Gwalior
21. Central India Agency	21. Bombay States	21. Bombay States	21. Hyderabad
22. Central Provinces States	22. Central India Agency	22. Central India Agency	22. Jammu and Kashmir
23. Hyderabad State	23. Central Provinces States	23. Central Province States	23. Mysore
24. Kashmir State	24. Gwalior State	24. Gwalior State	24. Rajputana
25. Madras States	25. Hyderabad State	25. Hyderabad States	25. Travancore
26. Mysore State	26. Kashmir State	26. Jammu and Kashmir State	
27. North-West Frontier Provinces States	27. Madras States	27. Madras States Agency	
28. Punjab States	28. Mysore State	28. Mysore State	
29. Rajputana Agency	29. North-West Frontier Province States Agencies and Tribal Areas	29. North-West Frontier Province States	
30. Sikkim State	30. Punjab States	30. Punjab States	
31. United Provinces States	31. Rajputana Agency	31. Punjab States Agency	
	32. Sikkim State	32. Rajputana Agency	
	33. United Provinces States	33. United Provinces States	
		34. Western Indian States Agency	

Exhibit 2.1   *(continued)*

1951	1961	1971
1. Ajmer	1. Andhra Pradesh	1. Andhra Pradesh
2. Assam	2. Assam	2. Assam
3. Bilaspur	3. Bihar	3. Bihar
4. Bhopal	4. Gujarat	4. Gujarat
5. Bihar	5. Jammu and Kashmir	5. Haryana
6. Bombay	6. Kerala	6. Himachal Pradesh
7. Coorg	7. Madhya Pradesh	7. Jammu and Kashmir
8. Delhi	8. Madras	8. Kerala
9. Himachal Pradesh	9. Maharashtra	9. Madhya Pradesh
10. Hyderabad	10. Mysore	10. Maharashtra
11. Kutch	11. Orissa	11. Mysore
12. Madras	12. Punjab	12. Nagaland
13. Madhya Bharat	13. Rajasthan	13. Orissa
14. Madhya Pradesh	14. Uttar Pradesh	14. Punjab
15. Mysore	15. West Bengal	15. Rajasthan
16. Orissa	Union Territories	16. Tamil Nadu
17. Punjab and East Pun-	16. Andaman and Nicobar	17. Uttar Pradesh
jab States Union	Islands	18. West Bengal Union Terri-
(PEPSU)	17. Delhi	tories
18. Punjab	18. Himachal Pradesh	19. Andaman and Nicobar
19. Rajasthan	19. Laccadive, Minicoy,	Islands
20. Saurastra	Amindivi Islands	20. Chandigarh
21. Uttar Pradesh	20. Manipur	21. Dadra and Nagar Haveli
22. Vindhya Pradesh	21. Tripura	22. Delhi
23. West Bengal	22. Dadra and Nagar Haveli	23. Goa, Daman, Diu
24. Manipur	23. Goa, Daman, Diu	24. Laccadive, Minicoy,
25. Tripura	24. Pondicherry	Amindivi Islands
26. Sikkim	25. North-East Frontier	25. Manipur
27. Travancore	Agency	26. Meghalaya
and Cochin	26. Nagaland	27. Arunachal Pradesh
28. Andaman and	27. Sikkim	28. Pondicherry
Nicobar Islands		29. Tripura

SOURCES: 1872 [7, 8, 9], 1881 [10], 1891 [11], 1901 [12], 1911 [13], 1921 [14], 1931 [15], 1941 [17], 1951 [21], 1961 [29], 1971 [32].

1872–1971. When the first all-India census was taken in 1872, India* was about twice as large as at present but was divided into only 11 provinces. At the time of the second census in 1881 there were 18 administrative units, including British Indian provinces and princely states. This number increased to 25 in 1891, 27 in 1901, 31 in 1911, 33 in 1921, and 34 in 1931. Thereafter the number dropped to 25 in 1941. In 1951 the number of Part A, Part B, and Part C states was 27. The number of states and territories was again 27 in 1961 and 29 in 1971.

* Including territories now in Pakistan, Bangladesh, Sri Lanka, Burma.

The boundaries of the British Indian provinces and the princely states in 1911 are shown in Map 2.1. The year 1911 has been chosen as a typical illustration of the administrative divisions of the country in the earlier decades of this century. A brief history of the major changes since 1911 may be noted. The territory now forming the independent and sovereign country of Burma was separated from India in the 1930s, and the 1941 census of India for the first time provided tables excluding the then British Burma and the Shan States.

The territory now constituting Pakistan (formerly West Pakistan) was created in 1947 by separating the then British Indian provinces of Sind and Baluchistan, the North-West Frontier Province, and about two-thirds of the British Indian province of the Punjab. Some of the princely states like Bhawalpur and Khaira were also merged into West Pakistan.

Immediately after independence in 1947, the constituent units of the Indian Union were classified into Part A states, Part B states, Part C states, and other territorial units [27]. The general pattern was that the former British Indian provinces (which were incorporated in the Indian Union) were transformed into Part A states; the larger of the former princely states were transformed into Part B states; the princely states of medium size and population (either singly or combined) also became Part B states; and the minor princely states and other special areas were designated Part C states (see Map 2.2). Map 2.3 reveals the changes that occurred in the decade 1951–1961.

The newly created Part A State of Madras and Part B State of Hyderabad were reorganized on the basis of the language spoken by the majority of inhabitants in each district. Thus 13 districts of the State of Madras and eight districts of the State of Hyderabad were joined together to form the big Telugu-speaking state called Andhra Pradesh. Twelve districts of Madras and one newly created district were combined into the compact Tamil-speaking State of Madras (now called Tamil Nadu). Two districts from Madras, three districts from Hyderabad, four districts from Bombay, the Part B State of Mysore, and the Part C State of Coorg were joined together to constitute the new Kanarese-speaking State of Mysore (also called Karnataka).

The erstwhile State of Bombay was reorganized into two states. Twelve districts from Bombay, seven districts from Hyderabad, and eight districts from the then State of Madhya Pradesh were combined into the large Marathi-speaking State of Maharashtra. Seven districts from Bombay were combined with the Part B States of Saurasthra and Kutch to form the Gujarati-speaking State of Gujarat.

14

Map 2.1 Administrative units of India: 1911

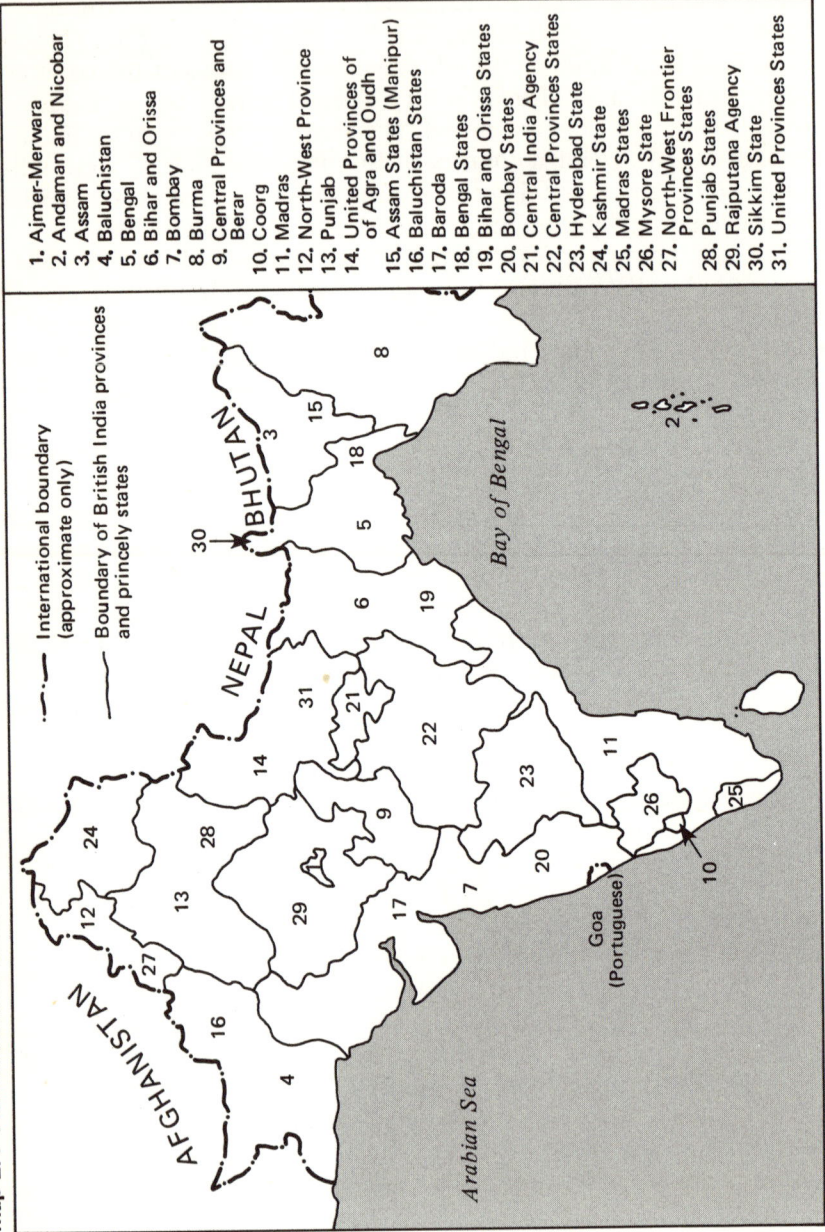

- - - International boundary (approximate only)
——— Boundary of British India provinces and princely states

1. Ajmer-Merwara
2. Andaman and Nicobar
3. Assam
4. Baluchistan
5. Bengal
6. Bihar and Orissa
7. Bombay
8. Burma
9. Central Provinces and Berar
10. Coorg
11. Madras
12. North-West Province
13. Punjab
14. United Provinces of of Agra and Oudh
15. Assam States (Manipur)
16. Baluchistan States
17. Baroda
18. Bengal States
19. Bihar and Orissa States
20. Bombay States
21. Central India Agency
22. Central Provinces States
23. Hyderabad State
24. Kashmir State
25. Madras States
26. Mysore State
27. North-West Frontier Provinces States
28. Punjab States
29. Rajputana Agency
30. Sikkim State
31. United Provinces States

AFGHANISTAN

NEPAL

BHUTAN

Bay of Bengal

Arabian Sea

Goa (Portuguese)

Map 2.2 Administrative units of the Indian Union: 1951

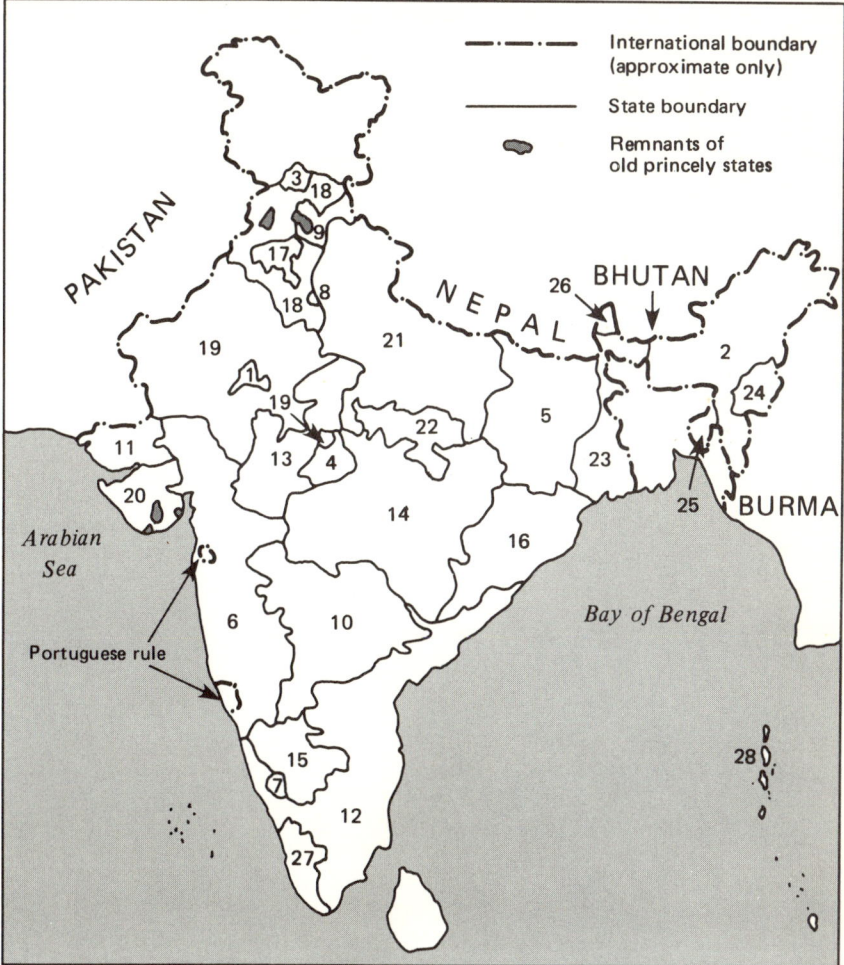

	International boundary (approximate only)
	State boundary
	Remnants of old princely states

PAKISTAN

NEPAL

BHUTAN

BURMA

Arabian Sea

Bay of Bengal

Portuguese rule

1. Ajmer	11. Kutch	21. Uttar Pradesh
2. Assam	12. Madras	22. Vindhya Pradesh
3. Bilaspur	13. Madhya Bharat	23. West Bengal
4. Bhopal	14. Madhya Pradesh	24. Manipur
5. Bihar	15. Mysore	25. Tripura
6. Bombay	16. Orissa	26. Sikkim
7. Coorg	17. PEPSU	27. Travancore
8. Delhi	18. Punjab	and Cochin
9. Himachal Pradesh	19. Rajasthan	28. Andaman
10. Hyderabad	20. Saurastra	and Nicobar Islands

Map 2.3 Administrative units of the Indian Union: 1961

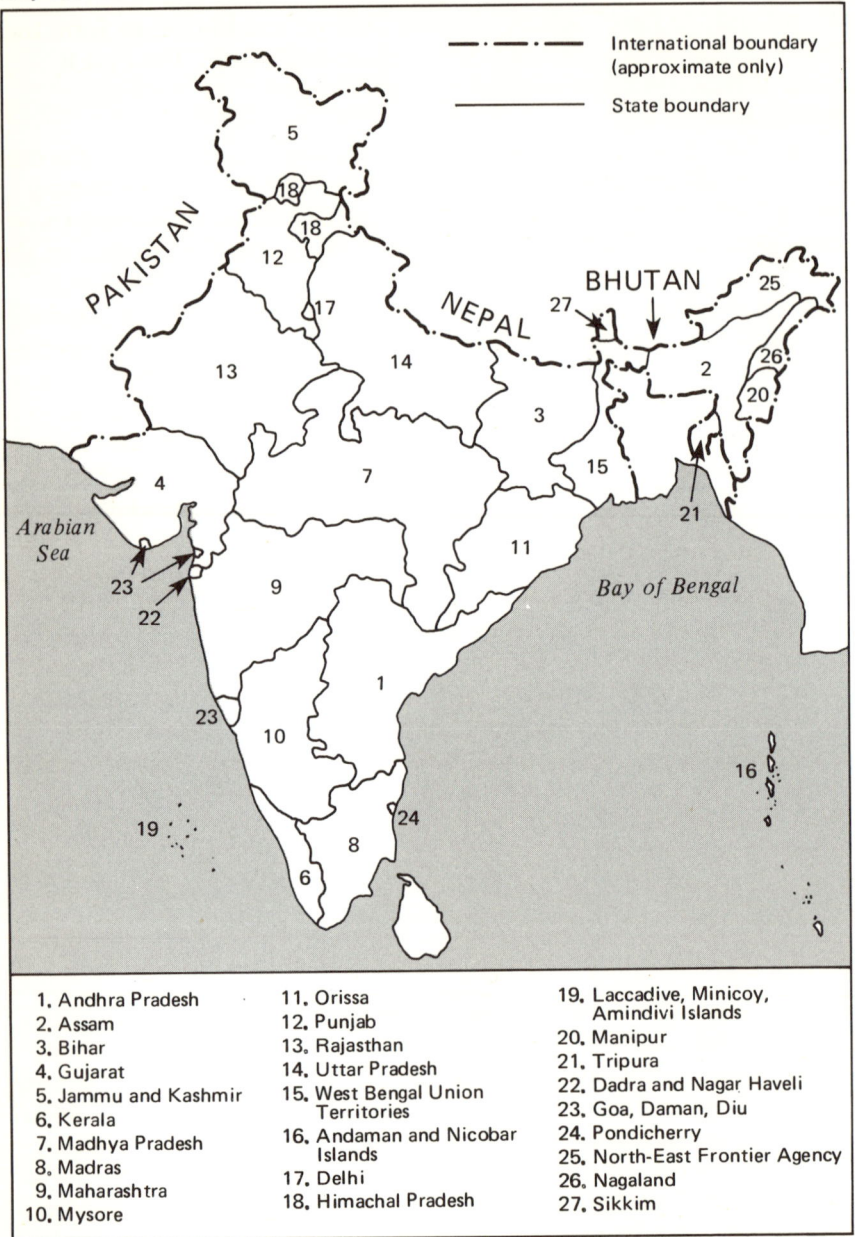

— · — · —	International boundary (approximate only)		
———	State boundary		

1. Andhra Pradesh
2. Assam
3. Bihar
4. Gujarat
5. Jammu and Kashmir
6. Kerala
7. Madhya Pradesh
8. Madras
9. Maharashtra
10. Mysore
11. Orissa
12. Punjab
13. Rajasthan
14. Uttar Pradesh
15. West Bengal Union Territories
16. Andaman and Nicobar Islands
17. Delhi
18. Himachal Pradesh
19. Laccadive, Minicoy, Amindivi Islands
20. Manipur
21. Tripura
22. Dadra and Nagar Haveli
23. Goa, Daman, Diu
24. Pondicherry
25. North-East Frontier Agency
26. Nagaland
27. Sikkim

The twelve remaining districts of the State of Madhya Pradesh were combined with the Part B States of Vindhya Pradesh and Madhya Bharat and the Part C States of Rewa, Indore, and Bhopal to form the large but sparsely populated State of Madhya Pradesh. The Part B State of Rajasthan was joined with Ajmer to make the State of Rajasthan.

Among the other changes may be mentioned the transfer of the major part of Manbhum District from Bihar to West Bengal, the carving out of the territorial unit called the North-East Frontier Agency (now called Arunachal Pradesh) from the State of Assam, the creation of the new State of Nagaland by merging the two districts in the erstwhile State of Assam, the creation of the territorial unit called Goa, Daman, and Diu from areas previously under Portuguese colonial rule, the creation of the territorial unit of Pondicherry which had hitherto been under French rule, the creation of the territorial unit of Himachal Pradesh by combining some hilly areas earlier included among the princely states of the Punjab, and the creation of the State of Punjab by combining the Part A State of Punjab and Part B State of PEPSU.

Changes in territorial boundaries did not stop in the year 1961. Extensive reorganization of Punjab and Assam has taken place since then. The State of Haryana was formed by carving out seven districts from the State of Punjab. Three districts from the State of Punjab were ceded to the Union Territory of Himachal Pradesh, which now enjoys the full status of a state in the Indian Union. The erstwhile State of Punjab kept the remaining Punjabi-speaking districts. The city of Chandigarh, built as a capital of the larger Punjab, remained a separate unit. The status of the Union Territories of Nagaland, Tripura, and Manipur was raised to that of a state. Moreover, a new union territory called Meghalaya was created by combining the two hilly districts of Assam—United Khasi Jaintia Hills and Garo Hills. The present State of Assam is composed of the remaining nine districts.

Current administrative divisions

Table 2.1 and Map 2.4 show the 21 states and eight union territories as defined for the 1971 census. It is these administrative divisions for which the age composition has been reconstructed. Though the administrative divisions existing up to the year 1971 have been taken into account, the age data for the 1971 census are not yet available. Hence the reconstruction of the age data covers the period 1881–1961. (Partially tabulated age data for the 1971 census were available in November 1972. A note on 1971 age distribution appears in the appendix.)

Table 2.1 States and union territories of India with area and population according to 1971 census

State or territory	Status	Number of districts	Area (km²)	1971 population (1000's)	Average density per km²	Average area of a district	Average population of a district (1000's)	Total population increase, 1881–1971 (%)
EASTERN ZONE		74	672,608	142,191	211.40	9,089	1,922	166.09
Assam^a	State	10	99,610	14,957	150.15	9,961	1,496	427.06
West Bengal	State	16	87,853	44,312	504.39	5,491	2,770	198.39
Bihar	State	17	173,876	56,353	324.10	10,228	3,315	109.75
Orissa	State	13	155,842	21,945	140.81	11,988	1,688	155.02
Nagaland	State	3	16,527	516	31.22	5,509	172	u
Manipur	State	5	22,356	1,073	47.00	4,471	215	u
Tripura	State	3	10,477	1,556	148.52	3,492	519	u
Arunachal Pradesh	UT^b	5	83,578	467	5.59	16,716	93	u
Meghalaya	State	2	22,489	1,012	45.00	11,244	506	266.65
CENTRAL ZONE		97	737,254	129,905	176.20	7,601	1,339	112.06
Madhya Pradesh	State	43	442,841	41,654	94.06	10,299	969	144.60
Uttar Pradesh	State	54	294,413	88,341	300.06	5,452	1,636	99.74
SOUTHERN ZONE		69	637,972	135,851	212.94	9,246	1,969	229.75
Andhra Pradesh	State	21	276,754	43,503	157.19	13,179	2,072	246.22
Kerala	State	10	38,864	21,347	549.27	3,876	2,135	u
Mysore	State	19	191,773	29,299	152.78	10,093	1,542	131.53
Tamil Nadu	State	14	130,069	41,199	316.75	9,291	2,943	157.84
Pondicherry	UT	4	480	472	983.33	120	118	u
Laccadive, Minicoy, Amindivi Islands	UT	1	32	31	968.75	32	31	u
WESTERN ZONE		46	504,237	77,183	153.07	10,961	1,678	208.74
Gujarat	State	19	195,984	26,697	136.22	10,315	1,405	175.62
Maharashtra	State	26	307,762	50,412	163.80	11,837	1,939	229.20
Dadra and Nagar Haveli	UT	1	491	74	150.71	491	74	u

19

NORTHERN ZONE		716,306	66	61,754	862.12	1,085	936	386.13
Jammu and Kashmir	State	222,236	10	4,617	20.77	22,224	462	u
Punjab	State	50,362	11	13,551	269.07	4,578	1,232	111.29
Rajasthan	State	342,214	26	25,766	75.29	13,162	991	u
Haryana	State	44,222	7	10,037	226.97	6,317	1,434	145.65
Himachal Pradesh	State	55,673	10	3,460	62.15	5,567	346	88.29
Chandigarh	UT	114	1	257	2,254.34	114	257	u
Delhi	UT	1,185	1	4,066	2,738.05	1,485	4,066	1,009.70
Andaman and Nicobar Islands	UT	8,293	1	115	13.87	8,293	115	686.16
Goa, Daman, Diu	UT	3,813	3	858	225.02	1,271	286	u
India		3,280,483	356	547,950	167.03	9,215	1,539	183.02

u—unavailable.

a The Mizo District of Assam was carved out of the state and constituted into a separate union territory on 21 January 1972—that is, after the first draft of this book was completed.

b UT—union territory.

Map 2.4 Administrative units of the Indian Union: 1971

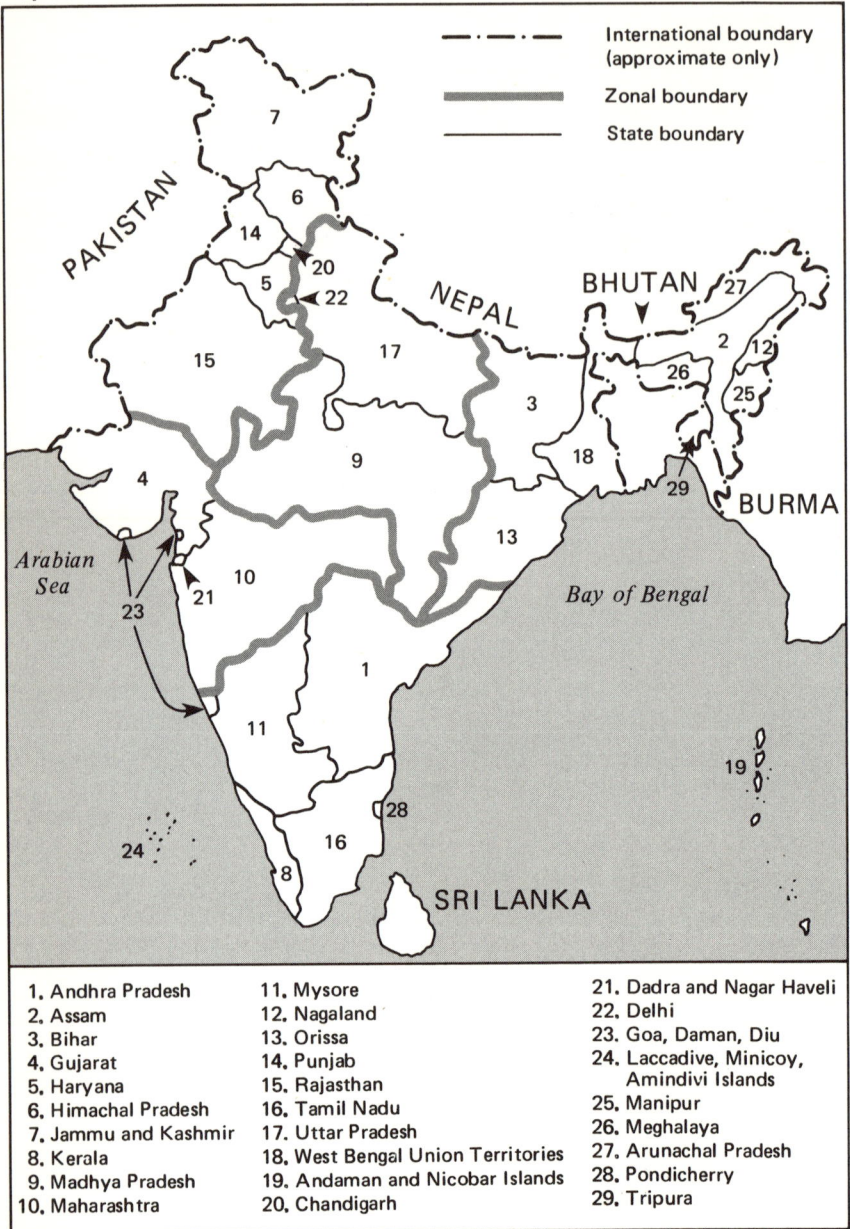

1. Andhra Pradesh	11. Mysore	21. Dadra and Nagar Haveli
2. Assam	12. Nagaland	22. Delhi
3. Bihar	13. Orissa	23. Goa, Daman, Diu
4. Gujarat	14. Punjab	24. Laccadive, Minicoy,
5. Haryana	15. Rajasthan	Amindivi Islands
6. Himachal Pradesh	16. Tamil Nadu	25. Manipur
7. Jammu and Kashmir	17. Uttar Pradesh	26. Meghalaya
8. Kerala	18. West Bengal Union Territories	27. Arunachal Pradesh
9. Madhya Pradesh	19. Andaman and Nicobar Islands	28. Pondicherry
10. Maharashtra	20. Chandigarh	29. Tripura

The states and territories vary widely in area and population. At one extreme are states like United Provinces with 88 million people; at the other are states like Nagaland with 0.50 million people. As regards area, Madhya Pradesh comprises 443,000 square kilometers while Tripura has only 10,000. The average density of population varies from 31 persons per square kilometer in Nagaland to 594 persons in Kerala. The 1961 census divided the country into five zones: Eastern, Central, Southern, Western, and Northern. We have adopted this division for estimating vital rates and also for demographic analysis. Each zone contains a number of states and union territories. The grouping of states and territories into the five zones is shown in Table 2.1. The variation in area and population among the zones is much narrower than that among the states. The Eastern Zone has the largest population (142 million); the Northern Zone has the smallest (62 million).

The districts are the most important administrative units in the country in the sense that their boundaries have undergone only minimal changes in the last hundred years. There are 356 districts in the whole country—the number of districts located in the different states and territories varying from 52 in United Provinces to two in Meghalaya. Map 2.5 shows the demarcation of districts and zones in India. Successive reorganization of states and territories has led to the transfer of some districts from one state to another. But changes in district boundaries of significant magnitude have been few and far between.

Strategy for regrouping age data

Since the districts are the lowest administrative units for which the census provides data on age and sex, our main strategy has been to compile age-sex data for the districts, reassemble them, and reconstruct the age composition for the respective states and territories. The compilation of age data for about 356 districts in India for nine census years is an unwieldy task. Labor has often been saved by collecting data for a whole province or princely state or for a group of districts together, whenever such groups of provinces happen to be wholly included in a newly created state. In other words, we built up from district-level data when it was necessary. When it was possible, we used higher-level data.

Sometimes changes occurred between two or more adjacent districts, all of which are now included in the same state. Such changes had no effect on the age composition in the state. Complications arose when changes occurred in districts such that the different parts of the

Map 2.5 Districts and zones of the Indian Union: 1971

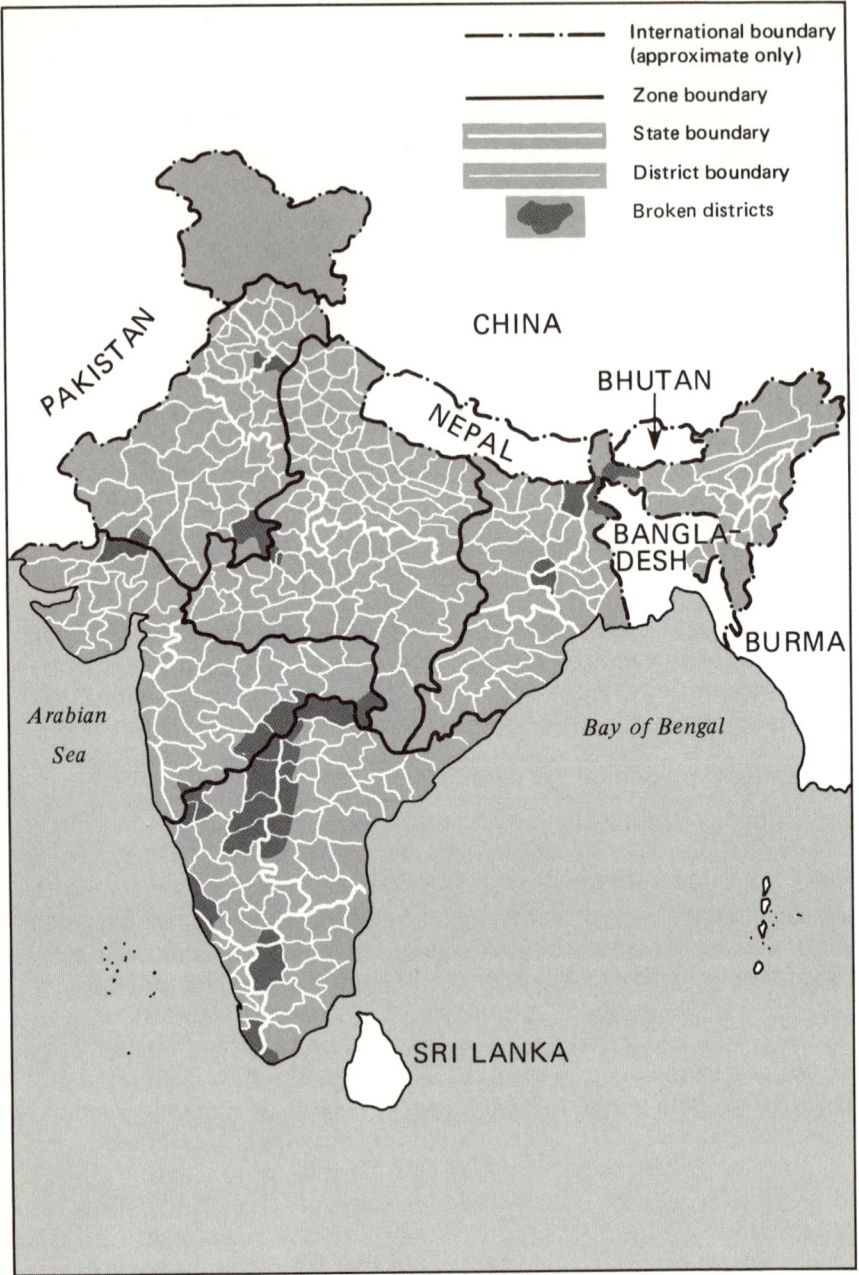

dismembered districts were incorporated into different states. There was no way to obtain the age composition for the parts of a district. The only avenue open to us was to take the total population of the relevant part of the district and distribute it according to the age distribution in the entire district as defined in the earlier census. This procedure introduces an element of estimation in the resultant age figures.

But the number of dismembered districts is small, and the magnitude of error resulting from such estimation is expected to be marginal. Table 2.2 lists the 16 districts that were fragmented during the period 1951–1961 and the fragments that were added to districts in other states. Map 2.5 shows the location of these districts. There were eight such districts in the Southern Zone (Bellary, Raichur, Gulbarga, Bidar, Nanded, South Kanara, Quilon, Trivandrum), one in the Central Zone (Kota), three in the Western Zone (Belgaum, Adilabad, Bidar), two in the Northern Zone (Kohistan, Banas Kantha), and two in the Eastern Zone (Manbhum, Purnea). The table provides information on the 1961 population in the two segments of such districts—the one that was transferred to some other state and the other that was retained in the original state. The age composition in the part of the district that contains the larger share of the district population must be close to the age composition in the entire district. Hence the error involved in the assumption of similarity between the two age compositions is small. The age composition in the part of the district that contains the smaller share of the population may have been markedly different from that in the whole district. But the size of the population involved in this case is small. Hence the effect of this difference on the accuracy of the ultimate age distribution could be only marginal.

Variation in boundaries of age intervals

As our endeavor in this study is to hammer out comparable age distributions in a uniform set of five-year age intervals, we interpolated the number of persons in five-year age intervals from those in ten-year or twenty-year age intervals. Before discussing the steps involved in this interpolation, we may briefly indicate the varying degrees of detail in which age tabulation was available at the provincial or district level in different census years (see References for Basic Tables at the end of this book):

1. At the level of the province (so called before 1951) and princely state, age data by marital status are available in quinquennial age intervals for all census years from 1881 through 1931.

2. Such information is available also for each of the major religious communities

Table 2.2 Percentage of population of dismembered districts incorporated into separate states: 1951–1961

Name of district in 1951	Transferred from	Transferred to	Transferred population		Nontransferred population as percentage of original district
			As percentage of original district	As percentage of state to which transferred	
Bellary	Madras	Andhra Pradesh	37.10	1.50	62.90
Raichur	Hyderabad	Andhra Pradesh	9.72	0.33	91.28
Gulbarga	Hyderabad	Andhra Pradesh	14.77	0.67	85.23
Bidar	Hyderabad	Andhra Pradesh	23.26	0.69	76.74
		Maharashtra	43.01	1.27	56.99
Nanded	Hyderabad	Andhra Pradesh	8.52	0.28	91.48
South Kanara	Madras	Kerala	14.77	1.60	85.23
Kota	Rajasthan	Madhya Pradesh	12.60	0.38	87.40
Quilon	Travancore Cochin	Madras	3.31	0.20	96.69
Trivandrum	Travancore Cochin	Madras	36.36	2.96	63.64
Belgaum	Hyderabad	Maharashtra	4.50	0.29	95.50
Adilabad	Hyderabad	Maharashtra	17.00	0.52	83.00
Coimbatore	Hyderabad	Mysore	4.77	0.76	95.23
Kohistan	Kohistan	Punjab	88.88	1.18	11.12
Banas Kantha	Gujarat	Rajasthan	6.28	0.33	94.72
Manbhum	Bihar	West Bengal	54.00	3.89	46.00
Purnea	Bihar	West Bengal	10.93	1.09	89.07

SOURCE: [27].

(Hindus, Muslims, Christians, Buddhists, Sikhs) in quinquennial age intervals for all provinces and princely states for the entire period 1881–1931.

3. For the years 1881 and 1891, five-year age distribution is available at the district level as well.

4. For the years 1901 and 1911, district-level age data are available in seven age groups: 0–4, 5–9, 10–14, 15–19, 20–39, 40–59, and 60+.

5. For the years 1921 and 1931, district-level age data are available in nine age groups: 0–4, 5–9, 10–14, 15–19, 20–29, 30–39, 40–49, 50–59, and 60+.

6. Data referred to in items 3, 4, and 5 are available in cross classification by marital status and major religious group.

7. For the year 1941, the original data are not available for the then British Indian provinces. Tables constructed on the basis of a 2 percent sample of the original enumeration slips and the reconstructed Y-sample tables* are available at both provincial level and district level in quinquennial age intervals by marital status. Also, single-year age data are available for all marital statuses combined at the level of provinces as well as districts for the then British Indian provinces. For some of the major princely states, five-year age data for the entire population are available at both state level and district level.

8. For the year 1951, age data by marital status are available† at the state and district levels in nine age intervals: 0–4, 5–14, 15–24, 25–34, 35–44, 45–54, 55–64, 65–74, and 75+. Single-year age data are also available for all marital statuses combined at both state level and district level.

9. For the year 1961, age data by marital status are available in quinquennial age intervals at both state level and district level. Single-year age data are also available for all marital statuses combined at both state level and district level.

10. For 1951 and 1961, age tables are available for total population, rural population, and urban population separately.

Decomposition of a broad age group into five-year age groups

So far as our central task of reconstructing the age data in quinquennial age intervals is concerned, the years 1901 and 1911 presented the problem of decomposing the two twenty-year age groups 20–39 and 40–59 into two sets of four five-year age groups. For this purpose we assumed that the pattern of distribution over the four five-year age groups within a twenty-year age group in a district is similar to that in the corresponding province or princely state. On the basis of this assumption, the five-year age distribution at the higher level was super-

---

* So called because the sample slips were preserved according to the direction of Census Commissioner Yeatts.

† For a 10 percent sample of the nondisplaced population and for the entire displaced population. For the latter, age tables are given for all marital statuses combined.

imposed on the twenty-year age distribution at the corresponding lower level to yield the five-year age distribution for the districts. To put it symbolically: let DP_{20-39} be the district population in the age interval 20–39; let HP_{20-39} be the population in the whole province in the age interval 20–39; let HP_{20-24}, HP_{25-29}, HP_{30-34}, and HP_{35-39} be the populations in the province in the respective five-year age intervals; and let DP_{20-24}, DP_{25-29}, DP_{30-34}, and DP_{35-39} be the required district populations in the same age intervals. Then

$$k_1 = HP_{20-24}/HP_{20-39}$$
$$k_2 = HP_{25-29}/HP_{20-39}$$
$$k_3 = HP_{30-34}/HP_{20-39}$$
$$k_4 = HP_{35-39}/HP_{20-39}$$

and

$$DP_{20-24} = k_1(DP_{20-39})$$
$$DP_{25-29} = k_2(DP_{20-39})$$
$$DP_{30-34} = k_3(DP_{20-39})$$
$$DP_{35-39} = k_4(DP_{20-39})$$

Note that our purpose is not to interpolate the five-year age distribution within a twenty-year age distribution; it is to reclaim as far as possible the original age distribution along with whatever biases it might initially contain. We have not, therefore, adopted any sophisticated interpolation technique involving the neighboring age groups. We simply assume that the internal distribution within a twenty-year age group is the same in the provincial population as in the district population. To examine whether it is actually so, we scrutinized the age data for the districts incorporated into West Bengal vis-à-vis the age data for the then Province of Bengal as a whole. We discovered some interesting differences in age distribution between the group of districts located in West Bengal and those located in East Bengal (now Bangladesh). It may be recalled that the Province of Bengal was partitioned on the basis of religion—the Hindu majority districts were included in West Bengal and the Muslim majority districts in East Bengal. In this part of the Indian subcontinent the Muslims had a younger age distribution than the Hindus. Therefore, for the purpose of decomposing a broader age group into five-year age groups, the use of the five-year age distribution of the Hindu population in Bengal was thought to be more appropriate than that of the total population of Bengal.

Table 2.3 sets out the distribution within the twenty-year age intervals for the Hindu and Muslim populations in Bengal and also for the

Table 2.3 **Percentage distribution of population within 20-year age groups, by region and by religion: Bengal, male, 1911**

Age group	Province of Bengal	West Bengal districts	Bangladesh districts	Bengal Muslims	Bengal Hindus
20–39	100.00	100.00	100.00	100.00	100.00
20–24	24.70	25.42	24.14	24.03	25.41
25–29	29.41	29.11	29.61	29.70	29.12
30–34	24.89	24.70	25.05	25.03	24.69
35–39	21.00	20.77	21.20	21.24	20.78
40–59	100.00	100.00	100.00	100.00	100.00
40–44	40.11	38.88	41.18	39.20	38.83
45–49	25.92	25.26	26.46	25.32	25.28
50–54	24.88	23.71	25.93	24.80	23.72
55–59	9.09	12.15	6.43	10.68	12.17

population in the districts of West Bengal and East Bengal separately. It reveals that the age distribution within the broad age group 20–39 in West Bengal districts is similar to that of the Hindu population of Bengal and unlike that of the Muslim population and the total population of the province. By the same token, the distribution within the age group 40–59 in West Bengal is similar to that of the Hindu population in Bengal and dissimilar from that of the total Bengal population.

Parent age distribution for different areas

This problem of using the age distribution of a particular community for the purpose of processing the district age data arose with respect to those states in the Indian Union that were created by partitioning an erstwhile British Indian province or a princely state, namely West Bengal, Maharashtra, Gujarat, Punjab, Haryana, and Himachal Pradesh. Table 2.4 shows which parent age distribution was used for interpolating the five-year age groups for each of these states. We have tried to select an age distribution that is likely to be similar to the expected age distribution in any given area. That is why we have selected the age distribution of the Sikh community for the State of Punjab and that of the Hindu community for the State of Haryana.

The method for decomposing the ten-year age groups of 1921 and 1931 into the corresponding pairs of five-year age groups was the same as discussed above, except that instead of disaggregating two twenty-year age groups we had to disaggregate four ten-year age groups—all into corresponding five-year age groups.

Table 2.4   Areas and religious groups used to estimate district age data for states created from partitioned provinces

Province or state and district	Area and religious group
West Bengal	
15 districts	Bengal: Hindu
Purulia	Bihar: all religions
Maharashtra	
Bombay group of districts	Bombay: Hindu
Hyderabad group of districts	Hyderabad: all religions
Central Provinces group of districts	Central Provinces and Berar: all religions
Gujarat	
Bombay group of districts	Bombay: Hindu
Princely states	Western India States Agency: all religions
Punjab	Punjab: Sikh
Haryana	Punjab: Hindu
Himachal Pradesh	Punjab States Agency: all religions

Semismoothed age data for 1931

In the age tables for 1931 the census commissioner made two important departures from the practice of previous commissioners: instead of recording age on the last birthday, he recorded age on the nearest birthday [15]; and instead of presenting the raw age data, he subjected them to a preliminary smoothing process and presented the partially smoothed data in census tables [15]. This has deprived demographers of the opportunity of using the raw age data for research. Moreover, it has reduced the comparability of the 1931 age data with those for other years. We have therefore made an attempt to unsmooth the 1931 age data and present the derived unsmoothed age distribution for the respective states and territories.

This anomaly in the 1931 age tables was brought to notice by Agarwala, who also unsmoothed the age data for the provinces and princely states as defined in 1931 [2]. But Agarwala presented the derived unsmoothed age data not in the conventional quinquennial age intervals but in alternate ternary and septenary age intervals: 4—6, 7—13, 14—16, and so forth. The usefulness of the derived unsmoothed figures is, however, enhanced if they are presented in the conventional quinquennial age intervals. Besides, Agarwala adjusted the data for the administrative divisions as defined in 1931. In the present study the unsmoothed age data have been presented for the states and territories as defined in the 1971 census.

In 1931 information as to age was collected on the basis of the following instructions [15:111] issued to the enumerators: "Enter the age as it was or will be on the birthday nearest to the date of final enumeration, i.e., to nearest approximate years. For infants less than 6 months old enter the word 'infant'." The explanation offered for this switch was that the returns in India were not really affected by such nice differences and that the ages which the enumerators either guessed or accepted as correct were recorded without any consideration as to whether they were as of the next birthday or last birthday and might therefore be assumed to be the ages on the nearest birthday. "The presumption that the age on the present occasion should be recorded to the nearest birthday was an innovation intended to recognize and make use of the actual practice which would be followed despite instructions to the contrary" [15:112].

Table 2.5 sets out the smoothing formula used in the 1931 census. It will be observed that the essence of the method lies in forming preliminary age groups of alternate three-year and seven-year intervals for

Table 2.5 Smoothing formula used in 1931 census

Intermediate age group for smoothing	Number of persons in age group	Age group for presentation in census tables	Number of persons obtained after smoothing	Formula[a]
0	a			
1	b			
2	c			
3	d			
4–6	e	0–5	N1	$a + b + c + d + (\frac{1}{2})e$
7–13	f	5–10	N2	$(\frac{1}{2})e + (\frac{1}{2})f$
14–16	g	10–15	N3	$(\frac{1}{2})f + (\frac{1}{2})g$
17–23	h	15–20	N4	$(\frac{1}{2})g + (\frac{1}{2})h$
24–26	i	20–25	N5	$(\frac{1}{2})h + (\frac{1}{2})i$
27–33	j	25–30	N6	$(\frac{1}{2})i + (\frac{1}{2})j$
34–36	k	30–35	N7	$(\frac{1}{2})j + (\frac{1}{2})k$
37–43	l	35–40	N8	$(\frac{1}{2})k + (\frac{1}{2})l$
44–46	m	40–45	N9	$(\frac{1}{2})l + (\frac{1}{2})m$
47–53	n	45–50	N10	$(\frac{1}{2})m + (\frac{1}{2})n$
54–56	o	50–55	N11	$(\frac{1}{2})n + (\frac{1}{2})o$
57–63	p	55–60	N12	$(\frac{1}{2})o + (\frac{1}{2})p$
64–66	q	60–65	N13	$(\frac{1}{2})p + (\frac{1}{2})q$
67–73	r	65–70	N14	$(\frac{1}{2})q + (\frac{1}{2})r$
74+	s	70+	N15	$(\frac{1}{2})r + s$

a   For application of smoothing formula to data on age at nearest birthday.
SOURCE: [16:111–114].

ages 5 through 74, and then adding half of one three-year age group and one seven-year age group to obtain the smoothed figure for the corresponding five-year age group. The assumptions underlying this method, as well as its limitations, are provided by the census commissioner himself [15:114]:

> The alternative ternary and septenary groups are considered to result in figures actually including all or all but a negligible proportion of those whose real age falls within them. . . . It is then assumed that within each group those less than an age with the digit 5 or 0, as the case may be, are equal to those of or over an age with that digit. The assumption clearly does not accurately represent the facts, since in age group 7 to 13 for instance there will be more people aged less than ten, than there are aged ten and over. It is justified, however, by the fact that it results in a demonstrably more accurate approximation to the actual figures.

The unsmoothing method

The steps in the unsmoothing operation may be briefly stated as follows:

1. Apply the 1931 smoothing formula on the raw single-year age data for 1961 and obtain the smoothed quinquennial age distribution ($S_{i, 1961}$).

2. Obtain the raw quinquennial age distribution for the same population ($R_{i, 1961}$).

3. Compare the raw quinquennial age groups with the smoothed quinquennial age groups and obtain the multipliers:

$$K_{i, 1961} = \frac{R_{i, 1961}}{S_{i, 1961}}$$

4. Multiply the smoothed age groups for 1931 by $K_{i, 1961}$ to obtain approximate estimates of the raw 1931 age distribution.

If the multipliers ($K_{i, 1961}$) are applied to the smoothed age distribution of 1961, then we get back exactly the raw age data for 1961. If the age data for any other year contain heapings and distortions similar to those in the year 1961, these multipliers could be used to derive the unsmoothed figures from the smoothed ones. To the extent that the heapings and distortions in a given year are dissimilar from those in 1961, the derived unsmoothed figures would differ from the original figures. It has been the experience of Indian actuaries and demographers that the biases in age data in India reveal some broad patterns common to all years [28].

The age recorded in 1931 relates to age on the nearest birthday— whereas in 1961 the recorded age relates to age on the last birthday. As a consequence of this difference the actual limits of the ternary and

Table 2.6 Boundary of preliminary age groups according to two definitions of age

Age group	Notation	According to age at nearest birthday		According to age at last birthday		Modification needed in smoothing formula
		Over exact age	Under exact age	Over exact age	Under exact age	
0	a	0	½	0	1	
1	b	½	1½	1	2	
2	c	1½	2½	2	3	
3	d	2½	3½	3	4	
4–6	e	3½	6½	4	7	$N1 = a + b + c + d + (1/3)e$
7–13	f	6½	13½	7	14	$N2 = (2/3)e + (3/7)f$
14–16	g	13½	16½	14	17	$N3 = (4/7)f + (1/3)g$
17–23	h	16½	23½	17	24	$N4 = (2/3)g + (3/7)h$
24–26	i	.	.	.	.	.
27–33	j	.	.	.	.	.
34–36	k	.	.	.	.	.
37–43	l	.	.	.	.	.
44–46	m	.	.	.	.	.
47–53	n	.	.	.	.	.
54–56	o	.	.	.	.	.
57–63	p	.	.	.	.	.
64–66	q	64½	66½	64	67	$N13 = (2/3)p + (3/7)q$
67–73	r	66½	73½	67	74	$N14 = (4/7)q + (1/3)r$
74+	s	73½		74		$N15 = (2/3)r + s$

septenary age groups in 1931 and 1961 differ as shown in Table 2.6. To apply the 1931 smoothing formula to the single-year age data of 1961, we should have to modify the smoothing formula as shown in column 5 of Table 2.6, which is somewhat different from the formula indicated in column 5 of Table 2.5.

Table 2.7 shows the unsmoothing of the 1931 census age distribution with and without modification of the limits of the preliminary age intervals for the male population of Uttar Pradesh. We do not have any firm evidence to show that the age groups in one set (except for 0–4) are nearer the original data than those in the other set. As regards the age group 0–4, the K_i multiplier with modified age boundary was near unity—implying that there was not much underenumeration in the age group 0–4. From the experience of underenumeration in age group 0–4 in all other census years, it seems that when people in India return ages, they do not make any subtle distinction between age on next birthday and age on last birthday or age on nearest birthday. Hence we thought it more expedient to apply the 1931 smoothing formula without taking account of definitional differences in the age recorded. As regards the sequence of the two operations of regrouping and unsmoothing, we have first regrouped the smoothed age

Table 2.7   Smoothed and unsmoothed 1931 age distributions: Uttar Pradesh, male

Age group	1931 census age distribution	Unsmoothed 1931 age distribution[a] Age boundary modified	Age boundary unmodified
0–5	12.87	12.38	11.27
5–10	12.70	13.14	13.57
10–15	12.47	12.05	12.40
15–20	9.10	8.51	8.79
20–25	8.34	7.72	7.55
25–30	8.86	8.44	8.94
30–35	7.86	7.87	7.72
35–40	6.59	6.17	6.62
40–45	5.98	6.56	6.42
45–50	4.51	4.09	4.41
50–55	4.02	4.89	4.94
55–60	2.39	1.98	2.09
60+	4.30	6.28	5.27
All age groups	100.00	100.00	100.00

a   Age distribution was unsmoothed by applying 1931 smoothing formula to 1961 age data. For details of unsmoothing procedure, see text.

data for each state and territory and then unsmoothed the resultant age distributions. Finally, the unsmoothed age distributions were adjusted upward or downward by suitable multiplying factors so that the total populations might agree with the corresponding totals for the redefined states and territories.

Result of unsmoothing operations

Table 2.8 provides the $K (I, J)$ multipliers computed in the manner discussed above. With respect to the male population, the $K (I, J)$ multipliers are generally the lowest for age group 55–59 and next to lowest for age group 0–4, implying that the smoothing in 1931 led to the largest increase in the number of persons in these two age groups. The $K (I, J)$ multipliers are less than unity for age groups 10–14, 15–19, 20–24, and 30–34 and are greater than unity for age groups 5–9, 25–29, 35–39, 40–44, 45–49, and 50–54. They are always highest for age group 60+, implying that the smoothing process had effected the biggest reduction in this age group. More or less the same pattern is observed in the multipliers for the female population—with some differences for age group 15–19.

But there are significant differences in the size of the multipliers among different states and territories. The multiplier for the male pop-

Table 2.8 *K* multipliers for unsmoothing 1931 census age data for five states

Age group	West Bengal	Uttar Pradesh	Andhra Pradesh	Maharashtra	Punjab
MALE					
0–4	0.8859127	0.9099153	0.8817372	0.9038449	0.8983106
5–9	1.1125626	1.1298918	1.0458811	1.0623824	1.0806199
10–14	0.9594077	0.9063874	1.0069928	0.9903362	0.9575060
15–19	0.9508010	0.9051352	0.9778640	0.9538842	0.8880713
20–24	0.9635016	0.9599099	0.8917215	0.9301842	0.9682954
25–29	1.0321713	1.0493982	1.0285781	1.0390340	1.0496341
30–34	0.9715812	0.9902181	1.0186329	0.9541778	1.0365342
35–39	1.0491975	1.0074082	0.9728190	1.0694643	0.9721356
40–44	1.0327286	1.0723031	1.1077714	1.0287583	1.1579771
45–49	1.0275318	1.0136464	0.9562739	1.0842333	0.9311515
50–54	1.0675622	1.2065434	1.2688595	1.0739255	1.3270477
55–59	1.0263800	0.8663686	0.8112474	1.0104821	0.7638409
60+	1.1381478	1.2205412	1.2532640	1.1662904	1.2774600
FEMALE					
0–4	0.8926953	0.8912027	0.8853339	0.9062685	0.8983672
5–9	1.1650756	1.1042912	1.0825132	1.0956323	1.0722194
10–14	0.8947083	0.9620155	0.9670243	0.9552027	0.9884491
15–19	0.9558397	0.9072829	0.9334622	0.9052809	0.9582888
20–24	0.9634605	0.9780539	0.9103498	0.9630671	0.9408972
25–29	1.0405244	1.0180019	1.0494672	1.0663372	1.0408411
30–34	0.9943188	0.9950708	1.0450422	0.9625093	0.9703973
35–39	1.0147584	1.0084629	0.9740796	1.0555886	1.0008742
40–44	1.0669986	1.0713641	1.1264190	1.0436235	1.0852576
45–49	0.9791484	1.0036416	0.9133902	1.0703414	0.9996461
50–54	1.1197156	1.1732277	1.3136618	1.0933489	1.2237543
55–59	0.9136646	0.8777653	0.7510659	0.9272936	0.8409978
60+	1.1761763	1.2221747	1.2577792	1.1770299	1.2205261

ulation for age group 0–4 is lowest for Bihar (0.87126) and Nagaland (0.87032) and highest for Andaman and Nicobar Islands (0.92073) and Madhya Pradesh (0.90403). Thus the range of variation in the multipliers for age group 0–4 is relatively narrow. But the variation in the multipliers for age group 60+ is much wider—from 1.09 for Kerala to 1.26 for Rajasthan. The pattern of regional variation in the multipliers for the females is similar to that for the males, indicating that the effects of smoothing varied more among regions than between sexes. We may thus infer that the comparability of the age data in different states was greatly lost as a result of the smoothing in 1931. This doubly justifies the elaborate computation involved in the unsmoothing exercise.

The question that remains unsolved is whether the pattern of interstate differences in age bias varies from census to census or remains unchanged over time. If it remains unchanged, then the construction of K (I, J) multipliers from 1961 age data and application of these multipliers on 1931 age data are justified. But if the pattern changes over time, then the validity of the results obtained becomes a matter of doubt.

Table 2.9 presents the age distribution for the male and female population in five states before and after unsmoothing. The most noticeable effect of unsmoothing is felt on age group 0—4 and next to that on age group 5—9. The effects of the unsmoothing operation on age groups 50—54 and 60+ are also conspicuous. It will be recalled that the smoothing process in 1931 was only a preliminary sort of adjustment for ironing out some of the most conspicuous biases in the age returns, as distinguished from the thorough and drastic smoothing resorted to by Indian actuaries for the purpose of constructing life tables from age data. Yet it is interesting that our unsmoothing brings into relief the most important errors in the census age data, which may be briefly stated as follows:

1. Conspicuous underenumeration in age group 0—4

2. Overenumeration in age group 5—9

3. Underenumeration of males in age groups 10—14, 15—19, and 20—24

4. Underenumeration of females in age groups 15—19 and 20—24

5. Conspicuous overenumeration in age groups 40—44, 50—54, and 60+

6. Conspicuous underenumeration in age group 55—59 for the female population

Besides, the variations in the nature and degree of bias among the different states and territories are apparent from a perusal of the two sets of percentage distributions in Table 2.9.

The usefulness of the unsmoothing exercise may be better appreciated if we examine the age ratios and sex ratios in the census age tables and the unsmoothed age tables. The age-ratio score for the male and female populations of Andhra Pradesh are 4 and 5 respectively for the census age distribution and 14 and 16 respectively for the unsmoothed age distribution. The sex-ratio score is 6 for the census data and 9 for the unsmoothed data.* The joint score is 27 for the census data and 58 for the unsmoothed age data. Though there are differences of degree among the states, the age-ratio scores, the sex-ratio scores, and consequently the joint scores are always smaller for the census age distribution than for the unsmoothed age distribution.

---

* See Chapter 3 for the definitions of age-ratio score and sex-ratio score.

Table 2.9 1931 census percentage age distribution for five states before and after unsmoothing

Age group	West Bengal		Uttar Pradesh		Andhra Pradesh		Maharashtra		Punjab	
	Census	Un-smoothed	Census	Un-smoothed	Census	Un-smoothed	Census	Un-smoothed	Census	Un-smoothed
MALE										
0—4	11.68	10.31	12.87	11.27	14.44	12.73	14.75	13.31	14.10	12.49
5—9	12.26	13.60	12.70	13.57	12.89	13.48	12.82	13.60	12.77	13.64
10—14	11.28	10.79	12.47	12.40	11.69	11.77	11.49	11.36	12.30	12.24
15—19	9.33	8.85	9.10	8.79	8.74	8.54	8.50	8.10	9.53	9.50
20—24	9.33	8.96	8.34	7.55	9.06	8.08	9.14	8.49	9.21	8.39
25—29	10.23	10.53	8.86	8.94	8.54	8.79	8.61	8.93	7.71	8.03
30—34	8.96	8.67	8.48	7.72	7.62	7.76	8.10	7.72	7.04	6.75
35—39	7.63	7.77	6.64	6.62	6.60	6.42	6.64	7.09	5.59	5.48
40—44	6.15	6.33	5.47	6.42	5.63	6.23	5.51	5.66	4.86	5.23
45—49	4.46	4.57	4.02	4.41	4.30	4.11	4.35	4.71	4.46	4.28
50—54	3.35	3.57	3.19	4.94	3.41	4.33	3.49	3.74	3.61	4.41
55—59	2.06	2.11	1.99	2.09	2.50	2.03	2.42	2.44	2.83	2.33
60+	3.47	3.94	3.23	5.27	4.58	5.73	4.17	4.86	6.00	7.24
All age groups	100.00	100.00	100.00	100.00	100.00	100.00	100.00	100.00	100.00	100.00
FEMALE										
0—4	13.52	12.03	19.16	12.82	15.64	13.86	16.15	14.64	16.45	14.73
5—9	12.39	14.39	13.83	13.78	12.47	13.51	12.71	13.93	13.36	14.27
10—14	10.63	9.48	11.40	10.44	10.99	10.64	11.15	10.66	12.27	12.08
15—19	10.64	10.14	9.89	7.65	9.37	8.75	9.23	8.30	9.33	8.91
20—24	10.38	9.97	10.26	8.88	10.10	9.21	9.76	9.40	9.06	8.50
25—29	9.65	10.01	8.52	8.97	9.11	9.57	8.56	9.13	9.50	7.85
30—34	7.92	7.85	7.34	7.99	7.33	7.66	7.49	7.21	6.50	6.28
35—39	6.13	6.21	5.28	6.33	5.87	5.72	6.04	6.38	5.39	5.38
40—44	5.18	5.51	4.23	6.33	4.95	5.58	5.06	5.29	4.76	5.15
45—49	3.89	3.80	3.10	4.18	3.80	3.47	3.94	4.22	4.16	4.14
50—54	3.31	3.70	2.54	4.69	3.14	4.13	3.16	3.45	3.34	4.08
55—59	2.16	1.97	1.66	1.92	2.38	1.79	2.38	2.21	2.55	2.14
60+	4.21	4.94	2.79	6.01	4.85	6.10	4.35	5.13	5.33	6.48
All age groups	100.00	100.00	100.00	100.00	100.00	100.00	100.00	100.00	100.00	100.00

This is what is expected. Since the biases in the original census returns of 1931 had been somewhat reduced by the smoothing operation, the age-ratio scores and sex-ratio scores were reduced. Because the unsmoothing operation reversed the process, the resultant age distributions regained some of the old biases in the original census age returns.

Y-sample tables and partially smoothed data: 1941

Two types of age data are available for 1941: 2 percent sample tables for the British Indian provinces and complete tabulation for a number of princely states. For the princely states, the age data were subjected to a preliminary smoothing operation before being presented in the census tables. We have attempted to regain the raw age figures from these two types of data.

Since 1941 was a war year, a drastic economy was effected in the tabulation and printing of the census information. Age data were tabulated for the then British Indian provinces on the basis of a 2 percent sample of the enumeration slips [17]. It was later discovered that these samples had not been drawn with an equal rigor for the different districts in the various provinces. After a few years the sample slips were used by the Indian Statistical Institute for correcting the errors of sampling and reconstructing the age data. These reconstructed age tables (called the Y-sample tables) are available for the following states: Andhra Pradesh (excluding districts transferred from Nizam's Territory of Hyderabad), Madhya Pradesh (excluding districts transferred from Central Provinces States and Central Indian Agency), Madras, West Bengal, Assam, Gujarat (excluding districts transferred from princely states of the West Indian Agency), Orissa, Bihar, Haryana, Punjab (excluding districts transferred from princely states of the Punjab States and Punjab States Agency), Maharashtra, Meghalaya, and Uttar Pradesh.

Three sets of figures are given in these reconstructed age tables. The first set shows the age distribution in five-year age groups by sex and marital status. The second set shows the literacy standard by age and sex, under the categories Illiterate, Literate, and Literate in English. The third set presents the single-year age distribution. Since the five-year age distribution in the sample tables had been subjected to a preliminary smoothing operation, we preferred to use the reconstructed single-year age figures and regrouped them into five-year age groups for our purpose.

The reader may profitably note in this connection the following

observations made in the census paper on Y-sample tables for West
Bengal [17:1].

No uniform method of estimation can be used for all the districts for two reasons.
Firstly, owing largely to conditions created by the war, the 2% slips were not
always properly extracted and sometimes properly stored after extraction and
were partly destroyed or lost. In consequence, available district samples were de-
fective, some of them being extremely so. Adjustments had therefore to be made
to eliminate as far as possible the effects of such defects.

In certain cases even tolerably satisfactory sample slips were not available. Adjustments had to be made therefore on the basis of the information contained in
the Sample Tables already published in the Census Report.

On the basis of the adjustments noted above, "weights" or "multipliers" were
determined to estimate from sample figures results for the whole population. The
figures given in these tables are such estimates.

One could see some pitfalls in the drawing of the samples and in
tracing and identifying the codes of some places. Nevertheless, it is
believed that the sampling errors were to some extent counterbalanced
by presumably higher quality of office work. Moreover, the use of the
district data gave the additional benefit of stratification.

The population covered by the Y-sample tables constituted about
half the total population of India in 1941. The remaining population
belonged mainly to the princely states. Most of the major princely
states, acting on the advice of the census commissioner, proceeded to
a full tabulation at their own expense [25]. The existence of a full age
record for Kashmir, Rajputana, Baroda, Gwalior, Mysore, Travancore,
and Cochin served the additional purpose of enabling the statisticians
to test the results of estimation against the complete data.

The advantage was not, however, unqualified. The age data for the
abovementioned areas had been presented not in raw form but after
having been subjected to a preliminary process of smoothing (compare
1931). In pursuance of the suggestions of the census actuary of 1931,
the census commissioner of 1941 advised the officers in charge in the
princely states to apply a smoothing formula to the raw age data and
then present them in the census tables. The formula used for smoothing was different from that used in 1931. The 1941 smoothing formula is given in Table 2.10 [19:130].

Such smoothing had been effected with respect to the states of
Cochin, Baroda, and Gwalior. As for the other states, it was not mentioned whether smoothing had been done or not. But an examination
of the census age tables strongly suggests that the age data for these
other states also had been smoothed. We have therefore derived the

Table 2.10 Formula for smoothing 1941 age data for selected princely states

Sorters' age group	Population	Formula	Compilers' age group
0	A	A	0
1	B	B	1
2	C	C	2
3	D	D	3
4	E	E	4
5	F	$F + G + (3/5)H$	5–9
6	G	$(2/5)H + (3/5)I$	10–14
7–11	H	$(2/5)I + (3/5)J$	15–19
12–16	I	$(2/5)J + (3/5)K$	20–24
17–21	J	$(2/5)K + (3/5)L$	25–29
22–26	K	$(2/5)L + (3/5)M$	30–34
27–31	L	$(2/5)M + (3/5)N$	35–39
32–36	M	$(2/5)N + (3/5)O$	40–44
37–41	N	$(2/5)O + (3/5)P$	45–49
42–46	O	$(2/5)P + (3/5)Q$	50–54
47–51	P	$(2/5)Q + (3/5)R$	55–59
52–56	Q	$(2/5)R + (3/5)S$	60–64
57–61	R	$(2/5)S + (3/5)T$	65–69
62–66	S	$(2/5)T + U$	70+
67–71	T		
72+	U		

SOURCE: [19:130].

raw age data by an unsmoothing formula analogous to that adopted for the year 1931. We have applied the 1941 smoothing formula to the single-year age data for 1961 and then estimated the raw age figures for 1941 according to the formula:

$$\text{Raw 1941} = \frac{\text{Raw 1961} \times \text{Smoothed 1941}}{\text{Smoothed 1961}}$$

For the states of Kerala, Mysore, and Madhya Pradesh the unsmoothed age data for some constituent areas were combined with the single-year age data as reconstructed from the Y samples for other areas. The hybrid nature of the resultant age figures might detract from their value and reliability, but this is all that could be done under the circumstances.

A word may be said about the manner in which the samples had been drawn by the census in areas where the age tables were provided not for the whole population but for a sample. As a typical case we may quote the following from the Baroda Census Report [19:125]:

For the purpose of collecting the sample, every one of the 11570 blocks of the State was ransacked. If a block had less than 30 slips, it was neglected, and where a block had more than 30 and less than 50 slips, the last slip in the rack was picked out, and marked $ on the back. Where a block had more than 50 slips and less than 75, then the 50th slip was so marked. For blocks of larger sizes, i.e., with 75 and more slips the principle adopted was to mark the first 25th slip, and then the 50th after that, i.e., the first 75th, then the 125th, and so on. In this way the selection went on throughout the State. Altogether 57298 slips were picked out in this manner—29585 males and 27713 females: the sex-ratio being 937 females to 1000 males. The sex-ratio for the whole population being 938, the sample may be accepted as representative.

For the states of Andhra Pradesh, Maharashtra, Kerala, and others, data obtained from Y-sample tables for some districts were added to those for other districts obtained from the unsmoothed age figures. Specifically, for Kerala the age data for the areas in the then princely states of Travancore and Cochin were unsmoothed as stated above. The unsmoothed figures were then added to the age-distributed population of the districts of Malabar obtained from Y-sample tables. The resultant age distribution was scaled down on the basis of the total population of the state as given by the 1961 census.

Madhya Pradesh presented one of the most complicated areas so far as the age data for 1941 were concerned. Of the 43 districts in the state, Y-sample tables were available for 14—i.e., those which had been in the then Central Provinces and Berar. Smoothed data were available for the six districts included in the then Princely State of Gwalior and three districts included in the Princely State of Rewa. These data were unsmoothed by us. The age data for Indore were collected from the Census of India, Paper 3 of 1954 [20:172]. These data were given in single-year ages from 0 to 16 and thence forwarded in five-year age groups 17–21, 22–26, 27–31, and so on. To recast the age composition in the conventional five-year age groups, we formed identical groups from the single-year age data of the 1961 census for the same district and worked out the ratio of the respective three-year totals and two-year totals in each of these five-year totals. By applying these ratios to the 1941 data for Indore, we derived the raw five-year age distribution for the district. Since the data for the remaining districts of the state were not available from any source whatsoever, we summed the age-distributed data already obtained by us and raised the totals thus obtained by suitable multiplying factors.

A similar procedure was adopted for Mysore. The census age data for the Princely State of Mysore were unsmoothed. Y-sample tables were obtained for the districts of Bijapur, Belgaum, Dharwar, and Kanara (previously in the State of Bombay), and Bellary and South Kanara (previously in the State of Madras). The data for the three districts Raichur, Gulbarga, and Bidar which had been parts of the Nizam's

Territory of Hyderabad were not available from any source. This leaves a big gap in the data for 1941.

A gap exists also in the age data for Punjab, Haryana, and Himachal Pradesh. Of the eleven districts in the Punjab, Y-sample tables were available for only six: Hoshiarpur, Jullundhur, Ludhiana, Ferozepur, Amritsar, and Gurudaspur. The small and medium-sized princely states included in what was then Punjab had not tabulated the age data. The only alternative left to us therefore was to add up the age figures for these six districts and scale up the resultant age distribution by a suitable multiplying factor. Evidently the multiplying factors were large in such cases. In the absence of relevant data this appears to be unavoidable.

As regards Haryana, Y-sample tables were available for five out of seven districts: Hissar, Rohtak, Karnal, Gurgaon, and Ambala. As regards Himachal Pradesh, Y-sample tables were available for two districts only (Simla and Kangra). No age data were available for the then princely states in the hills. We have constructed tables on the 1961 age data for the states of Madhya Pradesh, Andhra Pradesh, Maharashtra, and Mysore showing the differences in their age composition with and without those districts for which no age data were available for 1941. The differences were small. Presumably, similar differences for 1941 also would be small. We hypothesize that though the gaps in data were real and substantial in some cases, the effects of such gaps were not great.

The displaced population: 1951

The age data for 1951 were given in the census tables separately for the displaced population from Pakistan and the rest of the population (the nondisplaced or general population). For the nondisplaced population, age data are available for a 10 percent sample. (The sampling fraction was not strictly 10 percent in all cases; there are some variations from state to state.)

The registrar general's instruction [21:iii] for taking the samples was as follows:

Break each pad [of 100 enumeration slips] and stack the slips of the pad; and cut the stack as in a card game. Place the lower portion above the upper portion and then deal the slips into the pigeonholes. You should deal the slips into the pigeonholes in the order of 1, 2, 3, 4, 5, S, 6, 7, 8 and 9 respectively. All the time you should watch the slips of displaced persons. If you come across any slip of a displaced person, deal it in the pigeonhole of "Displaced Persons."

A displaced person was defined [21:iii] as "any person who has entered India having left or being compelled to leave his or her home in Western Pakistan on or after the first [of] March 1947 or his or her home in Eastern Pakistan on or after the 15th [of] October 1946 on account of civil disturbances or the fear of such disturbances or on account of the setting up of the two dominions of India and Pakistan."

With regard to the nondisplaced persons, the single-year age data of the sample population were grouped into the required series of quinquennial age intervals. The age figures thus obtained were expanded by suitable multiplying factors separately for the male and female population. The multiplying factors were obtained by relating the nondisplaced population of each state by sex (adjusted for changes in the administrative boundaries) to the sample population for the respective areas. If

$$N = \text{number of nondisplaced persons adjusted for boundary changes}$$

$$S = \text{effective sample size for area}$$

$$m = \text{multiplying factor}$$

$$sp(i) = \text{number of persons in age group } (i) \text{ in sample}$$

$$p(i) = \text{number of persons in age group } (i) \text{ in parent nondisplaced population}$$

then

$$m = \frac{N}{S}$$

and

$$p(i) = m[sp(i)]$$

With regard to the displaced persons, the census age tables for 1951 provide five-year age distribution for age groups 0–4, 5–9, and 10–14 and ten-year age distribution thereafter (15–24, 25–34, and so on). We first decomposed the ten-year age groups into the corresponding pairs of five-year age groups on the basis of the assumption that the internal distribution of two five-year age groups within a ten-year age group was the same for the displaced population as for the nondisplaced population in the particular state. Then the age-distributed displaced population was added to the age-distributed nondisplaced population of the respective states.

Of the 29 states and territories, separate account has been taken of the displaced population in seven: Assam, Meghalaya, West Bengal, Punjab, Haryana, Himachal Pradesh, and Delhi. For the remaining 22 states and territories, the entire population was assumed to have been

Table 2.11 **Percentage age distribution of displaced and nondisplaced male population in four states and territories: 1951**

Age group	West Bengal		Assam		Punjab		Delhi	
	Dis-placed	Nondis-placed	Dis-placed	Nondis-placed	Dis-placed	Nondis-placed	Dis-placed	Nondis-placed
0–4	6.94	10.79	8.17	15.83	4.63	16.45	3.66	19.31
5–9	10.95	11.15	11.88	14.74	12.73	12.54	11.30	10.89
10–14	13.67	11.58	12.44	11.45	14.35	11.90	13.81	10.55
15–59	65.85	61.67	62.86	53.62	57.22	51.37	63.65	54.08
60+	2.59	4.81	4.65	4.36	11.07	7.74	7.58	5.17
All age groups	100.00	100.00	100.00	100.00	100.00	100.00	100.00	100.00

nondisplaced—though there might have been a few displaced persons—and the multiplying factors were obtained by relating the total population by sex to the sample populations of the respective areas.

At the risk of a little digression, we may make a few comments on the age composition of the displaced population. Table 2.11 sets out a summarized age distribution of the displaced and nondisplaced population separately in four states and territories. Notice the significantly smaller proportion of children in age group 0—4 among the displaced population than among the nondisplaced population. Several reasons may be suggested to explain this.

First, there might have been a relatively greater undercount of children among the displaced population. The census of 1951 was the first after independence, and the census apparatus did not have sufficient time to adjust to the new situation. A comparison of the number of persons in age groups 0—4 in 1951 and 10—14 in 1961 indicates that both displaced and nondisplaced children in age group 0—4 were underenumerated. There might have been a greater undercount of children among the displaced population—owing to the unsettled conditions of life in refugee camps.

Second, a displaced person was defined as one who had left Pakistan in or after 1946. Children below 5 years of age in 1951 were born after 1946. Therefore children born to displaced parents after their arrival in India were excluded from the category of displaced population.

Third, there might also have occurred a higher incidence of mortality among children of this age group as a consequence of the extremely unfavorable environment in which the bulk of the newly arrived displaced people were compelled to live.

Finally, the abnormal conditions of life in the years immediately preceding and following migration might have depressed the level of fertility among the displaced people. The low proportion of children could not have been due to an age selectivity of refugee migration. When people left Pakistan, they would not have left their children back there. There is, however, the theoretical possibility that a high proportion of small families migrated. Hindu families in Pakistan encumbered with many children might have thought twice before deciding on migration. An inquiry into the age distribution of Hindus remaining in Pakistan would throw more light on this problem.

$$\mathcal{3}$$

The reconstructed age tables

Chapter 2 was devoted to an exposition of the methods adopted for reconstructing the age composition for the states and territories in India as defined in the 1971 census. This chapter presents the basic tables and indicates the probable magnitude of bias and distortion in the reconstructed age data.

Broad features of the age composition

Figures 3.1 and 3.2 depict the male and female age distributions in India in the nine successive censuses, 1881 through 1961. The story told by the graphs is clear, simple, and vivid. The gradient in the age curves is steep in the early ages, slow in the middle ages, and once again steep in the old ages. Basic tables showing the age distribution in percentage repeat the same story for the five zones and all states and territories in India and for both male and female populations. The young age distribution shown in nine successive censuses is unlikely to be an accidental feature or an enumeration freak. It is a persistent feature of Indian demography—revealed in bold relief in spite of enumeration errors and statistical manipulations.

The basic tables also reveal small but persistent differences in age structure in the different zones of India. The proportions in age sector 0–10 are lower in the Southern Zone than in the Eastern or Northern

Figure 3.1 Male age distribution: India, 1901—1961

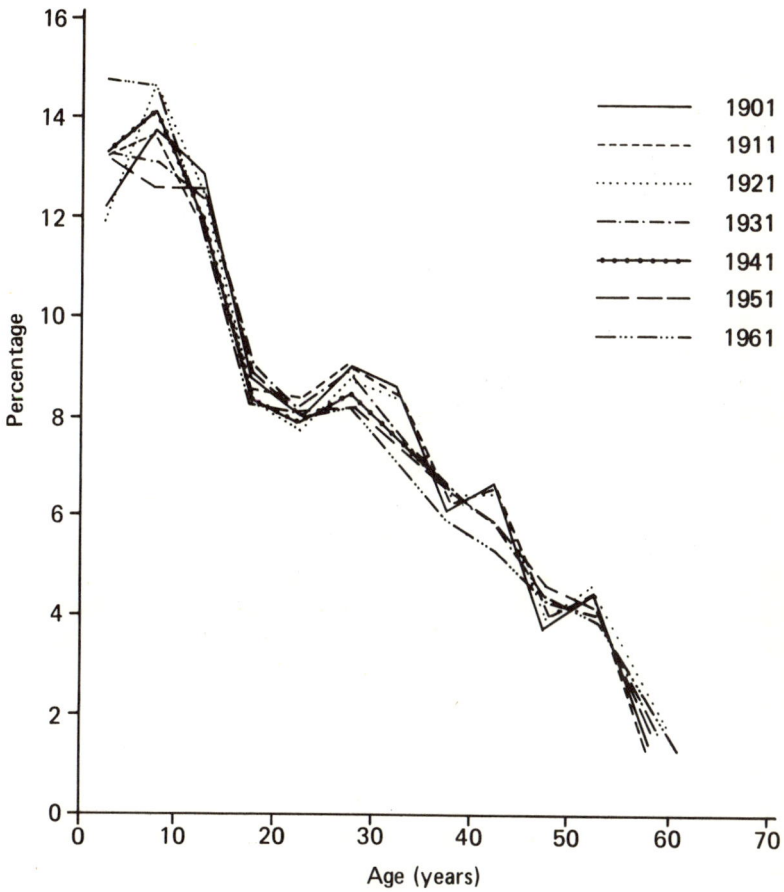

Figure 3.2 Female age distribution: India, 1901–1961

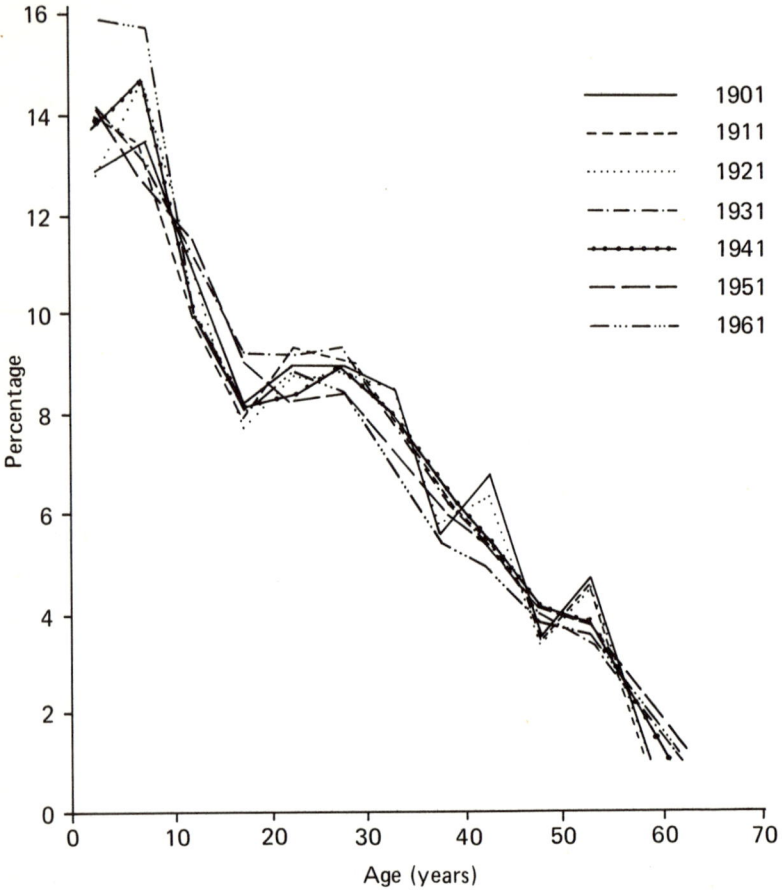

Zones, while the proportions in the higher ages are lower in the Eastern and Northern Zones. Although the age distributions in all the zones are remarkably younger than in the West European or North American countries, they are somewhat older in the Southern Zone than in the Northern and perhaps a little older in the Western Zone than in the Eastern.

Figures 3.3 and 3.4 provide a comparative picture of the age-sex structure in India and some other countries. The structural difference between the age composition in India on the one hand and that in Japan, the United States, Europe, or Great Britain on the other is striking. The Indian age pyramid has a conspicuously broader base, narrower middle, and thinner top than the others. Japan's age structure bears evidence of the drastic decline in birth rate in the 1950s. The narrow middle in the American and European age structure bears the mark of the decline in birth rates in the prewar years and war years.

Such structural differences in age composition at a particular time may also be studied in the context of changes that occurred during the fifty-year period 1911–1961. The triangular shape of the Indian age pyramid remained more or less unchanged during this period, but the British pyramid changed from a triangular shape to a columnar one. There is extensive documentation in the demographic literature of the reasons for such discrepant movement in the age distribution in India on the one hand and countries like Great Britain on the other—the basic reason being the persistence of a high birth rate in India and the steep decline in birth rates in Great Britain, Western Europe generally, North America, and Australia [93, 94].

Errors in the reconstructed age tables

The validity of these observations rests on the assumption that the errors in the reconstructed age composition in India are not so large as to vitiate all inferences drawn from them. It is, therefore, in the fitness of things that a brief examination be made of the nature and extent of errors in the age tables presented here for India and its states and territories. Such errors may be of two broad types—those arising out of computational manipulations in the process of reconstruction, and inherent errors in Indian age data arising out of the biases and misstatements in the census age returns.

In the computational procedure a continuous effort has been made to reduce the first kind of error to the minimum, so that the nature and magnitude of the second kind may remain unaffected in the

Figure 3.3 Comparative age structures for India, Japan, United States, and Europe: 1955–1961

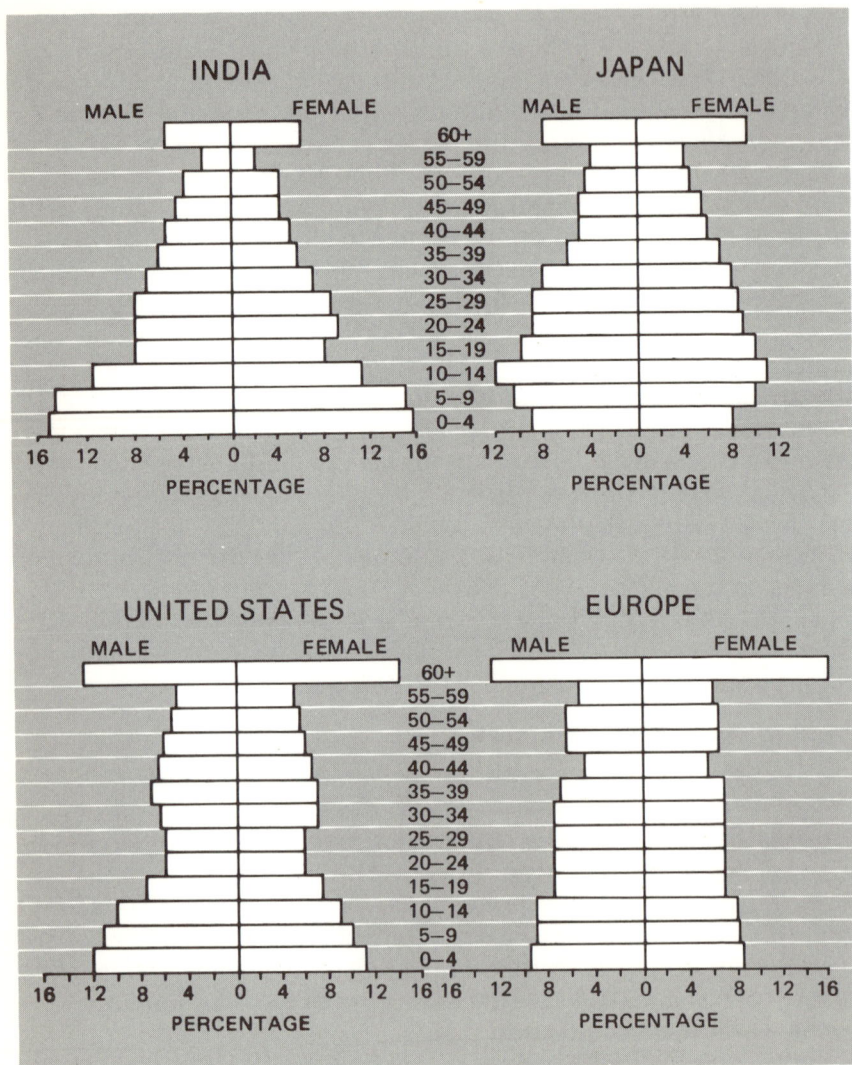

Figure 3.4 Age structural changes in India and Great Britain: 1911—1961

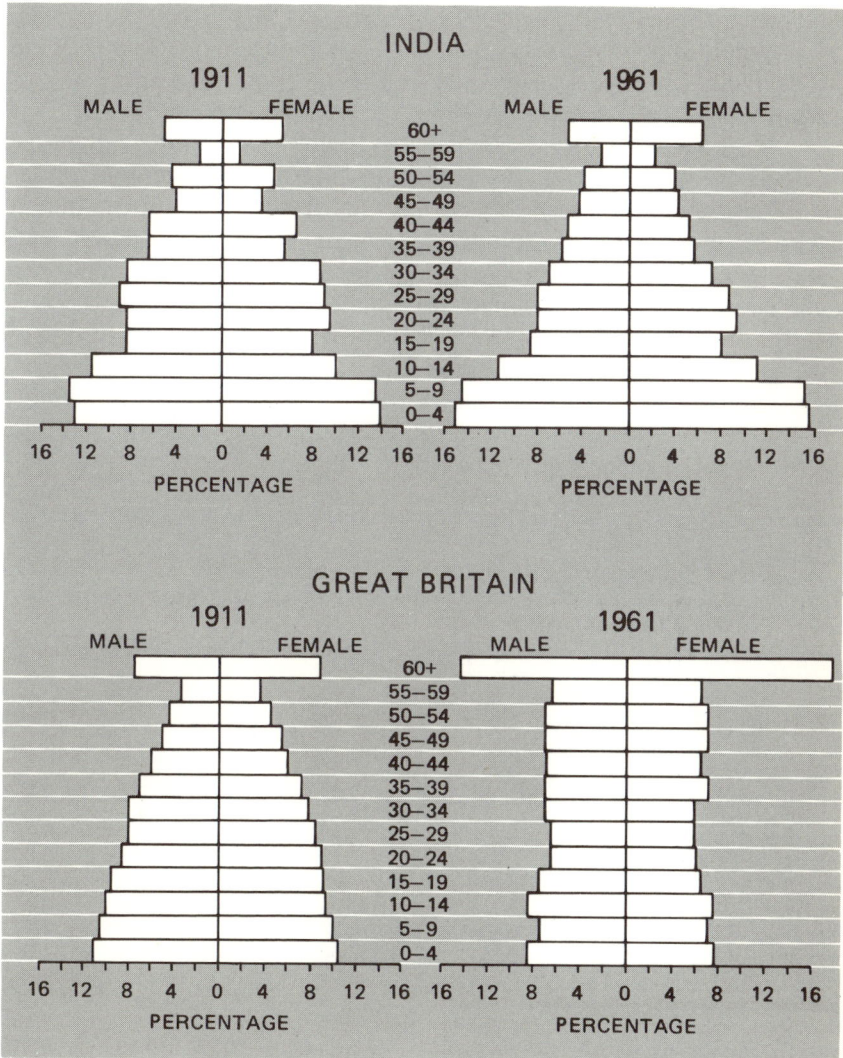

reconstructed age tables. In other words, our endeavor has been to ensure that the reconstructed age tables contain all the biases and distortions of the original census data.

Lack of universal coverage is one factor that may give rise to the first kind of error. Fortunately, the areas for which age data were not available for some of the census years were few; moreover, the size of the population involved was small. Data for Manipur and Tripura were not available for census years 1881 and 1891; those for Jammu and Kashmir were not available for 1881 and 1951; and those for the North-East Frontier Agency (Arunachal Pradesh) were not available for 1881 through 1921 and 1941. The inclusion or exclusion of these small areas is not expected to have any significant effect on the Indian age distribution in proportionate terms in the respective years.

To illustrate this point we computed the age distribution of the aggregate population in those areas for which age data have been available for all the census years. We then compared this age distribution with that of the total population in India for the year 1961 (Table 3.1). The two age distributions are strikingly similar, thus supporting our hypothesis that the inclusion or exclusion of the areas noted above is not expected to have any perceptible effect on the relative proportions of the total population in the different age groups.

Table 3.1 Percentage age distribution in the common set of states and territories and in India as a whole: 1961

Age group	Common set of states and territories		India	
	Male	Female	Male	Female
0—4	14.62	15.46	14.68	15.47
5—9	14.61	14.88	14.63	14.86
10—14	11.53	10.71	11.62	10.83
15—19	8.22	8.10	8.23	8.12
20—24	8.04	8.99	8.05	9.00
25—29	8.23	8.50	8.20	8.49
30—34	7.10	7.00	7.07	6.98
35—39	6.05	5.58	6.02	5.58
40—44	5.37	5.09	5.35	5.07
45—49	4.34	3.94	4.31	3.91
50—54	4.06	3.77	4.04	3.75
55—59	2.35	2.15	2.34	2.14
60+	5.48	5.83	5.47	5.81
All age groups	100.00	100.00	100.00	100.00
Population (millions)	203	191	226	213

Biases and distortions in the age data

Indian census actuaries have identified various types of errors in the census age returns arising out of a prejudice against or a preference for certain ages and digits, ignorance of age, and age-sex selective omissions in enumeration. It is necessary to have a measure of such distortion in the age composition we reconstructed. This will serve two purposes. First, it will tell us how much reliance can be placed on studies based on these reconstructed tables. Second, it will indicate whether the original biases and distortions in census age returns have been ironed out in the process of reconstruction or whether the raw character of the data has been properly preserved.

Among the various methods suggested to measure the degree of error in the age data, we have chosen the so-called United Nations Secretariat method of computing sex ratios and age ratios for five-year age groups [91]. We have selected this method because it is most suited to grouped data summarizing the combined effect of age preferences, digit preferences, and age misstatements. The following quotation from U.N. Manual II [91:42] may be relevant here:

The United Nations Secretariat method has the advantage over the method of Whipple, Myers and Bachi that the index which is obtained is affected by differential omission of persons in various age groups from the census count and by tendentious age misstatements as well as by digit preference, and is therefore more truly a reflection of the general accuracy of the age statistics. Also, it provides an indication of accuracy of the data in the form in which they are used for most purposes, that is, in age groups rather than single years. The methods applied to data by single years of age may in some cases show a fairly large amount of age misstatement which has little influence on the grouped data.

Age-ratio score and sex-ratio score

The age ratio for a given five-year age group (i) is a number obtained by multiplying 100 times a ratio in which the numerator is the number enumerated in the given age interval and the denominator is the mean of the numbers enumerated in the immediately lower and immediately higher age intervals—that is, in the $(i - 1)$th and $(i + 1)$th age intervals. The deviations of the products from 100—both positive and negative—are summed without regard to sign, and the sum is divided by the number of age intervals for which age ratios have been calculated to yield what is known as the age-ratio score. To put it symbolically, let

$$P_i = \text{number of persons enumerated in}$$
$$\text{age interval } (i)$$

P_{i-1} = number of persons enumerated in age
interval $(i - 1)$

P_{i+1} = number of persons enumerated in age
interval $(i + 1)$

R_i = age ratio for age interval (i)

ARS = age-ratio score for given age distribution

n = total number of age intervals (13) in
entire distribution

Then

$$R_i = \frac{200P_i}{P_{i-1} + P_{i+1}}$$

and

$$ARS^* = \frac{1}{n-3} \sum_{i=2}^{n-2} |R_i - 100|$$

If there are no violent fluctuations in mortality and fertility or big waves of migration (which is often age-selective) and if the number of persons in the successive age groups is gradually depleted through the incidence of mortality, the age ratio for any five-year age group should be approximately 100. A large deviation from 100 will be considered to be due mainly to misreporting of age or differential omission in enumeration of persons belonging to the given age group, or both.

The sex ratio for an age group (i) is defined as the number of males for 100 females in that age group. The mean difference between the sex ratios of all the pairs of successive age groups is called the sex-ratio score. In other words, let M_i and F_i be the number of males and females in age interval (i); let S_i be the sex ratio for age interval (i); and let SRS be the sex-ratio score for the entire sex-age distribution. Then

$$S_i = \frac{100M_i}{F_i}$$

and

$$SRS = \frac{1}{n-1} \sum_{i=2}^{n} |S_i - S_{i-1}|$$

---

* The denominator $n - 3$ (= 10) is explained as follows. The first age interval for which age ratio can be calculated is 5–9, 0–4 being the $(i - 1)$th age interval and 10–14 being the $(i + 1)$th. The age interval 50–54 is the last for which age ratio can be calculated, 45–49 and 55–59 being the $(i - 1)$th and $(i + 1)$th. The age interval 60+ is open-ended and hence must be excluded from calculation.

It is well known that the age curve is not linear. Hence even if the age data are completely accurate, the age ratio may deviate from 100 and the age-ratio score may have a nonzero value. Moreover, in all countries and cultures there are differential incidences of mortality for the two sexes in different age groups. Thus one can expect only a non-zero value for the sex-ratio score. The United Nations has suggested that an age-ratio score of 2.6 for males and 2.4 for females and a sex-ratio score of 1.5 be accepted as a standard for evaluating any given age distribution. They also think [91:42–43] that "on the whole more reliance should be placed on the sex-ratio score than on the age-ratio score for the two sexes." And so they suggest a standard joint score equal to 9.5 obtained by adding three times the sex-ratio score to the sum of the male and female age-ratio scores.

In the light of this let us have a look at the age ratios and sex ratios in India and its zones as worked out from the reconstructed age distribution in five-year age intervals. Figures 3.5 to 3.10 depict the trends in the age ratios and sex ratios over the 80-year period for the different age groups for India and its zones. Some typical features of the Indian census age data are immediately visible. There is an excess of both males and females in age intervals 5–9, 25–29, 30–34, 40–44, and 50–54. There is a visible undercount for both males and females in age intervals 0–4, 15–19, 35–39, and 45–49. In the age interval 10–14, there is an overcount of males and an undercount of females. Conversely, in the age interval 20–24 there is an overcount of females and an undercount of males.

Table 3.2 sets out the age-ratio scores, sex-ratio scores, and joint scores for the reconstructed age composition over the 80-year period 1881 through 1961. Even a quick glance at the table tells us of a steady decline in the value of the scores and hence a steady improvement in the quality of the age data in Indian censuses. But, as indicated earlier, the data for 1931, 1941, and 1951 present special problems. Therefore when we make inferences or derive estimates from the age data, we place greater reliance on the age data for the years 1881 through 1921 and the year 1961 than on those for 1931, 1941, or 1951.

Age ratios and sex ratios computed by Indian census actuary

It may be interesting at this stage to compare our age ratios and sex ratios with those computed by the Indian census actuary from the census age data for the then British Indian provinces and princely

Figure 3.5 Age ratios for India: 1881–1961

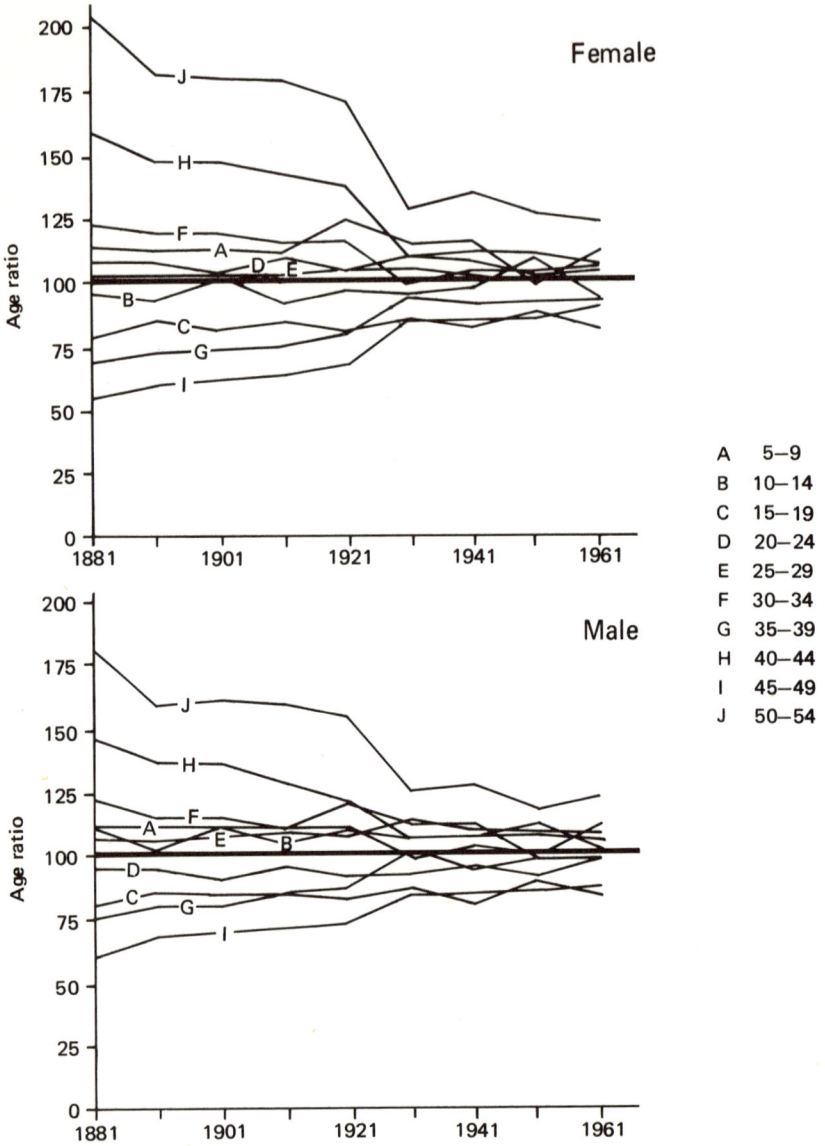

A	5–9
B	10–14
C	15–19
D	20–24
E	25–29
F	30–34
G	35–39
H	40–44
I	45–49
J	50–54

Figure 3.6 Age ratios for Eastern Zone: 1881—1961

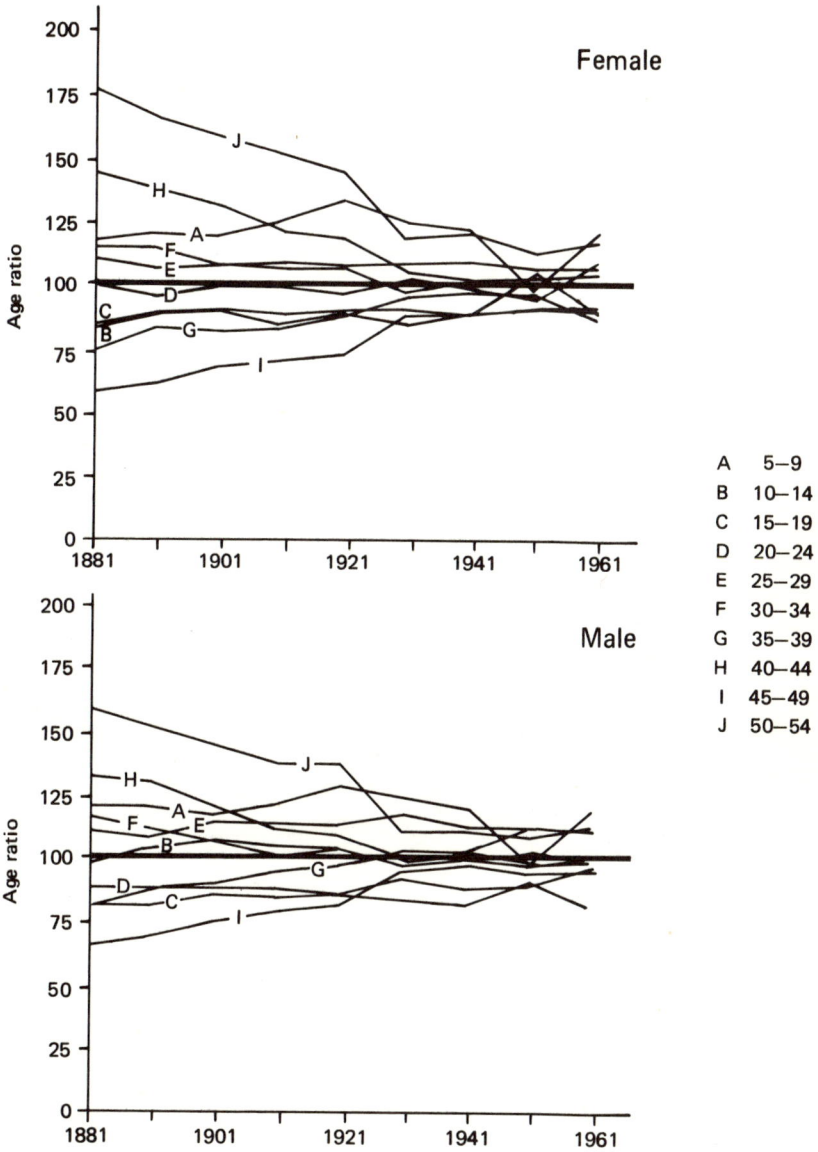

A	5—9
B	10—14
C	15—19
D	20—24
E	25—29
F	30—34
G	35—39
H	40—44
I	45—49
J	50—54

Figure 3.7 Age ratios for Central Zone: 1881–1961

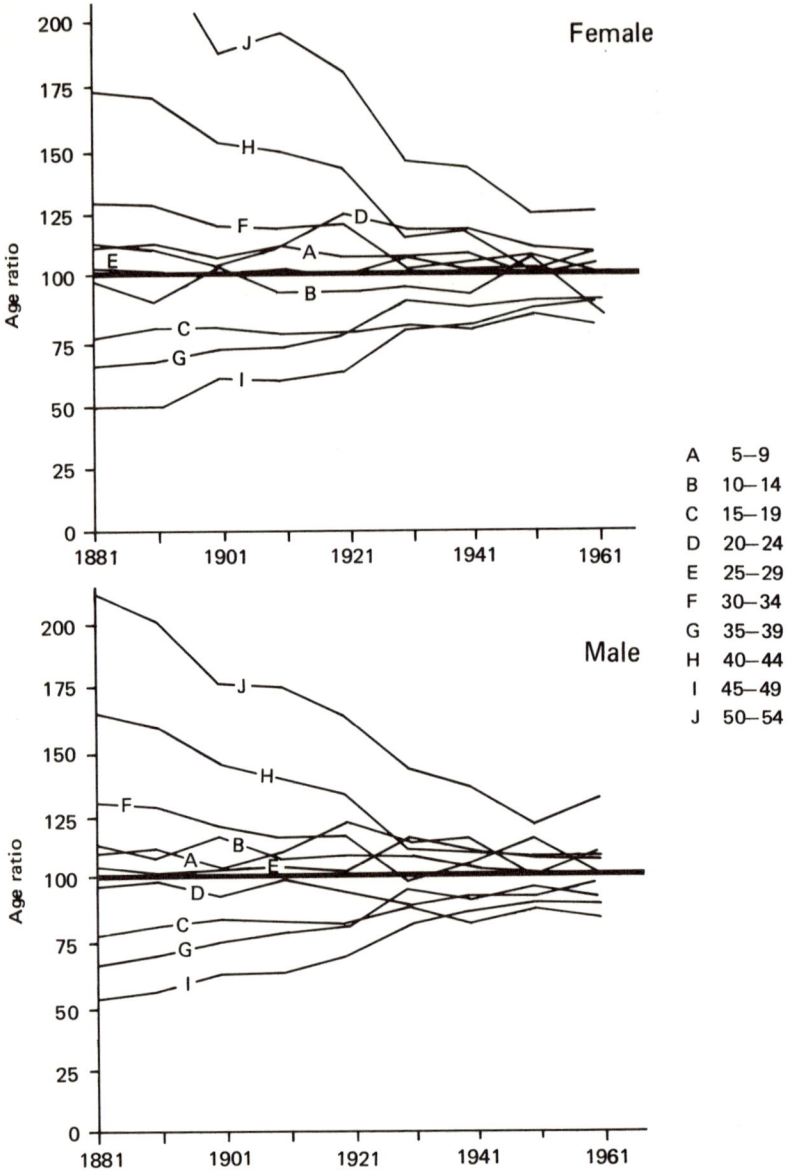

A	5–9
B	10–14
C	15–19
D	20–24
E	25–29
F	30–34
G	35–39
H	40–44
I	45–49
J	50–54

Figure 3.8 Age ratios for Southern Zone: 1881–1961

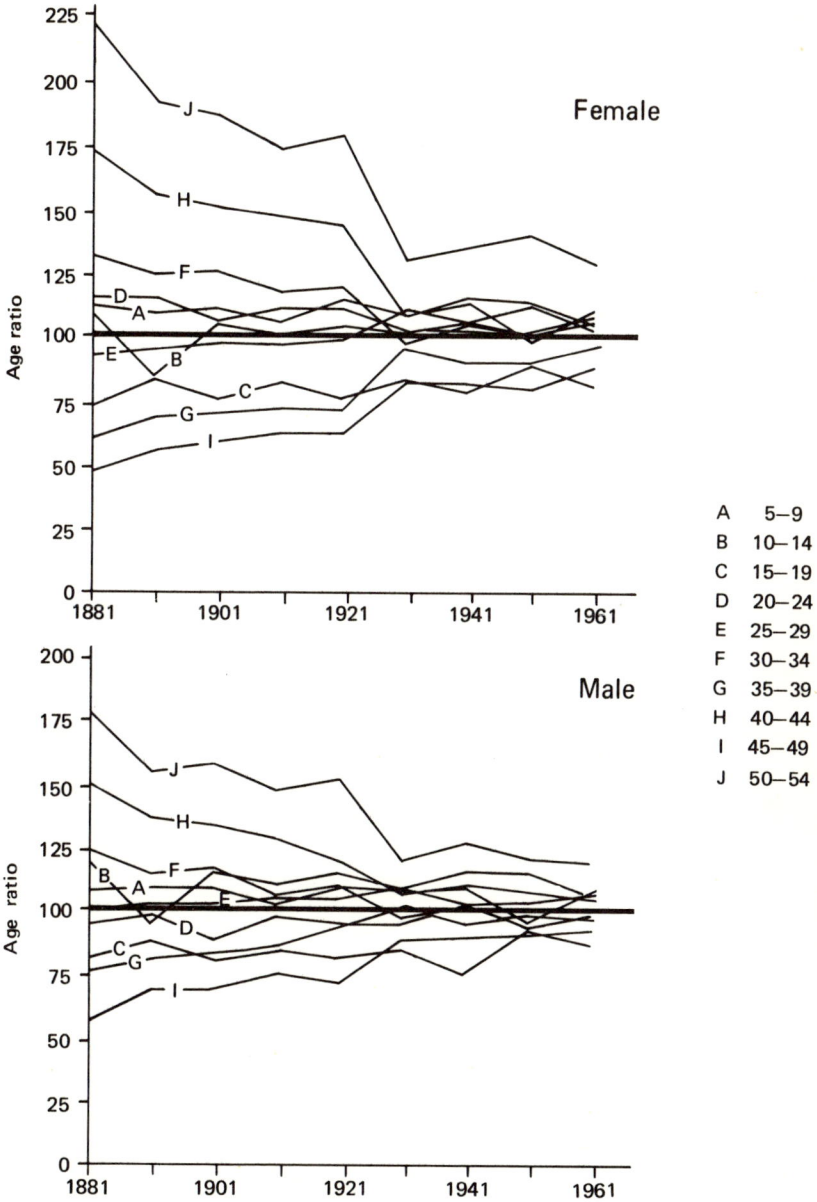

A	5–9
B	10–14
C	15–19
D	20–24
E	25–29
F	30–34
G	35–39
H	40–44
I	45–49
J	50–54

Figure 3.9 Age ratios for Western Zone: 1881—1961

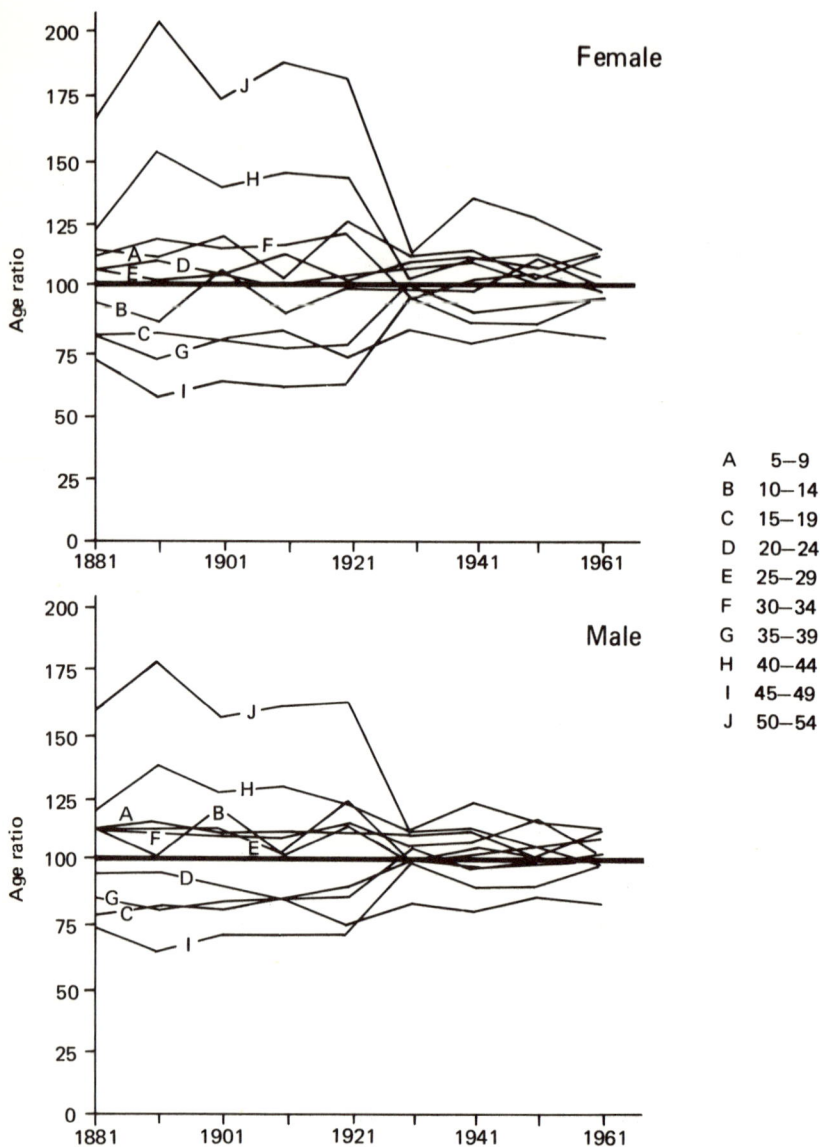

A	5—9
B	10—14
C	15—19
D	20—24
E	25—29
F	30—34
G	35—39
H	40—44
I	45—49
J	50—54

Figure 3.10 Age ratios for Northern Zone: 1881–1961

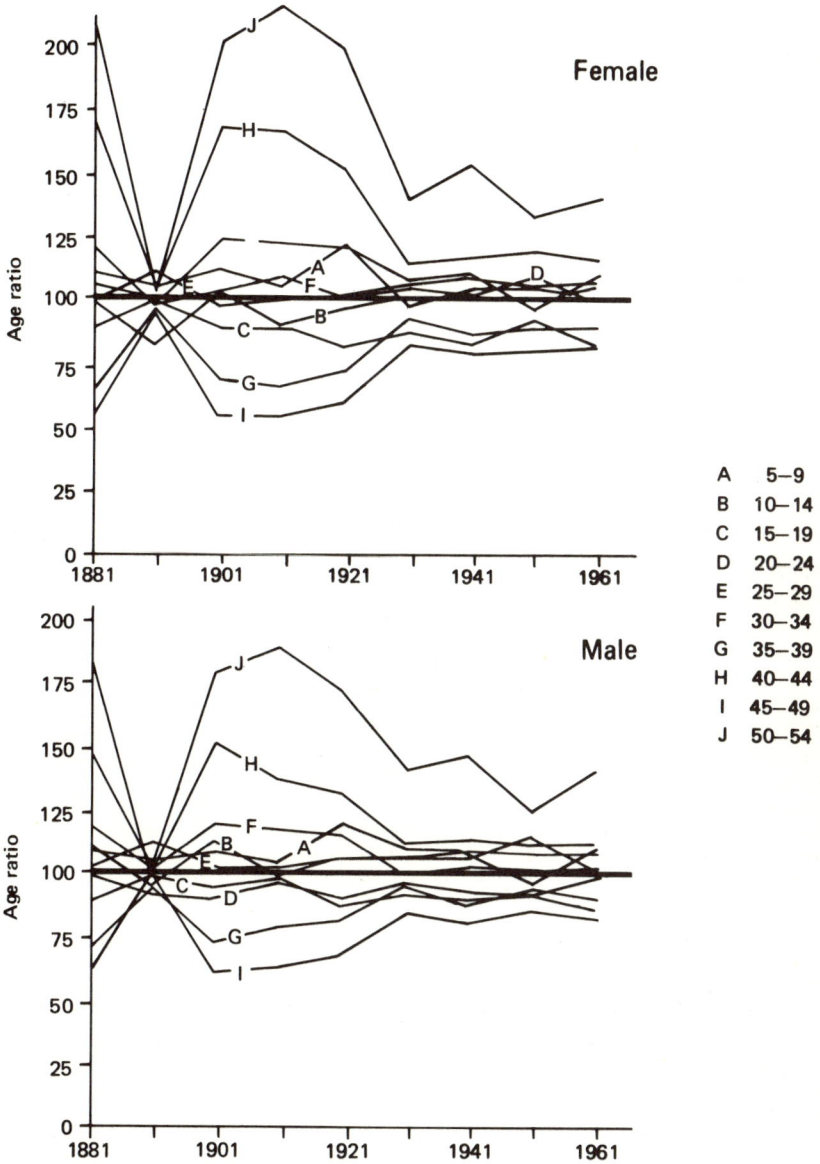

A	5–9
B	10–14
C	15–19
D	20–24
E	25–29
F	30–34
G	35–39
H	40–44
I	45–49
J	50–54

Table 3.2 Age-ratio score, sex-ratio score, and joint score: India and zones, 1881—1961

Zone	1881	1891	1901	1911	1921	1931	1941	1951	1961
INDIA									
Age-ratio score: male	26	20	22	18	19	10	10	8	8
Age-ratio score: female	31	26	25	25	24	11	13	9	10
Sex-ratio score	12	13	11	12	12	8	9	7	7
Joint score	94	85	80	80	79	45	50	38	38
EASTERN									
Age-ratio score: male	22	20	17	15	14	9	8	7	8
Age-ratio score: female	26	23	19	19	18	10	10	6	11
Sex-ratio score	13	11	11	12	11	10	10	6	10
Joint score	87	77	70	68	66	50	49	29	47
CENTRAL									
Age-ratio score: male	34	30	25	23	22	14	13	9	9
Age-ratio score: female	37	36	27	29	27	15	16	10	11
Sex-ratio score	11	13	9	11	11	10	9	8	7
Joint score	104	105	78	85	82	60	56	43	42
SOUTHERN									
Age-ratio score: male	27	18	21	16	17	9	11	8	7
Age-ratio score: female	39	31	29	24	26	10	13	12	10
Sex-ratio score	15	16	14	14	14	7	7	7	6
Joint score	111	97	93	81	86	41	47	42	34
WESTERN									
Age-ratio score: male	19	23	22	17	22	6	9	7	5
Age-ratio score: female	20	31	24	26	27	7	13	10	9
Sex-ratio score	10	15	12	15	14	7	12	9	7
Joint score	70	100	80	87	90	34	57	45	36
NORTHERN									
Age-ratio score: male	25	4	25	21	22	11	13	10	12
Age-ratio score: female	31	5	30	32	28	11	14	12	13
Sex-ratio score	14	8	12	16	14	5	8	7	6
Joint score	97	32	91	103	93	38	51	42	41

NOTE: Joint score = ARS (M) + ARS (F) + 3(SRS) where ARS is the age-ratio score and SRS is the sex-ratio score. Small discrepancies exist owing to rounding errors.

states for the census years 1901, 1911, and 1921 (Table 3.3) [28].*
The census actuary's figures are not strictly comparable with ours, because the boundaries of the areas to which the former relate are different from those to which our figures relate and also because the number of age intervals is 13 in our calculations and 15 in the census

---

* The scores in the census actuary's tables for 1931, 1941, 1951, and 1961 were calculated from smoothed age data and hence are not at all comparable to those we calculated from raw age data. Thus they are excluded from Table 3.3.

Table 3.3 Age-ratio score, sex-ratio score, and joint score calculated from original and reconstructed age data: India and selected areas, 1901–1921

Area	Original age data			Reconstructed age data		
	1901	1911	1921	1901	1911	1921
INDIA						
Age-ratio score: male	21.2	17.8	18.1	22	18	19
Age-ratio score: female	24.3	24.0	23.3	25	25	24
Sex-ratio score	9.9	10.9	12.2	11	12	12
Joint score	75.2	74.5	78.0	80	80	79
BIHAR						
Age-ratio score: male	u	15.1	13.9	18	17	15
Age-ratio score: female	u	17.8	16.7	20	20	18
Sex-ratio score	u	10.5	10.7	10	11	11
Joint score	u	64.4	62.7	69	69	66
UTTAR PRADESH						
Age-ratio score: male	25.8	23.3	20.6	26	23	21
Age-ratio score: female	28.3	27.7	25.2	28	28	25
Sex-ratio score	6.7	8.9	10.0	9	11	11
Joint score	74.2	86.7	75.8	81	83	73
MADRAS						
Age-ratio score: male	22.9	15.4	18.2	22	14	17
Age-ratio score: female	32.9	24.8	28.4	32	24	28
Sex-ratio score	11.9	11.8	12.1	14	12	15
Joint score	91.5	75.6	82.9	97	75	85
BOMBAY						
Age-ratio score: male	19.2	14.6	18.4	24	20	24
Age-ratio score: female	22.7	21.6	24.3	26	27	29
Sex-ratio score	9.7	13.5	13.9	12	14	14
Joint score	71.0	76.7	84.4	86	90	96
RAJASTHAN						
Age-ratio score: male	27.5	30.5	32.3	28	30	32
Age-ratio score: female	35.4	42.6	39.6	36	43	39
Sex-ratio score	10.7	14.3	14.9	14	18	17
Joint score	95.0	116.0	116.0	104	126	122

NOTE: Joint score = ARS (M) + ARS (F) + 3(SRS).

u—unavailable.

actuary's tables. We have modified the census actuary's calculations by excluding the last two age intervals, 60–64 and 65–69.

Notwithstanding the lack of strict comparability between the two sets of calculations, the similarity in the values of respective scores for 1901, 1911, and 1921 is striking. This shows that the degree and pattern of age biases in the reconstructed age tables are similar to those in the census age data. The process of reconstruction left the biases and distortions largely unaffected.

Age ratios and sex ratios for other countries

To provide a perspective to our present study of the age ratios and sex ratios in Indian age data, we have computed these ratios for some recent age data relating to a few statistically advanced countries as well as three relatively less advanced countries. In statistically advanced countries like the United States, Great Britain, and France, the sex-ratio scores are much smaller than in India. The age-ratio scores too are smaller; but the differences between the respective sets of age-ratio scores are narrower than those between the sets of sex-ratio scores. If it is assumed that the age distribution and age bias are identical for both sexes, then all sex ratios would be identical and the sex-ratio scores would be zero. The sex-ratio scores would depart from zero to the extent that male and female age distributions and the pattern of biases in them are different.

The low sex-ratio scores in the statistically advanced countries indicate that the differences in the true age distributions and in the pattern of errors in the age data for the two sexes are much smaller in advanced countries than in India. There are good reasons for the existence of some differences in the true age distribution of the male and female populations in the advanced countries because of past trends in fertility, mortality, migration, and other parameters. Part of the observed sex-ratio score in the advanced countries is explained by this factor.

The observed magnitudes of the age-ratio score in these countries—though smaller than in India—indicate a certain amount of bias in the age data of the advanced countries also. But the difference in the degree of bias for the two sexes is smaller in the advanced countries than in the statistically backward countries. Not only are the age distortions much larger in the Indian census data, but also such distortions are more dissimilar between the two sexes.

Age-sex selectivity in underenumeration

One of the basic causes that led to such biases and distortions in the age composition is age-selective and sex-selective underenumeration. A number of studies have been made by demographers on this aspect of Indian census data [15, 20, 28], but the point is sufficiently important to bear a brief repetition. Table 3.4 presents the ratios of the number of persons by sex in the age group (x + 10 to x + 14) in a given census year (t + 10) to that in the age group (x to x + 4) in the immediately preceding census (t) for each of nine census years. The number of persons from which these ratios are calculated is somewhat

Table 3.4 Ratios of sex-age selectivity due to underenumeration: India, 1891–1961

Age at earlier census	Age at later census	Year of later census							
		1891	1901	1911	1921	1931	1941	1951	1961
MALE									
0–4	10–14	0.97361	0.93824	1.00373	0.95451	1.12176	1.08136	1.07533	1.07169
5–9	15–19	0.64245	0.62057	0.64828	0.61179	0.65338	0.64343	0.72337	0.79253
10–14	20–24	0.72462	0.70452	0.68714	0.66483	0.72234	0.74070	0.76648	0.78585
15–19	25–29	1.17720	1.08584	1.10028	1.02566	1.18911	1.12547	1.19049	1.09890
FEMALE									
0–4	10–14	0.74518	0.74554	0.80074	0.76256	0.90757	0.87985	0.96902	0.94173
5–9	15–19	0.63088	0.59814	0.61637	0.56785	0.62754	0.62892	0.70814	0.75773
10–14	20–24	0.98176	0.97485	0.89590	0.86676	0.93927	0.91897	0.92510	0.91008
15–19	25–29	1.31082	1.17916	1.19099	1.10026	1.30356	1.19373	1.20923	1.14164

NOTE: See text for explanation of how ratios are calculated.

less than the corresponding number given in Basic Table 1 for the reason that whereas Basic Table 1 includes the population of all states and territories for which age data were available for any particular year, Table 3.4 includes the population of only those states and territories which are common in all nine census years. The states for which the population has been excluded are listed in Table 8.1 (Chapter 8). Assuming that there was no net migration, persons aged $x + 10$ in census year $t + 10$ are the survivors of persons aged x in census year t. Since life expectancy before 1921 was around 20–25 years, the ten-year survival ratio for age group 0–4 would be less than 0.75. But we find that the census survival ratio for males aged 0–4 was 0.97361 for 1881–1891, 0.93824 for 1881–1901, and so on. In the last four census decades, the census survival ratios were greater than 1, implying that there were more men in age group 10–14 in the latter census than those aged 0–4 in the earlier one. It is clear that the high census survival ratios both before and after 1921 glaringly reveal the large underenumeration in age group 0–4 in the respective census years.

Comparing the similar ratios for the female population with those for the male population, one can clearly see the sex selectivity in such underenumeration. Males aged 0–4 are consistently underenumerated more than females. And if one compares the similar ratios for other age groups, one visualizes the age selectivity in the underenumeration for both males and females.

The tables that follow set out the reconstructed age data for India, its five zones, and its 27 states and territories, as defined for the purpose of the 1971 census. They are called Basic Tables, because they constitute the most important end product of this treatise and are basic to the purpose of the study. For this reason they appear as part of the text, rather than in an appendix.

Basic Tables 1, 2, 3, and 4 present the age distribution in absolute numbers, in a time series dating from 1881 through 1971. Basic Tables 5, 6, 7, and 8 reduce the data to percentage distributions and are intended to facilitate comparison over time and space.

The method of reconstructing the age data has been discussed in Chapter 2, and their sources are indicated in the list of references that appears at the end of this volume.

Basic Table 1 Population by age and sex: India and zones, states, and territories, 1881–1971

INDIA — MALE

AGE	1881	1891	1901	1911	1921	1931	1941	1951	1961	1971
0–4	12686544	16446458	14681735	16776781	15156913	17994660	21399100	24137288	33179553	118893343
5–9	13902349	16797822	16503192	17297636	18661782	19959676	23195400	23089143	33064316	
10–14	12063451	13570456	15389662	14829346	15987445	17041836	19408400	22808689	26264354	25215770
15–19	8030545	9865259	10535263	10881354	10704920	12315251	12981900	16759288	18589511	21566954
20–24	7575837	9594949	9553302	10627711	9907038	11622938	12609000	14757853	18191589	20030824
25–29	8934729	10390242	10580563	11464388	11041879	12612347	13684800	15155397	18527847	35547036
30–34	8923050	10711681	10264509	10694717	10660771	10845493	12425900	13418519	15584890	
35–39	5793483	7227380	7331827	7994380	8200600	9582421	10538700	11806868	13602862	27520558
40–44	6564638	7855682	8003834	8270904	8127948	8404966	9532500	10761587	12084281	
45–49	3282296	4324443	4543618	4925361	5075462	6308401	7404400	8384569	9735462	17988252
50–54	4359855	5070135	5413604	5689236	5739972	5860648	7075600	7719382	9129000	
55–59	1563701	2055432	2170601	2292299	2365280	3106134	3839700	4794206	5283347	16873877
60+	4565686	5498845	5501791	6181329	6482389	6944128	8890700	9671048	12352548	
TOTAL	98646260	118892784	120473501	127925442	128112399	142598899	162986100	183263837	259989740	283936614

INDIA — FEMALE

AGE	1881	1891	1901	1911	1921	1931	1941	1951	1961	1971
0–4	13147909	17169298	15150344	17339425	15763453	18665598	21504400	23947685	32909384	111409503
5–9	12946033	15796559	15835212	16563067	18033995	18953632	22095300	22348446	31591339	
10–14	9600215	12769070	12806203	12238909	13256323	14427433	16506100	20733126	23022831	22241305
15–19	7221694	8981732	9563920	9921454	9543813	11468941	12084500	15756576	17277533	21524586
20–24	8692354	10296332	10434264	11486997	10648010	12475027	13166600	15122396	19129498	20477211
25–29	8843729	10333165	10457420	11255481	10807264	12346723	13519700	14435909	18046983	33525108
30–34	8573389	9929914	10105858	10496766	10389716	10252249	11870700	12857669	14852823	
35–39	5577934	6375975	6652172	6956230	7066299	8431245	9376900	10324071	11859684	23645374
40–44	6320675	7441843	7885538	8015584	7836359	7608376	8779300	9684532	10771861	
45–49	2945811	3688323	4082350	4266815	4333005	5448348	6318600	7115687	8321583	15364282
50–54	4483046	5046770	5480077	5655187	5540502	5323779	6441100	7130209	7978654	
55–59	1503515	1893441	2025842	2058098	2098179	2786263	3237900	4125934	4548697	15825826
60+	5605835	6705022	6558055	6987458	7002375	7264263	9149300	9941222	12353173	
TOTAL	94562339	114429444	117041255	123241471	122319293	135452234	154055800	173523462	212664033	264013195

Basic Table 1 *(continued)*

EASTERN ZONE   MALE

AGE	1881	1891	1901	1911	1921	1931	1941	1951	1961	1971
0-4	3779406	3847645	3795048	4113122	3601509	4435101	5241000	6081084	8537076	31369114
5-9	4070590	4415757	4321830	4779836	4912175	5293119	6034500	5748012	8967383	
10-14	3019580	3508288	3622466	3744209	3990985	4101109	4792400	5579758	6556583	6374210
15-19	2034420	2319509	2520418	2606138	2760677	2954021	3274000	4164737	4599965	5319487
20-24	1948977	2052255	2266572	2407341	2412937	2906107	3620900	3620900	4614500	5381735
25-29	2374945	2387200	2637500	2861707	2842701	3353655	3655700	3981484	4986541	9475286
30-34	2342188	2348569	2369846	2604397	2595186	2849301	3309400	3423591	4257492	
35-39	1650131	1821832	1824049	2083376	2188485	2514312	2931000	3057690	3646472	
40-44	1703825	1856269	1794930	1845738	1929926	2046968	2394600	2694367	3050476	7212634
45-49	925021	1041104	1116232	1185145	1305701	1594155	1929500	2156821	2511979	
50-54	1088060	1154287	1176247	1190633	1238269	1314105	1597300	1842388	2207680	4446680
55-59	448030	477522	516037	555365	516958	752630	952800	1233629	1396659	4021015
60+	1221951	1298975	1287453	1374168	1315590	1460503	1960800	2738373	2867404	
TOTAL	26607124	28529532	29266628	31357175	31611099	35575086	41145300	46322834	58199210	73600161

EASTERN ZONE   FEMALE

AGE	1881	1891	1901	1911	1921	1931	1941	1951	1961	1971
0-4	4033343	4162809	4050514	4383711	3832635	4656547	5373000	6151602	8750558	29930123
5-9	3757802	4237400	4220548	4669058	4786668	5043566	5714600	5532893	8696949	
10-14	2417806	2865356	3001066	3108640	3293275	3407173	3951800	5020862	5608766	5676690
15-19	1979386	2296496	2533224	2608966	2695901	3001203	3202700	4009060	4454227	5421270
20-24	2255356	2336772	2611993	2773347	2718493	3210928	3284500	3651083	4897950	5294493
25-29	2543140	2555587	2683412	2936322	2885133	3256538	3525400	3667759	4653811	8690828
30-34	2344505	2452602	2373054	2550477	2586930	2690607	3105300	3182637	3821574	
35-39	1518005	1700231	1715397	1832093	1956788	2180607	2570500	2666369	2997826	
40-44	1724571	1843773	1801174	1802277	1843966	1888225	2161600	2352212	2677061	5879252
45-49	662396	951006	1038134	1094934	1132727	1379747	1636200	1842511	2092506	
50-54	1178699	1205723	1248055	1260032	1212413	1237832	1510100	1696061	1946130	3744809
55-59	467014	499441	542557	576288	551920	720711	862000	1127616	1210679	3954665
60+	1706851	1782152	1743437	1799959	1659227	1711771	2233800	2859003	3126207	
TOTAL	26828954	26889648	29562565	31396084	31155086	34393903	39131500	43759668	54934244	68592130

Basic Table 1 *(continued)*

CENTRAL ZONE — MALE

AGE	1881	1891	1901	1911	1921	1931	1941	1951	1961	1971
0-4	4033573	4546923	4088354	4434167	4007438	4431263	5548400	6130153	8217880	29157196
5-9	4369742	4762161	4328481	4693440	4998862	5099727	5952520	6028713	7970477	
10-14	3677298	4040987	4241852	4069117	4223739	4513304	4783900	5836411	6302652	5694627
15-19	2511754	2804948	2956751	2998938	2855496	3242702	3276700	4125173	4447646	4774151
20-24	2639057	2868878	2806846	3203396	2700300	2895467	3186900	3695964	4357357	4828014
25-29	2927237	2996689	3018860	3013396	2891294	3321347	3571100	3855371	4463854	8524990
30-34	2980073	3152291	2993946	3081172	2894613	2846827	3275400	3519052	3937551	
35-39	1727399	1965752	1950926	2121103	2105382	2449653	2663800	3055977	3234410	6549401
40-44	2249100	2474488	2311438	2376357	2301820	2290142	2518400	2839530	2998953	
45-49	1003867	1134110	1234583	1286052	1349837	1628482	1909100	2189121	2390426	4486854
50-54	1519258	1617284	1586456	1614248	1594638	1703490	1931000	2047397	2383328	
55-59	436507	475067	572595	555697	592834	757213	953700	1228187	1271818	4456522
60+	1479394	1644579	1479547	1583387	1648462	1789999	2275500	1802821	3196053	
TOTAL	31761259	34484157	33570635	34934232	34164715	36969601	41819100	46353870	55212405	68471755

CENTRAL ZONE — FEMALE

AGE	1881	1891	1901	1911	1921	1931	1941	1951	1961	1971
0-4	4098258	4713228	4103357	4492092	4115578	4580881	5555900	6068252	8045753	26015274
5-9	3908002	4365472	3991472	4325420	4634487	4756228	5438000	5705093	7325847	
10-14	2912991	3019851	3419812	3166284	3273432	3532761	3803300	5065697	5216470	4710329
15-19	2112874	2330051	2511393	2406333	2307945	2495461	2794800	3730024	3964113	4853127
20-24	2726982	2911969	2913116	3076998	2720806	3091854	3219900	3729872	4579266	4750395
25-29	2758195	2930091	2908607	3061887	2758532	3075443	3435500	3526810	4287570	7908879
30-34	2753116	2956115	2846790	2928285	2782445	2681278	3079800	2305837	3526652	
35-39	1547776	1732150	1838228	1901448	1882031	2154456	2374100	2610433	2853381	5644158
40-44	2112559	2285158	2285243	2261908	2171149	2087304	2353900	2514483	2689067	
45-49	890476	952936	1156884	1132871	1154843	1410667	1643800	1874596	2078926	3710350
50-54	1488610	1579945	1605103	1592288	1516799	1501967	1763900	1816295	2004359	
55-59	414253	434245	553320	503208	529907	664960	826100	1033679	1123484	3930996
60+	1771676	2006585	1782128	1810184	1828946	1929550	2397400	1952438	3111636	
TOTAL	25445768	32217796	31915443	32659006	31676900	34162810	38703400	42933569	50906404	61523508

Basic Table 1 *(continued)*

SOUTHERN ZONE — MALE

AGE	1881	1891	1901	1911	1921	1931	1941	1951	1961	1971
0–4	2419333	3760260	3739931	4116800	3876849	4703186	5357500	5971148	7857848	⎱ 27456738
5–9	2767667	3513998	4051367	4085253	4314023	4856789	5750200	5736479	7757479	⎰
10–14	2724386	2714101	3725076	3808924	4030794	4340759	5163000	5927912	6664805	6287918
15–19	1783573	2131168	2349862	2728645	2699374	3376020	3128000	4623833	4656936	5649133
20–24	1704571	2142344	2069784	2580497	2569873	2917619	3211900	3904618	4501091	4883510
25–29	1792235	2209931	2296835	2599090	2708385	3043436	3123300	3777470	4423050	⎱ 8632426
30–34	1888097	2149426	2374007	2390278	2603407	2659848	2871000	3325760	3833381	⎰
35–39	1651739	1575665	1779388	1901003	2019943	2420773	2559000	2988097	3457586	⎱ 7036560
40–44	1413902	1726000	1940462	2045466	1966635	2129591	2454700	2798847	3113953	⎰
45–49	634414	963011	1127472	1296846	1259139	1567117	1894700	2227023	2499408	⎱ 4551422
50–54	864757	1105745	1331289	1431289	1474630	1431209	1807500	2107003	2318700	⎰
55–59	333363	459289	567631	656430	688752	824902	972900	1248600	1368126	⎱ 4151918
60+	968251	1285920	1447156	1753334	1870081	1538731	2282800	2686723	3218418	⎰
TOTAL	20546288	25731858	28800060	31193499	32081885	35910070	40576700	47223113	55670781	68649625

SOUTHERN ZONE — FEMALE

AGE	1881	1891	1901	1911	1921	1931	1941	1951	1961	1971
0–4	2556632	3965160	3938753	4299718	4063316	4914772	5332300	5993598	7827439	⎱ 26947992
5–9	2783006	3475390	4057260	4130403	4446136	4806547	5773300	5809069	7757713	⎰
10–14	2389545	2348662	3304911	3473840	3672595	4023562	4757400	5775359	6328260	6036621
15–19	1639898	2062695	2211938	2694463	2548467	3093684	3222600	4429713	4581601	5707155
20–24	2016941	2523415	2479130	2981104	3006864	3307026	3452700	4205244	4508301	5352008
25–29	1860481	2291108	2448894	2682126	2829743	3349756	3416800	3912622	4717292	⎱ 8644606
30–34	1929322	2267560	2533046	2577206	2693933	2702029	3038200	3447647	3847650	⎰
35–39	1631443	1342363	1557107	1681266	1689618	2215203	2428900	2764727	3186912	⎱ 6246038
40–44	1387951	1677697	1924270	2060349	2016363	1935979	2351200	2670900	2823585	⎰
45–49	564000	801762	969216	1108315	1113505	1379718	1644200	1915735	2159803	⎱ 4139276
50–54	588504	1181824	1370203	1469090	1529819	1405775	1667400	2123489	2204435	⎰
55–59	319176	415988	497380	569970	586443	761698	827700	1122595	1225139	⎱ 4128461
60+	1184953	1560648	1673399	1901603	1950008	2012895	2353400	2791569	3276163	⎰
TOTAL	20651852	25914272	28969507	31629453	32146807	35905644	40267400	46962267	54883293	67202157

Basic Table 1 *(continued)*

WESTERN ZONE — MALE

AGE	1881	1891	1901	1911	1921	1931	1941	1951	1961	1971
0-4	1655118	2049045	1536217	2274618	1923735	2406643	2751100	3329854	4658894	16664885
5-9	1800119	2039112	1979512	1975054	2368918	2531293	2873200	3250290	4532001	⎬
10-14	1593957	1623830	1955974	1644542	1986874	2138913	2396500	3174939	3631446	
15-19	1041288	1142951	1260512	1262686	1152725	1535263	1627300	2252166	2603807	3686266
20-24	1062748	1202517	1193425	1376569	1134597	1543037	1660700	2100915	2630379	3218960
25-29	1227739	1394554	1384071	1544554	1404162	1569161	1843400	2094890	2610333	2911691
30-34	1137818	1313632	1302673	1397237	1402630	1354094	1685700	1877076	2225123	5076804
35-39	800426	912883	943227	1044949	1053399	1244450	1370000	1622459	1896690	⎬
40-44	747351	988404	946351	1074228	1036437	1037008	1170500	1402620	1600956	3813665
45-49	470645	530487	545735	633783	628334	849511	918700	1039582	1337968	⎬
50-54	545495	678308	617271	728267	744037	708705	868600	933771	1148454	2454233
55-59	221467	233626	246727	276530	291104	434801	518400	592429	710294	2129305
60+	523953	681699	545309	727506	799375	859725	1145800	1159970	1505883	⎬
TOTAL	12828124	14791018	14457004	15960523	15926327	18212604	20829900	24821961	31092308	39955809

WESTERN ZONE — FEMALE

AGE	1881	1891	1901	1911	1921	1931	1941	1951	1961	1971
0-4	1728847	2176610	1617184	2379053	2026403	2498005	2780600	3270045	4561038	15707323
5-9	1701695	1936477	1938147	1894987	2309340	2425872	2783400	3163391	4365874	⎬
10-14	1254422	1286162	1645089	1348949	1662730	1880521	2909000	2880832	3209821	
15-19	971231	1061875	1159405	1174923	1039138	1450212	1504100	2063729	2347819	3128815
20-24	1133485	1306022	1290296	1490911	1217829	1618718	1821900	2134061	2715372	3102391
25-29	1150593	1305372	1270060	1453164	1324100	1509196	1792100	1973141	2498272	2897955
30-34	1041479	1227422	1252539	1363308	1318624	1226009	1504100	1747966	2016681	4750751
35-39	686929	768188	849916	899304	881306	1085548	1148800	1378446	1643820	⎬
40-44	682445	923824	936242	1024191	1000518	938232	1070000	1264755	1447820	3347733
45-49	439555	435612	494207	527775	528392	740122	792500	387786	1158431	⎬
50-54	542618	643371	628401	710991	692935	618995	810300	861085	994410	2130959
55-59	215622	195422	226665	233906	236831	375360	414400	483978	593527	2162144
60+	618548	789696	664236	819125	860182	869734	1191400	1334045	1600778	⎬
TOTAL	12171309	14056053	14029387	15317587	15098328	17236524	19704500	23443260	29152723	37228071

Basic Table 1 *(continued)*

NORTHERN ZONE   MALE

AGE	1881	1891	1901	1911	1921	1931	1941	1951	1961	1971
0-4	758845	2266207	1521888	1837020	1746506	2016758	2501100	2622677	3865145	⎫ 14056321
5-9	894038	2066520	1821754	1763094	2066965	2177272	2612300	2324168	3790806	⎭
10-14	848052	1683117	1844103	1559945	1754211	1946646	2272600	2287940	3067352	3124556
15-19	652363	1467541	1447507	1366188	1235710	1506451	1675900	1691784	2211603	2555598
20-24	619496	1327761	1215701	1262918	1087593	1358887	1473200	1432277	2056964	2281508
25-29	610626	1404143	1241576	1253586	1192404	1321403	1491100	1443697	2015062	⎫ 3767331
30-34	571798	1265093	1221401	1218446	1161114	1132834	1284400	1271797	1707314	⎭
35-39	362085	949171	814278	837464	829918	950809	1014900	1081050	1348330	⎫ 2863163
40-44	448565	808124	1008375	926457	890754	899665	994300	1025577	1301865	⎭
45-49	247806	654909	518545	522071	531240	667980	752400	771100	981141	⎫ 2020558
50-54	341432	513498	701128	723720	687633	702275	871000	788222	1057203	⎭
55-59	124139	409726	267436	247748	275346	336238	441900	491050	527112	⎫ 2088988
60+	371580	587034	741360	741786	848186	894618	1229800	1291665	1543301	⎭
TOTAL	6890825	15342844	14365052	14260443	14307580	15911836	18615100	18523004	25473158	32758023

NORTHERN ZONE   FEMALE

AGE	1881	1891	1901	1911	1921	1931	1941	1951	1961	1971
0-4	730578	2151114	1440268	1783836	1724771	2013598	2462600	2462072	3682466	⎫ 12628212
5-9	755383	1781547	1627584	1542365	1656643	1920120	2386000	2136542	3400202	⎭
10-14	625324	1246598	1435152	1140594	1533557	1582580	1885700	1988786	2620292	2645181
15-19	518229	1230515	1147807	1036239	951818	1230640	1360300	1532734	1900784	2400277
20-24	556463	1217995	1139582	1164035	983545	1245632	1387000	1401226	1999636	2143842
25-29	531029	1250796	1089249	1121239	1009024	1154707	1349900	1354240	1863563	⎫ 3469667
30-34	504650	1025929	1130154	1079861	1007149	943112	1143300	1172694	1522980	⎭
35-39	293474	832852	691173	641600	655991	794706	854600	903241	1157964	⎫ 2485810
40-44	413165	711148	938379	866439	804042	758144	842600	881722	1114213	⎭
45-49	188879	545947	423820	402668	403300	537729	601900	594752	776025	⎫ 1607211
50-54	284527	437807	632188	622553	588388	558944	695400	633093	808351	⎭
55-59	87427	348334	205890	174830	192972	263765	307700	357913	384921	⎫ 1615466
60+	323340	565859	690773	656193	703679	739915	972400	1003827	1207555	⎭
TOTAL	5812468	13349441	12562219	12232452	12234879	13743592	16249400	16412842	22438992	28995666

Basic Table 1 *(continued)*

ANDHRA PRADESH   MALE

AGE	1881	1891	1901	1911	1921	1931	1941	1951	1961	1971
0-4	776935	1088886	1176795	1373329	1196345	1551003	1749100	1885540	2490164	
5-9	858346	1092219	1351404	1439882	1461105	1642224	1987400	1914844	2535552	8895361
10-14	855891	889795	1262221	1329425	1414754	1434061	1827500	1982774	2152314	1891331
15-19	518184	621865	741828	870235	865054	1040468	772800	1406870	1511422	1680471
20-24	554657	682712	685302	862640	850126	984121	1057300	1233001	1422861	1598707
25-29	521423	644849	779027	893594	933121	1070404	1075500	1244217	1478453	
30-34	623878	708832	820028	835683	877255	945937	1053700	1145161	1313111	2796298
35-39	300976	383518	577740	630833	640928	781879	847200	946577	1066655	
40-44	465236	598311	684674	727254	687674	759623	937400	1023716	1076330	2289515
45-49	153325	224586	363287	430062	408780	500595	621400	722259	769025	
50-54	306889	387669	471394	512767	516013	527514	703200	777925	838735	1468828
55-59	72463	87833	178904	210756	213764	247229	294900	379409	393237	
60+	363707	439193	507497	652862	684301	698615	855000	1008272	1107812	1388152
TOTAL	6371910	7850268	9607091	10769322	10749220	12183673	13782400	15670565	18161671	22008663

ANDHRA PRADESH   FEMALE

AGE	1881	1891	1901	1911	1921	1931	1941	1951	1961	1971
0-4	823193	1164065	1269510	1443669	1275152	1665609	1685700	1916334	2513073	
5-9	827964	1056627	1333859	1440015	1536576	1624333	1584100	1930158	2559895	8715034
10-14	710633	733721	1079990	1160200	1241749	1279041	1591800	1830582	1968420	1780303
15-19	483272	600966	696785	845756	801198	1052121	949000	1390370	1482658	1756382
20-24	646162	838339	816288	1002970	980965	1106538	1135700	1339971	1574094	1730659
25-29	494421	624640	811884	904643	928029	1149719	1147400	1255161	1524455	
30-34	610041	741497	858047	898066	922353	920949	1122100	1206792	1282455	2771274
35-39	221683	291233	487814	550028	541105	637749	772100	867004	971336	
40-44	440123	563435	643318	708330	697650	671017	887200	980457	982922	2005954
45-49	118449	160564	289374	348531	347641	417418	504600	612286	671926	
50-54	326483	391591	457419	504793	519883	496749	628300	746863	800244	1353420
55-59	62709	69660	143845	173798	176510	214851	232500	321893	346404	
60+	428053	522916	570697	697291	702417	733806	866100	1046823	1135214	1381019
TOTAL	6193186	7739794	9458830	10678090	10671228	12019900	13506900	15444654	17821776	21494045

Basic Table 1 *(continued)*

ASSAM — MALE

AGE	1881	1891	1901	1911	1921	1931	1941	1951	1961	1971
0-4	249205	250724	254002	311173	333394	450851	543600	685485	936231	3539854
5-9	217034	242347	258030	312839	393844	442852	565100	644414	924728	
10-14	147243	177873	185243	209758	288742	331945	417900	505299	686935	660860
15-19	105772	118468	123192	147128	188245	236170	266800	346755	472157	581946
20-24	113636	126268	138758	156243	179849	245406	258300	347863	460549	586758
25-29	138486	147545	175370	194560	222722	238663	334200	373216	517510	981439
30-34	126375	146080	164353	179780	211054	243788	289200	331099	428939	
35-39	95239	112341	129101	149874	182734	218446	270400	289944	370839	693050
40-44	83048	108791	113713	129952	157145	167029	198000	251705	295256	
45-49	56305	53585	61053	76862	97702	125423	153300	183508	236517	437372
50-54	49975	68872	67633	80650	101978	106526	134000	118853	213722	
55-59	33142	25084	25823	32672	41388	57939	73500	79675	128084	403785
60+	56794	66649	58780	74234	91857	112830	146700	191868	271503	
TOTAL	1470254	1646627	1755051	2055725	2494154	3028068	3651000	4399684	5943430	7885064

ASSAM — FEMALE

AGE	1881	1891	1901	1911	1921	1931	1941	1951	1961	1971
0-4	262815	263175	264784	331330	347844	460913	540000	671125	971124	3471571
5-9	189404	234736	249397	309172	380871	422965	529200	616477	915866	
10-14	114582	142964	152093	178116	234574	274823	327000	419404	579586	612501
15-19	105483	121621	130017	153968	192674	251935	290600	349171	456517	552749
20-24	112768	122668	163201	176098	203272	263070	289200	373668	462700	546401
25-29	148858	125070	165597	185786	211714	245787	314800	346461	437719	791179
30-34	105578	131832	138654	155556	186852	190799	237600	265665	334592	
35-39	78497	79252	89064	86325	126838	150396	178900	198270	249491	492098
40-44	67919	87373	89734	98879	115562	118526	145600	170123	202238	
45-49	45015	35995	42666	50696	62757	81162	99500	110674	145481	303996
50-54	44238	47927	57370	65436	75593	78769	97100	121272	143862	
55-59	27834	18729	19443	24700	28854	38744	48000	55502	79415	301983
60+	64541	66749	58543	73039	73230	87655	111700	148236	205251	
TOTAL	1367532	1478091	1620587	1889101	2245635	2665544	3209400	3840048	5184342	7072478

Basic Table 1 *(continued)*

BIHAR — MALE

AGE	1881	1891	1901	1911	1921	1931	1941	1951	1961	1971
0-4	1511293	1894689	1743189	1832636	1614615	2020104	2370700	2841601	3552054	12505545
5-9	2102838	2265819	2046544	2235808	2308909	2510182	2786500	2435441	3827706	
10-14	1534514	1746155	1696014	1696140	1761695	1887108	2108900	2401873	2736432	2373066
15-19	949331	1063757	1112956	1100250	1178743	1246265	1364700	1625072	1794294	2029307
20-24	890497	938222	1001841	1005112	998043	1213127	1222600	1317442	1709556	2028806
25-29	1138874	1121609	1158943	1213882	1181200	1388143	1438900	1545195	1882076	3649584
30-34	1170460	1122105	1037683	1144114	1124552	1204237	1313400	1324247	1592733	
35-39	815483	860521	805711	892129	942135	1065188	1198900	1230019	1401155	2838993
40-44	848522	873526	803261	802688	843269	861788	944300	1072606	1153348	
45-49	485110	530760	504994	517355	583826	727235	851300	931350	1039048	1765572
50-54	554576	577723	530044	533724	543562	578073	673400	763636	852029	
55-59	222280	236770	234697	241722	244432	342102	432800	589008	563027	1656071
60+	619419	667220	619497	640337	630203	682296	917800	1414327	1197991	
TOTAL	13243197	13894876	13295374	13855897	13955184	15725848	17624200	19491817	23301449	28846944

BIHAR — FEMALE

AGE	1881	1891	1901	1911	1921	1931	1941	1951	1961	1971
0-4	2079153	2095790	1894586	1987305	1757089	2153282	2442500	2841433	3607931	11490527
5-9	1988020	2189235	2011872	2188842	2235545	2350147	2612300	2307084	3590900	
10-14	1237982	1461721	1426207	1408453	1437890	1580727	1761700	2194697	2343702	2117017
15-19	899645	1041357	1083915	1047050	1075349	1203306	1294600	1613141	1756041	2272586
20-24	1080796	1132085	1244400	1236549	1162772	1401103	1394600	1412156	2033101	2126425
25-29	1271896	1286148	1279900	1346171	1271800	1422848	1527800	1553166	1940246	3684035
30-34	1202523	1243511	1136202	1225947	1216655	1233686	1379200	1360802	1631460	
35-39	817667	904698	829104	884463	934020	1023101	1208300	1206140	1336771	2584934
40-44	873347	917503	859551	852943	869906	857536	959700	1068196	1159900	
45-49	473636	528258	509906	519702	538537	674275	799300	892495	972361	1562454
50-54	585123	608270	598490	591155	567194	541935	666500	763390	813843	
55-59	242981	263307	263504	267990	255923	351141	413500	560310	550580	1668447
60+	871025	940302	890799	904449	851344	839957	1092300	1521357	1410925	
TOTAL	13623770	14608885	14018836	14461019	14174024	15624044	17549900	19294367	23154161	27506425

Basic Table 1 *(continued)*

GUJARAT — MALE

AGE	1881	1891	1901	1911	1921	1931	1941	1951	1961	1971
0-4	596366	750359	432409	761914	664817	769013	979700	1147649	1660188	5987260
5-9	722747	782770	625037	611229	815430	857758	956500	1124730	1637145	
10-14	676572	598847	653363	479276	676905	740584	802800	1118041	1300065	1347737
15-19	469212	465158	490596	448436	406139	538679	593000	812503	922382	1122166
20-24	466802	491546	417338	453494	360040	497854	612500	716768	910367	959302
25-29	467269	499585	463288	496394	443962	470381	628700	671762	835505	1667542
30-34	409953	468462	428475	438439	431555	404244	540600	616252	712293	
35-39	310648	333563	320877	340187	343068	372229	414100	523683	599249	1221052
40-44	259262	345796	278007	323715	321082	341016	368500	456693	532158	
45-49	184597	182813	167334	201380	213868	270312	294900	309039	438788	811738
50-54	193491	236645	181730	217354	236281	247888	315300	294758	403362	
55-59	89963	81031	76452	90829	106612	134488	179700	180945	204545	685697
60+	151407	212040	119969	175205	213703	262160	374100	359099	481255	
TOTAL	4999689	5448675	4654875	5037852	5233462	5506646	7060400	8331922	10633902	13802494

GUJARAT — FEMALE

AGE	1881	1891	1901	1911	1921	1931	1941	1951	1961	1971
0-4	604505	780103	433783	776350	690919	791599	984100	1122273	1611950	5508037
5-9	667541	721315	590509	553054	760830	803022	905700	1062141	1516634	
10-14	548505	469656	545100	378691	568802	633634	704600	1011926	1123003	1182959
15-19	405530	368826	426848	375258	340003	476467	541000	743537	812538	1090961
20-24	454550	499307	429772	484352	385095	523031	638500	741241	931583	942254
25-29	434589	473352	434646	467462	410206	445014	587600	652870	805555	1568621
30-34	375352	441983	402279	432417	422293	336071	482000	583699	677234	
35-39	285861	291088	286490	296824	299917	342514	357300	456447	545345	1141599
40-44	250159	341458	293656	319771	321185	322288	355300	414842	515513	
45-49	180486	160775	163417	173729	189916	247980	263100	276663	393773	741685
50-54	196290	240018	195015	219507	225550	216486	295300	281265	346998	
55-59	93312	72339	75922	77900	85525	117733	141500	153982	178170	718865
60+	189336	261765	162436	210420	240886	272403	385200	429849	538952	
TOTAL	4686416	5141985	4439873	4765735	4941527	5583182	6641200	7930735	9999448	12894981

Basic Table 1   *(continued)*

HARYANA — MALE

AGE	1881	1891	1901	1911	1921	1931	1941	1951	1961	1971
0-4	261747	378759	271479	275987	297628	319261	381700	466834	666362	2474265
5-9	284478	304348	330100	273462	338075	344048	383100	370415	631951	
10-14	273365	271123	314921	272893	274825	319036	355800	374342	501111	534122
15-19	212851	268446	243576	250827	208692	255244	286300	282378	357366	401265
20-24	212537	237562	215892	208342	192104	208764	230500	237285	309489	330258
25-29	202222	236907	218450	203097	202469	211850	221600	231238	298942	531509
30-34	183122	163242	206867	182140	169964	173890	181000	201045	242429	
35-39	111278	166190	136184	126087	125413	140980	141000	156097	198936	433030
40-44	143331	81533	175516	142522	131443	132180	156800	153126	201515	
45-49	78301	118687	90342	85706	86516	101530	110200	125471	158707	323103
50-54	109705	45556	120380	110270	107504	99328	135000	129422	162497	
55-59	39469	84772	42185	41913	47421	50724	65600	84857	84820	349706
60+	110299	63145	121485	111723	131365	130019	167400	238160	258329	
TOTAL	2222705	2420870	2487377	2284969	2313419	2487154	2816000	3030720	4072654	5377258

HARYANA — FEMALE

AGE	1881	1891	1901	1911	1921	1931	1941	1951	1961	1971
0-4	227842	354311	256351	266116	290900	312836	395460	429905	625572	2165899
5-9	241817	253651	292125	233178	301023	292991	351100	341502	552242	
10-14	201286	203238	246402	197933	221053	258492	301600	326075	433138	444865
15-19	164570	234579	188163	181930	161041	196990	222100	246776	291243	370191
20-24	184927	203201	193212	180933	162674	189475	221600	232965	266212	309967
25-29	165884	217509	186037	169962	162692	178187	199700	218013	278684	514810
30-34	162587	122761	185518	157925	147230	138729	168500	179474	222106	
35-39	91657	153152	113203	98987	97799	113089	126300	137426	175349	381727
40-44	136140	62542	158172	128263	115512	105797	129900	138715	169917	
45-49	59532	108378	68713	63947	64840	78726	81400	92625	122748	240626
50-54	94039	30374	106624	90212	87533	75538	103800	101079	120005	
55-59	27776	78186	29572	28421	32238	36919	38900	55801	58329	231465
60+	100974	49365	111531	92224	98046	95017	116700	142924	171801	
TOTAL	1863231	2076181	2135623	1890031	1942581	2072846	2457700	2643280	3517346	4659550

Basic Table 1 *(continued)*

HIMACHAL PRADESH — MALE

AGE	1881	1891	1901	1911	1921	1931	1941	1951	1961	1971
0-4	110562	151536	106719	108515	106769	121220	147900	156263	205617	724574
5-9	124497	127956	120812	118463	128844	129709	156600	142444	195229	
10-14	115655	109176	122661	110403	114235	119778	140000	137709	165659	161017
15-19	89001	105198	93791	89365	88756	92171	101400	116817	116746	130173
20-24	85653	92735	81340	87990	77515	92274	81400	93130	110364	120290
25-29	85697	99981	88007	88194	83625	86067	86500	104037	110463	201859
30-34	84498	68268	67538	82217	82974	82072	76400	84811	98245	
35-39	53328	73149	61932	55245	68205	72477	76400	83965	86220	162144
40-44	65084	37487	71160	68887	65423	60638	66800	68311	73015	
45-49	34380	52750	51426	39508	44718	51951	60000	58615	66194	123963
50-54	48626	20042	59875	55278	52500	49046	62900	61666	63529	
55-59	17241	38691	20090	19479	26420	31423	37600	41047	44382	142937
60+	56023	32926	64824	70642	80790	75564	99300	101267	115204	
TOTAL	970245	1009895	1010175	994166	1020774	1064390	1193200	1250082	1450907	1766957

HIMACHAL PRADESH — FEMALE

AGE	1881	1891	1901	1911	1921	1931	1941	1951	1961	1971
0-4	111896	154009	108275	110085	109509	125733	141200	174050	204706	701478
5-9	115416	117140	118038	116063	121833	123550	148700	134256	189647	
10-14	89764	85317	79832	91230	93002	105938	124100	122315	156929	161757
15-19	75728	100166	82214	83824	82930	89545	93500	109637	120619	139813
20-24	81405	86343	77827	84430	76317	90467	86000	88382	118214	129098
25-29	79269	94258	82644	82118	79710	84417	94900	98677	116392	211534
30-34	78212	54860	51736	79300	73933	68492	79800	79007	95010	
35-39	43448	67354	63443	46838	55037	63883	64100	68890	78180	149303
40-44	62246	28074	29573	63304	57988	49598	62100	58783	65665	
45-49	25978	45446	42112	28948	33193	41282	42400	44377	51514	95497
50-54	41914	13665	13897	44237	42799	39181	42200	44315	50426	
55-59	11782	34843		13005	17242	21977	17800	30254	28446	104997
60+	50327	26724	57645	59452	63733	60547	73000	82775	85345	
TOTAL	867385	908199	909825	902834	907226	964610	1069800	1135918	1361093	1693477

Basic Table 1 *(continued)*

JAMMU - KASHMIR   MALE

AGE	1881	1891	1901	1911	1921	1931	1941	1951	1961	1971
0-4	u	159013	155415	167384	177348	189580	203800	u	267364	
5-9	u	140051	159748	167966	191697	200876	239000	u	271654	1021461
10-14	u	98081	139890	138704	156017	164714	188400	u	210768	
15-19	u	78248	92452	106193	108150	136846	145500	u	169912	214794
20-24	u	76213	81452	100749	99126	120300	120400	u	149241	189623
25-29	u	77745	87730	98901	106505	126628	122600	u	157540	182954
30-34	u	82394	99823	99547	109258	114132	116600	u	144564	
35-39	u	57990	69572	69880	75057	95561	101200	u	126396	314527
40-44	u	63051	77200	76252	71558	76140	85200	u	106414	
45-49	u	36526	39109	42308	41496	53718	62300	u	75234	235961
50-54	u	43981	53807	56361	57939	51040	64600	u	73953	
55-59	u	14554	15749	17339	19851	26036	31800	u	37073	145985
60+	u	62322	64819	80721	82203	76230	98600	u	106480	153010
TOTAL	u	990169	1136766	1222305	1296205	1431801	1577000	u	1896633	2458315

JAMMU - KASHMIR   FEMALE

AGE	1881	1891	1901	1911	1921	1931	1941	1951	1961	1971
0-4	u	156729	153204	161898	172870	186581	192900	u	260643	
5-9	u	125060	149587	156278	175887	175232	212600	u	255407	959061
10-14	u	71712	113410	112912	122827	135494	157300	u	183400	
15-19	u	68339	79779	96137	97584	123207	123200	u	149565	180251
20-24	u	78573	83031	100583	104959	116776	114200	u	149285	168584
25-29	u	74840	81633	91600	101743	121246	121500	u	160152	176112
30-34	u	75701	83417	85666	88799	93913	105800	u	127275	
35-39	u	46868	53416	55372	55737	74117	85000	u	98456	286023
40-44	u	55827	67581	67279	62003	59969	70200	u	80391	
45-49	u	26041	31529	31195	30458	40090	46900	u	51752	184615
50-54	u	33467	40373	43813	44184	38323	47800	u	51012	
55-59	u	9910	12651	11172	11897	17475	20800	u	22518	100383
60+	u	47639	52985	56325	59206	55584	71500	u	74487	103288
TOTAL	u	870706	1002596	1070230	1128154	1238407	1369700	u	1664343	2158317

u—unavailable.

Basic Table 1 *(continued)*

KERALA — **MALE**

AGE	1881	1891	1901	1911	1921	1931	1941	1951	1961	1971
0-4	u	405703	420598	489991	519843	708624	776100	983293	1279056	4345630
5-9	u	384974	433053	468493	522434	646277	775200	812008	1241616	
10-14	u	356848	421215	449013	503828	610205	743200	847539	1127300	1127154
15-19	u	278762	303113	348514	369482	419261	497500	738012	690161	977917
20-24	u	248118	254627	306406	326970	402213	451400	623417	678523	664398
25-29	u	261483	275002	306564	324385	358200	384100	510131	604396	1205148
30-34	u	227737	257961	267883	291118	311411	332400	409521	522579	
35-39	u	207476	219495	241242	256069	313393	330700	398687	507585	995794
40-44	u	169228	180993	193231	217090	234370	270900	313867	380032	
45-49	u	118826	121923	143093	160090	211132	249200	300084	359958	639977
50-54	u	106158	119448	127361	143042	156993	198100	239365	278552	
55-59	u	61646	60772	76080	83927	126526	144500	180671	219870	631833
60+	u	124796	123246	141554	162174	210342	290000	350306	472259	
TOTAL	u	2951855	3191466	3559425	3879458	4702251	5443300	6681901	8361927	10587851

KERALA — **FEMALE**

AGE	1881	1891	1901	1911	1921	1931	1941	1951	1961	1971
0-4	u	428025	435674	496736	520666	703300	761800	958459	1248711	4249997
5-9	u	369638	420811	456213	509867	618954	762400	789952	1202117	
10-14	u	323676	386938	417800	478030	589350	725200	847047	1108958	1210250
15-19	u	291637	312440	363702	385626	453143	533600	773082	743029	1012068
20-24	u	281997	295057	345786	378284	459271	483900	684374	755359	723166
25-29	u	276450	291469	321661	354751	409971	432600	555072	687236	1282815
30-34	u	225584	264363	278167	297427	326551	372500	442573	551412	
35-39	u	174760	184986	210163	222507	307768	346700	405289	503342	960662
40-44	u	158225	176777	194444	216153	222894	273800	323860	372257	
45-49	u	102043	106175	126767	142856	201222	240900	283161	350021	624649
50-54	u	109011	124090	135510	149979	154859	199500	247305	281129	
55-59	u	58226	55035	70116	74932	118929	141100	186454	222466	695917
60+	u	149050	150981	171183	191591	237857	314300	365589	514361	
TOTAL	u	2948322	3204796	3588248	3922669	4804099	5588300	6867217	8541788	10759524

u—unavailable.

Basic Table 1 (continued)

MADHYA PRADESH — MALE

AGE	1881	1891	1901	1911	1921	1931	1941	1951	1961	1971
0-4	1212953	1301319	1002002	1512656	1195224	1485596	1664000	1766900	2654026	9369838
5-9	1298878	1479652	1073794	1326732	1558442	1550737	1792600	1767397	2361904	⎰
10-14	1010182	1152337	1089541	991118	1243154	1270239	1892000	1581918	1773121	1716177
15-19	665526	727475	787183	757884	695280	943997	522000	1150624	1326354	1526955
20-24	689482	740046	723163	817671	756208	920961	901900	1050055	1351430	1552574
25-29	789365	848757	793115	946005	788095	985101	1112800	1150663	1470378	2791783
30-34	871792	943573	807386	943656	864446	828013	1046600	1063755	1253330	⎰
35-39	506655	568591	539936	620198	622358	718093	817700	914890	1000752	2013843
40-44	651687	733880	577986	633534	674619	611681	671500	828483	874319	⎰
45-49	253176	289973	301027	327956	348905	475663	503600	599554	722865	1314655
50-54	378872	419293	365470	412002	412711	410796	510900	512317	672858	⎰
55-59	93333	98210	139518	133291	137344	210426	263000	280381	354104	1169509
60+	365203	402296	272628	368588	416628	411384	584200	588062	762763	⎰
TOTAL	8787804	9705402	8472749	9791291	9713414	10622587	12180000	13255004	16578204	21455334

MADHYA PRADESH — FEMALE

AGE	1881	1891	1901	1911	1921	1931	1941	1951	1961	1971
0-4	1262580	1401765	1014694	1572657	1263666	1550664	1682800	1745639	2644114	8834258
5-9	1195557	1399538	1021837	1274691	1511386	1499142	1725100	1715704	2280806	⎰
10-14	788185	850479	893758	802963	1011224	1065390	1150800	1409595	1501401	1503641
15-19	583645	640140	711088	667194	647121	888420	516000	1069395	1222426	1568317
20-24	745718	836742	826282	939819	762193	993087	989200	1080429	1444301	1550431
25-29	785525	854285	797987	963047	810232	954765	1133900	1107328	1380067	2556381
30-34	781852	863505	771516	893479	863882	793036	981400	1049687	1123703	⎰
35-39	432334	480142	515193	549871	561794	659868	720100	819475	878631	1765060
40-44	570054	621376	592243	626016	635288	591495	642900	737466	830307	⎰
45-49	206627	214673	317745	301844	301568	423212	470000	546387	645589	1180076
50-54	365507	387460	402868	437464	419502	393475	516000	493637	610707	⎰
55-59	88537	88408	147665	130598	132833	211007	260100	291495	319700	1240621
60+	435904	521178	375143	490031	531647	509509	722300	750396	907452	⎰
TOTAL	8241825	9169712	8380019	9649674	9453336	10533070	11810600	12816663	15794204	20198785

Basic Table 1 *(continued)*

MAHARASHTRA   MALE

AGE	1881	1891	1901	1911	1921	1931	1941	1951	1961	1971
0-4	1058752	1298686	1103838	1512704	1258918	1637630	1771400	2182205	2993694	⎤ 10660743
5-9	1077212	1256342	1354475	1363825	1553488	1673495	1916700	2125560	2890354	⎦
10-14	914585	1024953	1302611	1167266	1309969	1398329	1593700	2056838	2328074	2335665
15-19	572076	677753	769916	814250	746586	996584	1034300	1439663	1679413	2094282
20-24	596946	710971	776087	923075	774557	1045183	1048200	1384147	1717916	1949672
25-29	760470	894969	920783	1048160	960200	1098780	1214700	1423128	1772719	⎤ 3404668
30-34	728265	845150	874198	958798	971075	949850	1145100	1260824	1510511	⎦
35-39	489778	579320	622350	702762	710331	872221	955900	1098776	1298437	⎤ 2588964
40-44	480089	642608	668344	750513	715335	695992	800000	945927	1067370	⎦
45-49	285648	347674	378401	432403	414466	579199	623800	730543	897726	⎤ 1640130
50-54	352004	441663	435541	510913	507756	460817	553300	639013	744087	⎦
55-59	131504	152595	170275	185701	184492	300313	338700	411484	505120	⎤ 1442227
60+	372646	469659	425340	552301	585672	597555	771700	791871	1023461	⎦
TOTAL	7828435	9342343	9802129	10922671	10692865	12305958	13769500	16490039	20428882	26116351

MAHARASHTRA   FEMALE

AGE	1881	1891	1901	1911	1921	1931	1941	1951	1961	1971
0-4	1124342	1396507	1183401	1602703	1335484	1706406	1795500	2147772	2943712	⎤ 10182424
5-9	1034154	1215162	1347638	1341933	1548510	1622850	1877700	2101250	2844798	⎦
10-14	705917	816506	1099989	970258	1094128	1241887	1383300	1868906	2083924	1942909
15-19	565301	673049	732557	799665	698535	973805	961100	1320192	1533120	2008417
20-24	681935	806715	860524	1006559	832734	1095637	1183400	1392820	1781185	1952988
25-29	716004	832020	892414	985702	913894	1064182	1204500	1322411	1690123	⎤ 3177622
30-34	666127	785439	850260	927891	896631	839938	1022100	1154267	1331521	⎦
35-39	401068	477100	563426	602480	581389	743034	791500	921999	1056889	⎤ 2202691
40-44	432286	582366	642586	704420	679133	615944	714700	849913	930942	⎦
45-49	259509	274837	330790	354046	338476	492142	529400	611123	763539	⎤ 1387184
50-54	346328	403353	433386	491484	467385	402509	515000	579820	649573	⎦
55-59	122310	123083	150743	156006	151506	257627	272900	329946	414843	⎤ 1441649
60+	429612	527931	501800	608705	619296	597331	806200	904196	1060664	⎦
TOTAL	7484893	8914068	9589514	10551852	10156801	11653342	13063300	15512525	19124836	24295884

Basic Table 1 *(continued)*

MYSORE MALE

AGE	1881	1891	1901	1911	1921	1931	1941	1951	1961	1971
0-4	633824	381150	829609	838155	816316	931952	1070100	1296813	1749993	
5-9	843425	820942	925995	847656	909994	1030785	1131800	1236790	1796194	6252402
10-14	880315	559488	873324	844174	841024	903653	1029800	1265933	1451331	1406026
15-19	570128	483817	522426	612055	541332	637969	707300	995421	995421	1198654
20-24	551127	513280	466236	577138	563389	593857	707700	833975	964246	1026268
25-29	622281	555699	536237	586970	592274	648282	667560	793458	934362	
30-34	607238	514138	530064	526702	557398	574265	584700	702256	808017	1796397
35-39	431649	395869	421792	422691	456685	564885	529800	628104	730545	
40-44	466613	400247	435660	454015	392840	458670	498200	564628	668184	1445320
45-49	176074	240737	281133	291942	271091	314280	387100	449550	521003	
50-54	252013	250206	298085	317871	301723	300018	359700	417264	480144	935531
55-59	101759	113365	145544	139973	150588	145885	179500	239728	263655	
60+	235763	257978	315830	368459	396064	395951	440800	503687	677828	911502
TOTAL	6373209	5992916	6582105	6827801	6793718	7445458	8294000	9866923	12040923	14971900

MYSORE FEMALE

AGE	1881	1891	1901	1911	1921	1931	1941	1951	1961	1971
0-4	662427	917204	853290	875401	863211	972793	1087600	1303415	1738179	
5-9	855048	818839	926216	864287	929306	1025611	1170900	1285014	1814587	6183717
10-14	792494	489349	763353	775097	764695	830416	965000	1262107	1393473	1271318
15-19	511395	458843	469359	580334	496984	598244	639000	868787	925052	1155982
20-24	629637	576573	522611	629467	628765	650101	711900	865761	1008657	1099851
25-29	620645	548669	536652	567812	582850	658927	700700	800267	964216	
30-34	587903	518135	542096	538837	512055	561722	585600	675410	793382	1745199
35-39	345532	334474	373508	353692	337100	415774	475000	529180	618369	
40-44	421758	369898	422353	439389	382032	397742	448000	494002	566300	1207207
45-49	153375	197344	247735	241536	237921	246385	301200	355694	405210	
50-54	288237	264097	303934	316962	312289	299814	314100	384252	431575	789094
55-59	105172	105388	133405	117380	126463	126471	141900	190708	212812	
60+	307524	333007	378137	397266	410210	403534	420400	520436	674007	874746
TOTAL	6281187	5931820	6472649	6697450	6583881	7187534	7961300	9535033	11545849	14327114

Basic Table 1 *(continued)*

NAGALAND — MALE

AGE	1881	1891	1901	1911	1921	1931	1941	1951	1961	1971
0-4	u	9905	6438	10389	9594	11717	12900	15177	22332	
5-9	u	8391	7406	10558	10732	12351	13400	16653	25713	99368
10-14	u	5274	4390	7855	8983	11138	13300	14307	24430	26159
15-19	u	3582	3235	5505	6504	7203	8200	8337	17954	27145
20-24	u	4002	4162	5010	5051	6223	6200	7755	16170	25111
25-29	u	5854	5183	6290	6204	6700	5900	7422	15089	
30-34	u	6177	4789	5813	5645	6859	6100	6623	13654	37479
35-39	u	6745	3993	4846	4887	5605	5900	4732	12549	
40-44	u	4498	3910	5670	5545	5554	5600	6835	11303	25697
45-49	u	2425	2313	3354	3448	3855	3900	4226	7554	
50-54	u	2379	2426	3520	3980	3673	3500	4014	7038	15581
55-59	u	741	984	1426	1635	1724	1400	2063	3777	
60+	u	2226	2244	4819	7571	6934	7500	7907	13464	19544
TOTAL	u	62199	51473	74796	79738	89536	93800	106551	191027	276084

NAGALAND — FEMALE

AGE	1881	1891	1901	1911	1921	1931	1941	1951	1961	1971
0-4	u	10289	6710	10633	10209	12439	13300	14909	23344	
5-9	u	7405	6806	10924	10457	12094	13800	16150	24486	96337
10-14	u	4853	3937	7110	8223	10220	9800	12397	22755	23776
15-19	u	4605	3479	5237	6666	7820	9300	11077	19015	20580
20-24	u	4915	5260	6597	5561	6770	6300	6904	14614	20292
25-29	u	6306	5550	6960	5792	6254	7600	7364	14430	
30-34	u	6239	4647	5827	6225	7277	6400	9296	13105	30666
35-39	u	5020	2579	3235	4226	5103	6500	4493	10334	
40-44	u	4366	3562	5404	5730	5493	5500	6784	9712	21324
45-49	u	1826	1827	2770	3111	3435	2700	3762	5674	
50-54	u	2110	2357	3577	3976	3802	3500	4082	5858	12417
55-59	u	600	889	1349	1517	1809	2500	1471	3179	
60+	u	2134	2474	4619	7370	6792	3600	7735	11667	14973
TOTAL	u	60668	50077	74242	79063	89308	95800	106424	178173	240365

u—unavailable.

Basic Table 1 *(continued)*

ORISSA — MALE

AGE	1881	1891	1901	1911	1921	1931	1941	1951	1961	1971
0-4	630568	626126	670326	768406	620848	813022	793900	898309	1214705	
5-9	685671	751892	734120	853116	858784	869941	974000	933439	1259308	4669591
10-14	514883	657376	672401	709975	765824	714983	820900	834759	975884	
15-19	348766	436655	467101	462253	473515	521923	512500	634228	704873	916824
20-24	354470	367455	384683	401804	378682	487360	460400	554942	705179	744268
25-29	372489	364716	445005	485264	448177	553506	567600	601858	761326	792280
30-34	371290	382513	398446	457372	415195	474089	588900	513795	658796	146880
35-39	224807	264166	309374	356637	347845	402704	479600	502835	550971	
40-44	269783	327147	302893	313656	318836	343948	427800	446315	481236	1090341
45-49	112663	139004	190423	202160	220742	255431	312000	334689	390355	
50-54	183982	198618	199869	208558	207625	245231	309300	327605	398005	722753
55-59	54615	57227	88498	94456	93366	127858	156700	182523	218220	636146
60+	184647	195436	194961	221975	200788	232259	332900	427595	451658	
TOTAL	4309134	4768331	5058100	5535632	5350227	6042255	6706500	7242892	8770586	11041083

ORISSA — FEMALE

AGE	1881	1891	1901	1911	1921	1931	1941	1951	1961	1971
0-4	659611	671549	708648	803867	648418	849214	830000	955533	1274164	
5-9	641894	734501	734464	854214	873607	880620	982100	939734	1278786	4626478
10-14	418579	555864	590104	638674	710677	626555	724500	821703	858601	
15-19	331522	425388	479905	477828	495014	571417	514700	614090	722607	864149
20-24	390522	406470	449642	491343	479971	586731	555500	610395	772253	792002
25-29	371105	384317	462253	534903	524974	629381	539600	618289	762253	861571
30-34	375111	413086	410547	487130	483689	521552	612200	591366	636173	
35-39	191424	242258	299582	351442	371327	414216	475200	495695	500791	1428366
40-44	287494	334410	317616	339926	365276	385009	459800	427574	475624	
45-49	96700	118283	185092	207118	226134	262635	307500	309745	364603	970090
50-54	204217	217657	221151	235594	233348	262618	334500	343139	381657	
55-59	51360	55540	97368	106809	105289	143595	164300	179913	207668	675529
60+	275460	286265	288445	314395	290635	313258	447300	494878	543080	685347
TOTAL	4295599	4839688	5244817	5843243	5803359	6448801	7061500	7433054	8778260	10903532

Basic Table 1 *(continued)*

PUNJAB — MALE

AGE	1881	1891	1901	1911	1921	1931	1941	1951	1961	1971
0-4	407350	655942	494761	469473	494261	548161	696100	690194	878560	2978285
5-9	461504	541827	537765	480799	557992	601881	713300	621802	912077	
10-14	434310	424049	517859	453032	480866	536173	634600	613282	746670	774302
15-19	331357	417737	394968	365285	345718	419014	471200	450982	555793	602095
20-24	301683	374158	323114	323981	310901	371172	400200	382205	479810	485314
25-29	304256	378155	334063	290287	320692	353928	399400	371785	434283	759167
30-34	287102	257782	317053	287766	280708	298676	334100	317413	353188	
35-39	187736	256031	226035	240067	222610	239760	271400	262923	281335	610536
40-44	227032	147647	265746	211977	215866	230724	275700	248103	284463	
45-49	128440	205586	152950	152615	161825	184305	212500	203238	223400	459060
50-54	173073	85043	199498	183254	184726	196270	241300	214411	248103	
55-59	64357	152344	84491	79818	94435	99477	130200	148390	130859	597756
60+	195850	129949	260521	233578	295427	318843	439000	417053	471103	
TOTAL	3504090	4031247	4108824	3771932	3966027	4398384	5219000	4941781	5999544	7266515

PUNJAB — FEMALE

AGE	1881	1891	1901	1911	1921	1931	1941	1951	1961	1971
0-4	372487	585744	436751	427918	466413	531359	666000	622372	803259	2616980
5-9	377234	445893	448105	395172	482404	517066	646700	553319	788435	
10-14	314704	301052	381674	302185	357508	433784	517000	537129	643925	665484
15-19	261024	355695	293760	243902	245824	328932	375900	430767	476953	532471
20-24	271863	325336	287133	259151	244445	307191	357600	366104	435204	428198
25-29	265897	335790	294801	266630	253060	283221	349800	319733	392906	707556
30-34	248818	204168	284387	235949	232863	227316	289000	264501	316507	
35-39	150286	234148	195972	156774	168552	193643	212800	216803	250409	547426
40-44	202057	112511	236431	188439	187392	185380	213400	210533	242333	
45-49	97968	175138	126304	112127	121127	149442	167100	153542	184461	369967
50-54	138740	57623	168344	141115	149632	146151	184900	161041	181581	
55-59	45638	126124	61795	52768	63311	77954	86500	101575	97774	416463
60+	162516	101824	220719	179938	214442	232177	316000	308800	321669	
TOTAL	2909232	3361046	3436176	2959068	3186973	3613616	4381000	4219219	5135456	6284545

Basic Table 1 *(continued)*

RAJASTHAN — MALE

AGE	1881	1891	1901	1911	1921	1931	1941	1951	1961	1971
0-4	u	893266	468886	792464	640999	798953	1094000	1160460	1643491	5980141
5-9	u	928195	647415	695503	818895	858901	1061400	1080986	1580028	
10-14	u	758552	724303	555533	699721	767660	899500	1049863	1279501	
15-19	u	573118	601903	529677	456879	566373	616100	747550	875760	1190257
20-24	u	524418	493149	521247	376097	524989	578500	629938	855754	981913
25-29	u	590051	492386	553970	449588	503013	606300	655068	871616	947588
30-34	u	619318	489825	547099	491792	430806	533000	595118	749925	1622903
35-39	u	380431	308645	328386	321604	375126	388300	538098	558492	
40-44	u	471516	402381	412887	387350	378188	377400	498428	555018	1182921
45-49	u	226559	188689	192870	186294	261024	342000	339083	401007	
50-54	u	315557	264925	307145	271339	293440	347500	347875	458845	835252
55-59	u	113236	101564	84819	82796	122368	167600	193645	204679	
60+	u	294753	219418	235106	246024	279769	405500	507771	529966	743408
TOTAL	u	6689070	5403989	5756206	5429378	6160610	7274700	8313883	10564082	13484383

RAJASTHAN — FEMALE

AGE	1881	1891	1901	1911	1921	1931	1941	1951	1961	1971
0-4	u	873466	460850	796229	655740	817770	1004400	1130906	1596834	5401722
5-9	u	814478	595500	618664	747043	775504	971400	1020191	1435813	
10-14	u	571249	574659	414397	539403	618035	742300	905619	1063472	
15-19	u	449752	487095	412380	345281	465608	509300	681938	756642	996328
20-24	u	505704	480211	522221	372837	512534	566800	639228	881803	992695
25-29	u	509082	427539	494290	392898	461504	547800	656355	807600	934607
30-34	u	558185	447345	505439	447029	395066	472500	590017	678866	1497237
35-39	u	317446	267744	273962	268403	333905	344100	439761	493817	
40-44	u	446985	398916	406424	368489	344799	349300	433733	507538	1065420
45-49	u	182578	162089	159665	147174	219290	251200	274394	330449	
50-54	u	300353	264725	294218	254621	251597	305600	298578	372296	715773
55-59	u	92885	85653	66493	65252	105173	138100	153521	159920	
60+	u	336963	237775	262921	259100	236579	386400	429650	506460	677641
TOTAL	u	5959126	4890101	5227303	4863270	5587364	6589200	7656891	9591520	12281423

u—unavailable.

Basic Table 1 *(continued)*

TAMIL NADU   MALE

AGE	1881	1891	1901	1911	1921	1931	1941	1951	1961	1971
0-4	1008574	1384521	1312929	1415325	1344345	1511607	1762200	1805502	2310519	⎤ 7862278
5-9	1065896	1215863	1340915	1329222	1420490	1537503	1855800	1772837	2160347	⎦
10-14	988180	907970	1168326	1186312	1271188	1392840	1562500	1831666	1917727	1841548
15-19	695261	739724	782475	897841	925506	978322	1150400	1474214	1438680	1771662
20-24	558787	698234	663619	834313	826388	932428	932400	1214225	1419095	1576455
25-29	647531	743900	706429	811872	858605	966546	996400	1229664	1390254	⎤ 2801925
30-34	656581	658719	758954	760010	877636	828235	900200	1068822	1176243	⎦
35-39	519114	588802	560361	606237	666261	820616	851300	1014729	1140189	⎤ 2279770
40-44	482053	558214	639105	670966	669025	676922	748200	891236	977985	⎦
45-49	305015	378762	361129	431749	419178	541110	637000	755130	839795	⎤ 2279770...
50-54	305655	361112	442362	473024	513852	446774	546500	672449	712404	⎦ 1490321
55-59	159141	196445	182211	229621	241473	311262	354000	448792	485410	⎤ 1204062
60+	368781	463953	500583	590459	627542	633823	697000	824458	947330	⎦
TOTAL	7801169	8936819	9419398	10236951	10659489	11577988	13057000	15003724	16910578	20828021

TAMIL NADU   FEMALE

AGE	1881	1891	1901	1911	1921	1931	1941	1951	1961	1971
0-4	1071012	1455846	1380279	1483912	1404287	1573070	1797200	1815390	2295584	⎤ 7701010
5-9	1099994	1230286	1376364	1369888	1470387	1537649	1855900	1803945	2147248	⎦
10-14	886418	801916	1074630	1120743	1188121	1324755	1475400	1835623	1837663	1752698
15-19	645231	711249	733354	904681	864659	987176	1007000	1377474	1414683	1761650
20-24	741142	856506	845174	1002881	1018850	1091116	1121200	1315138	1552508	1777409
25-29	745415	837529	808889	888010	964110	1131139	1136100	1302122	1523621	⎤ 2812171
30-34	731378	782344	868540	862136	962098	892807	958000	1122872	1205635	⎦
35-39	464228	535896	510799	567383	588906	803912	835100	963254	1081362	⎤ 2048826
40-44	526630	586139	681822	718186	720528	644326	742200	867581	891062	⎦
45-49	292176	341811	325932	391482	385087	514693	597500	664594	761554	⎤ 1355766
50-54	373784	417125	484760	511825	547668	454323	525500	745069	681878	⎦
55-59	151295	182714	165095	208676	208538	301447	312200	423540	439925	⎤ 1161617
60+	449316	555675	577584	635863	645790	637698	753500	858721	939252	⎦
TOTAL	8177479	9295036	9833232	10665665	10969029	11894111	13210500	15115323	16775975	20371147

Basic Table 1 *(continued)*

UTTAR PRADESH — MALE

AGE	1881	1891	1901	1911	1921	1931	1941	1951	1961	1971
0-4	2820620	3245604	3086352	2921511	2812214	2945667	3884400	4363253	5563854	19787358
5-9	3070764	3282509	3254687	3366708	3440420	3548990	4132600	4261316	5608573	
10-14	2867116	2888650	3152311	3077999	2980585	3243065	3394700	4254493	4529531	3978450
15-19	1852828	2077473	2169568	2159269	2099288	2298705	2354700	2974549	3161292	3247196
20-24	1949575	2128832	2083683	2181267	2005020	1974446	2285000	2645909	3005927	3275440
25-29	2137872	2147932	2225745	2257391	2103199	2336246	2458000	2704708	2993476	5733207
30-34	2108281	2208718	2186560	2137516	2030167	2018814	2228800	2455297	2684221	
35-39	1220544	1397161	1410990	1500910	1483024	1731605	1846100	2141087	2233658	4535558
40-44	1597413	1740608	1733452	1742823	1627201	1678561	1846900	2011042	2124634	
45-49	750691	844137	933556	958096	1000932	1152819	1405500	1589567	1667561	3172199
50-54	1140386	1197991	1220985	1202246	1181927	1292694	1420100	1535080	1710470	
55-59	343174	376857	433077	422406	455490	546787	690700	947806	917714	3287013
60+	1114191	1242283	1206919	1214799	1231834	1378615	1691300	1214759	2433290	
TOTAL	22573455	24778755	25097886	25142941	24451301	26147014	29639100	33098866	38634201	47016421

UTTAR PRADESH — FEMALE

AGE	1881	1891	1901	1911	1921	1931	1941	1951	1961	1971
0-4	2835678	3311443	3088663	2919435	2851912	3030217	3873100	4322613	5401639	17181016
5-9	2712445	2965934	2969635	3050729	3123101	3257086	3712900	3989389	5045041	
10-14	2124806	2169372	2526054	2363321	2262208	2467371	2669500	3656102	3715069	3206688
15-19	1529229	1689911	1800305	1739139	1660824	1807041	1979200	2660629	2731687	3284810
20-24	1981264	2075227	2086834	2137179	1958613	2098767	2230700	2649443	3134965	3199964
25-29	1972270	2065805	2110620	2098840	1942300	2120678	2301600	2419482	2907503	5352498
30-34	1571264	2092610	2075274	2034806	1918563	1888242	2098400	2255150	2502829	
35-39	1115442	1252008	1323035	1351577	1320237	1494588	1654000	1799958	1974750	3879098
40-44	1542505	1663782	1692990	1635892	1535861	1495809	1711000	1777017	1858760	
45-49	684449	738263	839139	831027	853275	987455	1173800	1328209	1438337	2530274
50-54	1123103	1192485	1202235	1154824	1097297	1108492	1247500	1322658	1393652	
55-59	325716	345837	405655	372410	397074	453953	566000	742184	803784	2690375
60+	1335772	1485407	1406985	1320153	1297299	1420041	1675100	1202042	2204184	
TOTAL	21253943	23048084	23527424	23009332	22218564	23629740	26892800	30116876	35112200	41324723

Basic Table 1 *(continued)*

WEST BENGAL — MALE

AGE	1881	1891	1901	1911	1921	1931	1941	1951	1961	1971
0-4	966081	1038765	1058126	1112282	938384	1031187	1440000	1491065	2595490	9665223
5-9	1046856	1125552	1215682	1293291	1253503	1359810	1615300	1584247	2724281	
10-14	809181	904541	1021092	1067052	1100677	1078910	1365500	1661946	1974981	2216092
15-19	620695	684724	782892	851104	864858	884440	1073000	1467748	1498793	1770149
20-24	579908	605498	708470	804697	809866	895643	1085800	1312326	1609883	1785916
25-29	711690	734893	817796	919858	934116	1052642	1265500	1367774	1688976	3068843
30-34	663669	677421	732126	779537	797144	867147	1099200	1176852	1460073	
35-39	505370	567876	567876	654324	675107	776922	944100	963543	1222268	2366857
40-44	494863	533350	546889	565332	574027	632610	793500	860065	1037795	
45-49	267113	310190	343365	368189	380259	456432	591900	662717	784487	1382279
50-54	295176	305279	361231	346591	359787	356866	461700	543371	685555	
55-59	133292	155540	159931	177523	127229	210675	280300	362209	454982	1180628
60+	355570	359895	393502	409639	358191	393751	529500	651656	860911	
TOTAL	7449464	8003295	8708978	9349419	9173148	9997035	12543300	14105519	18599144	23435987

WEST BENGAL — FEMALE

AGE	1881	1891	1901	1911	1921	1931	1941	1951	1961	1971
0-4	1007651	1094113	1110998	1170206	986949	1071046	1467700	1528551	2655347	9371230
5-9	961349	1049917	1160148	1233106	1201946	1280949	1499000	1525448	2683466	
10-14	634378	684003	788663	826629	840525	843727	1072600	1466203	1661058	1880556
15-19	631335	688583	798352	878033	869082	902531	1043600	1334523	1387221	1621059
20-24	659662	662249	713835	820505	817971	887437	992700	1162205	1493854	1577865
25-29	736279	739039	733857	818610	820422	890830	974500	1066108	1379290	2516926
30-34	649066	648117	651767	639989	654551	698824	831600	888611	1115076	
35-39	419924	459976	475603	485366	493190	552391	671700	709017	833092	1648665
40-44	488234	490850	508443	479790	459145	490250	563000	633567	763341	
45-49	242310	261800	296292	301330	286292	337837	409000	492332	562520	1087385
50-54	341048	324068	354017	347300	313065	329098	390900	434595	556797	
55-59	141877	159461	155869	168887	152589	175187	222300	312049	347557	1172338
60+	487605	477979	483266	479599	405473	439894	542300	641252	888516	
TOTAL	7400718	7740155	8231110	8649350	8301200	8900001	10684300	12194461	16327135	20876024

Basic Table 1 *(continued)*

ANDAMAN-NICOBAR   MALE

AGE	1881	1891	1901	1911	1921	1931	1941	1951	1961	1971
0-4	269	378	297	1054	876	1709	u	2372	5105	22406
5-9	193	234	248	959	839	1476	u	1481	3900	
10-14	178	163	191	609	842	1105	u	1729	2711	4835
15-19	147	142	213	544	938	794	u	1595	2374	8513
20-24	588	914	974	1448	1738	1881	u	3179	5306	9674
25-29	1943	1725	1721	2145	2933	3345	u	2485	6428	13051
30-34	3076	2670	2636	3187	3821	2589	u	1243	3945	
35-39	1703	2077	1959	2480	3473	2379	u	1595	3030	6910
40-44	1895	2397	2278	2658	2376	1592	u	1046	2124	
45-49	643	822	1051	1464	1211	1156	u	922	1614	2832
50-54	853	1013	1213	1345	765	774	u	601	1136	
55-59	195	202	375	529	286	350	u	311	599	1806
60+	557	638	966	1148	695	552	u	496	1032	
TOTAL	12640	13375	14122	19570	20793	19702	u	19055	39304	70027

ANDAMAN-NICOBAR   FEMALE

AGE	1881	1891	1901	1911	1921	1931	1941	1951	1961	1971
0-4	251	377	268	1015	750	1795	u	2116	5106	21300
5-9	145	273	201	834	721	1299	u	1458	3842	
10-14	127	141	173	602	734	836	u	1590	2386	3844
15-19	76	100	153	530	544	741	u	1316	1971	4709
20-24	127	159	147	622	473	869	u	910	2420	4426
25-29	291	211	198	743	735	1083	u	1337	2574	5538
30-34	317	286	275	629	635	766	u	888	1611	
35-39	227	191	151	519	565	725	u	855	1330	2734
40-44	184	243	240	420	321	492	u	460	850	
45-49	65	60	89	252	228	365	u	307	657	1330
50-54	88	100	127	233	148	266	u	136	493	
55-59	23	11	30	96	106	126	u	153	280	1225
60+	67	82	82	394	333	398	u	340	724	
TOTAL	1988	2234	2134	6889	6293	9761	u	11916	24244	45106

u--unavailable.

Basic Table 1 *(continued)*

MALE — DELHI

AGE	1881	1891	1901	1911	1921	1931	1941	1951	1961	1971
0-4	19186	27691	24628	23197	29501	39583	65200	148926	203751	⎱ 829981
5-9	23559	24143	25914	26901	31462	41857	58900	108521	159827	⎰
10-14	24722	21536	24469	29380	28547	39285	54400	112744	163403	234354
15-19	19154	24794	20817	24841	27515	36803	55400	94057	136026	231443
20-24	19623	22675	20754	20609	31850	41388	62200	83719	152306	199062
25-29	18451	21304	20940	19137	29525	39917	54700	81519	142218	⎱ 314567
30-34	17076	14089	20295	19677	26418	33258	43300	73410	118963	⎰
35-39	9743	15380	11910	17799	17029	26905	36600	59967	96951	⎱ 225125
40-44	13118	6890	15872	14452	19114	21795	32400	57609	81540	⎰
45-49	6685	9801	7580	9064	10391	15452	23200	44693	56599	⎱ 126248
50-54	10028	3222	11092	11412	13625	13151	9900	34848	50276	⎰
55-59	3032	6129	3357	4380	4423	6210	9100	23111	25259	⎱ 96735
60+	9408	3939	10293	10016	12377	13893	20000	57414	62219	⎰
TOTAL	193785	201593	217921	230865	281777	369497	535200	986538	1489378	2257515

FEMALE — DELHI

AGE	1881	1891	1901	1911	1921	1931	1941	1951	1961	1971
0-4	18353	26855	24837	21590	29339	38859	67700	104839	191412	⎱ 741257
5-9	20916	20325	24064	23010	28453	35777	53550	84274	178658	⎰
10-14	19570	16030	19175	21937	19764	33637	43400	97648	139428	185196
15-19	16907	21984	16796	18066	19158	26358	36300	83616	105762	182174
20-24	18268	18838	18168	16717	22313	29189	40600	74547	118918	154032
25-29	15979	19317	16595	16639	18921	26132	36200	61462	107829	⎱ 238088
30-34	15033	10254	17063	15582	17295	19596	27000	59695	83216	⎰
35-39	7883	13884	9302	9667	10463	16069	22300	40361	61753	⎱ 149350
40-44	12722	5209	13836	12730	12658	12601	17700	39958	48369	⎰
45-49	5401	9366	5612	6786	6508	8899	12900	29814	35101	⎱ 80444
50-54	9834	2325	10010	8958	9619	8154	11100	28080	33071	⎰
55-59	2231	6386	2322	2971	3032	4267	5600	13762	17524	⎱ 77642
60+	9523	3344	10118	8333	9152	10011	13200	39478	47793	⎰
TOTAL	172620	174117	187898	182986	206675	266749	382700	757534	1169234	1808183

u—unavailable.

Basic Table 1 *(continued)*

MANIPUR — MALE

AGE	1881	1891	1901	1911	1921	1931	1941	1951	1961	1971
0–4	u	u	22637	27919	26903	35117	40300	44482	60633	228891
5–9	u	u	20630	27053	29233	31727	41400	39497	61618	
10–14	u	u	13915	19271	22713	24940	29900	33681	47755	
15–19	u	u	9930	14513	17327	18791	20400	23882	31034	
20–24	u	u	9314	10649	13450	18366	18800	24673	30412	51060
25–29	u	u	11599	13261	16656	17905	18500	23262	30769	47262
30–34	u	u	10717	12254	12196	15578	19100	19318	27248	39647
35–39	u	u	8935	10215	10560	12394	14600	16886	22298	62071
40–44	u	u	9757	10959	10436	10567	13100	14253	18955	
45–49	u	u	5771	6482	6488	6965	8800	10650	13164	48763
50–54	u	u	6056	6802	8400	7461	7400	10600	13923	
55–59	u	u	2453	2756	3451	4455	4700	6716	8524	31134
60+	u	u	7918	8532	10306	11549	12200	15785	20655	32847
TOTAL	u	u	139632	170666	188119	215815	249200	293685	387058	541675

MANIPUR — FEMALE

AGE	1881	1891	1901	1911	1921	1931	1941	1951	1961	1971
0–4	u	u	23200	28517	27885	36337	37000	40541	61271	227051
5–9	u	u	19847	27006	28745	31920	39600	37560	60107	
10–14	u	u	12844	19074	21984	24337	26300	37096	45671	
15–19	u	u	11434	15830	19318	20612	24900	23035	32647	
20–24	u	u	12805	14163	16324	21715	23100	26631	34522	52936
25–29	u	u	13510	14943	17002	20163	22000	23025	33505	45535
30–34	u	u	11311	12511	13454	16764	19800	20396	27644	39043
35–39	u	u	6277	6943	9132	12133	15500	16730	19994	61915
40–44	u	u	9906	11033	11318	11744	13200	16841	19481	
45–49	u	u	5079	5656	6147	7147	9600	12802	12556	43213
50–54	u	u	6555	7301	9059	8510	10500	11090	14681	
55–59	u	u	2474	2756	3458	4530	5200	8461	7916	28904
60+	u	u	9591	9823	12071	13879	16200	19742	22584	32481
TOTAL	u	u	144833	175556	195897	229791	262900	293950	392979	531078

u–unavailable.

Basic Table 1 *(continued)*

MEGHALAYA — MALE

AGE	1881	1891	1901	1911	1921	1931	1941	1951	1961	1971
0-4	21859	27436	27008	33204	32355	39064	39600	47386	58550	221223
5-9	17991	21796	25373	28129	32267	32976	38800	41155	54718	
10-14	13759	17069	19250	20598	24890	26455	36000	34300	43675	46220
15-19	9856	12323	13736	16243	18274	21874	28400	26541	33702	39836
20-24	9966	11090	11658	13467	14924	19787	24200	26591	33839	41069
25-29	13406	12583	14713	16770	18480	22316	25100	27542	34366	68880
30-34	12394	12273	13771	15496	15881	18765	23500	23701	30209	
35-39	9232	10412	10878	12919	13750	15682	17500	20776	24904	48808
40-44	7609	8957	9436	10788	11358	12391	12300	17559	20695	
45-49	3830	5140	5125	6382	7063	8620	8300	12077	14799	29169
50-54	4351	5416	5641	6696	6840	8252	8000	10886	14167	
55-59	4701	2160	2169	2712	2809	3647	3400	4541	6595	25762
60+	6121	7549	6767	9816	10123	11850	10200	12876	17480	
TOTAL	135075	154204	165525	193220	209014	241679	275300	305931	384699	520967

MEGHALAYA — FEMALE

AGE	1881	1891	1901	1911	1921	1931	1941	1951	1961	1971
0-4	24113	27893	27809	33897	32988	38768	42500	45211	59028	219589
5-9	17135	21606	24362	27357	31493	32442	38300	39377	54575	
10-14	11885	16251	18200	19274	22960	24989	29900	30938	40505	45480
15-19	11401	14942	17498	20017	22739	23531	25200	28352	32933	42476
20-24	11632	14385	16102	17793	19031	22817	25300	28117	34586	44286
25-29	14402	14707	16407	18772	19821	21465	25000	28040	35230	57220
30-34	12227	12817	13740	15718	15394	15953	18500	20558	26290	
35-39	10573	8817	8692	8723	10450	12141	14400	16250	18278	38250
40-44	7577	9271	9132	9975	10630	10869	11500	13998	16518	
45-49	4735	4844	4389	5114	5772	7063	8600	9677	11096	22291
50-54	4073	5691	5866	6600	6396	7251	7100	8943	11261	
55-59	2962	2104	2020	2492	2441	2885	6000	4147	4738	21140
60+	8220	8723	7258	9948	8871	10145	15400	12031	15263	
TOTAL	140935	161961	171475	195780	208986	230321	267700	285069	360301	490732

Basic Table 1 (continued)

MALE — TRIPURA

AGE	1881	1891	1901	1911	1921	1931	1941	1951	1961	1971
0-4	u	u	13322	17113	20416	29416	u	49342	95410	
5-9	u	u	14045	19042	24903	29687	u	46998	88237 ⌉	348541
10-14	u	u	10161	13560	19461	22625	u	38828	65388 ⌋	
15-19	u	u	7376	9442	13211	15925	u	27421	43533	
20-24	u	u	7686	10318	13113	16303	u	24120	43524	67996
25-29	u	u	8891	11822	15146	19728	u	29649	50178	56401
30-34	u	u	7961	10031	13519	16040	u	23792	41515 ⌉	54856
35-39	u	u	6181	8432	11467	14637	u	25482	38825 ⌋	98316
40-44	u	u	5071	6693	9310	11221	u	21956	30220 ⌉	72028
45-49	u	u	3188	4361	6173	8587	u	15600	24846 ⌋	
50-54	u	u	3347	4092	6097	7036	u	11620	27752 ⌉	47802
55-59	u	u	1482	2098	2148	3626	u	6092	13280 ⌋	
60+	u	u	3784	4816	6551	8101	u	14689	33525	55186
TOTAL	u	u	92495	121820	161515	202932	u	335589	591237	801126

FEMALE — TRIPURA

AGE	1881	1891	1901	1911	1921	1931	1941	1951	1961	1971
0-4	u	u	13779	17956	21253	30025	u	46199	96812	
5-9	u	u	13652	18437	24004	28857	u	45333	87863 ⌉	339264
10-14	u	u	9018	11310	16442	19438	u	34489	55885 ⌋	
15-19	u	u	8624	10903	15059	17711	u	31480	46280	
20-24	u	u	6748	10279	13591	18225	u	27457	50910	63540
25-29	u	u	6938	10177	13608	16581	u	27414	50116	57050
30-34	u	u	6162	7799	10110	12132	u	22757	36661 ⌉	58794
35-39	u	u	4496	5596	7605	9461	u	17861	28748 ⌋	88983
40-44	u	u	3230	4327	6399	7567	u	13333	23913 ⌉	60088
45-49	u	u	1883	2548	3987	5231	u	10598	18042 ⌋	
50-54	u	u	2249	3069	3782	5122	u	8802	18036 ⌉	40221
55-59	u	u	990	1305	1849	2342	u	5335	9135 ⌋	
60+	u	u	3061	4087	5233	6426	u	12382	28367	47276
TOTAL	u	u	80830	107793	142922	179518	u	303440	550768	755216

u—unavailable.

Basic Table 2 Population by age and sex: Goa, Daman, and Diu, 1900—1971

Age group	1900[a]	1910[a]	1921	1931	1941[b]	1950[a]	1961	1971
MALE								
0—4	27,529	29,054	28,420	29,603		31,919	37,605	166,455
5—9	34,539	31,787	32,823	35,158		34,787	42,270	
10—14	32,470	30,351	30,833	32,986		37,870	38,805	43,572
15—19	21,842	23,551	20,338	24,900		27,274	28,180	
0—20					140,915			
20—24	17,827	19,841	16,496	20,268		21,864	25,992	41,131
25—29	19,332	19,347	17,692	18,736		20,876	22,579	34,811
30—34	16,730	16,900	16,886	17,376		17,766	20,084	57,260
35—39	14,719	15,809	14,962	16,676		16,694	16,344	
40—44	15,026	14,904	13,730	15,800		15,682	15,914	38,298
45—49	11,894	11,286	11,056	12,791		13,970	13,106	
50—54	10,628	10,643	10,460	11,523		10,503	12,459	25,556
55—59	6,706	6,956	6,455	7,508		10,012	8,739	
21+					139,260			
60+	14,197	16,413	15,937	16,056		20,924	20,457	24,131
Total	243,439	246,842	236,088	259,381	280,175	280,141	302,534	431,214
FEMALE								
0—4	28,385	30,150	28,774	30,040		35,804	37,024	160,325
5—9	33,596	30,689	32,240	33,700		38,078	40,913	
10—14	30,924	29,025	28,217	30,150		35,297	36,836	40,014
15—19	21,966	24,996	21,944	25,226		27,986	27,018	
0—20					140,803			
20—24	21,125	24,918	22,298	24,309		24,887	26,543	35,513
25—29	22,775	23,951	23,072	23,361		23,497	23,901	34,035
30—34	19,922	20,388	21,038	22,187		21,747	21,795	54,614
35—39	15,202	16,398	16,398	18,287		19,830	18,451	
40—44	16,899	16,814	16,020	18,495		19,799	19,265	39,252
45—49	11,640	12,005	12,254	13,441		14,663	15,235	
50—54	13,500	13,775	12,933	13,894		13,285	16,376	30,104
55—59	7,189	7,843	7,369	7,940		12,876	10,667	
21+					162,758			
60+	20,956	21,774	22,259	21,299		28,169	30,109	32,700
Total	264,079	272,380	264,816	282,329	303,561	315,918	324,133	426,557

NOTE: Data unavailable for 1881 and 1891 censuses.

a   The census was taken a year earlier than usual during this decade in the three Portuguese territories.

b   Age data were given only in two broad groups in the 1941 census.

Basic Table 3 Population by age and sex: Dadra and Nagar Haveli, 1900–1971

Age group	1900[a]	1910[a]	1921	1931	1941[b]	1951	1961	1971
MALE								
0–4	1,360	2,219	2,026	2,600		2,817	5,012	⎫
5–9	2,123	2,177	2,754	3,007		2,841	4,502	⎬ 16,882
10–14	1,687	1,509	2,237	2,544		2,731	3,307	⎭
15–19	1,176	1,224	1,112	1,510		1,775	2,012	2,864
0–20					10,989			
20–24	1,096	1,246	1,007	1,537		1,581	2,096	2,512
25–29	980	1,338	1,240	1,698		1,892	2,609	2,717
30–34	870	1,092	1,059	1,325		1,547	2,219	⎫ 4,594
35–39	888	1,097	1,128	1,657		1,595	2,004	⎭
40–44	671	872	1,045	1,206		1,291	1,468	⎫ 3,649
45–49	539	728	822	1,098		1,019	1,454	⎭
50–54	367	441	576	676		825	1,045	⎫ 2,365
55–59	180	243	357	507		526	629	⎭
21+					10,020			
60+	449	568	645	652		905	1,167	1,381
Total	12,386	14,754	16,008	20,017	21,009	21,345	29,524	36,964
FEMALE								
0–4	1,454	2,398	2,138	2,721		2,790	5,376	⎫
5–9	2,012	1,939	2,643	2,762		3,453	4,243	⎬ 16,862
10–14	1,577	1,333	1,772	1,969		2,201	2,894	⎭
15–19	1,150	1,376	1,011	1,791		1,676	2,161	2,947
0–20					10,364			
20–24	1,101	1,486	1,100	1,735		1,716	2,604	3,013
25–29	905	1,237	1,275	1,758		1,754	2,594	2,713
30–34	906	1,063	1,022	1,256		1,391	1,926	⎫ 4,508
35–39	715	896	1,057	1,327		1,210	1,586	⎭
40–44	658	739	822	794		1,144	1,366	⎫ 3,443
45–49	378	466	689	710		868	1,119	⎭
50–54	376	412	464	551		645	895	⎫ 2,090
55–59	197	285	345	364		487	514	⎭
21+					9,068			
60+	465	636	702	505		852	1,161	1,630
Total	11,894	14,266	15,040	18,243	19,432	20,187	28,439	37,206

NOTE: Data unavailable for 1881 and 1891 censuses.

a The census was taken a year earlier than usual during this decade in the two Portuguese territories.

b Age data were given only in two broad groups in the 1941 census.

Basic Table 4   Population by age and sex: Pondicherry and Laccadive, Minicoy, and Amindivi Islands, 1961 and 1971

Age group	Pondicherry		Islands	
	1961	1971	1961	1971
MALE				
0—4	26,366 ⎤		1,750 ⎤	
5—9	22,032 ⎬	94,247	1,738 ⎬	6,820
10—14	19,518 ⎦		1,615 ⎦	
15—19	14,165	20,405	1,087	1,454
20—24	15,378	19,162	988	1,267
25—29	14,680	16,382	905	1,300
30—34	12,642 ⎬	30,601	789 ⎬	2,057
35—39	11,898		713	
40—44	10,877 ⎬	24,713	545 ⎬	1,448
45—49	9,137		450	
50—54	8,393 ⎬	16,079	472 ⎬	886
55—59	5,647		307	
60+	12,614	15,523	576	846
Total	183,347	237,112	11,935	16,078
FEMALE				
0—4	26,196 ⎤		1,697 ⎤	
5—9	22,215 ⎬	92,072	1,652 ⎬	6,162
10—14	18,996 ⎦		1,410 ⎦	
15—19	15,027	20,491	1,152	1,561
20—24	16,470	19,550	1,173	1,523
25—29	16,728	19,528	1,035	1,395
30—34	13,468 ⎬	31,145	828 ⎬	2,002
35—39	11,733		739	
40—44	10,436 ⎬	21,981	598 ⎬	1,408
45—49	8,530		552	
50—54	8,174 ⎬	15,435	435 ⎬	912
55—59	5,052		280	
60+	12,707	14,393	622	769
Total	185,732	234,595	12,173	15,732

NOTE: For these territories age data are not available for other years.

Basic Table 5 Percentage distribution of population by age and sex: India and states and territories, 1881–1971

Age group	1881	1891	1901	1911	1921	1931	1941	1951	1961	1971
INDIA—MALE										
0–4	12.86	13.85	12.19	13.11	11.83	12.62	13.13	13.17	14.68	
5–9	14.09	14.13	13.70	13.52	14.57	14.00	14.23	12.60	14.63	41.88
10–14	12.23	11.41	12.77	11.59	12.48	11.95	11.91	12.45	11.62	
15–19	8.14	8.30	8.74	8.51	8.36	8.64	7.97	9.14	8.23	8.88
20–24	8.09	8.07	7.93	8.31	7.73	8.15	7.74	8.05	8.05	7.60
25–29	9.06	8.74	8.78	8.96	8.62	8.84	8.40	8.27	8.20	7.16
30–34	9.05	8.56	8.52	8.36	8.32	7.61	7.62	7.32	7.07	
35–39	5.87	6.08	6.09	6.25	6.40	6.72	6.47	6.44	6.02	12.52
40–44	6.65	6.61	6.64	6.47	6.34	5.89	5.85	5.87	5.35	
45–49	3.33	3.64	3.77	3.85	3.96	4.42	4.54	4.58	4.31	9.69
50–54	4.42	4.26	4.49	4.45	4.48	4.11	4.34	4.21	4.04	
55–59	1.59	1.73	1.80	1.79	1.85	2.18	2.36	2.62	2.34	6.33
60+	4.63	4.63	4.57	4.83	5.06	4.87	5.45	5.28	5.47	5.94
Total	100.00	100.00	100.00	100.00	100.00	100.00	100.00	100.00	100.00	100.00
INDIA—FEMALE										
0–4	13.85	15.00	12.94	14.07	12.89	13.78	13.96	13.80	15.47	
5–9	13.63	13.80	13.53	13.44	14.74	13.99	14.34	12.88	14.86	42.20
10–14	10.11	9.41	10.94	9.93	10.84	10.65	10.71	11.95	10.83	
15–19	7.60	7.85	8.17	8.05	7.80	8.47	7.84	9.08	8.12	8.42
20–24	9.15	9.00	8.92	9.32	8.71	9.21	8.55	8.71	9.00	8.15
25–29	9.31	9.03	8.93	9.13	8.84	9.12	8.78	8.32	8.49	7.76
30–34	9.03	8.68	8.63	8.52	8.49	7.57	7.71	7.41	6.98	
35–39	5.35	5.57	5.68	5.64	5.78	6.22	6.09	5.95	5.58	12.70
40–44	6.66	6.50	6.74	6.50	6.41	5.62	5.70	5.58	5.07	
45–49	3.10	3.22	3.49	3.46	3.54	4.02	4.10	4.10	3.91	8.96
50–54	4.72	4.41	4.69	4.59	4.53	3.93	4.18	4.11	3.75	
55–59	1.58	1.65	1.73	1.67	1.72	2.06	2.10	2.38	2.14	5.82
60+	5.90	5.86	5.60	5.67	5.72	5.36	5.94	5.73	5.81	5.99
Total	100.00	100.00	100.00	100.00	100.00	100.00	100.00	100.00	100.00	100.00

Basic Table 5 *(continued)*

Age group	1881	1891	1901	1911	1921	1931	1941	1951	1961	1971
EASTERN ZONE—MALE										
0—4	14.20	13.49	12.97	13.12	11.39	12.47	12.74	13.13	14.67	42.62
5—9	15.30	15.48	14.77	15.24	15.54	14.88	14.67	12.41	15.41	
10—14	11.35	12.30	12.38	11.94	12.63	11.53	11.65	12.05	11.27	8.66
15—19	7.65	8.13	8.61	8.31	8.73	8.30	7.96	8.99	7.90	7.23
20—24	7.33	7.19	7.74	7.68	7.63	8.17	7.48	7.82	7.93	7.31
25—29	8.93	8.37	9.01	9.13	8.99	9.43	8.88	8.60	8.57	12.87
30—34	8.80	8.23	8.10	8.31	8.21	8.01	8.04	7.39	7.32	
35—39	6.20	6.39	6.29	6.66	6.92	7.07	7.12	6.60	6.27	9.80
40—44	6.40	6.51	6.13	5.89	6.11	5.75	5.82	5.82	5.24	
45—49	3.48	3.65	3.81	3.78	4.13	4.48	4.69	4.66	4.32	6.04
50—54	4.09	4.05	4.02	3.80	3.92	3.69	3.88	3.98	3.79	
55—59	1.68	1.67	1.76	1.77	1.64	2.12	2.32	2.66	2.40	5.47
60+	4.59	4.55	4.40	4.38	4.16	4.11	4.76	5.91	4.93	
Total	100.00	100.00	100.00	100.00	100.00	100.00	100.00	100.00	100.00	100.00
EASTERN ZONE—FEMALE										
0—4	15.03	14.41	13.70	13.96	12.30	13.54	13.73	14.06	15.93	42.20
5—9	14.16	14.67	14.28	14.87	15.36	14.66	14.60	12.64	15.83	
10—14	9.01	9.92	10.15	9.90	10.57	9.91	10.10	11.47	10.21	8.42
15—19	7.38	7.95	8.57	8.31	8.65	8.73	8.18	9.16	8.11	8.15
20—24	8.41	8.09	8.84	8.83	8.73	9.34	8.39	8.34	8.92	7.76
25—29	9.48	8.85	9.08	9.35	9.26	9.47	9.01	8.38	8.47	12.70
30—34	8.74	8.49	8.03	8.12	8.30	7.85	7.94	7.27	6.96	
35—39	5.66	5.89	5.80	5.84	6.28	6.34	6.57	6.09	5.46	8.96
40—44	6.43	6.38	6.09	5.74	5.92	5.49	5.52	5.38	4.87	
45—49	3.21	3.29	3.51	3.49	3.64	4.01	4.18	4.21	3.81	5.82
50—54	4.39	4.17	4.22	4.01	3.89	3.60	3.86	3.88	3.54	
55—59	1.74	1.73	1.84	1.84	1.77	2.10	2.20	2.58	2.20	5.99
60+	6.36	6.17	5.90	5.73	5.33	4.98	5.71	6.53	5.69	
Total	100.00	100.00	100.00	100.00	100.00	100.00	100.00	100.00	100.00	100.00

Basic Table 5 *(continued)*

CENTRAL ZONE—MALE

Age group	1881	1891	1901	1911	1921	1931	1941	1951	1961	1971
0—4	12.70	13.19	12.18	12.69	11.73	11.99	13.27	13.22	14.88	⎫
5—9	13.76	13.81	12.89	13.44	14.63	13.79	14.17	13.01	14.44	⎬ 42.58
10—14	12.21	11.72	12.64	11.65	12.36	12.21	11.44	12.59	11.42	⎭
15—19	7.93	8.13	8.81	8.35	8.36	8.77	7.84	8.90	8.13	8.32
20—24	8.31	8.32	8.36	8.58	7.90	7.83	7.62	7.97	7.89	6.97
25—29	9.22	8.69	8.99	9.17	8.46	8.98	8.54	8.32	8.08	7.05
30—34	9.38	9.14	8.92	8.82	8.47	7.70	7.83	7.59	7.13	⎫ 12.45
35—39	5.44	5.70	5.81	6.07	6.16	6.63	6.37	6.59	5.86	⎭
40—44	7.08	7.18	6.89	6.80	6.74	6.19	6.02	6.13	5.43	⎫ 9.57
45—49	3.16	3.29	3.68	3.68	3.95	4.40	4.57	4.72	4.33	⎭
50—54	4.78	4.69	4.73	4.62	4.67	4.61	4.62	4.42	4.32	⎫ 6.55
55—59	1.37	1.38	1.71	1.59	1.74	2.05	2.28	2.65	2.30	⎭
60+	4.66	4.77	4.41	4.53	4.83	4.84	5.44	3.89	5.79	6.51
Total	100.00	100.00	100.00	100.00	100.00	100.00	100.00	100.00	100.00	100.00

CENTRAL ZONE—FEMALE

Age group	1881	1891	1901	1911	1921	1931	1941	1951	1961	1971
0—4	13.89	14.63	12.86	13.75	12.99	13.41	14.36	14.13	15.80	⎫
5—9	13.25	13.55	12.51	13.24	14.63	13.92	14.05	13.29	14.39	⎬ 42.28
10—14	9.88	9.37	10.72	9.69	10.33	10.34	9.87	11.80	10.25	⎭
15—19	7.16	7.23	7.87	7.37	7.29	7.89	7.22	8.69	7.79	7.66
20—24	9.25	9.04	9.13	9.42	8.59	9.05	8.32	8.69	9.00	7.89
25—29	9.35	9.09	9.11	9.38	8.71	9.00	8.88	8.21	8.42	7.72
30—34	9.33	9.18	8.92	8.97	8.78	7.85	7.96	7.70	7.12	⎫ 12.86
35—39	5.25	5.38	5.76	5.82	5.94	6.31	6.13	6.08	5.61	⎭
40—44	7.16	7.09	7.16	6.93	6.85	6.11	6.08	5.86	5.28	⎫ 9.17
45—49	3.02	2.96	3.62	3.47	3.65	4.13	4.25	4.37	4.08	⎭
50—54	5.05	4.90	5.03	4.88	4.79	4.40	4.56	4.23	3.94	⎫ 6.03
55—59	1.40	1.35	1.73	1.54	1.67	1.95	2.13	2.41	2.21	⎭
60+	6.01	6.23	5.58	5.54	5.77	5.65	6.19	4.55	6.11	6.39
Total	100.00	100.00	100.00	100.00	100.00	100.00	100.00	100.00	100.00	100.00

Basic Table 5 *(continued)*

SOUTHERN ZONE—MALE

Age group	1881	1891	1901	1911	1921	1931	1941	1951	1961	1971
0–4	11.78	14.61	12.99	13.11	12.08	13.10	13.20	12.64	14.11	⎫
5–9	13.47	13.66	14.07	13.01	13.45	13.52	14.17	12.15	13.93	⎬ 40.00
10–14	13.26	10.55	12.93	12.13	12.56	12.09	12.72	12.55	11.97	⎭
15–19	8.68	8.28	8.16	8.69	8.41	8.57	7.71	9.58	8.37	9.16
20–24	8.30	8.33	7.19	8.22	8.01	8.12	7.92	8.27	8.09	8.23
25–29	8.72	8.57	7.98	8.28	8.44	8.48	7.70	8.00	7.95	7.11
30–34	9.19	8.35	8.24	7.61	8.11	7.41	7.08	7.04	6.89	⎫
35–39	6.09	6.12	6.18	6.06	6.30	6.74	6.31	6.33	6.21	⎬ 12.57
40–44	6.88	6.71	6.74	6.52	6.13	5.93	6.05	5.93	5.59	⎭
45–49	3.09	3.74	3.91	4.13	3.92	4.36	4.67	4.72	4.49	⎱ 10.25
50–54	4.21	4.30	4.62	4.56	4.60	3.99	4.45	4.46	4.17	⎰
55–59	1.62	1.78	1.97	2.09	2.15	2.30	2.40	2.64	2.46	6.63
60+	4.71	5.00	5.02	5.59	5.83	5.40	5.63	5.69	5.78	6.05
Total	100.00	100.00	100.00	100.00	100.00	100.00	100.00	100.00	100.00	100.00

SOUTHERN ZONE—FEMALE

Age group	1881	1891	1901	1911	1921	1931	1941	1951	1961	1971
0–4	12.38	15.30	13.60	13.59	12.64	13.69	13.24	12.76	14.26	⎫
5–9	13.48	13.41	14.01	13.06	13.83	13.39	14.34	12.37	14.13	⎬ 40.10
10–14	11.57	9.06	11.41	10.98	11.42	11.21	11.81	12.30	11.53	⎭
15–19	7.94	7.96	7.64	8.52	7.93	8.61	8.00	9.43	8.35	8.98
20–24	9.77	9.74	8.56	9.43	9.35	9.21	8.57	8.95	8.94	8.49
25–29	9.01	8.84	8.45	8.48	8.80	9.33	8.49	8.33	8.60	7.97
30–34	9.34	8.75	8.74	8.15	8.38	7.53	7.55	7.34	7.01	⎫
35–39	4.99	5.18	5.37	5.32	5.26	6.17	6.03	5.89	5.81	⎬ 12.86
40–44	6.72	6.47	6.64	6.51	6.27	5.39	5.84	5.69	5.14	⎭
45–49	2.73	3.09	3.35	3.50	3.46	3.84	4.08	4.08	4.01	⎱ 9.30
50–54	4.79	4.56	4.73	4.64	4.76	3.92	4.14	4.52	4.01	⎰
55–59	1.55	1.61	1.72	1.80	1.82	2.12	2.06	2.39	2.23	6.16
60+	5.74	6.02	5.79	6.01	6.07	5.61	5.85	5.94	5.97	6.14
Total	100.00	100.00	100.00	100.00	100.00	100.00	100.00	100.00	100.00	100.00

Basic Table 5 *(continued)*

Age group	1881	1891	1901	1911	1921	1931	1941	1951	1961	1971
WESTERN ZONE—MALE										
0—4	12.90	13.85	10.63	14.25	12.08	13.21	13.21	13.41	14.98	⎫
5—9	14.03	13.79	13.69	12.37	14.87	13.90	13.79	13.09	14.58	⎬ 41.71
10—14	12.43	10.98	13.53	10.32	12.48	11.74	11.51	12.79	11.68	⎭
15—19	8.12	7.73	8.72	7.91	7.24	8.43	7.81	9.07	8.37	9.23
20—24	8.28	8.13	8.25	8.62	7.12	8.47	7.97	8.46	8.46	8.06
25—29	9.57	9.43	9.57	9.68	8.82	8.62	8.85	8.44	8.40	7.29
30—34	8.87	8.88	9.01	8.75	8.81	7.43	8.09	7.56	7.16	⎫ 12.71
35—39	6.24	6.17	6.52	6.53	6.61	6.83	6.58	6.54	6.10	⎭
40—44	5.83	6.68	6.55	6.73	6.51	5.69	5.62	5.65	5.15	⎫ 9.54
45—49	3.67	3.59	3.77	3.97	3.95	4.66	4.41	4.19	4.30	⎭
50—54	4.25	4.59	4.27	4.56	4.67	3.89	4.17	3.76	3.69	⎫ 6.14
55—59	1.73	1.58	1.71	1.73	1.83	2.39	2.49	2.39	2.28	⎭
60+	4.08	4.61	3.77	4.56	5.02	4.72	5.50	4.64	4.84	5.32
Total	100.00	100.00	100.00	100.00	100.00	100.00	100.00	100.00	100.00	100.00
WESTERN ZONE—FEMALE										
0—4	14.20	15.49	11.53	15.53	13.42	14.49	14.11	13.95	15.65	⎫
5—9	13.98	13.78	13.81	12.37	15.30	14.07	14.13	13.49	14.98	⎬ 42.19
10—14	10.31	9.15	11.73	8.81	11.01	10.91	10.61	12.29	11.01	⎭
15—19	7.98	7.55	8.26	7.67	6.88	8.41	7.63	8.80	8.05	8.41
20—24	9.34	9.29	9.20	9.73	8.07	9.39	9.25	9.10	9.31	8.33
25—29	9.45	9.29	9.46	9.49	8.77	8.76	9.09	8.42	8.57	7.79
30—34	8.56	8.73	8.93	8.88	8.73	7.11	7.63	7.46	6.90	⎫ 12.76
35—39	5.64	5.47	6.06	5.87	5.84	6.30	5.83	5.88	5.64	⎭
40—44	5.61	6.57	6.67	6.69	6.63	5.44	5.43	5.39	4.97	⎫ 8.99
45—49	3.62	3.10	3.52	3.45	3.50	4.29	4.02	3.79	3.97	⎭
50—54	4.46	4.58	4.48	4.64	4.59	3.59	4.11	3.67	3.43	⎫ 5.72
55—59	1.77	1.39	1.62	1.53	1.57	2.18	2.10	2.06	2.04	⎭
60+	5.09	5.62	4.73	5.35	5.70	5.05	6.05	5.69	5.49	5.81
Total	100.00	100.00	100.00	100.00	100.00	100.00	100.00	100.00	100.00	100.00

Basic Table 5 *(continued)*

NORTHERN ZONE—MALE

Age group	1881	1891	1901	1911	1921	1931	1941	1951	1961	1971
0—4	11.59	14.77	10.59	12.88	12.21	12.67	13.44	14.16	15.17	42.91
5—9	12.97	13.47	12.68	12.36	14.45	13.68	14.03	12.55	14.88	
10—14	12.31	10.97	12.84	10.94	12.26	12.23	12.21	12.35	12.04	
15—19	9.47	9.56	10.08	9.58	8.64	9.47	9.00	9.13	8.68	9.54
20—24	8.99	8.65	8.46	8.86	7.60	8.54	7.91	7.73	8.08	7.80
25—29	8.86	9.15	8.64	8.79	8.33	8.30	8.01	7.79	7.91	6.96
30—34	8.30	7.85	8.50	8.54	8.12	7.12	6.90	6.87	6.70	11.50
35—39	5.25	6.19	5.67	5.87	5.80	5.98	5.45	5.84	5.29	
40—44	6.51	5.27	7.02	6.50	6.23	5.65	5.34	5.54	5.11	8.74
45—49	3.60	4.27	3.61	3.66	3.71	4.20	4.04	4.16	3.85	
50—54	4.95	3.35	4.88	5.08	4.81	4.41	4.68	4.26	4.15	6.17
55—59	1.80	2.67	1.86	1.74	1.92	2.11	2.37	2.65	2.07	
60+	5.39	3.83	5.16	5.20	5.93	5.62	6.61	6.97	6.06	6.38
Total	100.00	100.00	100.00	100.00	100.00	100.00	100.00	100.00	100.00	100.00

NORTHERN ZONE—FEMALE

Age group	1881	1891	1901	1911	1921	1931	1941	1951	1961	1971
0—4	12.57	16.11	11.47	14.58	14.10	14.65	15.16	15.00	16.41	43.55
5—9	13.00	13.35	12.96	12.61	15.18	13.97	14.68	13.02	15.15	
10—14	10.76	9.35	11.42	9.32	11.06	11.52	11.60	12.12	11.68	
15—19	8.92	9.22	9.14	8.47	7.78	8.95	8.37	9.28	8.47	9.12
20—24	9.57	9.12	9.07	9.52	8.04	9.06	8.54	8.54	8.91	8.28
25—29	9.14	9.37	8.67	9.17	8.25	8.40	8.31	8.25	8.31	7.40
30—34	8.68	7.69	8.76	8.83	8.23	6.86	7.04	7.14	6.79	11.97
35—39	5.05	6.24	5.50	5.25	5.36	5.78	5.26	5.50	5.16	
40—44	7.11	5.33	7.47	7.08	6.57	5.52	5.19	5.37	4.97	8.57
45—49	3.25	4.10	3.37	3.29	3.30	3.91	3.70	3.62	3.46	
50—54	4.90	3.28	5.03	5.09	4.81	4.07	4.28	3.86	3.60	5.54
55—59	1.50	2.61	1.64	1.43	1.58	1.92	1.89	2.18	1.72	
60+	5.56	4.24	5.50	5.36	5.75	5.38	5.98	6.12	5.38	5.57
Total	100.00	100.00	100.00	100.00	100.00	100.00	100.00	100.00	100.00	100.00

Basic Table 5 *(continued)*

Age group	1881	1891	1901	1911	1921	1931	1941	1951	1961	1971
ANDHRA PRADESH—MALE										
0—4	12.19	13.87	12.25	12.75	11.13	12.73	12.69	12.03	13.71 ⎫	
5—9	13.47	13.91	14.07	13.37	13.59	13.48	14.42	12.22	13.96 ⎬	40.42
10—14	13.43	11.33	13.14	12.34	13.16	11.77	13.26	12.65	11.85 ⎭	
15—19	8.13	7.92	7.72	8.08	8.05	8.54	5.61	8.98	8.36	8.59
20—24	8.70	8.70	7.13	8.01	7.91	8.08	7.67	7.87	7.83	7.64
25—29	8.18	8.21	8.11	8.30	8.68	8.79	7.80	7.94	8.14	7.26
30—34	9.79	9.03	8.61	7.76	8.16	7.76	7.65	7.31	7.23 ⎫	
35—39	4.72	4.89	6.01	5.86	5.96	6.42	6.15	6.04	5.87 ⎬	12.71
40—44	7.30	7.62	7.13	6.75	6.40	6.23	6.80	6.53	5.93 ⎭	
45—49	2.41	2.86	3.78	3.99	3.80	4.11	4.51	4.61	4.23 ⎫	
50—54	4.82	4.94	4.91	4.76	4.80	4.33	5.10	4.96	4.62 ⎬	10.40
55—59	1.14	1.12	1.86	1.96	1.99	2.03	2.14	2.42	2.17 ⎭	6.67
60+	5.71	5.59	5.28	6.06	6.37	5.73	6.20	6.43	6.10	6.31
Total	100.00	100.00	100.00	100.00	100.00	100.00	100.00	100.00	100.00	100.00
ANDHRA PRADESH—FEMALE										
0—4	13.29	15.04	13.42	13.52	11.95	13.86	12.48	12.41	14.10 ⎫	
5—9	13.37	13.65	14.10	13.49	14.40	13.51	14.69	12.50	14.42 ⎬	40.55
10—14	11.47	9.48	11.42	10.87	11.64	10.64	11.79	11.85	11.05 ⎭	
15—19	7.80	7.77	7.37	7.92	7.51	8.75	7.03	9.00	8.32	8.28
20—24	10.43	10.44	8.63	9.39	9.19	9.21	8.41	8.68	8.83	8.17
25—29	7.98	8.12	8.58	8.47	8.70	9.57	8.49	8.13	8.55	8.05
30—34	9.85	9.58	9.07	8.41	8.64	7.66	8.31	7.81	7.20 ⎫	
35—39	3.58	3.84	5.16	5.15	5.07	5.72	5.72	5.61	5.45 ⎬	12.89
40—44	7.11	7.28	6.80	6.63	6.54	5.58	6.57	6.35	5.52 ⎭	
45—49	1.91	2.07	3.06	3.26	3.26	3.47	3.74	3.96	3.77 ⎫	
50—54	5.27	5.06	4.84	4.73	4.87	4.13	4.65	4.84	4.49 ⎬	9.33
55—59	1.01	0.90	1.52	1.63	1.65	1.79	1.72	2.08	1.93 ⎭	6.30
60+	6.91	6.76	6.03	6.53	6.58	6.10	6.41	6.78	6.37	6.43
Total	100.00	100.00	100.00	100.00	100.00	100.00	100.00	100.00	100.00	100.00

Basic Table 5 *(continued)*

ASSAM—MALE

Age group	1881	1891	1901	1911	1921	1931	1941	1951	1961	1971
0–4	16.95	15.23	14.47	15.14	13.57	14.89	14.89	15.58	15.75	⎫
5–9	14.76	14.72	14.70	15.22	15.79	14.62	15.48	14.65	15.56	⎬ 44.89
10–14	10.01	10.80	10.55	10.20	11.50	10.96	11.45	11.48	11.56	⎭
15–19	7.19	7.19	7.02	7.16	7.55	7.80	7.31	7.88	7.94	8.38
20–24	7.73	7.67	7.91	7.60	7.21	8.10	7.07	7.91	7.75	7.38
25–29	9.42	8.96	9.99	9.46	8.93	9.54	9.15	8.48	8.71	7.44
30–34	8.46	8.99	9.36	8.75	8.46	8.05	7.92	7.53	7.22	⎱ 12.45
35–39	6.48	6.82	7.36	7.29	7.33	7.21	7.41	6.59	6.24	⎰
40–44	5.65	6.61	6.48	6.32	6.30	5.52	5.42	5.72	4.97	⎱ 8.78
45–49	3.83	3.25	3.48	3.74	3.92	4.14	4.20	4.17	3.99	⎰
50–54	3.40	4.18	3.85	3.92	4.09	3.52	3.67	3.84	3.60	⎱ 5.55
55–59	2.25	1.52	1.47	1.59	1.68	1.91	2.01	1.81	2.16	⎰
60+	3.86	4.05	3.35	3.61	3.68	3.73	4.02	4.36	4.57	5.12
Total	100.00	100.00	100.00	100.00	100.00	100.00	100.00	100.00	100.00	100.00

ASSAM—FEMALE

Age group	1881	1891	1901	1911	1921	1931	1941	1951	1961	1971
0–4	19.22	17.81	16.34	17.54	15.49	17.29	16.83	17.48	18.73	⎫
5–9	13.85	15.88	15.39	16.37	16.96	15.87	16.49	16.05	17.67	⎬ 49.08
10–14	8.38	9.67	9.39	9.43	10.45	10.31	10.19	10.92	11.19	⎭
15–19	7.71	8.23	8.02	8.15	8.58	9.45	9.05	9.09	8.81	8.66
20–24	8.25	8.30	10.07	9.32	9.05	9.87	9.01	9.73	8.92	7.81
25–29	10.89	8.46	10.22	9.83	9.43	9.22	9.81	8.87	8.44	7.73
30–34	7.72	8.92	8.56	8.23	8.32	7.16	7.40	6.92	6.45	⎱ 11.19
35–39	5.74	5.36	5.50	4.57	5.65	5.64	5.57	5.16	4.81	⎰
40–44	4.97	5.91	5.54	5.23	5.15	4.45	4.54	4.43	3.90	⎱ 6.96
45–49	3.29	2.44	2.63	2.68	2.79	3.04	3.10	2.88	2.81	⎰
50–54	3.23	3.24	3.54	3.46	3.37	2.96	3.03	3.16	2.77	⎱ 4.30
55–59	2.04	1.27	1.20	1.31	1.28	1.45	1.50	1.45	1.53	⎰
60+	4.72	4.52	3.61	3.87	3.48	3.29	3.48	3.86	3.96	4.27
Total	100.00	100.00	100.00	100.00	100.00	100.00	100.00	100.00	100.00	100.00

Basic Table 5 *(continued)*

BIHAR—MALE

Age group	1881	1891	1901	1911	1921	1931	1941	1951	1961	1971
0–4	14.43	13.64	13.11	13.23	11.57	12.85	13.45	14.58	15.24	⎱ 43.35
5–9	15.88	16.31	15.39	16.14	16.55	15.96	15.81	12.49	16.43	
10–14	11.59	12.57	12.76	12.24	12.62	12.00	11.97	12.32	11.74	8.23
15–19	7.17	7.66	8.37	7.94	8.45	7.92	7.74	8.34	7.70	7.04
20–24	6.72	6.75	7.54	7.25	7.15	7.71	6.94	6.76	7.34	7.03
25–29	8.60	8.07	8.72	8.76	8.46	8.83	8.16	7.93	8.08	⎱ 12.65
30–34	8.84	8.08	7.80	8.26	8.06	7.66	7.45	6.79	6.84	
35–39	6.16	6.19	6.06	6.44	6.75	6.77	6.80	6.31	6.01	⎱ 9.84
40–44	6.41	6.29	6.04	5.79	6.04	5.48	5.36	5.50	4.95	
45–49	3.66	3.82	3.80	3.73	4.18	4.62	4.83	4.78	4.46	⎱ 6.12
50–54	4.19	4.13	3.99	3.85	3.90	3.68	3.82	3.92	3.66	
55–59	1.68	1.70	1.77	1.74	1.75	2.18	2.46	3.02	2.42	⎱ 5.74
60+	4.68	4.80	4.66	4.62	4.52	4.34	5.21	7.26	5.14	
Total	100.00	100.00	100.00	100.00	100.00	100.00	100.00	100.00	100.00	100.00

BIHAR—FEMALE

Age group	1881	1891	1901	1911	1921	1931	1941	1951	1961	1971
0–4	15.26	14.35	13.51	13.74	12.40	13.78	13.92	14.73	15.58	⎱ 41.77
5–9	14.59	14.99	14.35	15.14	15.77	15.04	14.88	11.96	15.51	
10–14	9.09	10.01	10.17	9.74	10.14	10.12	10.04	11.37	10.12	7.70
15–19	6.60	7.13	7.73	7.24	7.59	7.70	7.38	8.36	7.58	8.26
20–24	7.93	7.75	8.88	8.55	8.20	8.97	7.93	7.32	8.78	7.23
25–29	9.34	8.80	9.13	9.31	8.97	9.11	8.70	8.05	8.38	⎱ 13.39
30–34	8.83	8.49	8.10	8.48	8.58	7.90	7.86	7.05	7.05	
35–39	6.00	6.19	5.91	6.12	6.59	6.55	6.88	6.25	5.77	⎱ 9.40
40–44	6.41	6.28	6.13	5.90	6.14	5.49	5.47	5.54	5.04	
45–49	3.48	3.62	3.57	3.59	3.80	4.32	4.55	4.63	4.20	⎱ 5.68
50–54	4.29	4.16	4.27	4.09	4.00	3.47	3.80	3.96	3.51	
55–59	1.78	1.80	1.88	1.85	1.81	2.25	2.36	2.90	2.38	⎱ 6.07
60+	6.39	6.44	6.35	6.25	6.01	5.32	6.22	7.88	6.09	
Total	100.00	100.00	100.00	100.00	100.00	100.00	100.00	100.00	100.00	100.00

Basic Table 5 *(continued)*

GUJARAT—MALE

Age group	1881	1891	1901	1911	1921	1931	1941	1951	1961	1971
0—4	11.93	13.77	9.29	15.12	12.70	13.02	13.88	13.77	15.61	⎫
5—9	14.46	14.37	13.43	12.13	15.58	14.52	13.55	13.50	15.40	⎬ 43.38
10—14	13.58	10.99	14.04	9.51	12.93	12.54	11.37	13.42	12.23	⎭
15—19	9.38	8.54	10.54	8.90	7.76	9.12	8.40	9.75	8.67	9.76
20—24	9.32	9.02	8.97	9.00	6.88	8.43	8.68	8.60	8.56	8.13
25—29	9.35	9.17	9.95	9.85	8.48	7.96	8.90	8.06	7.85	6.95
30—34	8.19	8.60	9.20	8.70	8.25	6.84	7.66	7.40	6.70	⎫ 12.08
35—39	6.21	6.12	6.89	6.75	6.56	6.30	5.87	6.29	5.61	⎭
40—44	5.19	6.35	5.97	6.43	6.14	5.77	5.22	5.48	5.00	⎫ 8.85
45—49	3.70	3.36	3.59	4.00	4.09	4.58	4.18	3.71	4.13	⎭
50—54	3.87	4.34	3.90	4.31	4.51	4.20	4.47	3.54	3.79	⎫ 5.88
55—59	1.80	1.49	1.64	1.80	2.04	2.28	2.55	2.17	1.92	⎭
60+	3.03	3.89	2.58	3.48	4.08	4.44	5.30	4.31	4.53	4.97
Total	100.00	100.00	100.00	100.00	100.00	100.00	100.00	100.00	100.00	100.00

GUJARAT—FEMALE

Age group	1881	1891	1901	1911	1921	1931	1941	1951	1961	1971
0—4	12.90	15.17	9.77	16.29	13.98	14.18	14.82	14.15	16.12	⎫
5—9	14.24	14.03	13.30	11.60	15.40	14.38	13.64	13.39	15.17	⎬ 42.72
10—14	11.70	9.13	12.28	7.95	11.51	11.44	10.61	12.76	11.23	⎭
15—19	8.66	7.56	9.61	7.87	6.89	8.53	8.15	9.38	8.13	9.17
20—24	9.70	9.71	9.68	10.16	7.79	9.37	9.61	9.35	9.32	8.45
25—29	9.27	9.21	9.79	9.81	8.30	7.97	8.85	8.23	8.06	7.31
30—34	8.01	8.60	9.06	9.07	8.55	6.91	7.26	7.36	6.77	⎫ 12.16
35—39	6.10	5.66	6.45	6.23	6.07	6.13	5.38	5.76	5.45	⎭
40—44	5.34	6.64	6.61	6.71	6.50	5.77	5.35	5.23	5.16	⎫ 8.85
45—49	3.85	3.13	3.68	3.65	3.84	4.44	3.96	3.49	3.94	⎭
50—54	4.19	4.67	4.39	4.61	4.56	3.88	4.45	3.55	3.49	⎫ 5.75
55—59	1.99	1.41	1.71	1.63	1.73	2.11	2.13	1.94	1.78	⎭
60+	4.04	5.09	3.66	4.42	4.87	4.88	5.80	5.42	5.39	5.58
Total	100.00	100.00	100.00	100.00	100.00	100.00	100.00	100.00	100.00	100.00

Basic Table 5 *(continued)*

HARYANA—MALE

Age group	1881	1891	1901	1911	1921	1931	1941	1951	1961	1971
0—4	11.78	15.65	10.91	12.08	12.87	12.84	13.55	15.40	16.36	⎫
5—9	12.80	12.57	13.27	11.97	14.61	13.83	13.60	12.22	15.52	⎬ 46.02
10—14	12.30	11.22	12.66	11.94	11.88	12.83	12.63	12.35	12.31	⎭
15—19	9.58	11.09	9.79	10.98	9.02	10.26	10.17	9.32	8.77	9.93
20—24	9.56	9.81	8.68	9.12	8.30	8.39	8.19	7.83	7.60	7.46
25—29	9.10	9.79	8.78	8.89	8.75	8.52	7.87	7.63	7.34	6.14
30—34	8.24	6.74	8.32	7.97	7.35	6.99	6.43	6.63	5.95	⎫
35—39	5.01	6.86	5.48	5.52	5.42	5.67	5.01	5.48	4.88	⎬ 9.89
40—44	6.45	3.37	7.06	6.24	5.68	5.31	5.57	5.05	4.95	⎫
45—49	3.52	4.90	3.63	3.75	3.74	4.08	3.91	4.14	3.90	⎬ 8.05
50—54	4.94	1.88	4.84	4.83	4.65	3.99	4.79	4.27	3.99	⎫
55—59	1.78	3.50	1.70	1.83	2.05	2.04	2.33	2.80	2.08	⎬ 6.01
60+	4.96	2.61	4.88	4.89	5.68	5.24	5.94	6.87	6.34	6.50
Total	100.00	100.00	100.00	100.00	100.00	100.00	100.00	100.00	100.00	100.00

HARYANA—FEMALE

Age group	1881	1891	1901	1911	1921	1931	1941	1951	1961	1971
0—4	12.23	17.06	12.00	14.08	14.97	15.09	16.09	16.26	17.79	⎫
5—9	12.98	12.46	13.68	12.34	15.50	14.13	14.29	12.92	15.70	⎬ 46.48
10—14	10.80	9.79	11.54	10.47	11.38	12.47	12.28	12.34	12.31	⎭
15—19	8.83	11.30	8.81	9.63	8.29	9.50	9.04	9.34	8.28	9.55
20—24	9.93	9.79	9.05	9.57	8.37	9.14	9.02	8.81	8.42	7.95
25—29	9.12	10.48	8.71	8.99	8.38	8.60	8.13	8.25	7.92	6.65
30—34	8.73	5.91	8.69	8.36	7.58	6.69	6.86	6.79	6.31	⎫
35—39	4.93	7.38	5.30	5.24	5.03	5.46	5.14	5.20	4.99	⎬ 11.05
40—44	7.31	3.01	7.41	6.79	5.95	5.10	5.29	5.25	4.83	⎫
45—49	3.20	5.22	3.22	3.38	3.34	3.80	3.31	3.50	3.49	⎬ 8.19
50—54	5.05	1.46	4.99	4.77	4.51	3.64	4.22	3.82	3.41	⎫
55—59	1.49	3.77	1.38	1.50	1.66	1.78	1.58	2.11	1.66	⎬ 5.16
60+	5.42	2.38	5.22	4.88	5.05	4.58	4.75	5.41	4.88	4.97
Total	100.00	100.00	100.00	100.00	100.00	100.00	100.00	100.00	100.00	100.00

Basic Table 5 *(continued)*

HIMACHAL PRADESH—MALE

Age group	1881	1891	1901	1911	1921	1931	1941	1951	1961	1971
0—4	11.40	15.01	10.56	10.92	10.46	11.39	12.40	12.50	14.17	⎫
5—9	12.83	12.67	11.96	11.92	12.62	12.19	13.12	11.39	13.46	⎬ 41.01
10—14	11.92	10.81	12.14	11.11	11.19	11.25	11.73	11.02	11.42	⎭
15—19	9.17	10.42	9.28	8.99	8.69	8.66	8.50	9.34	8.05	9.11
20—24	8.83	9.18	8.05	8.85	7.59	8.67	6.82	7.45	7.61	7.37
25—29	8.83	9.90	8.71	8.87	8.19	8.09	7.25	8.32	7.61	6.81
30—34	8.71	6.76	8.67	8.27	8.13	7.71	6.40	6.78	6.77	⎫ 11.42
35—39	5.50	7.24	6.13	5.56	6.68	6.81	6.40	6.72	5.94	⎭
40—44	6.71	3.71	7.04	6.93	6.41	5.70	5.60	5.46	5.03	⎫ 9.17
45—49	3.54	5.22	3.95	3.97	4.38	4.88	5.03	4.69	4.56	⎭
50—54	5.01	1.98	5.09	5.56	5.14	4.61	5.27	4.93	4.38	⎫ 7.02
55—59	1.78	3.83	1.99	1.96	2.59	2.95	3.15	3.28	3.06	⎭
60+	5.77	3.26	6.42	7.11	7.91	7.10	8.32	8.10	7.94	8.09
Total	100.00	100.00	100.00	100.00	100.00	100.00	100.00	100.00	100.00	100.00

HIMACHAL PRADESH—FEMALE

Age group	1881	1891	1901	1911	1921	1931	1941	1951	1961	1971
0—4	12.90	16.96	11.90	12.19	12.07	13.03	13.20	15.32	15.04	⎫
5—9	13.31	12.90	12.99	12.86	13.43	12.81	13.90	11.82	13.93	⎬ 41.42
10—14	10.35	9.39	10.97	10.10	10.25	10.98	11.60	10.77	11.53	⎭
15—19	8.73	11.03	9.04	9.28	9.14	9.28	8.74	9.65	8.86	9.55
20—24	9.39	9.51	8.55	9.35	8.41	9.38	8.04	7.78	8.69	8.26
25—29	9.14	10.38	9.08	9.10	8.79	8.75	8.87	8.69	8.55	7.62
30—34	9.02	6.04	9.06	8.78	8.15	7.10	7.46	6.96	6.98	⎫ 12.49
35—39	5.01	7.42	5.69	5.19	6.07	6.62	5.99	6.06	5.74	⎭
40—44	7.18	3.09	6.97	7.01	6.39	5.14	5.80	5.17	4.82	⎫ 8.82
45—49	2.99	5.00	3.25	3.21	3.66	4.28	3.96	3.91	3.78	⎭
50—54	4.83	1.50	4.63	4.90	4.72	4.06	3.94	3.90	3.70	⎫ 5.64
55—59	1.36	3.84	1.53	1.44	1.90	2.28	1.66	2.66	2.09	⎭
60+	5.80	2.94	6.34	6.59	7.03	6.28	6.82	7.30	6.27	6.20
Total	100.00	100.00	100.00	100.00	100.00	100.00	100.00	100.00	100.00	100.00

Basic Table 5 *(continued)*

Age group	1881	1891	1901	1911	1921	1931	1941	1951	1961	1971
JAMMU-KASHMIR—MALE										
0—4	u	16.06	13.67	13.69	13.68	13.24	12.73	u	14.10	
5—9	u	14.14	14.05	13.74	14.79	14.03	15.16	u	14.33	⎱ 41.55
10—14	u	9.91	12.31	11.35	12.04	11.50	11.95	u	11.11	
15—19	u	7.90	8.13	8.69	8.34	9.56	9.23	u	8.96	8.74
20—24	u	7.70	7.17	8.24	7.65	8.40	7.63	u	7.87	7.71
25—29	u	7.85	7.72	8.09	8.22	8.84	7.77	u	8.31	7.44
30—34	u	8.32	8.78	8.14	8.43	7.97	7.39	u	7.62	⎱ 12.79
35—39	u	5.86	6.12	5.72	5.79	6.67	6.42	u	6.66	
40—44	u	6.37	6.79	6.24	5.52	5.32	5.40	u	5.61	⎱ 9.60
45—49	u	3.69	3.44	3.46	3.20	3.75	3.95	u	3.97	
50—54	u	4.44	4.73	4.61	4.47	3.56	4.10	u	3.90	⎱ 5.94
55—59	u	1.47	1.39	1.42	1.53	1.82	2.02	u	1.95	
60+	u	6.29	5.70	6.60	6.34	5.32	6.25	u	5.61	6.23
Total	u	100.00	100.00	100.00	100.00	100.00	100.00	u	100.00	100.00
JAMMU-KASHMIR—FEMALE										
0—4	u	18.00	15.28	15.13	15.32	15.10	14.08	u	15.66	
5—9	u	14.36	14.92	14.60	15.59	14.15	15.52	u	15.35	⎱ 44.44
10—14	u	8.24	11.31	10.55	10.89	10.94	11.48	u	11.02	
15—19	u	7.85	7.96	8.98	8.65	9.95	8.99	u	8.99	8.35
20—24	u	9.02	8.28	9.40	9.30	9.43	8.34	u	8.97	7.81
25—29	u	8.60	8.14	8.56	9.02	9.79	8.87	u	9.62	8.16
30—34	u	8.69	8.32	8.00	7.87	7.58	7.72	u	7.65	⎱ 13.25
35—39	u	5.38	5.33	5.17	4.94	5.98	6.21	u	5.92	
40—44	u	6.41	6.74	6.29	5.50	4.84	5.13	u	4.83	⎱ 8.55
45—49	u	2.99	3.14	2.91	2.70	3.24	3.42	u	3.11	
50—54	u	3.84	4.03	4.09	3.92	3.09	3.49	u	3.06	⎱ 4.65
55—59	u	1.14	1.26	1.04	1.05	1.41	1.52	u	1.35	
60+	u	5.47	5.28	5.26	5.25	4.49	5.22	u	4.48	4.71
Total	u	100.00	100.00	100.00	100.00	100.00	100.00	u	100.00	100.00

u—unavailable.

Basic Table 5 *(continued)*

KERALA—MALE

Age group	1881	1891	1901	1911	1921	1931	1941	1951	1961	1971
0–4	u	13.74	13.18	13.77	13.40	15.07	14.26	14.72	15.30	⎱ 41.04
5–9	u	13.04	13.57	13.16	13.47	13.74	14.24	12.15	14.85	⎰
10–14	u	12.09	13.20	12.61	12.99	12.97	13.65	12.68	13.48	10.65
15–19	u	9.44	9.50	9.79	9.52	8.91	9.14	10.60	8.25	9.24
20–24	u	8.41	7.98	8.61	8.43	8.55	8.29	9.33	8.11	6.27
25–29	u	8.86	8.62	8.61	8.36	7.62	7.06	7.63	7.23	⎱ 11.38
30–34	u	7.72	8.08	7.53	7.50	6.62	6.11	6.13	6.25	⎰
35–39	u	7.03	6.88	6.78	6.60	6.66	6.08	5.97	6.07	⎱ 9.41
40–44	u	5.73	5.67	5.43	5.60	4.98	4.98	4.77	4.54	⎰
45–49	u	4.03	3.82	4.02	4.13	4.49	4.58	4.49	4.31	⎱ 6.04
50–54	u	3.60	3.74	3.58	3.69	3.34	3.64	3.58	3.33	⎰
55–59	u	2.09	1.90	2.14	2.14	2.56	2.65	2.70	2.63	5.97
60+	u	4.23	3.86	3.98	4.18	4.47	5.33	5.24	5.65	5.97
Total	u	100.00	100.00	100.00	100.00	100.00	100.00	100.00	100.00	100.00

KERALA—FEMALE

Age group	1881	1891	1901	1911	1921	1931	1941	1951	1961	1971
0–4	u	14.52	13.59	13.84	13.27	14.64	13.63	13.96	14.62	⎱ 39.50
5–9	u	12.54	13.13	12.71	13.00	12.88	13.64	11.50	14.07	⎰
10–14	u	10.98	12.07	11.64	12.19	12.27	12.98	12.33	12.98	11.25
15–19	u	9.89	9.75	10.14	9.83	9.43	9.55	11.26	8.70	9.41
20–24	u	9.56	9.21	9.64	9.64	9.56	8.66	9.97	8.84	6.72
25–29	u	9.38	9.09	8.96	9.04	8.53	7.74	8.08	8.05	⎱ 11.92
30–34	u	7.65	8.25	7.75	7.58	6.80	6.67	6.44	6.46	⎰
35–39	u	5.93	5.77	5.86	5.67	6.41	6.20	5.90	5.89	⎱ 8.93
40–44	u	5.37	5.52	5.42	5.51	4.64	4.90	4.79	4.36	⎰
45–49	u	3.46	3.31	3.53	3.64	4.19	4.31	4.12	4.12	⎱ 5.80
50–54	u	3.70	3.87	3.78	3.82	3.22	3.57	3.60	3.29	⎰
55–59	u	1.97	1.72	1.95	1.91	2.48	2.52	2.72	2.60	6.47
60+	u	5.06	4.71	4.77	4.88	4.95	5.62	5.32	6.02	6.47
Total	u	100.00	100.00	100.00	100.00	100.00	100.00	100.00	100.00	100.00

u—unavailable.

Basic Table 5 *(continued)*

MADHYA PRADESH—MALE

Age group	1881	1891	1901	1911	1921	1931	1941	1951	1961	1971
0—4	13.80	13.41	11.83	15.45	12.30	13.73	13.66	13.33	16.01	⎫
5—9	14.78	15.25	12.67	13.55	16.04	14.33	14.72	13.33	14.25	⎬ 43.67
10—14	11.50	11.87	12.86	10.12	12.80	11.74	11.41	11.93	10.70	⎭
15—19	7.58	7.50	9.29	7.74	7.79	8.72	7.57	8.68	8.00	8.00
20—24	7.85	7.63	8.54	8.35	7.16	8.51	7.40	7.92	8.15	7.12
25—29	8.98	8.75	9.36	9.66	8.11	9.10	9.14	8.68	8.87	7.23
30—34	9.92	9.72	9.53	9.64	8.90	7.65	8.59	8.03	7.56	⎫ 13.01
35—39	5.77	5.86	6.37	6.33	6.41	6.64	6.71	6.90	6.04	⎬
40—44	7.42	7.56	6.82	6.47	6.95	5.65	5.51	6.25	5.27	⎫ 9.39
45—49	2.88	2.99	3.55	3.35	3.59	4.40	4.13	4.52	4.36	⎬
50—54	4.31	4.32	4.31	4.21	4.25	3.80	4.19	3.87	4.06	⎫ 6.13
55—59	1.06	1.01	1.65	1.36	1.41	1.94	2.16	2.12	2.14	⎬
60+	4.16	4.15	3.22	3.76	4.29	3.80	4.80	4.44	4.60	5.45
Total	100.00	100.00	100.00	100.00	100.00	100.00	100.00	100.00	100.00	100.00

MADHYA PRADESH—FEMALE

Age group	1881	1891	1901	1911	1921	1931	1941	1951	1961	1971
0—4	15.32	15.29	12.10	16.30	13.36	14.72	14.25	13.62	16.74	⎫
5—9	14.51	15.26	12.18	13.21	15.98	14.23	14.61	13.39	14.44	⎬ 43.74
10—14	9.56	9.27	10.66	8.32	10.69	10.11	9.74	11.00	9.51	⎭
15—19	7.08	6.98	8.48	6.91	6.84	8.43	6.91	8.34	7.80	7.44
20—24	9.05	9.13	9.85	9.74	8.06	9.43	8.38	8.43	9.14	7.76
25—29	9.54	9.43	9.51	9.98	8.63	9.06	9.60	8.64	8.74	7.68
30—34	9.49	9.42	9.20	9.26	9.13	7.53	8.31	8.19	7.11	⎫ 12.66
35—39	5.25	5.24	6.14	5.70	5.94	6.26	6.10	6.39	5.56	⎬
40—44	6.92	6.78	7.06	6.49	6.72	5.62	5.44	5.75	5.26	⎫ 8.74
45—49	2.50	2.34	3.79	3.13	3.19	4.02	3.98	4.26	4.06	⎬
50—54	4.43	4.23	4.80	4.53	4.44	3.74	4.37	3.85	3.87	⎫ 5.84
55—59	1.07	0.96	1.76	1.35	1.40	2.00	2.20	2.27	2.02	⎬
60+	5.29	5.68	4.47	5.08	5.62	4.84	6.12	5.85	5.75	6.14
Total	100.00	100.00	100.00	100.00	100.00	100.00	100.00	100.00	100.00	100.00

Basic Table 5 *(continued)*

Age group	1881	1891	1901	1911	1921	1931	1941	1951	1961	1971
MAHARASHTRA—MALE										
0–4	13.52	13.90	11.26	13.85	11.77	13.31	12.86	13.23	14.65	⎫
5–9	13.76	13.45	13.82	12.49	14.53	13.60	13.92	12.89	14.15	⎬ 40.82
10–14	11.69	10.97	13.29	10.69	12.25	11.36	11.57	12.47	11.40	⎭
15–19	7.31	7.25	7.85	7.45	6.98	8.10	7.51	8.73	8.22	8.94
20–24	7.63	7.61	7.92	8.45	7.24	8.49	7.61	8.39	8.41	8.02
25–29	9.71	9.58	9.39	9.60	8.98	8.93	8.82	8.63	8.68	7.47
30–34	9.30	9.05	8.92	8.78	9.08	7.72	8.32	7.65	7.39	⎫ 13.04
35–39	6.26	6.20	6.35	6.43	6.64	7.09	6.94	6.66	6.36	⎭
40–44	6.23	6.88	6.82	6.87	6.69	5.66	5.82	5.74	5.22	⎫ 9.91
45–49	3.65	3.72	3.86	3.96	3.88	4.71	4.53	4.43	4.39	⎭
50–54	4.50	4.73	4.44	4.68	4.75	3.74	4.02	3.88	3.64	⎫ 6.28
55–59	1.68	1.63	1.74	1.70	1.73	2.44	2.46	2.50	2.47	⎭
60+	4.76	5.03	4.34	5.06	5.48	4.86	5.60	4.80	5.01	5.52
Total	100.00	100.00	100.00	100.00	100.00	100.00	100.00	100.00	100.00	100.00
MAHARASHTRA—FEMALE										
0–4	15.02	15.67	12.34	15.19	13.15	14.64	13.75	13.85	15.39	⎫
5–9	13.82	13.63	14.05	12.72	15.25	13.93	14.37	13.55	14.87	⎬ 41.91
10–14	9.43	9.16	11.47	9.20	10.77	10.66	10.61	12.05	10.90	⎭
15–19	7.55	7.55	7.64	7.58	6.88	8.36	7.37	8.51	8.02	8.00
20–24	9.11	9.05	8.97	9.54	8.20	9.40	9.06	8.98	9.31	8.26
25–29	9.57	9.33	9.31	9.34	9.00	9.13	9.22	8.51	8.84	8.04
30–34	8.90	8.81	8.87	8.79	8.82	7.21	7.82	7.51	6.96	⎫ 13.08
35–39	5.36	5.35	5.88	5.71	5.72	6.38	6.06	5.94	5.74	⎭
40–44	5.78	6.53	6.70	6.68	6.69	5.29	5.47	5.48	4.87	⎫ 9.07
45–49	3.47	3.08	3.45	3.36	3.33	4.22	4.05	3.94	3.99	⎭
50–54	4.63	4.52	4.52	4.66	4.60	3.45	3.94	3.74	3.40	⎫ 5.71
55–59	1.63	1.38	1.57	1.48	1.49	2.21	2.09	2.13	2.17	⎭
60+	5.74	5.92	5.23	5.77	6.10	5.13	6.17	5.83	5.55	5.93
Total	100.00	100.00	100.00	100.00	100.00	100.00	100.00	100.00	100.00	100.00

Basic Table 5 *(continued)*

MYSORE—MALE

Age group	1881	1891	1901	1911	1921	1931	1941	1951	1961	1971
0—4	9.95	14.70	12.60	12.28	12.02	12.52	12.90	13.14	14.53	⎫
5—9	13.23	13.70	14.07	12.41	13.39	13.84	13.65	12.53	14.92	⎬ 41.76
10—14	13.81	9.34	13.27	12.36	12.38	12.14	12.42	12.83	12.05	⎭
15—19	8.95	8.17	7.94	8.96	7.97	8.57	8.53	9.47	8.27	9.39
20—24	8.65	8.56	7.08	8.45	8.34	8.04	8.53	8.45	8.01	8.01
25—29	9.78	9.27	8.15	8.60	8.72	8.71	8.05	8.04	7.76	6.85
30—34	9.53	8.58	8.05	7.71	8.20	7.71	7.05	7.12	6.71	⎱ 12.00
35—39	6.77	6.61	6.41	6.19	6.72	6.78	6.39	6.37	6.07	⎰
40—44	7.32	6.68	6.62	6.65	5.78	6.16	6.01	5.72	5.55	⎱ 9.65
45—49	2.76	4.02	4.27	4.28	3.99	4.22	4.67	4.56	4.33	⎰
50—54	3.95	4.18	4.53	4.66	4.44	4.03	4.34	4.23	3.99	⎱ 6.25
55—59	1.60	1.89	2.21	2.05	2.22	1.96	2.16	2.43	2.19	⎰
60+	3.70	4.30	4.80	5.40	5.83	5.32	5.31	5.10	5.63	6.09
Total	100.00	100.00	100.00	100.00	100.00	100.00	100.00	100.00	100.00	100.00

MYSORE—FEMALE

Age group	1881	1891	1901	1911	1921	1931	1941	1951	1961	1971
0—4	10.55	15.46	13.18	13.07	13.11	13.53	13.66	13.67	15.05	⎫
5—9	13.61	13.80	14.31	12.90	14.11	14.27	14.71	13.48	15.72	⎬ 43.16
10—14	12.62	8.25	11.79	11.57	11.61	11.55	12.12	13.24	12.07	⎭
15—19	8.14	7.74	7.25	8.66	7.55	8.32	8.03	9.11	8.01	8.87
20—24	10.02	9.72	8.07	9.40	9.55	9.04	8.94	9.08	8.74	8.07
25—29	9.88	9.25	8.29	8.48	8.85	9.17	8.80	8.39	8.35	7.68
30—34	9.36	8.73	8.38	8.05	7.78	7.82	7.36	7.08	6.87	⎱ 12.18
35—39	5.50	5.64	5.77	5.28	5.12	5.78	5.97	5.55	5.36	⎰
40—44	6.72	6.24	6.53	6.56	5.80	5.53	5.63	5.18	4.90	⎱ 8.43
45—49	2.44	3.33	3.83	3.61	3.61	3.43	3.78	3.73	3.51	⎰
50—54	4.59	4.45	4.70	4.73	4.74	4.17	3.95	4.03	3.74	⎱ 5.51
55—59	1.67	1.78	2.06	1.75	1.92	1.76	1.78	2.00	1.84	⎰
60+	4.90	5.61	5.84	5.93	6.23	5.61	5.28	5.46	5.84	6.10
Total	100.00	100.00	100.00	100.00	100.00	100.00	100.00	100.00	100.00	100.00

Basic Table 5 *(continued)*

Age group	1881	1891	1901	1911	1921	1931	1941	1951	1961	1971
NAGALAND—MALE										
0–4	u	15.92	12.51	13.89	12.03	13.09	13.75	14.24	11.69	} 35.99
5–9	u	13.49	14.39	14.12	13.46	13.79	14.29	15.63	13.46	
10–14	u	8.48	8.53	10.50	11.27	12.44	14.18	13.43	12.79	
15–19	u	5.76	6.28	6.96	8.16	8.04	8.74	8.29	9.40	9.47
20–24	u	6.43	8.09	6.75	6.28	6.95	6.61	7.28	8.46	9.83
25–29	u	9.41	10.07	8.41	7.78	7.48	6.29	6.97	7.90	9.10
30–34	u	9.93	9.30	7.77	7.08	7.66	6.50	6.22	7.15	} 13.58
35–39	u	10.84	7.76	6.48	6.13	6.26	6.29	4.44	6.57	
40–44	u	7.23	7.60	7.58	6.95	6.20	5.97	6.41	5.92	} 9.31
45–49	u	3.90	4.49	4.48	4.32	4.31	4.16	3.97	3.95	
50–54	u	3.82	4.71	4.71	4.99	4.10	3.73	3.77	3.68	} 5.64
55–59	u	1.19	1.91	1.91	2.05	1.93	1.49	1.94	1.98	
60+	u	3.58	4.36	6.44	9.49	7.74	8.00	7.42	7.05	7.08
Total	u	100.00	100.00	100.00	100.00	100.00	100.00	100.00	100.00	100.00
NAGALAND—FEMALE										
0–4	u	16.96	13.40	14.32	12.91	13.93	13.88	14.01	13.10	} 40.08
5–9	u	12.21	13.59	14.71	13.23	13.54	14.41	15.18	13.74	
10–14	u	8.00	7.86	9.58	10.40	11.44	10.23	11.65	12.77	
15–19	u	7.59	6.95	7.05	8.43	8.76	9.71	10.41	10.67	9.89
20–24	u	8.10	10.50	8.89	7.03	7.58	6.58	6.49	8.20	8.56
25–29	u	10.39	11.08	9.37	7.33	7.00	7.93	6.92	8.10	8.44
30–34	u	10.28	9.28	7.85	7.87	8.15	6.68	8.73	7.36	} 12.76
35–39	u	8.27	5.15	4.36	5.35	5.71	6.78	4.22	5.80	
40–44	u	7.20	7.11	7.28	7.25	6.15	5.74	6.37	5.45	} 8.87
45–49	u	3.01	3.65	3.73	3.93	3.85	2.82	3.53	3.18	
50–54	u	3.48	4.71	4.82	5.03	4.26	3.65	3.84	3.29	} 5.17
55–59	u	0.99	1.78	1.82	1.92	2.03	2.61	1.38	1.78	
60+	u	3.52	4.94	6.22	9.32	7.61	8.98	7.27	6.55	6.23
Total	u	100.00	100.00	100.00	100.00	100.00	100.00	100.00	100.00	100.00

u—unavailable.

Basic Table 5 *(continued)*

Age group	1881	1891	1901	1911	1921	1931	1941	1951	1961	1971
ORISSA—MALE										
0–4	14.64	13.13	13.25	13.88	11.60	13.46	11.84	12.40	13.85	⎫
5–9	15.92	15.77	14.51	15.41	16.05	14.40	14.52	12.89	14.36	⎬ 42.29
10–14	11.95	13.79	13.29	12.83	14.31	11.83	12.24	12.22	11.13	⎭
15–19	8.09	9.16	9.23	8.35	8.85	8.64	7.64	8.76	8.04	8.30
20–24	8.24	7.71	7.61	7.26	7.08	8.07	6.86	7.66	8.04	6.74
25–29	8.64	7.65	8.80	8.77	8.38	9.16	8.46	8.31	8.68	7.18
30–34	8.62	8.02	7.88	8.26	7.76	7.85	8.33	7.09	7.51	⎫ 13.30
35–39	5.22	5.54	6.12	6.44	6.50	6.66	7.15	6.94	6.28	⎭
40–44	6.26	6.86	5.99	5.67	5.96	5.69	6.38	6.16	5.49	⎫ 9.88
45–49	2.61	2.92	3.76	3.65	4.13	4.23	4.65	4.62	4.45	⎭
50–54	4.27	4.17	3.95	3.77	3.88	4.06	4.61	4.52	4.54	⎫ 6.55
55–59	1.27	1.20	1.75	1.71	1.75	2.12	2.34	2.52	2.49	⎭
60+	4.27	4.10	3.85	4.01	3.75	3.84	4.96	5.90	5.15	5.76
Total	100.00	100.00	100.00	100.00	100.00	100.00	100.00	100.00	100.00	100.00
ORISSA—FEMALE										
0–4	15.35	13.88	13.51	13.76	11.16	13.17	11.75	12.92	14.51	⎫
5–9	14.94	15.18	14.00	14.62	15.04	13.66	13.91	12.69	14.57	⎬ 42.43
10–14	9.75	11.49	11.25	10.93	12.24	9.72	10.26	11.10	9.78	⎭
15–19	7.72	8.79	9.15	8.18	8.52	8.86	7.29	8.30	8.23	7.93
20–24	9.09	8.27	8.57	8.41	8.26	9.10	7.87	8.25	8.80	7.26
25–29	8.65	7.94	8.81	9.15	9.04	9.76	9.26	8.35	8.68	7.90
30–34	8.73	8.54	7.83	8.34	8.33	8.09	8.67	7.99	7.25	⎫ 13.10
35–39	4.46	5.01	5.71	6.01	6.39	6.42	6.73	6.70	5.70	⎭
40–44	6.69	6.91	6.06	5.82	6.29	5.97	6.51	5.78	5.42	⎫ 8.90
45–49	2.25	2.44	3.53	3.54	3.89	4.07	4.35	4.18	4.15	⎭
50–54	4.75	4.50	4.22	4.03	4.02	4.07	4.74	4.64	4.35	⎫ 6.19
55–59	1.20	1.15	1.86	1.83	1.81	2.23	2.33	2.43	2.37	⎭
60+	6.41	5.91	5.50	5.38	5.00	4.89	6.33	6.68	6.19	6.29
Total	100.00	100.00	100.00	100.00	100.00	100.00	100.00	100.00	100.00	100.00

Basic Table 5 *(continued)*

PUNJAB—MALE

Age group	1881	1891	1901	1911	1921	1931	1941	1951	1961	1971
0—4	11.62	16.27	12.04	12.45	12.46	12.46	13.34	13.97	14.64	
5—9	13.17	13.44	13.09	12.75	14.07	13.68	13.67	12.58	15.20	40.99
10—14	12.39	10.52	12.60	12.01	12.12	12.19	12.16	12.41	12.45	
15—19	9.46	10.36	9.61	9.68	8.72	9.53	9.03	9.13	9.26	10.65
20—24	8.61	9.28	7.86	8.59	7.84	8.44	7.67	7.73	8.00	8.29
25—29	8.68	9.38	8.13	7.70	8.09	8.05	7.65	7.52	7.24	6.68
30—34	8.19	6.39	7.72	7.63	7.08	6.79	6.40	6.42	5.89	
35—39	5.36	6.35	5.50	6.36	5.61	5.45	5.20	5.32	4.69	10.45
40—44	6.48	3.66	6.47	5.62	5.44	5.25	5.28	5.02	4.74	
45—49	3.67	5.22	3.72	4.05	4.08	4.19	4.07	4.11	3.72	8.40
50—54	4.94	2.11	4.86	4.86	4.66	4.46	4.62	4.34	4.14	
55—59	1.84	3.78	2.06	2.12	2.38	2.26	2.49	3.00	2.18	6.32
60+	5.59	3.22	6.34	6.19	7.45	7.25	8.41	8.44	7.85	8.22
Total	100.00	100.00	100.00	100.00	100.00	100.00	100.00	100.00	100.00	100.00

PUNJAB—FEMALE

Age group	1881	1891	1901	1911	1921	1931	1941	1951	1961	1971
0—4	12.80	17.43	12.71	14.46	14.63	14.70	15.20	14.75	15.64	
5—9	12.97	13.27	13.04	13.35	15.14	14.31	14.81	13.19	15.35	41.64
10—14	10.82	8.96	11.11	10.21	11.22	12.00	11.80	12.73	12.54	
15—19	8.97	10.58	8.55	8.24	7.71	9.10	8.58	9.50	9.29	10.59
20—24	9.34	9.68	8.36	8.76	7.67	8.50	8.16	8.68	8.47	8.47
25—29	9.14	9.99	8.58	9.01	7.94	7.84	7.98	7.58	7.65	6.81
30—34	8.55	6.07	8.28	7.97	7.31	6.29	6.61	6.27	6.16	
35—39	5.17	6.97	5.70	5.30	5.29	5.36	4.86	5.14	4.88	11.26
40—44	6.95	3.35	6.88	6.37	5.88	5.13	4.87	4.99	4.72	
45—49	3.37	5.21	3.68	3.79	3.80	4.14	3.81	3.64	3.59	8.71
50—54	4.77	1.71	4.90	4.77	4.70	4.04	4.22	3.82	3.54	
55—59	1.57	3.75	1.80	1.78	1.99	2.16	1.97	2.41	1.90	5.89
60+	5.59	3.03	6.42	5.98	6.73	6.43	7.11	7.32	6.26	6.63
Total	100.00	100.00	100.00	100.00	100.00	100.00	100.00	100.00	100.00	100.00

Basic Table 5 *(continued)*

RAJASTHAN—MALE

Age group	1881	1891	1901	1911	1921	1931	1941	1951	1961	1971
0—4	u	13.35	8.68	13.77	11.81	12.97	13.88	13.96	15.56	⎱ 44.35
5—9	u	13.88	11.98	12.08	15.08	13.94	14.59	13.00	14.96	⎰
10—14	u	11.34	13.40	9.65	12.89	12.46	12.36	12.63	12.11	8.83
15—19	u	8.57	11.14	9.20	8.41	9.19	8.47	8.99	8.29	7.28
20—24	u	7.84	9.13	9.06	6.93	8.52	7.95	7.58	8.10	7.03
25—29	u	8.82	9.11	9.62	8.28	8.16	8.33	7.88	8.25	⎱ 12.04
30—34	u	9.26	9.06	9.50	9.06	6.99	7.33	7.16	7.10	⎰
35—39	u	5.69	5.71	5.70	5.92	6.09	5.34	6.11	5.29	⎱ 8.77
40—44	u	7.05	7.46	7.16	7.13	6.14	5.19	6.00	5.25	⎰
45—49	u	3.39	3.49	3.35	3.43	4.24	3.91	4.08	3.80	⎱ 6.19
50—54	u	4.72	4.90	5.34	5.00	4.76	4.78	4.18	4.34	⎰
55—59	u	1.69	1.88	1.47	1.52	1.99	2.30	2.33	1.94	⎱ 6.19
60+	u	4.41	4.06	4.08	4.53	4.54	5.57	6.11	5.02	5.52
Total	u	100.00	100.00	100.00	100.00	100.00	100.00	100.00	100.00	100.00

RAJASTHAN—FEMALE

Age group	1881	1891	1901	1911	1921	1931	1941	1951	1961	1971
0—4	u	14.66	9.42	15.23	13.48	14.64	15.24	14.77	16.65	⎱ 43.98
5—9	u	13.67	12.18	11.84	15.36	13.88	14.74	13.32	14.97	⎰
10—14	u	9.59	11.75	7.93	11.09	11.06	11.27	11.83	11.09	8.11
15—19	u	7.55	9.96	7.89	7.10	8.33	7.73	8.91	7.89	8.08
20—24	u	8.49	9.82	9.99	7.67	9.17	8.60	8.35	9.19	7.61
25—29	u	8.54	8.74	9.46	8.08	8.26	8.31	8.57	8.42	⎱ 12.19
30—34	u	9.37	9.15	9.67	9.19	7.07	7.17	7.71	7.08	⎰
35—39	u	5.33	5.48	5.24	5.52	5.98	5.22	5.74	5.15	⎱ 6.68
40—44	u	7.50	8.16	7.78	7.58	6.17	5.30	5.66	5.29	⎰
45—49	u	3.06	3.31	3.05	3.03	3.92	3.81	3.58	3.45	⎱ 5.83
50—54	u	5.04	5.41	5.63	5.24	4.50	4.64	3.90	3.88	⎰
55—59	u	1.56	1.75	1.27	1.34	1.88	2.10	2.04	1.67	⎱ 5.83
60+	u	5.65	4.86	5.03	5.33	5.13	5.86	5.61	5.28	5.52
Total	u	100.00	100.00	100.00	100.00	100.00	100.00	100.00	100.00	100.00

u—unavailable.

Basic Table 5 *(continued)*

Age group	1881	1891	1901	1911	1921	1931	1941	1951	1961	1971
TAMIL NADU—MALE										
0—4	12.93	15.49	13.94	13.83	12.61	13.06	13.50	12.03	13.66	⎱ 37.75
5—9	13.66	13.61	14.24	12.98	13.33	13.28	14.21	11.82	12.77	⎰
10—14	12.67	10.16	12.40	11.59	11.93	12.03	11.97	12.21	11.31	
15—19	8.91	8.28	8.31	8.77	8.66	8.45	8.81	9.83	8.51	8.84
20—24	7.68	7.81	7.05	8.15	7.75	8.05	7.62	8.09	8.39	8.51
25—29	8.30	8.32	7.50	7.93	8.05	8.35	7.63	8.20	8.22	7.57
30—34	8.42	7.82	8.06	7.42	8.23	7.15	6.89	7.12	6.96	⎱ 13.45
35—39	6.65	6.59	5.95	5.92	6.25	7.09	6.52	6.76	6.74	⎰
40—44	6.18	6.25	6.78	6.55	6.28	5.85	5.73	5.94	5.78	⎱ 10.95
45—49	3.91	4.24	3.83	4.22	3.93	4.67	4.88	5.03	4.97	⎰
50—54	3.92	4.05	4.70	4.62	4.82	3.86	4.19	4.48	4.21	⎱ 7.15
55—59	2.04	2.20	1.93	2.24	2.27	2.69	2.71	2.99	2.87	⎰
60+	4.73	5.19	5.31	5.77	5.89	5.47	5.34	5.50	5.60	5.78
Total	100.00	100.00	100.00	100.00	100.00	100.00	100.00	100.00	100.00	100.00
TAMIL NADU—FEMALE										
0—4	13.10	15.66	14.04	13.91	12.80	13.23	13.60	12.01	13.71	⎱ 37.80
5—9	13.45	13.24	14.00	12.84	13.40	12.93	14.05	11.93	12.80	⎰
10—14	10.84	8.63	10.93	10.51	10.83	11.14	11.17	12.14	10.95	
15—19	7.89	7.65	7.46	8.48	7.88	8.30	8.33	9.25	8.43	8.60
20—24	9.06	9.21	8.60	9.40	9.29	9.17	8.49	8.70	9.25	8.65
25—29	9.12	9.01	8.23	8.33	8.79	9.51	8.60	8.61	9.08	8.73
30—34	8.94	8.42	8.83	8.08	8.77	7.51	7.25	7.43	7.19	⎱ 13.80
35—39	5.68	5.77	5.19	5.32	5.37	6.76	6.32	6.37	6.45	⎰
40—44	6.43	6.31	6.93	6.73	6.57	5.42	5.62	5.74	5.31	⎱ 10.06
45—49	3.57	3.68	3.31	3.67	3.51	4.33	4.52	4.40	4.54	⎰
50—54	4.57	4.49	4.93	4.80	4.99	3.82	3.98	4.93	4.06	⎱ 6.66
55—59	1.85	1.97	1.68	1.96	1.90	2.53	2.36	2.80	2.62	⎰
60+	5.50	5.98	5.87	5.96	5.89	5.36	5.70	5.68	5.60	5.70
Total	100.00	100.00	100.00	100.00	100.00	100.00	100.00	100.00	100.00	100.00

Basic Table 5 *(continued)*

UTTAR PRADESH—MALE

Age group	1881	1891	1901	1911	1921	1931	1941	1951	1961	1971
0–4	12.28	13.10	12.30	11.62	11.50	11.27	13.11	13.18	14.40	⎫
5–9	13.37	13.25	12.97	13.39	14.07	13.57	13.94	12.87	14.52	⎬ 42.08
10–14	12.48	11.66	12.56	12.24	12.19	12.40	11.45	12.85	11.72	⎭
15–19	8.07	8.38	8.64	8.59	8.59	8.79	7.94	8.99	8.18	8.46
20–24	8.49	8.59	8.30	8.68	8.20	7.55	7.71	7.99	7.78	6.91
25–29	9.31	8.67	8.87	8.98	8.60	8.94	8.29	8.17	7.75	6.97
30–34	9.18	8.91	8.71	8.50	8.30	7.72	7.52	7.42	6.95	⎱ 12.19
35–39	5.31	5.64	5.62	5.97	6.07	6.62	6.23	6.47	5.78	⎰
40–44	6.95	7.02	6.91	6.93	6.65	6.42	6.23	6.08	5.50	⎱ 9.65
45–49	3.27	3.41	3.72	3.81	4.09	4.41	4.74	4.80	4.32	⎰
50–54	4.96	4.83	4.86	4.78	4.83	4.94	4.79	4.64	4.43	⎱ 6.75
55–59	1.49	1.52	1.73	1.68	1.86	2.09	2.33	2.86	2.38	⎰
60+	4.85	5.01	4.81	4.83	5.04	5.27	5.71	3.67	6.30	6.99
Total	100.00	100.00	100.00	100.00	100.00	100.00	100.00	100.00	100.00	100.00

UTTAR PRADESH—FEMALE

Age group	1881	1891	1901	1911	1921	1931	1941	1951	1961	1971
0–4	13.34	14.37	13.13	12.69	12.84	12.82	14.40	14.35	15.38	⎫
5–9	12.76	12.87	12.62	13.26	14.06	13.78	13.81	13.25	14.37	⎬ 41.58
10–14	10.00	9.41	10.74	10.27	10.18	10.44	9.93	12.14	10.58	⎭
15–19	7.20	7.33	7.65	7.56	7.47	7.65	7.36	8.83	7.78	7.76
20–24	9.32	9.00	8.87	9.29	8.82	8.88	8.29	8.80	8.93	7.95
25–29	9.28	8.96	8.97	9.12	8.74	8.97	8.56	8.03	8.28	7.74
30–34	9.27	9.08	8.82	8.84	8.63	7.99	7.80	7.49	7.13	⎱ 12.95
35–39	5.25	5.43	5.62	5.87	5.94	6.33	6.15	5.95	5.62	⎰
40–44	7.26	7.22	7.20	7.11	6.91	6.33	6.36	5.90	5.29	⎱ 9.39
45–49	3.22	3.20	3.57	3.61	3.84	4.18	4.36	4.41	4.10	⎰
50–54	5.28	5.17	5.11	5.02	4.94	4.69	4.64	4.39	3.97	⎱ 6.12
55–59	1.53	1.50	1.72	1.62	1.79	1.92	2.10	2.46	2.29	⎰
60+	6.28	6.44	5.98	5.74	5.84	6.01	6.23	3.99	6.28	6.81
Total	100.00	100.00	100.00	100.00	100.00	100.00	100.00	100.00	100.00	100.00

Basic Table 5 *(continued)*

Age group	1881	1891	1901	1911	1921	1931	1941	1951	1961	1971
WEST BENGAL—MALE										
0—4	12.97	12.98	12.15	11.90	10.23	10.31	11.48	10.57	13.95	41.24
5—9	14.05	14.06	13.96	13.83	13.66	13.60	12.88	11.23	14.65	
10—14	10.86	11.30	11.72	11.41	12.00	10.79	10.88	11.78	10.62	
15—19	8.33	8.56	8.99	9.10	9.43	8.85	8.55	10.41	8.06	9.46
20—24	7.78	7.57	8.13	8.61	8.83	8.96	8.66	9.30	8.66	7.55
25—29	9.55	9.18	9.39	9.84	10.18	10.53	10.09	9.70	9.08	7.62
30—34	8.91	8.46	8.41	8.34	8.69	8.67	8.76	8.34	7.85	13.09
35—39	6.78	7.09	6.52	7.00	7.36	7.77	7.53	6.83	6.57	
40—44	6.64	6.66	6.28	6.05	6.26	6.33	6.33	6.10	5.58	10.10
45—49	3.59	3.88	3.94	3.94	4.15	4.57	4.72	4.70	4.22	
50—54	3.96	3.81	4.15	3.71	3.92	3.57	3.68	3.85	3.69	5.90
55—59	1.79	1.94	1.84	1.90	1.39	2.11	2.23	2.57	2.45	
60+	4.77	4.50	4.52	4.38	3.90	3.94	4.22	4.62	4.63	5.04
Total	100.00	100.00	100.00	100.00	100.00	100.00	100.00	100.00	100.00	100.00
WEST BENGAL—FEMALE										
0—4	13.62	14.14	13.50	13.53	11.89	12.03	13.74	12.53	16.26	44.88
5—9	12.99	13.56	14.09	14.26	14.48	14.39	14.03	12.51	16.44	
10—14	8.57	8.84	9.58	9.56	10.13	9.48	10.04	12.02	10.17	
15—19	8.53	8.90	9.70	10.15	10.47	10.14	9.77	10.94	8.50	9.01
20—24	8.91	8.56	8.67	9.49	9.85	9.97	9.29	9.53	9.15	7.76
25—29	9.95	9.55	8.92	9.46	9.88	10.01	9.12	8.74	8.45	7.56
30—34	8.77	8.37	7.92	7.40	7.89	7.85	7.78	7.29	6.83	12.06
35—39	5.67	5.94	5.78	5.61	5.94	6.21	6.29	5.81	5.10	
40—44	6.60	6.34	6.18	5.55	5.53	5.51	5.30	5.20	4.68	7.90
45—49	3.27	3.38	3.60	3.48	3.45	3.80	3.83	4.04	3.45	
50—54	4.61	4.19	4.30	4.02	3.77	3.70	3.66	3.56	3.41	5.21
55—59	1.92	2.06	1.89	1.95	1.84	1.97	2.08	2.56	2.13	
60+	6.59	6.18	5.87	5.54	4.88	4.94	5.08	5.26	5.44	5.61
Total	100.00	100.00	100.00	100.00	100.00	100.00	100.00	100.00	100.00	100.00

Basic Table 5 *(continued)*

ANDAMAN-NICOBAR—MALE

Age group	1881	1891	1901	1911	1921	1931	1941	1951	1961	1971
0—4	2.13	2.83	2.10	5.39	4.21	8.67	u	12.45	12.99	} 32.00
5—9	1.53	1.75	1.76	4.90	4.04	7.49	u	7.77	9.92	
10—14	1.41	1.22	1.35	3.11	4.05	5.61	u	9.07	6.90	} 6.90
15—19	1.16	1.06	1.51	2.78	4.51	4.03	u	8.37	6.04	
20—24	7.82	6.83	6.90	7.40	8.36	9.55	u	16.68	13.50	12.16
25—29	15.37	12.90	12.19	10.96	14.11	16.98	u	13.04	16.35	13.81
30—34	24.34	19.96	18.67	16.29	18.38	13.14	u	6.52	10.04	} 18.64
35—39	13.47	15.53	13.87	12.67	16.70	12.07	u	8.37	7.71	
40—44	14.99	17.92	16.13	13.58	11.43	8.08	u	5.49	5.40	} 9.87
45—49	5.09	6.15	7.44	7.48	5.82	5.87	u	4.84	4.11	
50—54	6.75	7.57	8.59	6.87	3.68	3.93	u	3.15	2.89	} 4.04
55—59	1.54	1.51	2.66	2.70	1.38	1.78	u	1.63	1.52	
60+	4.41	4.77	6.84	5.87	3.34	2.80	u	2.60	2.63	2.58
Total	100.00	100.00	100.00	100.00	100.00	100.00	u	100.00	100.00	100.00

ANDAMAN-NICOBAR—FEMALE

Age group	1881	1891	1901	1911	1921	1931	1941	1951	1961	1971
0—4	12.63	16.88	12.56	14.73	11.92	18.39	u	17.76	21.06	} 47.22
5—9	7.29	12.22	9.42	12.11	11.46	13.31	u	12.24	15.85	
10—14	6.39	6.31	8.11	8.74	11.66	8.56	u	13.34	9.84	} 8.52
15—19	3.82	4.48	7.17	7.69	8.64	7.59	u	11.04	8.13	
20—24	6.39	7.12	6.89	9.03	7.52	8.90	u	7.64	9.98	10.44
25—29	14.64	9.44	9.28	10.79	11.68	11.10	u	11.22	10.62	9.81
30—34	15.95	12.80	12.89	9.13	10.09	7.85	u	7.45	6.64	} 12.28
35—39	11.42	8.55	7.08	7.53	8.98	7.43	u	7.18	5.49	
40—44	9.26	10.88	11.25	6.10	5.10	5.04	u	3.86	3.51	} 6.06
45—49	3.27	2.69	4.17	3.66	3.62	3.74	u	2.58	2.71	
50—54	4.43	4.48	5.95	3.38	2.35	2.73	u	1.56	2.03	} 2.95
55—59	1.16	0.49	1.41	1.39	1.68	1.29	u	1.28	1.15	
60+	3.37	3.67	3.84	5.72	5.29	4.08	u	2.85	2.99	2.72
Total	100.00	100.00	100.00	100.00	100.00	100.00	u	100.00	100.00	100.00

u—unavailable.

Basic Table 5 *(continued)*

Age group	1881	1891	1901	1911	1921	1931	1941	1951	1961	1971
DELHI—MALE										
0–4	9.90	13.74	11.30	10.05	10.47	10.71	12.18	15.10	13.68	36.77
5–9	12.16	11.98	11.89	11.65	11.17	11.33	11.01	11.00	13.42	
10–14	12.76	10.68	11.23	12.73	10.13	10.63	10.15	11.43	10.97	10.38
15–19	9.88	12.30	9.55	10.76	9.76	9.96	10.35	9.53	9.13	10.25
20–24	10.13	11.25	9.52	8.93	11.30	11.20	11.62	9.09	10.23	8.82
25–29	9.52	10.57	9.61	8.29	10.48	10.80	10.22	8.26	9.55	13.93
30–34	8.81	6.99	9.31	8.52	9.38	9.00	8.09	7.44	7.99	
35–39	5.03	7.63	5.47	7.71	6.04	7.28	6.84	6.08	6.51	9.97
40–44	6.77	3.42	7.28	6.26	6.78	5.90	6.05	5.84	5.47	
45–49	3.45	4.86	3.48	3.93	3.69	4.18	4.33	4.53	3.80	5.59
50–54	5.17	1.60	5.09	4.94	4.84	3.56	3.72	3.53	3.38	
55–59	1.56	3.04	1.54	1.90	1.57	1.68	1.70	2.34	1.70	4.29
60+	4.85	1.95	4.72	4.34	4.39	3.76	3.74	5.82	4.18	
Total	100.00	100.00	100.00	100.00	100.00	100.00	100.00	100.00	100.00	100.00
DELHI—FEMALE										
0–4	10.63	15.42	13.22	11.80	14.20	14.57	16.38	13.84	16.37	40.99
5–9	12.12	11.67	12.81	12.57	13.77	13.41	13.98	11.12	15.28	
10–14	11.34	9.21	10.21	11.99	9.56	11.56	11.34	12.89	11.92	10.24
15–19	9.79	12.63	8.94	9.87	9.27	9.88	9.49	11.04	9.05	10.08
20–24	10.58	10.82	9.67	9.14	10.80	10.94	10.66	9.84	10.17	8.52
25–29	9.26	11.09	8.83	9.09	9.15	9.80	9.46	8.11	9.22	13.17
30–34	8.71	5.89	9.08	8.52	8.37	7.35	7.06	7.88	7.12	
35–39	4.57	7.97	4.95	5.28	5.06	6.02	5.83	5.33	5.28	8.26
40–44	7.37	2.99	7.36	6.96	6.12	4.72	4.63	5.27	4.14	
45–49	3.13	5.38	2.99	3.71	3.15	3.34	3.37	3.94	3.00	4.45
50–54	5.70	1.34	5.33	4.90	4.65	3.06	2.90	3.71	2.83	
55–59	1.29	3.67	1.24	1.62	1.47	1.60	1.46	1.82	1.53	4.29
60+	5.52	1.92	5.38	4.55	4.43	3.75	3.45	5.21	4.09	
Total	100.00	100.00	100.00	100.00	100.00	100.00	100.00	100.00	100.00	100.00

Basic Table 5 *(continued)*

Age group	1881	1891	1901	1911	1921	1931	1941	1951	1961	1971
MANIPUR—MALE										
0—4	u	u	16.21	16.36	14.30	16.27	16.17	15.68	15.67	
5—9	u	u	14.77	15.85	15.54	14.70	16.61	13.92	15.92	42.25
10—14	u	u	9.97	11.29	12.07	11.56	12.00	11.87	12.35	
15—19	u	u	7.11	8.50	9.21	8.71	8.19	8.42	8.02	9.43
20—24	u	u	6.67	6.24	7.15	8.51	7.54	8.70	7.86	8.73
25—29	u	u	8.31	7.77	8.85	8.30	7.42	8.20	7.95	7.32
30—34	u	u	7.68	7.18	6.48	7.22	7.66	6.81	7.04	11.46
35—39	u	u	6.40	5.99	5.61	5.74	5.86	5.95	5.76	
40—44	u	u	6.99	6.42	5.55	4.90	5.26	5.02	4.90	9.00
45—49	u	u	4.13	3.80	3.45	3.23	3.53	3.75	3.41	
50—54	u	u	4.34	3.99	4.47	3.46	2.97	3.74	3.60	5.75
55—59	u	u	1.76	1.61	1.83	2.06	1.89	2.37	2.20	
60+	u	u	5.67	5.00	5.48	5.35	4.90	5.56	5.34	6.06
Total	u	u	100.00	100.00	100.00	100.00	100.00	100.00	100.00	100.00
MANIPUR—FEMALE										
0—4	u	u	16.02	16.24	14.23	15.81	14.07	13.79	15.59	
5—9	u	u	13.70	15.38	14.67	13.89	15.06	12.78	15.30	42.75
10—14	u	u	8.87	10.86	11.22	10.59	10.00	12.62	11.62	
15—19	u	u	7.89	9.02	9.86	8.97	9.47	7.84	8.31	9.97
20—24	u	u	8.84	8.07	8.33	9.45	8.79	9.06	8.78	8.57
25—29	u	u	9.33	8.51	8.68	8.77	8.37	7.83	8.53	7.35
30—34	u	u	7.81	7.13	6.87	7.30	7.53	6.94	7.03	11.66
35—39	u	u	4.33	3.95	4.66	5.28	5.90	5.69	5.09	
40—44	u	u	6.84	6.28	5.78	5.11	5.02	5.73	4.96	8.14
45—49	u	u	3.51	3.22	3.14	3.11	3.65	4.36	3.20	
50—54	u	u	4.53	4.16	4.62	3.70	3.99	3.77	3.74	5.44
55—59	u	u	1.71	1.57	1.77	1.97	1.98	2.88	2.01	
60+	u	u	6.62	5.60	6.16	6.04	6.16	6.72	5.85	6.12
Total	u	u	100.00	100.00	100.00	100.00	100.00	100.00	100.00	100.00

u—unavailable.

Basic Table 5 *(continued)*

MEGHALAYA—MALE

Age group	1881	1891	1901	1911	1921	1931	1941	1951	1961	1971
0—4	16.18	17.79	16.32	17.18	15.48	16.16	14.38	15.49	15.22	⎱ 42.46
5—9	13.32	14.13	15.33	14.56	15.44	13.64	14.09	13.45	14.22	⎰
10—14	10.19	11.07	11.63	10.66	11.91	10.95	13.08	11.21	11.35	8.87
15—19	7.30	7.99	8.30	8.41	8.74	9.05	10.32	8.68	8.76	7.65
20—24	7.38	7.19	7.04	6.97	7.14	8.19	8.79	8.69	8.02	7.83
25—29	9.92	8.16	8.89	8.68	8.84	9.23	9.12	9.00	8.93	⎱ 13.22
30—34	9.18	7.96	8.32	8.02	7.60	7.76	8.54	7.75	7.85	⎰
35—39	6.83	6.75	6.57	6.69	6.58	6.49	6.36	6.79	6.47	⎱ 9.37
40—44	5.63	5.81	5.70	5.58	5.43	5.13	4.47	5.74	5.38	⎰
45—49	2.84	3.33	3.10	3.30	3.38	3.57	3.01	3.95	3.85	⎱ 5.60
50—54	3.22	3.51	3.41	3.47	3.27	3.41	2.91	3.56	3.68	⎰
55—59	3.48	1.40	1.31	1.40	1.34	1.51	1.24	1.48	1.71	⎱ 4.95
60+	4.53	4.90	4.09	5.08	4.84	4.90	3.71	4.21	4.54	⎰
Total	100.00	100.00	100.00	100.00	100.00	100.00	100.00	100.00	100.00	100.00

MEGHALAYA—FEMALE

Age group	1881	1891	1901	1911	1921	1931	1941	1951	1961	1971
0—4	17.11	17.22	16.22	17.31	15.78	16.83	15.88	15.86	16.38	⎱ 44.75
5—9	12.16	13.34	14.21	13.97	15.07	14.09	14.31	13.82	15.15	⎰
10—14	8.43	10.03	10.61	9.84	10.99	10.85	11.17	10.85	11.24	9.27
15—19	8.09	9.23	10.20	10.28	10.88	10.22	9.41	9.95	9.14	8.66
20—24	8.25	8.88	9.39	9.09	9.11	9.91	9.45	9.86	9.60	9.02
25—29	10.22	9.08	9.57	9.59	9.48	9.32	9.34	9.84	9.78	⎱ 11.66
30—34	8.68	7.91	8.01	8.03	7.37	6.93	6.91	7.21	7.30	⎰
35—39	7.50	5.39	5.07	4.46	5.00	5.27	5.38	5.70	5.07	⎱ 7.79
40—44	5.38	5.72	5.33	5.10	5.09	4.72	4.30	4.91	4.58	⎰
45—49	3.36	2.99	2.56	2.61	2.76	3.07	3.21	3.18	3.08	⎱ 4.54
50—54	2.89	3.51	3.42	3.37	3.06	3.15	2.65	3.14	3.13	⎰
55—59	2.10	1.30	1.18	1.27	1.17	1.25	2.24	1.45	1.32	⎱ 4.31
60+	5.83	5.39	4.23	5.08	4.24	4.40	5.75	4.22	4.24	⎰
Total	100.00	100.00	100.00	100.00	100.00	100.00	100.00	100.00	100.00	100.00

Basic Table 5 *(continued)*

Age group	1881	1891	1901	1911	1921	1931	1941	1951	1961	1971
TRIPURA—MALE										
0–4	u	u	14.40	14.05	12.64	14.50	u	14.70	16.14	⎫
5–9	u	u	15.18	15.63	15.42	14.63	u	14.00	14.92	⎬ 43.51
10–14	u	u	10.99	11.13	12.05	11.15	u	11.57	11.06	⎭
15–19	u	u	7.97	7.75	8.18	7.85	u	8.17	7.36	8.49
20–24	u	u	8.31	8.47	8.12	8.03	u	7.19	7.36	7.04
25–29	u	u	9.61	9.70	9.38	9.72	u	8.83	8.49	6.85
30–34	u	u	8.61	8.23	8.37	7.90	u	7.09	7.02	⎫ 12.27
35–39	u	u	6.68	6.92	7.10	7.21	u	7.59	6.57	⎭
40–44	u	u	5.48	5.49	5.76	5.53	u	6.54	5.11	⎫ 8.99
45–49	u	u	3.45	3.58	3.82	4.23	u	4.65	4.20	⎭
50–54	u	u	3.62	3.36	3.77	3.47	u	3.46	3.85	⎫ 5.97
55–59	u	u	1.60	1.72	1.33	1.79	u	1.82	2.25	⎭
60+	u	u	4.09	3.95	4.06	3.99	u	4.38	5.67	6.88
Total	u	u	100.00	100.00	100.00	100.00	u	100.00	100.00	100.00
TRIPURA—FEMALE										
0–4	u	u	17.05	16.66	14.87	16.73	u	15.23	17.58	⎫
5–9	u	u	16.89	17.10	16.80	16.07	u	14.94	15.95	⎬ 44.92
10–14	u	u	11.16	10.49	11.50	10.83	u	11.37	10.15	⎭
15–19	u	u	10.67	10.11	10.54	9.87	u	10.37	8.40	8.41
20–24	u	u	8.35	9.54	9.51	10.15	u	9.05	9.24	7.55
25–29	u	u	8.58	9.44	9.52	9.46	u	9.03	9.10	7.79
30–34	u	u	7.62	7.24	7.07	6.76	u	7.50	6.66	⎫ 11.78
35–39	u	u	5.56	5.19	5.32	5.27	u	5.89	5.22	⎭
40–44	u	u	4.00	4.01	4.48	4.22	u	4.39	4.34	⎫ 7.96
45–49	u	u	2.33	2.36	2.79	2.91	u	3.49	3.28	⎭
50–54	u	u	2.78	2.85	2.65	2.85	u	2.90	3.27	⎫ 5.33
55–59	u	u	1.22	1.21	1.29	1.30	u	1.76	1.66	⎭
60+	u	u	3.79	3.79	3.66	3.58	u	4.08	5.15	6.26
Total	u	u	100.00	100.00	100.00	100.00	u	100.00	100.00	100.00

u—unavailable.

Basic Table 6 Percentage distribution of population by age and sex: Goa, Daman, and Diu, 1900–1971

Age group	1900[a]	1910[a]	1921	1931	1941[b]	1950[a]	1961	1971
MALE								
0–4	11.31	11.77	12.04	11.41		11.39	12.43	38.60
5–9	14.19	12.88	13.90	13.55		12.42	13.97	
10–14	13.34	12.30	13.06	12.72		13.52	12.83	
15–19	8.97	9.54	8.61	9.60		9.74	9.31	10.10
0–20					50.30			
20–24	7.32	8.04	6.99	7.81		7.80	8.59	9.54
25–29	7.94	7.84	7.49	7.23		7.45	7.46	8.07
30–34	6.87	6.85	7.15	6.70		6.34	6.65	13.28
35–39	6.05	6.40	6.34	6.44		5.96	5.40	
40–44	6.17	6.04	5.82	6.09		5.60	5.26	8.88
45–49	4.89	4.57	4.68	4.93		4.99	4.33	
50–54	4.37	4.31	4.43	4.44		3.75	4.12	5.93
55–59	2.75	2.81	2.73	2.89		3.57	2.89	
21+					49.70			
60+	5.83	6.65	6.76	6.19		7.47	6.76	5.60
Total	100.00	100.00	100.00	100.00	100.00	100.00	100.00	100.00
FEMALE								
0–4	10.75	11.07	10.87	10.64		11.33	11.42	37.59
5–9	12.72	11.27	12.17	11.94		12.05	12.62	
10–14	11.71	10.66	10.66	10.68		11.17	11.36	
15–19	8.32	9.18	8.29	8.94		8.86	8.34	9.38
0–20					46.38			
20–24	8.00	9.15	8.42	8.61		7.88	8.19	8.33
25–29	8.62	8.79	8.71	8.27		7.44	7.38	7.98
30–34	7.54	7.49	7.94	7.86		6.88	6.73	12.80
35–39	5.76	5.89	6.19	6.48		6.28	5.69	
40–44	6.40	6.17	6.05	6.55		6.27	5.94	9.20
45–49	4.41	4.40	4.63	4.76		4.64	4.70	
50–54	5.11	5.06	4.88	4.92		4.20	5.05	7.06
55–59	2.72	2.88	2.78	2.81		4.08	3.29	
21+					53.62			
60+	7.94	7.99	8.41	7.54		8.92	9.29	7.66
Total	100.00	100.00	100.00	100.00	100.00	100.00	100.00	100.00

NOTE: Data unavailable for 1881 and 1891 censuses.

a The census was taken a year earlier than usual during this decade in the three Portuguese territories.

b Age data were given only in two broad groups in the 1941 census.

Basic Table 7 Percentage distribution of population by age and sex: Dadra and Nagar Haveli, 1900—1971

Age group	1900[a]	1910[a]	1921	1931	1941[b]	1950[a]	1961	1971
MALE								
0—4	10.98	15.04	12.66	12.99		13.20	16.98	45.67
5—9	17.14	14.75	17.20	15.02		13.31	15.25	
10—14	13.62	10.23	13.97	12.71		12.79	11.20	
15—19	9.49	8.30	6.95	7.54		8.32	6.81	7.75
0—20					52.31			
20—24	8.85	8.44	6.29	7.68		7.41	7.10	6.80
25—29	7.91	9.07	7.75	8.48		8.86	8.84	7.35
30—34	7.02	7.40	6.62	6.62		7.25	7.52	12.43
35—39	7.17	7.44	7.05	8.28		7.47	6.79	
40—44	5.42	5.91	6.53	6.02		6.05	4.97	9.87
45—49	4.35	4.93	5.13	5.49		4.77	4.92	
50—54	2.96	2.99	3.60	3.38		3.87	3.54	6.40
55—59	1.45	1.65	2.23	2.53		2.46	2.13	
21+					47.69			
60+	3.62	3.85	4.02	3.26		4.24	3.95	3.73
Total	100.00	100.00	100.00	100.00	100.00	100.00	100.00	100.00
FEMALE								
0—4	12.22	16.82	14.21	14.92		13.82	18.90	45.32
5—9	16.92	13.59	17.57	15.14		17.11	14.92	
10—14	13.26	9.34	11.78	10.79		10.90	10.18	
15—19	9.67	9.64	6.72	9.82		8.30	7.60	7.92
0—20					53.33			
20—24	9.26	10.42	7.31	9.51		8.50	9.16	8.10
25—29	7.60	8.67	8.48	9.64		8.69	9.12	7.29
30—34	7.62	7.45	6.80	6.88		6.89	6.77	12.12
35—39	6.01	6.28	7.03	7.27		5.99	5.58	
40—44	5.53	5.18	5.47	4.35		5.67	4.80	9.25
45—49	3.18	3.27	4.58	3.89		4.30	3.93	
50—54	3.16	2.89	3.09	3.02		3.20	3.15	5.62
55—59	1.66	2.00	2.29	2.00		2.41	1.80	
21+					46.67			
60+	3.91	4.46	4.67	2.77		4.22	4.09	4.38
Total	100.00	100.00	100.00	100.00	100.00	100.00	100.00	100.00

NOTE: Data unavailable for 1881 and 1891 censuses.

a The census was taken a year earlier than usual during this decade in the two Portuguese territories.

b Age data were given only in two broad groups in the 1941 census.

Basic Table 8   Percentage distribution of population by age and sex: Pondicherry and Laccadive, Minicoy, and Amindivi Islands, 1961 and 1971

	Pondicherry		Islands	
Age group	1961	1971	1961	1971
MALE				
0–4	14.38 ⎫		14.66 ⎫	
5–9	12.02 ⎬ 39.75		14.56 ⎬ 42.42	
10–14	10.64 ⎭		13.53 ⎭	
15–19	7.73	8.61	9.11	9.04
20–24	8.39	8.08	8.28	7.88
25–29	8.01	6.91	7.58	8.09
30–34	6.89 ⎫ 12.91		6.61 ⎫ 12.79	
35–39	6.49 ⎭		5.97 ⎭	
40–44	5.93 ⎫ 10.42		4.57 ⎫ 9.01	
45–49	4.98 ⎭		3.77 ⎭	
50–54	4.58 ⎫ 6.78		3.95 ⎫ 5.51	
55–59	3.08 ⎭		2.57 ⎭	
60+	6.88	6.54	4.84	5.26
Total	100.00	100.00	100.00	100.00
FEMALE				
0–4	14.10 ⎫		13.94 ⎫	
5–9	11.96 ⎬ 39.25		13.57 ⎬ 39.17	
10–14	10.23 ⎭		11.58 ⎭	
15–19	8.09	8.73	9.46	9.92
20–24	8.87	8.33	9.64	9.68
25–29	9.01	8.32	8.50	8.87
30–34	7.25 ⎫ 13.28		6.80 ⎫ 12.73	
35–39	6.32 ⎭		6.07 ⎭	
40–44	5.62 ⎫ 9.37		4.92 ⎫ 8.95	
45–49	4.59 ⎭		4.54 ⎭	
50–54	4.40 ⎫ 6.58		3.57 ⎫ 5.80	
55–59	2.72 ⎭		2.30 ⎭	
60+	6.84	6.14	5.11	4.88
Total	100.00	100.00	100.00	100.00

NOTE: For these territories age data are not available for other years.

4

Age distribution
and the hypothesis of quasi stability

Looking at the age distribution in India and its zones, states, and territories for the period 1881 through 1961, one cannot but be impressed by the essential similarity of the age structures in the respective areas over the eighty-year period. Take for instance the age segment 0–10 for India. The percentage of population in this age segment ranged only from 25.77 to 29.31 for males and from 26.68 to 30.33 for females. One can hardly expect any real population (as distinct from a theoretical population) to show a greater similarity in the proportion of population in a particular age segment over such a long period. The proposition is equally true for other age segments. Furthermore, it is true not only for the country as a whole but for each of its five zones and, to a lesser extent, for each of the states and territories.

Along with the basic similarity of the age structures, small but systematic variations are observed in the age group 0–4 in three different periods. In the decades 1891–1901 and 1911–1921 the proportion of population in the age group 0–4 decreased somewhat. During the period 1921–1961 this proportion increased, first slowly and then at a faster rate. The increase in the proportion of the 0–4 age group was evidently a consequence of the secular decline in mortality that had started in the third decade of this century, accelerated during the 1950s, and has been continuing to this day. The converse effect was

produced by a rise in mortality during the decades 1891—1901 and
1911—1921. There is ample evidence to confirm the occurrence of extensive epidemics throughout the country during these two decades
[13]. It is also well known that when the incidence of overall mortality goes up, there occurs a more than proportionate increase in the
number of deaths among infants and children—so that the percentage
of population in the age group 0—4 goes down.*

Overshadowing such small variations, the constancy of the age distribution in India stands out in bold relief when studied in contrast to
the age distribution in countries that have had a nonstable population
during these years. The West European and North American countries
fall in this category. The typical behavior of the age distribution in
such countries is marked by a steep fall in the proportion of population in younger ages, a remarkable increase in the proportion of people
in old ages, and a slight increase in the proportion in the middle ages.

The broad difference between the behavior of the age distribution
in India and its zones on the one hand and that in the West European
and North American countries on the other is widely known. That the
aging of the population in the latter group of countries is due to a decline in fertility is also extensively documented [93]. The hypothesis
that the near constancy of the age distribution in India is due to a sub-
stantively unchanged fertility over a long period accompanied by fluctuations in mortality before 1921 and a secular decline in mortality
since 1921 has been made by several authors in the last two decades
[58, 75, 86, 110]. But such hypotheses have hitherto been made on
the basis of an overall observation of the age distribution in different
years—mostly at the national level and without proper study of any
possible impact on the age distribution of changes in administrative
boundaries or changes in the manner of collecting and presenting census age data. There is therefore a need to probe into the hypotheses of
stability or quasi stability of Indian age distributions at both national
and subnational levels—taking into account whatever changes occurred
in the administrative boundaries and in the age groups in which the
census age tables were presented.

This need is all the greater because, though the age distribution for
different years is substantially similar, no two age distributions (i.e., at
two different times) are exactly identical. For the purpose of testing

---

*   An unresolved question is whether the proportionate decrease in the age group
0—4 was an effect exclusively of a rise in mortality, or whether there occurred
a temporary decline in the birth rate also—possibly as a consequence of epidemics.

the hypothesis of quasi stability* of Indian age distributions, we need an index to measure the dissimilarity between two age distributions and also a standard against which to compare the dissimilarity in any given case. Such a standard would tell us how much discrepancy between two or more age distributions could be accommodated within the broad framework of quasi stability and what the limit is beyond which such discrepancies cannot go without affecting the validity of the assumption of a quasi-stable population. An attempt has been made in the following pages to develop an index of dissimilarity and to fix a standard value of this index that separates stable or quasi-stable populations from nonstable ones.

The L curve and indices of dissimilarity

A convenient diagrammatic framework for visualizing the total discrepancy between two age distributions is made possible by the use of the Lorenz curve (L curve) [59]. This curve plots the cumulated proportions of one population against those of another over the same age groups; the age groups are arranged in ascending order beginning with 0–4. Figure 4.1 illustrates the method of comparison. We have taken the female age distribution of India (1901) as the base and those of India (1961) and the United States (1950) as the ones to be compared with the base (Table 4.1).

If the Indian age distribution for 1961 were identical with that for 1901, then the L curve for India (1961) would be identical with the diagonal OZ. Since the age distributions are identical, all the cumulated proportions for the sets of corresponding age segments are equal and the plotted points corresponding to each set of X and Y lie on the diagonal which we may conveniently call the S line. If, however, a given age distribution q_i is younger than the base age distribution p_i, the cumulated Q_i values would be larger than the cumulated P_i values and the L curve would lie above the S line. The L curve for India (1961) is a case in point. The curve representing the United States female age distribution (1950) illustrates how an L curve depicting an older age distribution lies below the S line.

Following Gini [54], we can derive from the L curve five summary measures which can be used to ascertain the nature and extent of the

---

* By a quasi-stable population we mean a population with a history of constant fertility (both level and pattern) and constant mortality (both level and pattern) up to a certain time and thereafter a changing level of mortality, the age pattern of mortality remaining restricted within a family of model life tables.

Figure 4.1　L curves showing age distribution of India females (1961) and United States females (1950) with India females (1901) as base

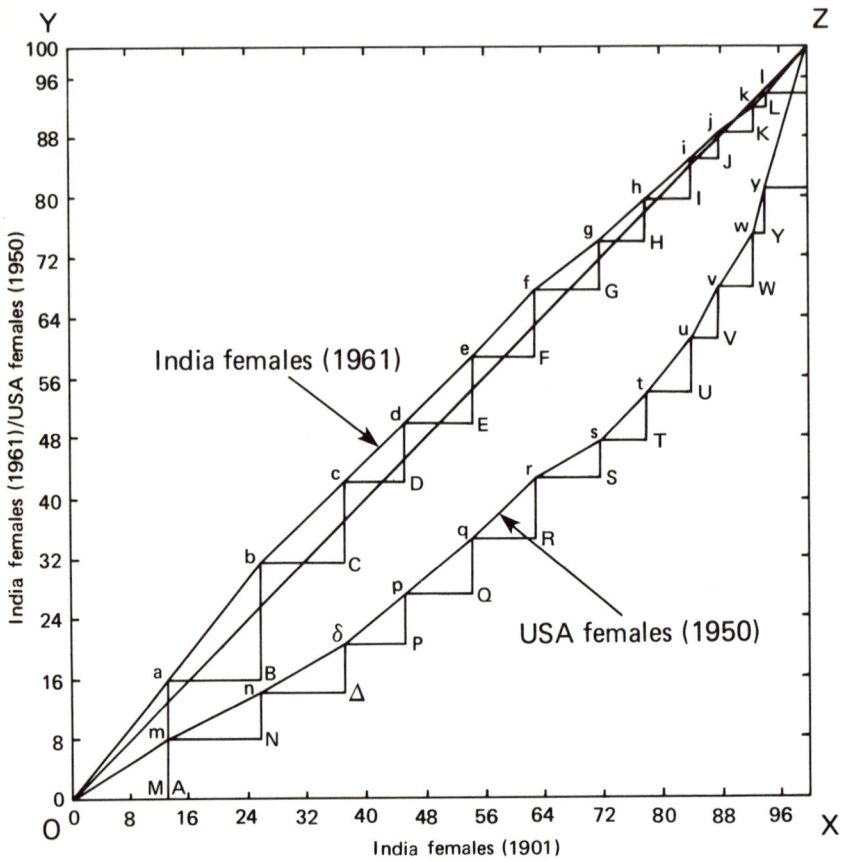

Table 4.1 Cumulative percentage of total population up to various ages: India, female (1901 and 1961), and United States, female (1950)

Up to age	India, female (1901): base	India, female (1961)	United States, female (1950)
0	0	0	0
5	12.94	15.47	8.23
10	26.47	30.33	14.37
15	37.42	41.16	20.63
20	45.59	49.28	27.67
25	54.50	59.28	35.07
30	63.44	66.76	42.61
35	72.07	73.75	47.51
40	77.75	79.32	53.98
45	84.49	84.39	61.10
50	87.98	88.30	68.17
55	92.67	92.05	74.81
60	94.40	94.19	80.79
100	100.00	100.00	100.00

SOURCES: India 1901 and 1961: Basic Table 5; United States 1950: [92:98].

dissimilarity between two age distributions. The five measures are as follows:

$$|D| = \text{aggregate dissimilarity}$$

$$= \tfrac{1}{2} \sum_{1}^{n} |p_i - q_i|$$

$$|C| = \text{concentration dissimilarity}$$

$$= \tfrac{1}{2} \sum_{1}^{n} |p_i Q_{i-1} - q_i P_{i-1}|$$

$$C = \text{net concentration dissimilarity}$$

$$= \tfrac{1}{2} \sum_{1}^{n} (p_i Q_{i-1} - q_i P_{i-1})$$

$$D_p = \text{partial dissimilarity}$$

$$= \tfrac{1}{2} \sum_{1}^{6} (p_i - q_i)$$

$$C_p = \text{partial concentration dissimilarity}$$

$$= \tfrac{1}{2} \sum_1^6 (p_i\, Q_{i-1} - q_i\, P_{i-1})$$

where

p_i = base proportional age distribution

q_i = given proportional age distribution to be compared with base proportional age distribution

i = any age group

n = number of age groups (13 in the present case)

$$Q_{i-1} = \sum_1^{i-1} q_i$$

$$P_{i-1} = \sum_1^{i-1} p_i$$

Test of the indices

The validity of the preceding formulations has been tested on the basis of some historical evidence drawn from the male and female age distributions of seven advanced countries for which fairly reliable age data are available over a long period and in which both fertility and mortality are known to have declined over the period considered here [92]. The seven countries are Austria, Canada, France, Germany, Great Britain, Sweden, and the United States.

We have computed for each country the values of $|D|$, D_p, $|C|$, C, and C_p for the relevant pairs of age distribution. The pairing is done by successively taking the age distribution of each year as the base (p_i) and the age distribution of all other years in the same set* as the ones to be compared (q_i). For instance, age data for Canada are available for six census years: 1901, 1911, 1921, 1931, 1941, and 1951. Taking the age distribution of 1901 as the base, we have five pairs: 1901 and 1911, 1901 and 1921, 1901 and 1931, 1901 and 1941, and 1901 and 1951. Taking the age distribution of 1911 as the base, we again get five combinations—of which one (1911 and 1901) is common

---

* A set refers to the available male age distributions or the available female age distributions of a country for different years.

with one (1901 and 1911) of the previous five pairs—so that we have really four new pairs. In this way we have obtained 15 pairs of age distribution in all ($\overset{6}{\underset{2}{C}} = 15$). The number of such combinations for each of the other countries has been determined by the number of years for which age data are available. Thus we have obtained 21 combinations for Austria, 15 combinations each for Canada, Germany (prepartition), and the United States, 45 combinations for France, and 55 combinations each for Great Britain and Sweden.

For convenience the computed values of $|D|$, $|C|$, and C for the female population of the United States are reproduced in Table 4.2. In this table the base year (p_i) appears in the first column and the reference years in the others. Each row sets out the computed values of the measures relating to the reference years indicated in the row. Similarly, each column indicates the values for the reference years compared with the base years indicated in the first column.

The inductive generalization is that with any earlier year as base, aggregate dissimilarity for each successive year goes on increasing rapidly—thus revealing that the age distributions for successive years are more and more dissimilar from those of earlier years. Corroborative evidence is found in the same values read down each column.

Reading along the rows in panels 2 and 3 from right to left, we find that the values of concentration dissimilarity and absolute values of net concentration dissimilarity with an earlier year as base increase for each successive year compared with the base.

It will further be observed that although $|C|$ is not always equal to the absolute magnitudes of C, the differences are small. The implication is that the enclosed areas between the L curve and S line lie predominantly on one side of the S line (in this case above the S line)— and only small fragments lie on the other side. Moreover, the negative values of the net concentration dissimilarity show that the age distribution in successive years has kept on getting older—a finding also suggested in the values of D_p and C_p (not shown here). This finding is consistent with the history of decline in fertility in the United States during the period under review. It is remarkable that all the trends noted in Table 4.2 are uniform and unbroken. It is also remarkable that the distance measures for the male age distributions reveal similarly uniform and unbroken trends. This experience is repeated in the other six countries for which distance measures have been computed. To save space, we have not reproduced the elaborate matrices of the distance measures for these countries. But the computed values of $|D|$,

Table 4.2   Matrix of distances between age distributions of different years: United States, 1900–1940

Base year	Reference year				
	1950	1940	1930	1920	1910
$|D|$ MALE					
1900	0.1166	0.1021	0.0680	0.0467	0.0264
1910	0.0997	0.0837	0.0516	0.0331	
1920	0.0746	0.0682	0.0311		
1930	0.0698	0.0445			
1940	0.0574				
$|D|$ FEMALE					
1900	0.1454	0.1201	0.0745	0.0458	0.0220
1910	0.1257	0.1004	0.0548	0.0261	
1920	0.1011	0.0777	0.0348		
1930	0.0829	0.0510			
1940	0.0589				
$|C|$ MALE					
1900	0.1541	0.1440	0.0858	0.0571	0.0309
1910	0.1345	0.1156	0.0668	0.0411	
1920	0.1017	0.0902	0.0365		
1930	0.0827	0.0596			
1940	0.0437				
$|C|$ FEMALE					
1900	0.1858	0.1629	0.0939	0.0532	0.0277
1910	0.1633	0.1374	0.0682	0.0349	
1920	0.1365	0.1116	0.0442		
1930	0.1058	0.0707			
1940	0.0516				
C MALE					
1900	−0.1386	−0.1440	−0.0858	−0.0535	−0.0294
1910	−0.1125	−0.1156	−0.0572	−0.0248	
1920	−0.0875	−0.0902	−0.0323		
1930	−0.0566	−0.0583			
1940	−0.0014				
C FEMALE					
1900	−0.1707	−0.1629	−0.0939	−0.0513	−0.0262
1910	−0.1473	−0.1374	−0.0682	−0.0254	
1920	−0.1223	−0.1116	−0.0427		
1930	−0.0819	−0.0694			
1940	−0.0163				

NOTE: See text for definitions of $|D|$, $|C|$, and C.

|C|, and C for the female population with the earliest year as base are set out in Table 4.3 for each of the later years for which age data were available. Though there are small gaps in the data on changes in fertility in these countries during the period, the occurrence of a secular decline in fertility is well documented [93]. As a consequence of this decline the age distribution has become older and older over the decades—an aging that is truly reflected in the distance measures set out in this table.*

Computed distance measures for India

Corresponding to the nine age distributions for the male population and nine age distributions for the female population, there are 36 values for each of the indices $|D|$, $|C|$, C, D_p, and C_p so that there are 180 values for the male population and another 180 values for the female population. These 360 values have been computed for India, its five zones, and its 29 states and territories. For purposes of illustration, three of the five distance measures for the female and male age distribution in India are set out in Tables 4.4 and 4.5, respectively. A comparative study of the distance measures in India and the advanced countries reveals the following:

1. The distances between the age distributions for any given state at two different times are significantly smaller in India than in the advanced countries. (See Figures 4.2, 4.3, and 4.4.)

2. Whichever year is taken as base, the distance measures for successive census years reveal a very slowly rising trend or nearly constant values. The contrast with the rapidly rising values of the distance measures in the advanced countries is sharp and vivid.

3. The differences between the values of $|C|$ and C for corresponding age distributions corroborate the previous finding that there are large errors in Indian census age data.

Distance measures for hypothetical quasi-stable populations

Decisive evidence in support of the hypothesis of constant fertility in India is provided by a comparison between the distance measures for Indian age distributions and those for hypothetical age distributions subjected to conditions of constant fertility and changing mortality.

---

* We have repeated this exercise for many other countries, among them Australia, Belgium, Bulgaria, Denmark, Greece, Italy, the Netherlands, Norway, and Portugal. We have found similarly uniform and convincing trends in the values of these measures, which are consistent with the known trends of decline in fertility and mortality.

Table 4.3 Aggregate dissimilarity, concentration dissimilarity, and net concentration dissimilarity for six advanced countries: female

Country and base year	Index	Reference year and value of index									
Great Britain (1851)		1957	1939	1931	1921	1911	1901	1891	1881	1871	1861
	$|D|$	0.2125	0.1832	0.1399	0.0984	0.0590	0.0289	0.0146	0.0155	0.0158	0.0109
	$|C|$	0.2603	0.2361	0.1860	0.1272	0.0696	0.0350	0.0143	0.0161	0.0175	0.0119
	C	-0.2584	-0.2361	-0.1860	-0.1272	-0.0696	-0.0350	-0.0097	0.0056	-0.0011	-0.0029
Sweden (1850)		1950	1940	1930	1920	1910	1900	1890	1880	1870	1860
	$|D|$	0.1603	0.1426	0.0897	0.0596	0.0506	0.0548	0.0485	0.0321	0.0450	0.0315
	$|C|$	0.1947	0.1859	0.1280	0.0797	0.0655	0.0765	0.0641	0.0457	0.0443	0.0378
	C	-0.1864	-0.1859	-0.1280	-0.0774	-0.0526	-0.0463	-0.0385	-0.0238	-0.0121	-0.0008
Austria (1870)		1951	1939	1934	1927	1920	1910	1900	1890	1880	
	$|D|$	0.1988	0.1798	0.1459	0.1185	0.0910	0.0405	0.0302	0.0249	0.0204	
	$|C|$	0.2556	0.2397	0.2020	0.1602	0.1328	0.0479	0.0423	0.0339	0.0298	
	C	-0.2550	-0.2353	-0.1971	-0.1602	-0.1328	-0.0065	-0.0047	-0.0083	-0.0067	
France (1851)		1950	1931	1921	1911	1901	1891	1881	1872	1861	
	$|D|$	0.1243	0.0699	0.0616	0.0321	0.0262	0.0281	0.0302	0.0263	0.0124	
	$|C|$	0.1632	0.1002	0.0905	0.0426	0.0297	0.0366	0.0374	0.0346	0.0136	
	C	-0.1443	-0.0908	-0.0905	-0.0409	-0.0274	-0.0208	-0.0146	0.0214	0.0020	
Germany (1880)		1933	1925	1910	1900	1890					
	$|D|$	0.1547	0.0959	0.0211	0.0117	0.0175					
	$|C|$	0.1823	0.1167	0.0227	0.0132	0.0174					
	C	-0.1823	-0.1128	-0.0160	-0.0043	-0.0055					
Canada (1901)		1951	1941	1931	1921	1911					
	$|D|$	0.0944	0.0785	0.0385	0.0279	0.0227					
	$|C|$	0.1211	0.1038	0.0467	0.0328	0.0210					
	C	-0.0965	-0.1038	-0.0452	-0.0088	-0.0010					

Table 4.4 Matrix of distances between age distributions of census years: India, female, 1881–1961

Base year	Reference year							
	1961	1951	1941	1931	1921	1911	1901	1891
$|D|$								
1881	0.0568	0.0571	0.0396	0.0409	0.0304	0.0158	0.0235	0.0199
1891	0.0439	0.0575	0.0376	0.0420	0.0307	0.0165	0.0281	
1901	0.0497	0.0442	0.0355	0.0347	0.0148	0.0180		
1911	0.0485	0.0476	0.0347	0.0322	0.0252			
1921	0.0419	0.0471	0.0258	0.0361				
1931	0.0326	0.0287	0.0176					
1941	0.0291	0.0291						
1951	0.0418							
$|C|$								
1881	0.0334	0.0355	0.0254	0.0296	0.0142	0.0096	0.0121	0.0096
1891	0.0281	0.0296	0.0215	0.0248	0.0107	0.0075	0.0114	
1901	0.0326	0.0263	0.0222	0.0209	0.0079	0.0074		
1911	0.0288	0.0275	0.0216	0.0214	0.0085			
1921	0.0271	0.0242	0.0162	0.0205				
1931	0.0191	0.0143	0.0106					
1941	0.0163	0.0127						
1951	0.0177							
C								
1881	0.0202	-0.0040	0.0040	0.0067	0.0011	0.0012	-0.0028	0.0060
1891	0.0140	-0.0021	-0.0021	0.0006	-0.0050	-0.0047	-0.0088	
1901	0.0231	0.0067	0.0068	0.0095	0.0040	0.0040		
1911	0.0189	0.0028	0.0027	0.0054	-0.0001			
1921	0.0191	0.0027	0.0029	0.0055				
1931	0.0138	-0.0026	-0.0025					
1941	0.0160	-0.0002						
1951	0.0163							

NOTE: See text for definitions of $|D|$, $|C|$, and C.

Table 4.5 Matrix of distances between age distributions of census years: India, male, 1881—1961

Base year	Reference year 1961	1951	1941	1931	1921	1911	1901	1891
|D|								
1881	0.0516	0.0503	0.0381	0.0334	0.0285	0.0218	0.0210	0.0184
1891	0.0366	0.0472	0.0342	0.0318	0.0298	0.0168	0.0233	
1901	0.0552	0.0419	0.0407	0.0298	0.0191	0.0199		
1911	0.0434	0.0374	0.0314	0.0243	0.0251			
1921	0.0448	0.0409	0.0285	0.0282				
1931	0.0345	0.0265	0.0188					
1941	0.0254	0.0239						
1951	0.0373							
|C|								
1881	0.0341	0.0320	0.0267	0.0234	0.0161	0.0120	0.0106	0.0092
1891	0.0254	0.0267	0.0227	0.0200	0.0132	0.0088	0.0085	
1901	0.0316	0.0248	0.0238	0.0189	0.0096	0.0085		
1911	0.0278	0.0231	0.0197	0.0149	0.0092			
1921	0.0264	0.0200	0.0160	0.0156				
1931	0.0199	0.0128	0.0113					
1941	0.0135	0.0108						
1951	0.0184							
C									
1881	0.0076	−0.0085	−0.0062	−0.0049	−0.0069	−0.0044	−0.0047	0.0029
1891	0.0046	−0.0113	−0.0091	−0.0078	−0.0097	−0.0072	−0.0075	
1901	0.0122	−0.0040	−0.0016	−0.0003	−0.0022	0.0002		
1911	0.0118	−0.0041	−0.0019	−0.0005	−0.0024			
1921	0.0143	−0.0018	0.0006	0.0019				
1931	0.0123	−0.0036	−0.0013					
1941	0.0134	−0.0023						
1951	0.0157							

Figure 4.2 Values of |D| for India and zones contrasted to those for some advanced countries: female, 1861–1961

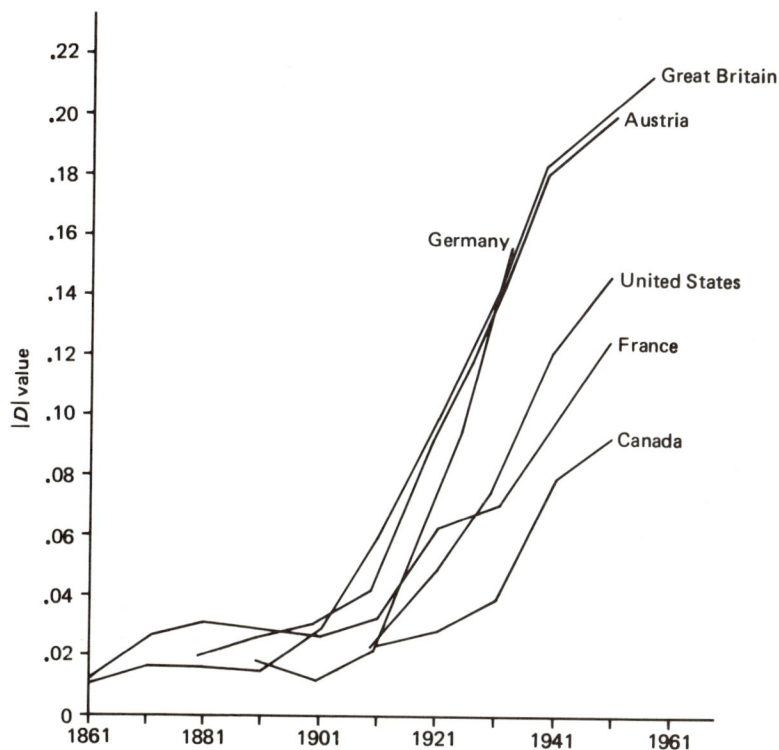

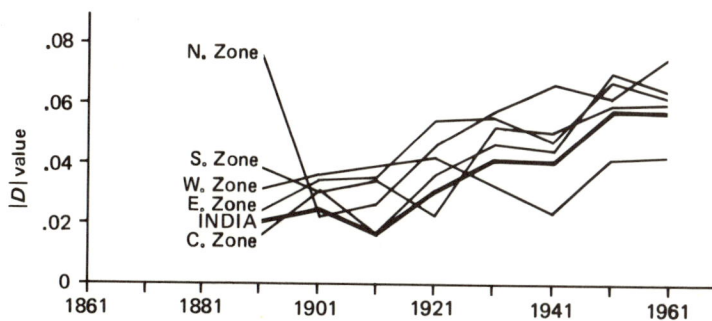

Figure 4.3 Values of |C| for India and zones contrasted to those for some
advanced countries: female, 1861–1961

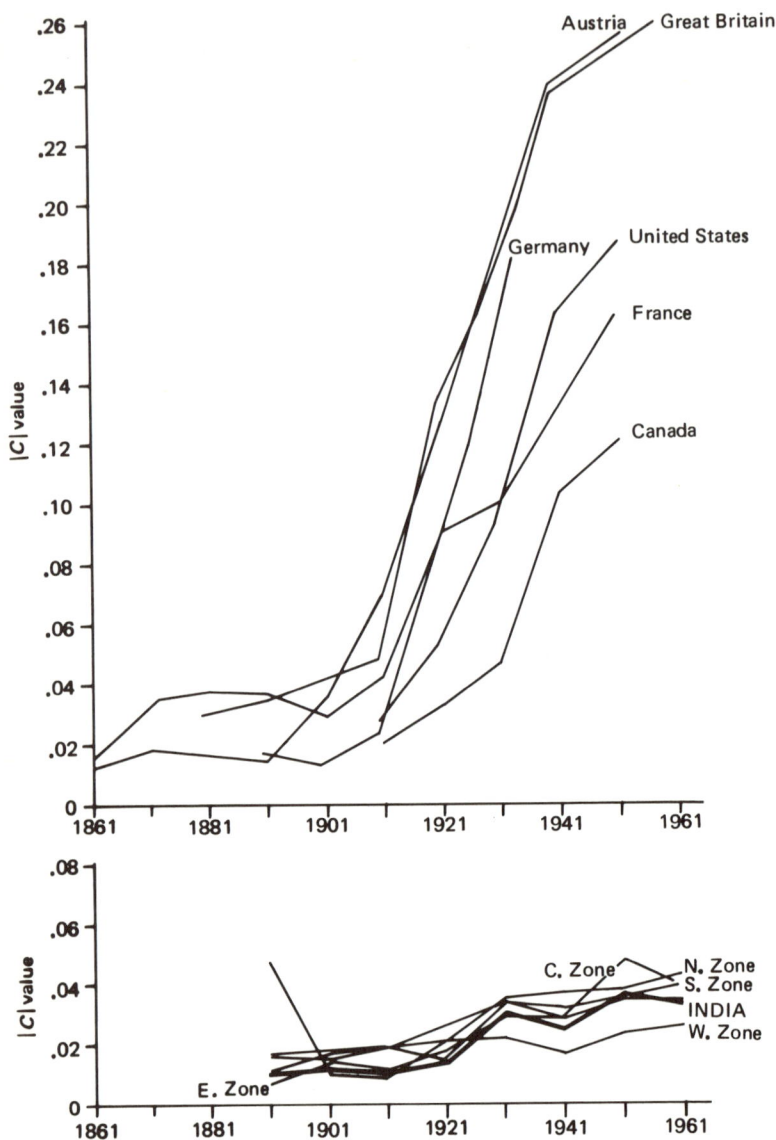

Figure 4.4   Values of C for India and zones contrasted to those for some
advanced countries: female, 1861–1961

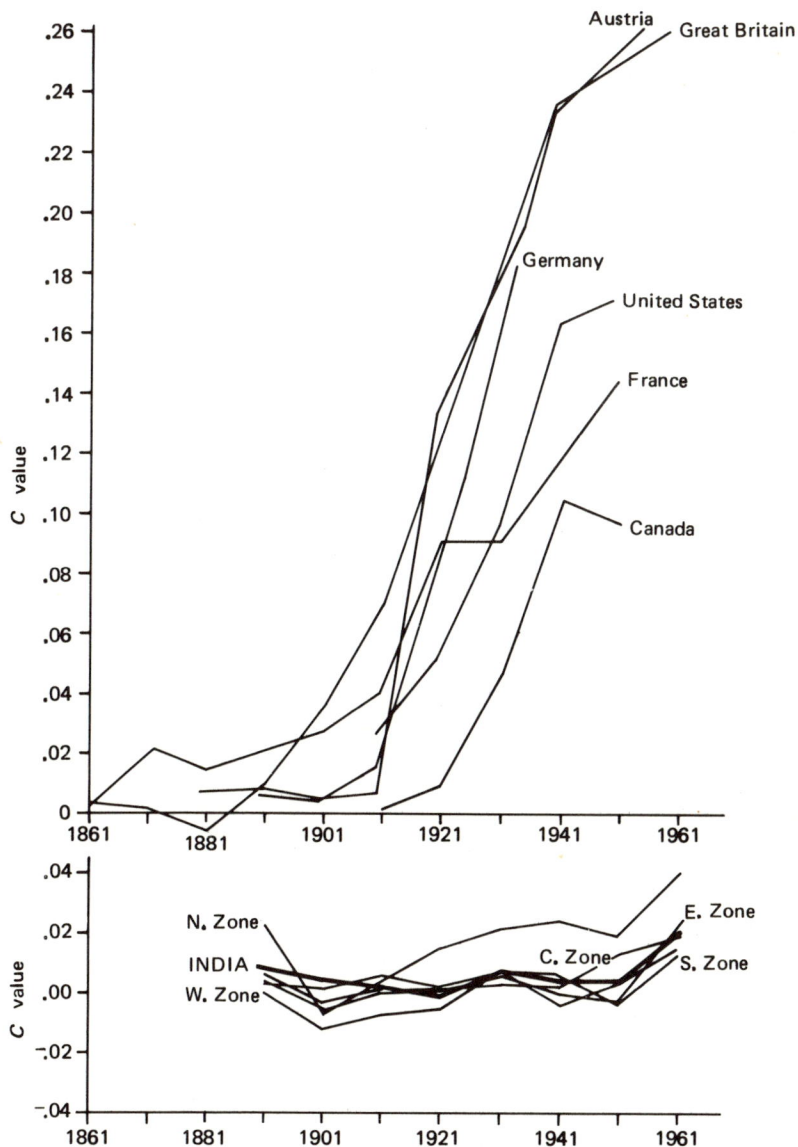

We generated 12 sets of such age distributions—corresponding to three levels of fertility (gross reproduction rate or GRR = 3.0, 3.2, 3.4) and four different assumptions (A, B, C, D) about the likely course of mortality changes. The distance measures were then computed for these simulated age distributions. The values of one distance measure ($|D|$) are set out in Table 4.6. Though the other four distance measures are not shown here, the features and trends that emerge from them are similar to those that emerge from an examination of the values of $|D|$. Two significant inferences are drawn from this table:

1. If fertility remains unchanged, the pattern of variation in the distance measures is different for different courses of mortality changes.
2. If the course of mortality changes is given, the distance measures are almost invariant with different levels of fertility—provided that the level remains unchanged over the period under consideration.

It follows that the changes in the Indian age structure are similar to the expected changes in an age distribution subjected to conditions of constant fertility and declining mortality. The average rate of mortality decline in India since 1951 has been faster than that in the advanced countries over the past hundred years. Hence the effect of declining mortality on the distance between age distributions must have been quantitatively larger in India than in the advanced countries for similar periods. If such effects of mortality decline are eliminated from the observed values of the distance measures in India, the residues in

Table 4.6 Aggregate dissimilarity between actual age distribution and simulated age distribution under assumptions of constant fertility and changing mortality

GRR	Mortality assumption[a]	Year compared					
		1961	1951	1941	1931	1921	1911
3.00	A	0.0384	0.0237	0.0235	0.0196	0.0179	0.0000
3.00	B	0.0295	0.0222	0.0243	0.0234	0.0248	0.0001
3.00	C	0.0437	0.0321	0.0303	0.0231	0.0199	0.0000
3.00	D	0.0549	0.0335	0.0236	0.0120	0.0044	0.0036
3.20	A	0.0390	0.0235	0.0235	0.0200	0.0182	0.0001
3.20	B	0.0294	0.0217	0.0242	0.0241	0.0253	0.0001
3.20	C	0.0440	0.0317	0.0306	0.0238	0.0202	0.0000
3.20	D	0.0549	0.0333	0.0236	0.0123	0.0045	0.0038
3.40	A	0.0393	0.0230	0.0237	0.0206	0.0186	0.0000
3.40	B	0.0295	0.0214	0.0242	0.0242	0.0257	0.0001
3.40	C	0.0442	0.0313	0.0306	0.0244	0.0206	0.0001
3.40	D	0.0554	0.0336	0.0239	0.0127	0.0043	0.0037

a   For the time path of mortality changes under the various assumptions see Table 6.9.

such values may be looked upon as a consequence of changes in fertility. Such residues are much smaller in Indian age distributions than in those of the advanced countries.

To sum up, the distances between age distributions in India for successive census years are significantly smaller than those for advanced countries for which there is a well-documented evidence of a decline in fertility. Moreover, the pattern of variation in the distance measures differs from what could be expected under conditions of changing fertility; in fact, the pattern resembles the expected variation when fertility remains constant and mortality undergoes changes similar to such changes in India.

Effect of differences in fertility on the index

Attempts may now be made to quantify the relationship between a difference in fertility and the distance measures and to find the size of a distance measure corresponding to a given difference in fertility. We have adopted the following method:

1. We selected six stable age distributions corresponding to six different levels of fertility (GRR = 2.00, 2.25, 2.50, 3.00, 3.50, 4.00) and a given level of mortality—defined by a life expectancy of 20 years [42]. We then computed the distances for the 15 possible combinations of age distributions from these six stable populations. This process was repeated for four other mortality levels (e_0 = 30, 40, 50, 57.5 years), and indices of distance were similarly obtained for each mortality level (Table 4.7).

2. Correlations were made between the size of these 15 distance measures and the proportionate difference in GRR for the two corresponding age distributions—separately for each of the five mortality levels. It was found that the relationship between the distance measures and the differences in GRR is linear and the correlation is strong. On the basis of this experience it has been possible to set up equations expressing quantitatively how much difference in GRR would be associated with a given value of the distance measure. (A change in fertility and a difference in fertility are two different concepts. But here they have been used synonymously.)

3. The observed distances between Indian age distributions for successive census years were then fed into these estimating equations to yield estimates of any possible change in India's GRR.

Table 4.8 sets out the computed values of parameters a and b of the regression equation $y = a + bx$, where x stands for $\Delta GRR/GRR$ and y stands for $|D|$, D_p, and $|C|$ successively for stable populations at different levels of mortality.

The regression lines between $\Delta GRR/GRR$ (x) on the one hand and $|D|$, $|C|$ (= C), and D_p (y) on the other are depicted in Figure 4.5. Note that the correlations are strong and the relationship between a differ-

Figure 4.5 Regression of ΔGRR/GRR on |D|, D_p, and C

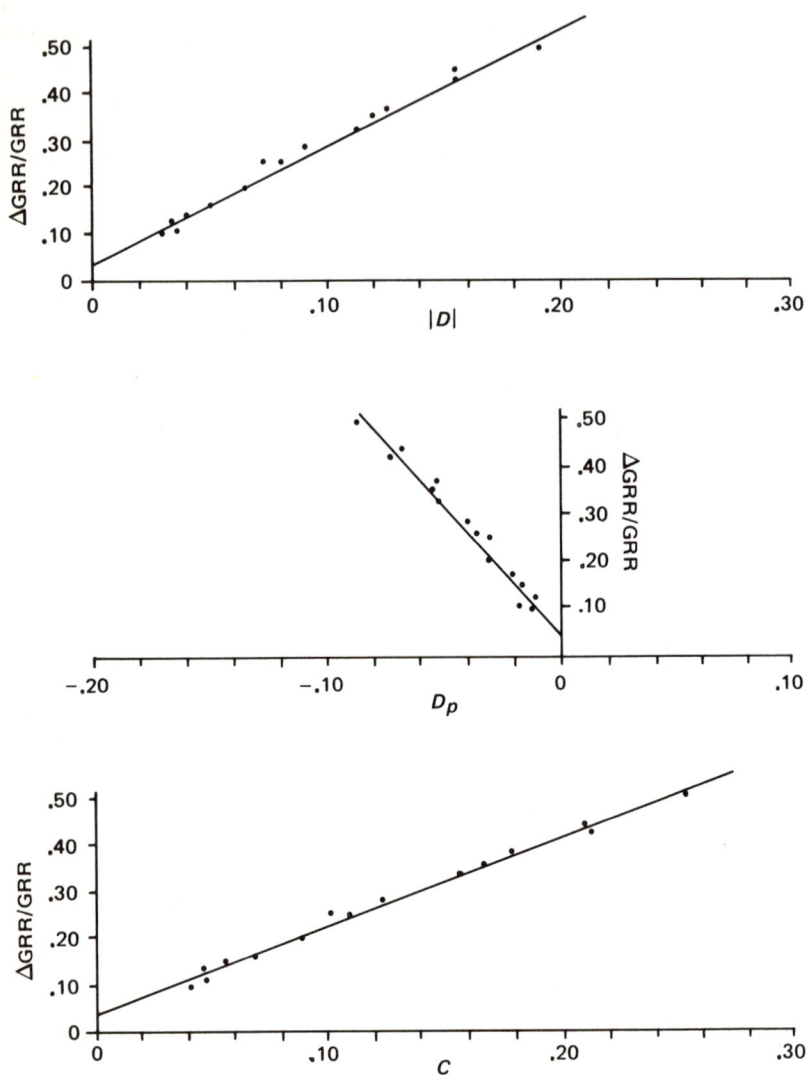

Table 4.7 Aggregate dissimilarity between stable age distributions corresponding to proportionate differences in GRR underlying such age distributions, by mortality level

GRR of compared populations		ΔGRR/GRR	Indices of aggregate dissimilarity				
Higher	Lower		$e_0 = 20$	$e_0 = 30$	$e_0 = 40$	$e_0 = 50$	$e_0 = 57.5$
2.50	2.25	0.100	0.0308	0.0307	0.0309	0.0308	0.0309
2.25	2.00	0.111	0.0349	0.0352	0.0352	0.0354	0.0352
4.00	3.50	0.125	0.0357	0.0349	0.0341	0.0338	0.0332
3.50	3.00	0.143	0.0427	0.0418	0.0411	0.0407	0.0403
3.00	2.50	0.167	0.0519	0.0519	0.0514	0.0509	0.0505
2.50	2.00	0.200	0.0657	0.0659	0.0659	0.0662	0.0661
4.00	3.00	0.250	0.0784	0.0764	0.0752	0.0745	0.0735
3.00	2.25	0.280	0.0826	0.0826	0.0823	0.0817	0.0813
3.50	2.50	0.286	0.0946	0.0937	0.0924	0.0912	0.0904
3.00	2.00	0.333	0.1175	0.1173	0.1173	0.1171	0.1165
3.50	2.25	0.357	0.1248	0.1244	0.1233	0.1220	0.1209
4.00	2.50	0.375	0.1303	0.1283	0.1257	0.1247	0.1236
3.50	2.00	0.429	0.1592	0.1591	0.1583	0.1574	0.1561
4.00	2.25	0.438	0.1605	0.1590	0.1566	0.1548	0.1535
4.00	2.00	0.500	0.1943	0.1936	0.1916	0.1902	0.1881

ence in fertility and the distance measure is close. In Table 4.8 the correlation between ΔGRR/GRR and each of $|D|$, $|C|$, or C is positive; that between ΔGRR/GRR and D_p is negative. This fits in well with the logic of the distance measures. With greater differences in fertility, higher values of $|D|$ and $|C|$ are expected.

Substituting the observed distance measures for India in these equations we find that the expected change in the gross reproduction rate in India is less than 5 percent in most cases, although there are excep-

Table 4.8 Computed values of coefficients *a* and *b*

Mortality level (e_0) in years	ΔGRR/GRR and $|D|$		ΔGRR/GRR and D_p		ΔGRR/GRR and $|C|$	
	a	*b*	*a*	*b*	*a*	*b*
20	0.0381	2.4874	0.0388	−5.2647	0.0375	1.8619
30	0.0393	2.5090	0.0399	−5.4414	0.0373	1.8805
40	0.0386	2.5231	0.0402	−5.5930	0.0373	1.9001
50	0.0383	2.5449	0.0412	−5.7007	0.0374	1.9133
57.5	0.0427	2.5353	0.0409	−5.8093	0.0374	1.9289

NOTE: See text for definitions of parameters.

tions here and there. With regard to the age distribution in 1961, the larger values of the distance measures are possibly a consequence of the substantial decrease in mortality during the period 1951–1961.

5

Rate of natural increase
and the hypothesis of quasi stability

In the last chapter, we found that the behavior of the age distribution in India over the 80-year period satisfies one necessary condition of quasi stability. In this chapter we investigate the rate of natural increase in India and examine whether it is in keeping with the concept of quasi stability.

Two kinds of quasi stability

There are two distinct phases in the behavior of the rate of natural increase. Prior to 1921 the rate fluctuated widely from one decade to the next. But since 1921 the rate has been monotonically increasing. This warrants a hypothesis of quasi stability in a somewhat broader sense than that in which the term has been hitherto used. Until now, the term quasi stability has been used to describe a situation in which fertility remains constant but mortality declines monotonically [38, 49]. In the present study, we do not restrict the concept to situations of declining mortality only but extend it to situations of both rising mortality and declining mortality—fertility having remained the same. The natural increase in India reveals the characteristics of quasi stability of the first kind in the decades after 1921 and those of the second kind in the decades before 1921. The prevalence of a long period of cyclical fluctuations in mortality prior to the onset of a secular decline in mortality has probably been characteristic of all developing countries—if not of developed countries also in earlier periods [48]. The long-term rate of population growth must have been very low in almost all countries. Otherwise, the present populations would be much larger than they are. There are three different combinations of fertility and mortality that would lead to a low growth rate in the long run:

1. Constant fertility and constant mortality—at levels conducive to a low rate of increase
2. Constant fertility and fluctuating mortality—so that the high growth rates in some years combined with low or negative growth rates in others produce a low growth rate in the long run [85]
3. Fluctuating fertility and constant mortality—so that, here again, the positive and negative growth rates in successive periods jointly produce a low long-term growth rate

The recorded history of India and of many other countries provides evidence of famines, epidemics, pestilences, and wars in different phases of their development [22]. The hypothesis of constant mortality is therefore untenable. In countries like India the nearly constant age distribution precludes the plausibility of the third alternative also. Hence the second alternative may be taken as the most general and likely combination of fertility and mortality trends in the past. By broadening the concept of quasi stability as stated above, the analytical frame may be made more useful to handle both situations—the monotonic decline in mortality in the immediate past and fluctuations in mortality prior to that.

Components of population increase

A comparison of the size of population in a state at the beginning and at the end of a decade gives the overall increase in population in the state during the decade. This overall increase has four components: the increase due to greater accuracy in the census count; the increase due to boundary changes; the increase due to migration to and from the area; and the natural increase.* To obtain the natural increase, we have to eliminate the other three components. These components and their quantitative impact on the census population in India are discussed in the following paragraphs.

---

* Of course, the population of a state can stay the same size or decrease, and similarly any of the components can act in a neutral or negative manner.

Accuracy in census counts

Census operations started in 1872 and improved in coverage and accuracy with each successive census. By 1891 or 1901 coverage was almost universal. It is therefore assumed that the increase in the resident census population over a decade may be taken as a tolerably good measure of the increase in actual population [29]. It must be admitted, however, that improvement in enumeration from one census to the next is not inevitable. Moreover, if there is a change in the direction of enumeration errors between two consecutive censuses, the resulting error in the rate of population increase may be large even though the absolute magnitude of error in each census is relatively small. This is exactly what happened in the 1941 census. Although in most years the census figures suffer from underenumeration, in 1941 there was an evident inflation of the population count for Punjab and Bengal. However, the fact that we have a series of population figures for 11 consecutive decennial censuses at the national, provincial, district, subdivision, police station, and village levels and that by and large the figures of total population for different years at all these levels are consistent with one another lends a considerable degree of dependability to these data.

Increase due to boundary changes

Changes in the boundaries of states and territories were discussed in Chapter 2. Such changes necessitate adjustment of the total population so that the rate of increase of population may be correctly measured. With regard to the total population for the period 1901–1961, we did not make any adjustments on our own but depended entirely on the time-series data presented in the 1961 census [29]. Adjustment for the six census years 1901 through 1951 according to the newly defined areal unit was done by the Census of India (1961) with the actual census counts in the respective censuses at all levels—provinces, princely states, districts, subdivisions, police stations, unions, and villages. In the large majority of cases, changes in the boundary of a state or territory did not involve the partition of the lowest administrative unit. Therefore, in the reconstruction of the total population for the constituent areas, no element of estimation was involved.* It was only

---

* Note the following quotation from the Census of India [27:4–5]: "*Estimation of data*—As a result of reorganization of States, Districts and Census tracts have sometimes been broken up and portions transferred from one State to another. Villages and towns, however, have not been affected. Since the data contained

with respect to a negligibly small number of people that the boundary changes led to the partition of a village and the share of the population in the fragmented areas had to be estimated.

The adjustment of population in previous censuses had been done by the census commissioner carefully and thoroughly. The population of a transferred area for any census year was estimated on the assumption that the proportion of the population in the area transferred to the total population of the relevant district (in which it was situated at the time of the transfer) was the same in the particular year as it was in 1951 [29].

We calculated the total population for 1881 and for 1891 on the basis of population data given in the census for the provinces and princely states that constituted the respective zones in the two years. In the absence of a good base map showing the small administrative divisions in 1881 and 1891, it was difficult to match the geographical area of a new political unit with that of an old one. Under the circumstances we used the total population figures for the provinces and princely states reconstructed by the Census of India (1901) for the years 1881 and 1891 [12]. Each zone contained a number of provinces and princely states as a whole and some fragmented areas. It was simple to identify most of the provinces and princely states as belonging to one zone or another. We reconstructed the aggregate population of those administrative units the location of which could be firmly identified in a zone from the figures adjusted by the 1901 census. Then we assumed that the population in the areas that could not be identified had grown at a rate equal to that of the population in areas that could be identified. On the basis of this assumption the population of the unidentified areas was obtained by backward projection.

International migration

To obtain the rate of natural increase for India as a whole, we treated the Indian population as closed to international migration for the period 1881 to 1941. There had always been a slight foreign influx in the population of India. There also occurred a small outflow of persons born in India to foreign territories, mainly in Africa and Asia. But as Kingsley Davis [47] has observed, whatever the economic and political importance of such movements to and from India, their demographic significance was small. The situation changed considerably in

---

in the present table are available by individual villages and towns in the published census records, it has been possible to recast the figures of the original count without resorting to estimations except in a few cases."

1951 and 1961 because of the partition of India and migration of displaced persons to and from Pakistan.

For the decade 1941–1951 the census commissioner estimated a net migration into India of about 600,000 to 800,000 persons or about one-sixth of 1 percent of the total population [22]. This conclusion was based on the following findings. The number of displaced persons from Pakistan enumerated in the 1951 census was 7.20 million. From the Pakistan Census Bulletin, it was found that nearly 7.15 million displaced persons from India were enumerated in Pakistan. Moreover, there were about 1.20 million Pakistan-born persons in East India who were not registered as displaced persons. It is difficult to ascertain the precise period of their migration to India. In addition to migrants to and from Pakistan, there was earlier in the decade an influx of Indians returning to India who had earlier migrated to countries like Burma and Malaya. It is extremely difficult to take all these factors into proper account and provide any precise estimate of net migration. We have therefore accepted the census commissioner's estimate and assumed that the net immigration into India was 700,000 during the decade 1941–1951 [22]. To obtain the sex composition of the migrants, we processed the birthplace data of the male and female population born outside India (but enumerated in India in the 1951 census [21]) and thus divided the net migrants by sex. It was observed that males and females constituted 55.20 percent and 44.80 percent respectively of all immigrants. On this basis, 700,000 net migrants were divided into 386,000 males and 314,000 females.

For the decade 1951–1961, our estimates of net international migration were prepared from the following data made available by the Census of India (1961) [31]:

1. The estimated number of net migrants (both sexes) in the census paper on age tables, which puts the figures at 3.14 million [28]

2. Data on birthplace of the persons enumerated in various states and territories

3. Data on duration of stay of the migrant population in the place of enumeration classified into five groups: less than 1 year, 1–5 years, 6–10 years, 11–15 years, and 16 years and more [31]

We assumed that the sex composition and zonal distribution of the net international migrants are the same as those of all in-migrants during the period. We then divided net migrants into three duration groups according to the proportionate division of all in-migrants during the period. Then we applied the reverse survival method to the number of net in-migrants in each duration group and obtained the original cohort of migrants. Finally we estimated the net growth due to migration by assuming a 2 percent natural growth rate per year among migrants for the average period of their stay in India.

Internal migration

Though the volume of short-distance migration in India may be quite impressive,* long-distance migration is still very limited. For the purpose of estimating the contribution of internal migration to the growth of population in the zones, we made use of Zachariah's study [112] on migration to and from the provinces and princely states of India in the three decades 1901–1911, 1911–1921, and 1921–1931.† For the decades 1891–1901 and 1931–1941 we extrapolated from Zachariah's estimates. For the decade 1881–1891 we ignored migration altogether. For the decade 1941–1951 we used the estimates provided by the Indian census actuary [19]. And for the decade 1951–1961 we prepared our own estimates from the birthplace data given in the 1951 and 1961 census tables.

Before using Zachariah's estimates of net migration, we made some modifications necessitated by subsequent changes in the boundaries of administrative divisions. We took his estimates for different provinces or princely states and then regrouped these figures into different zones as demarcated in the 1961 census. In the case of a fragment cut off from one province or princely state and merged into another in the same zone, we made no modification of the original estimates for the relevant areal unit. But in the case of a fragment cut off from one province or princely state and added to another in a different zone, we allocated the number of migrants to the different parts of the divided province on the basis of the proportionate share of the total population falling in the respective parts. A possible source of error in such regrouping of migrants according to changed boundaries of states lies in the fact that a movement that was considered an act of migration may cease to be really so as a result of regrouping of territories. And, conversely, a movement that was not considered an act of migra-

---

*   In 1961, the number of people enumerated outside the state of birth was 25 million and the number of those enumerated outside the place of birth was 145 million [31].

†   We are aware of the limitations of this study. Zachariah himself has referred to some of them. A further refinement of the migration estimates is both necessary and possible even under the existing constraints of insufficient data. However, the contribution of migration to the overall population increase in the zones is so small that a slightly better estimate of migration is not expected to lead to any appreciable improvement in the estimated rate of natural increase of the zonal population.

tion may need to be redefined as migration as a result of cession of part of the territory to another areal unit. So far as our calculations were concerned, the amount of error on this account was negligibly small.

For the purpose of estimating migration in the decade 1951–1961, the overall migrational growth has been broken into two components, the zone's share of international migration and its share of internal migration. To determine the zone's share of international migration, we processed the data on birthplace and duration of stay (from the 1961 census) to yield the number of migrants to each zone coming from outside India during 1951–1961. The net migrational growth for India has been apportioned according to the proportion of such migrants in the zone to the total migrants to India from outside India. To determine the zone's share of internal migration, the following steps have been taken:

1. We constructed birthplace–enumeration place matrices from the census data of 1951 (Table 5.1) and 1961 (Table 5.2).

2. From these two matrices we obtained the number of net lifetime migrants to each zone in 1951 and 1961 on the basis of the following relationships:

$$I(t) = E(t) - 0(t)$$

where $I(t)$ = net lifetime migrants to zone in year t

$E(t)$ = number of persons enumerated in zone in year t but born in other zones

$0(t)$ = number of persons born in zone but enumerated in other zones in year t

3. We obtained the number of net surviving migrants of the decade 1951–1961 on the basis of the following relation:

$$M(1951-1961) = I(1961) - (S)[I(1951)]$$

where M = net surviving migrants of decade 1951–1961 in a zone

S = proportion of lifetime migrants of 1951 who survived up to 1961 (assuming a crude death rate of 20 persons per 1,000)

4. Once we obtained the number of net surviving migrants, we estimated the net growth due to internal migration by assuming a 2 percent rate of natural increase per year among the migrants for the average period of their stay in the respective zones.

Natural increase

Once we isolated the component of migration in the total population, we calculated the rate of natural increase per person per year (r) as follows:

Table 5.1 Birthplace–enumeration place matrix for male and female population by zone: 1951

Birthplace	Enumeration place						Andaman and Nicobar Islands
	Eastern Zone	Central Zone	Southern Zone	Western Zone	Northern Zone	All zones	
Eastern Zone							
Male	43,528,952	129,813	13,644	16,032	15,522	43,703,963 }	2,569
Female	41,645,203	198,487	10,955	7,218	10,107	41,871,970	
Central Zone							
Male	400,818	49,161,160	54,606	362,280	266,851	50,245,715 }	1,152
Female	223,474	45,625,183	58,837	126,362	289,608	46,323,464	
Southern Zone							
Male	73,944	61,107	47,000,991	370,651	13,755	47,520,448 }	4,277
Female	51,652	75,214	46,754,977	279,291	9,983	47,171,117	
Western Zone							
Male	18,738	77,805	84,102	19,749,625	21,722	19,952,003 }	122
Female	14,778	74,668	120,596	18,934,253	17,292	19,161,587	
Northern Zone							
Male	107,863	291,848	25,878	157,043	1,626,909	16,852,241 }	304
Female	57,040	329,113	13,524	87,755	14,722,503	15,209,935	
Andaman and Nico- bar Islands; French and Portuguese settlements; foreign countries							
Male	2,213,563	443,595	74,383	326,650	1,818,870	a }	a
Female	1,794,181	360,600	43,419	2,433,955	1,516,764	a	
Total							
Male	46,343,878	50,165,328	47,253,604	20,982,281	18,406,340	183,151,431 }	30,971
Female	43,786,328	46,663,265	47,002,308	19,678,834	16,566,257	173,696,992	

a The Andaman and Nicobar Islands were considered to be outside the country. Hence persons enumerated in these places and in foreign countries did not come within the purview of our study. However, those who were born in these places and enumerated in any of the zones have been duly taken into consideration and shown in the earlier columns in this row.

SOURCE: [21:248–59].

Table 5.2 Birthplace–enumeration place matrix for male and female population by zone: 1961

Birthplace	Enumeration place					
	Eastern Zone	Central Zone	Southern Zone	Western Zone	Northern Zone	All zones
Eastern Zone						
Male	54,814,384	196,603	28,651	31,838	36,534	55,108,010
Female	52,245,670	310,826	36,798	18,068	28,341	52,639,703
Central Zone						
Male	525,454	53,964,650	22,111	527,472	520,464	55,560,151
Female	348,297	49,522,310	14,238	251,852	493,699	50,630,396
Southern Zone						
Male	113,818	71,287	55,337,264	559,815	42,671	56,124,855
Female	85,200	37,227	54,515,423	447,272	25,284	55,110,406
Western Zone						
Male	35,622	178,846	128,261	29,406,903	33,792	29,783,424
Female	23,311	204,771	181,917	27,989,787	41,052	28,440,838
Northern Zone						
Male	167,916	403,475	38,427	224,200	23,237,553	24,071,571
Female	93,750	478,455	21,756	141,604	20,459,459	21,195,024
Andaman and Nicobar Islands; French and Portuguese settlements; foreign countries						
Male	2,627,552	397,544	116,067	342,080	1,673,356	5,156,591
Female	2,215,102	352,815	113,161	304,140	1,440,945	4,426,163
Total						
Male	58,284,746	55,212,405	55,670,781	31,092,303	25,544,366	225,804,606
Female	55,011,330	50,906,404	54,883,293	29,152,723	22,488,780	212,442,530

SOURCE: [31:16–71].

$$r = \frac{1}{10} \log_e \left(\frac{P_t}{P_0}\right)$$

where P_0 and P_t are the populations corrected for migration and boundary changes in two successive censuses.

The rates of natural increase reveal some important features in the dynamics of population growth in India (Table 5.3). Before 1921 there were positive rates of growth around 0.5 percent and slightly negative rates or nearly zero rate of growth in alternate decades. Since 1921 there has been an uninterrupted positive rate of population growth mainly as a consequence of some development in the socioeconomic and physical infrastructures. The transport system had been considerably developed, making it easier to rush food to famine areas in critical times. Elementary public health measures had been introduced; famines, pestilences, and epidemics were substantially eradicated; and there ensued a period of monotonic decline in mortality. This broad pattern is true for India as well as all its zones, although the rates of increase varied from zone to zone.

Recalling our basic point of inquiry, we note that the observed growth rates in India after 1921 are consistent with the conventional concept of quasi stability. And the observed growth rates before 1921 are consistent with the extended concept of quasi stability.

A pertinent question arises in this connection: What growth rate is to be associated with a quasi-stable age distribution at any given time? In a period when mortality rates are changing, the instantaneous growth rate differs from the period growth rate. This difference is predictable for a quasi-stable population of the conventional kind which reveals a regular upward trend in the growth rate, and the instantaneous growth rate may be approximated by taking the average of growth rates of some past years or decades and extrapolating them to the given moment. But in a quasi-stable population of the second kind, there is no regular trend in the rate of natural increase and extrapolation from past rates is impossible. The growth rate for a particular time may be zero, high positive, or high negative even though the long-term growth rate is low positive. The age distribution represents the long-term consequences of fertility and mortality conditions that produce a low and positive growth rate. To associate such an age distribution with the short-term effects of a sudden increase in mortality rates is neither theoretically sound nor practically helpful.

A practical solution lies in taking a twenty-year period as the basis of calculation so that the resultant growth rate represents the full

Table 5.3 Annual rate of natural increase: India and zones, 1881–1961

Period	India	Eastern	Central	Southern	Western	Northern
MALE						
1881–1891	0.007810	0.006172	0.007614	0.005885	0.017726	0.013078
1891–1901	-0.000743	0.004684	-0.002775	0.007487	-0.013302	-0.008415
1901–1911	0.006001	0.006768	0.004458	0.009504	0.009039	-0.000824
1911–1921	0.000076	0.000930	-0.001609	0.002637	-0.000548	0.000246
1881–1901	0.003533	0.005428	0.002420	0.006685	-0.001064	0.002253
1891–1911	0.002676	0.005728	0.000841	0.008450	-0.002131	0.004620
1901–1921	0.003086	0.003850	0.001425	0.006025	0.004245	-0.000289
1921–1931	0.010618	0.011591	0.008339	0.011165	0.012993	0.010909
1931–1941	0.012969	0.013011	0.012774	0.012479	0.012985	0.015572
1941–1951	0.013006	0.011951	0.010295	0.015111	0.013623	0.014913
1951–1961	0.018923	0.018850	0.017854	0.016669	0.020469	0.021924
FEMALE						
1881–1891	0.010511	0.004318	0.008223	0.014935	0.011797	0.015114
1891–1901	0.000168	0.004316	-0.001477	0.007402	-0.010998	-0.008412
1901–1911	0.005262	0.006001	0.002532	0.000407	0.008253	-0.003500
1911–1921	-0.000806	-0.001000	-0.001375	0.000186	-0.001567	-0.000113
1881–1901	0.005340	0.005372	0.003419	0.007402	0.000408	0.003351
1891–1911	0.002715	0.005160	0.000527	0.008405	-0.001373	-0.005956
1901–1921	0.002228	0.002500	-0.000136	0.005634	0.003343	-0.001806
1921–1931	0.010088	0.009704	0.007664	0.010836	0.012748	0.011933
1931–1941	0.012436	0.011331	0.012818	0.011630	0.013188	0.016472
1941–1951	0.013148	0.011637	0.010283	0.015476	0.015421	0.016251
1951–1961	0.018457	0.020644	0.016919	0.015558	0.020485	0.021700

Figure 5.1 Rate of natural increase: India and Eastern Zone, 1881—1961

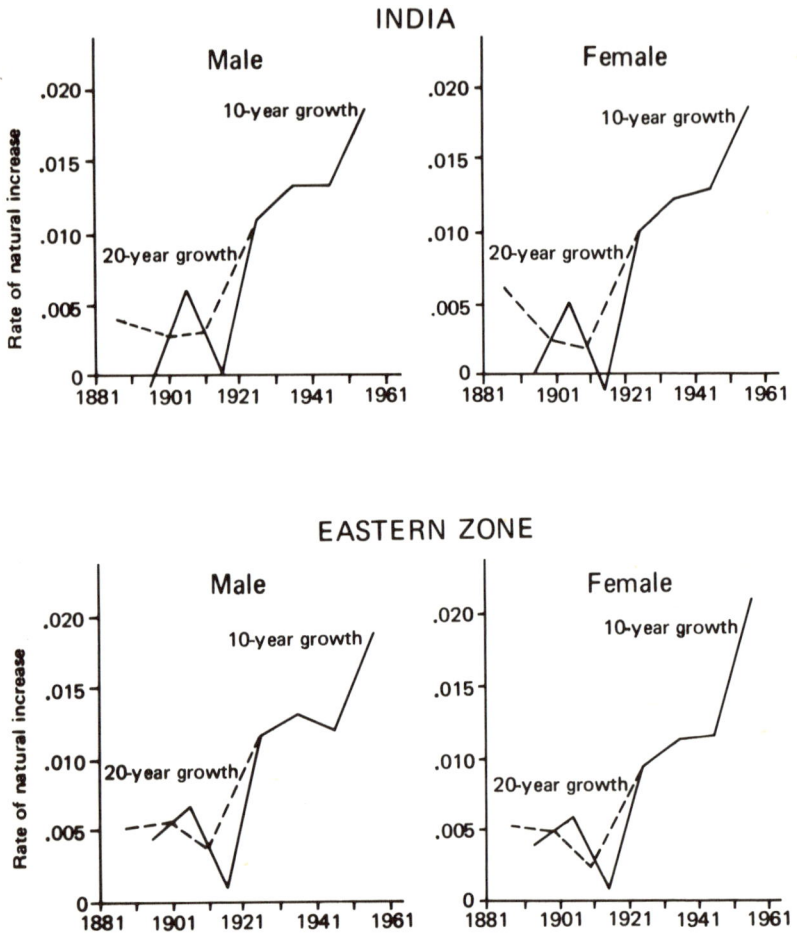

Figure 5.2 Rate of natural increase: Central and Southern Zones, 1881—1961

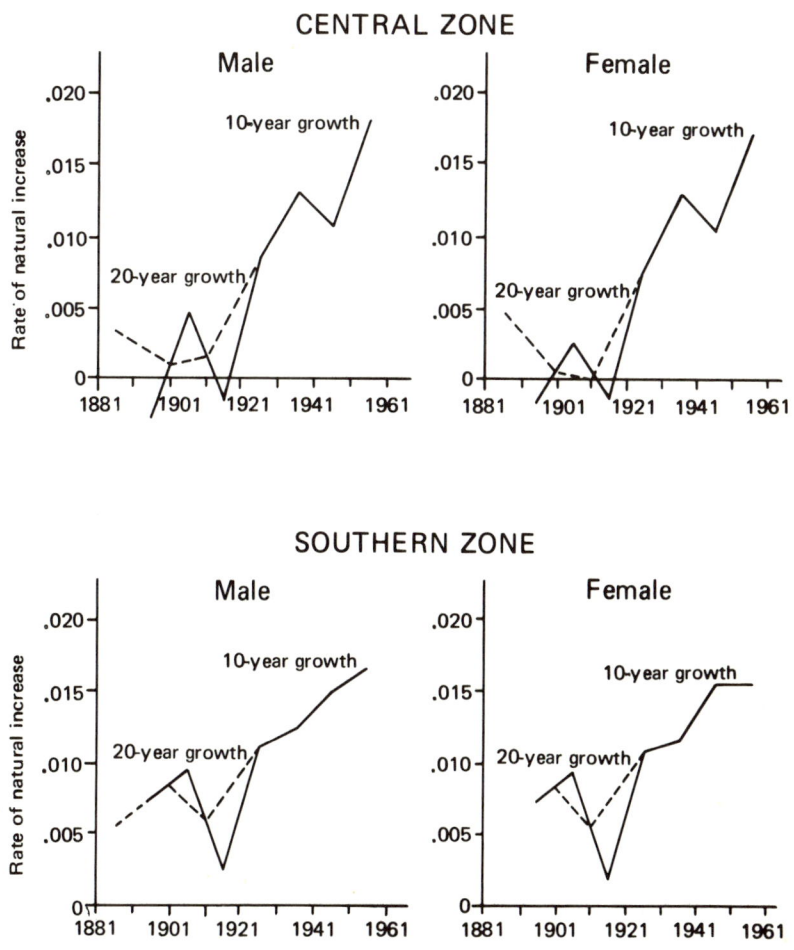

Figure 5.3 Rate of natural increase: Western and Northern Zones, 1881—1961

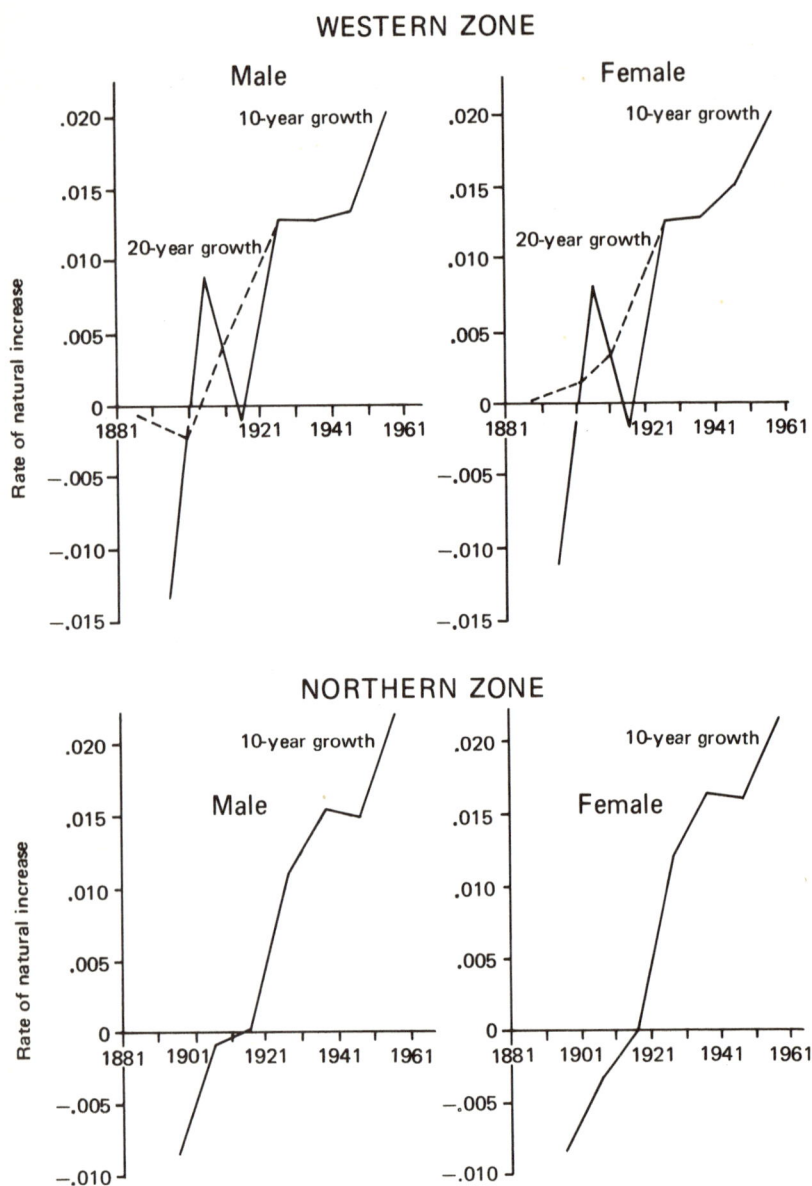

WESTERN ZONE

NORTHERN ZONE

range of high growth rate, zero growth rate, or negative growth rate. Table 5.3 and Figures 5.1 to 5.3 reveal that fluctuations in the decennial growth rate before 1921 are considerably ironed out when the rate is calculated on the basis of a twenty-year period.

⑥

Methodology used
to estimate fertility and mortality

One of the stated objectives of this study is to derive estimates of fertility and mortality in India by using the reconstructed age distribution obtained from census data on age and sex. United Nations Manual IV [99] lays down some new techniques for estimating the birth rate, death rate, gross reproduction rate, and life expectancy from incomplete data. (For a brief summary of these new methods see Coale [41].) From among a battery of new methods, we have selected two that are exclusively dependent on the information available in census tables: the method based on the quasi-stable population model and the method of forward projection.

The stable estimates are derived by drawing on the extensive tabulations of stable populations prepared by the Office of Population Research [42] and then correcting them for changes in mortality. Two observed parameters of the population for which estimates are required—the decennial growth rate and the age distribution—are used to identify the exact stable population implied by them. Once the stable population is identified, it is just a routine computation to read off the other parameters relating to this population. If we had dependable data on other parameters—gross reproduction rate, expectation of life at birth, childhood mortality, mean age—we could use any two of them (two nonredundant parameters, of course) to locate the exact stable population by interpolation from the above tabulations and derive the other variables. But under existing conditions of data availability, the growth rate and age distribution obtained from the census data seem to be the best estimating parameters we can hope to use.

The OPR stable populations

Since the stable population tables prepared by the Office of Population Research (OPR) hold a key position in our process of estimation, a brief discussion of their construction may be useful. For a full discussion the reader is referred to the original text [41]. Each stable age distribution is a combination of a model life table and a rate of natural increase according to Lotka's first fundamental equation,

$$c(a) = be^{-ra}p(a)$$

Since the age distributions are given in five-year intervals, the exact expression for the proportion in each age interval is

$$\int_{a_1}^{a_2} c(a)da = b \int_{a_1}^{a_2} e^{-ra}p(a)da$$

$$= be^{-r\bar{a}} \int_{a_1}^{a_2} p(a)da$$

The birth rate has been evaluated according to the relation

$$b = \frac{1}{\int_0^w e^{-ra}p(a)da}$$

The proportion of population in the age interval has been evaluated according to the relation

$$\int_{a_1}^{a_2} c(a)da = \frac{e^{-r\bar{a}} \int_{a_1}^{a_2} p(a)da}{\int_0^w e^{-ra}p(a)da}$$

The death rate has been obtained by subtracting the growth rate from the birth rate according to the relation

$$d = b - r$$

where b = birth rate of stable population

$c(a)$ = proportion of population at age a

r = intrinsic rate of natural increase

$p(a)$ = probability of survival from birth to age a

a_1 = lower limit of an age interval

a_2 = upper limit of an age interval

$\bar{a}$ = $(a_1 + a_2)/2$ for age intervals 0–5 to 75–80 and
$\bar{a} = 80 + e_{80}$ for age interval 80+

d = death rate of stable population

w = upper limit of highest age interval

The gross reproduction rate for each stable population has been cal-culated on the basis of the familiar relationship between the maternity schedule $m(a)$ and the intrinsic rate of natural increase given in Lotka's second fundamental equation:

$$\int_0^w e^{-ra} p(a)m(a)da = 1$$

It has been recognized that the same rate of natural increase (along with a given mortality schedule) may be associated with different val-ues of gross reproduction rate depending on different age patterns of fertility. Though a particular fertility schedule in conjunction with a given mortality schedule produces a unique age distribution, the same age distribution could be produced by a family of fertility schedules' working in conjunction with a given mortality schedule. Families of fertility schedules have therefore been differentiated according to the mean age of the schedules. Values of gross reproduction rate for each stable population have been provided corresponding to four such mean ages: 27, 29, 31, and 33 years. Various other parameters like net repro-duction rate, mean age of population, proportion of population in the age interval 15–44, and dependency ratio have been calculated by suitably applying the known relationships between these latter vari-ables and those obtained above.

A distinctive feature of these stable populations is that the life tables associated with them are differentiated not only according to the *level* of mortality but also according to the *age pattern* of mor-tality. With respect to the level of mortality, tabulations for the fe-male population have been made for 24 different values of e_0 varying from 20.0 years to 77.5 years at intervals of 2.5 years. Tabulations for the male population have been made also for 24 different values of e_0 varying from 18.03 years to 73.90 years. With respect to the age pat-tern of mortality, four families of life tables have been differentiated on the basis of the experience gathered from 326 life tables relating to different countries and periods. Close scrutiny of these tables reveals that the variation of mortality rate with age shows distinctive patterns; the life tables tend to cluster around four different lines representing distinct age patterns in different geographical regions: East, West, North, and South. Four sets of stable age distributions were provided corresponding to these four families.

Now a question arises: Which set of life tables represents the mortablity conditions in India—and, consequently, which set of stable age distributions is to be used for deriving estimates for India and its regions? Coale and Demeny suggest that the West life tables represent the wider mortality experience from the standpoint of heterogeneity of countries and cultures. The South, East, and North model life tables represent rather specific mortality experiences. In the absence of any knowledge about the Indian mortality pattern, it may be safer to impute the West pattern of mortality to India. Accordingly, we have used the West set of stable age distributions for our present purpose. Later in this chapter we return to a detailed discussion of the appropriateness of using the other three sets.

The estimation technique

The technique of deriving stable estimates by using the observed growth rate and age distribution as input parameters is illustrated in Table 6.1. The essence of the method is to identify the particular stable population determined by the given growth rate and cumulative proportion in any age sector. The identification is done by linear interpolation in two stages from the tabulations of stable population with different growth rates and at different levels of mortality prepared by the Office of Population Research. After the stable popula-

Table 6.1 Stable estimates of birth rate, death rate, gross reproduction rate, and life expectancy at birth: West Bengal, female, 1901
($r = 0.00532$)

Age segment used for estimation	Percentage of population in age segment	Stable estimate			
		BR	DR	GRR	e_0
0–5	13.50	40.28	34.96	2.489	28.79
0–10	27.59	52.53	47.21	3.211	21.84
0–15	37.17	46.93	41.61	2.877	24.53
0–20	46.87	46.15	40.83	2.831	24.93
0–25	55.55	45.36	39.96	2.780	25.46
0–30	64.46	47.85	42.53	2.932	24.06
0–35	72.38	50.47	45.15	3.087	22.73

tion is identified, the various vital rates are read off from the relevant columns of the model stable populations.

Note that the estimates made from different age sectors vary considerably from one another—a consequence of age distortions in Indian censuses, as well as past changes in mortality. Most of the differences in the estimated stable rates are due to biases in age data. If one wished to judge which stable estimates are nearer the true value, one would have to know the relative magnitude of enumeration error in the different age sectors. Valuable studies have been made on this subject by the Indian census actuaries and others. Special mention may be made of Vaidyanathan's study in the actuarial report of the 1931 census [109].

As these studies indicate, there is a considerable amount of regional variation and census-to-census variation in age preference and digital preference in the age returns. This variation results in different patterns of movement of the age ratios and sex ratios over the quinquennial age groups. However, beyond these complex variations a broad pattern of age bias does emerge for all the years and all the regions (summarized in Chapter 3). In considering the impact of age distribution on the stable estimates derived therefrom, one has to remember that the absolute number of persons in lower age groups is larger than in higher ones. This influences to a varying degree the quantitative effect of a proportionately equal deficit or excess in different age groups on the cumulative proportions of the population up to age 35.

Bringing all these factors to bear upon the stable estimates, we may hypothesize that the estimate based on the proportion of the population aged 0—5 is an underestimate whereas that based on the proportion aged 0—10 is an overestimate. The estimates based on proportions in the age groups 0—15, 0—30, and 0—35 are near the true values; those based on proportions in the age groups 0—20 and 0—25 are possibly somewhat lower than the true values.

It should be appreciated that the age distortions affect our estimates only to the extent that they carry people across the upper boundary of any age sector—e.g., when people below 35 years of age are carried up to higher ages or when people above 35 years of age are carried down to ages below 35. Age distortions within the broad age span of 0—35 do not affect our estimates made on the basis of the population proportion therein. The sequence of estimates made from the successive age sectors suggests that the undercount of infants and children in age group 0—5 results less from omissions than from an overstatement of their ages. If it were predominantly a case of omission, the estimated birth rate would tend to rise continuously in the successive age sectors. As the sum of the proportions in all age intervals is 100 in any case, the relative importance of the undercount in age group 0—5 would gradually diminish. If there were an undercount in higher age groups also, the effect of the undercount in age group 0—5 on the stable esti- mate derived therefrom would be limited to the extent of the rela- tively greater undercount in this age group (i.e., 0—5). And this effect would similarly diminish in successive age sectors. However, the phe- nomenon observed here is that the estimates go up and down and then up again. Such a sequence lends support to the hypothesis that the true stable birth rate lies between the limits indicated.*

An alternative method

A different method was used by the Indian census actuary (1961) for applying the stable technique to Indian age data. This method consists of deriving a life table from the reported age distribution and growth rate and then finding a birth rate consistent with this derived life table and growth rate. This method may be stated as follows. Starting from the stable age distribution,

$$c(a) = be^{-ra}p(a)$$

we obtain

$$c(a)e^{ra} = bp(a)$$

That is, multiplying the reported age distribution by the factor e^{ra} we get a life table with radix b. Since age group 0—5 is often severely mis- reported, we may use the expectation of life at age 10, instead of the expectation of life at age 0, for finding the mortality level. Once the level of mortality is found, we use the model life table for getting the detailed values of $p(a)$. Then, by using the formula

---

* This method was suggested in the U.N. Population Studies No. 42 [92:12—28, 61—72]. The limitations of the method are recognized. The technique of using the cumulated age proportions takes care of the relative underenumeration in age group 0—4 and relative overenumeration in age group 5—9. But when whole families are missed by the census enumerator, this method does not serve as a corrective. If there is proportionate underenumeration in all ages, only the growth rate is affected—not the age distribution. This method tries to find a so- lution to the problem of age-selective underenumeration. To cope with the problem of sex-selective underenumeration, we constructed estimates sepa- rately for the male and the female population and examined their consistency. (See Chapter 7.)

$$b = \frac{1}{\int_0^W e^{-ra}p(a)da}$$

we find the birth rate. Table 6.2 illustrates this method. The estimate of the female birth rate for West Bengal (1901) determined according to this method is 54.99.

It may seem at first sight that this method gives a single estimate and hence is superior. But it gives a single estimate precisely because we have chosen a single life table on the basis of the computed value of e_{10}. If we had chosen a life table on the basis of the estimated values of e_5, e_{15}, e_{20}, and so forth, each life table would have been different from the others and we would have obtained a separate estimate of b in each case. In the method discussed earlier we do not know the mortality level. We therefore apply cumulative age proportions up to different ages and get correspondingly different mortality levels and different birth rates. As a matter of fact, in the alternative method we plug in the same values or parameters as in the earlier method. The only difference is that we return a roundabout way via the so-called reported life table. Thus we take the additional step of deflating the age distribution that is assumed to be stable and then convert it into a stationary age distribution. Finally, the likelihood that a small error in ℓ_{10} produces a big error in e_{10}—and hence in the life table—makes the method less acceptable to us. When we make estimates from Indian age data, we always remember that there may be biases in the data and, hence, errors in the estimates derived from them. Rather than presenting a single value as The Estimate, we prefer to provide a range of values within which the real value is expected to lie.

Age pattern of mortality in India

We may now turn to the question of the applicability of the West life tables to Indian conditions in preference to other regional model life tables. In the absence of reliable information on the age pattern of mortality in India, we fall back on indirect evidence in support of the assumption that the West pattern of mortality describes Indian conditions better than others.

Comparative estimates of the vital rates have been derived for the female population in India (1911) in conjunction with each of the four sets of model life tables and corresponding stable populations (Table 6.3). Estimates of the birth rate made by using the East or South life tables are around 55 per 1,000. They seem to be too high and extremely deviant from estimates hitherto made by demographers.

Table 6.2 Estimates of birth rate and life expectancy at age 10 by alternative method: West Bengal, female, 1901 ($r = 0.00532$)

Age group	$c(a, a + 5)$	$(a + 2.5)$	$r(a + 2.5)$	$e^{r(a + 2.5)}$	$\dfrac{c(a, a + 5)}{e^{r(a + 2.5)}} \times$	$(_5L_a)/\ell_0$	$e^{-r(a + 2.5)}/\ell_0 \times (_5L_a)/\ell_0$
0–5	0.1350	2.5	0.013300	1.0134	0.136807	2.915048	2.876503
5–10	0.1409	7.5	0.039900	1.0407	0.146635	2.319046	2.228352
10–15	0.0958	12.5	0.066500	1.0688	0.102387	2.171768	2.031969
15–20	0.0970	17.5	0.093100	1.0976	0.106464	2.034077	1.853204
20–25	0.0867	22.5	0.119700	1.1272	0.097725	1.871041	1.659902
25–30	0.0892	27.5	0.146300	1.1575	0.103253	1.694925	1.464298
30–35	0.0792	32.5	0.172900	1.1887	0.094149	1.516044	1.275380
35–40	0.0578	37.5	0.199500	1.2208	0.070562	1.338875	1.096719
40–45	0.0618	42.5	0.226100	1.2537	0.077479	1.170729	0.933819
45–50	0.0360	47.5	0.252700	1.2875	0.046350	1.015103	0.788430
50–55	0.0430	52.5	0.279300	1.3222	0.056855	0.858696	0.649445
55–60	0.0189	57.5	0.305900	1.3578	0.025663	0.692931	0.510334
60–65	0.0260	62.5	0.332500	1.3944	0.036256	0.515954	0.370019
65–70	0.0171	67.5	0.359100	1.4320	0.024488	0.341046	0.238161
70–75	0.0096	72.5	0.385700	1.4706	0.014118	0.192137	0.130652
75–80	0.0044	77.5	0.412300	1.5103	0.006645	0.084013	0.055627
80+	0.0016	82.5	0.438900	1.5510	0.002482	0.032470	0.020935
					1.148318		18.183749

NOTE: $\ell_{10} = 1/10\ (0.146635 + 0.102387) = 0.0249022$

$T_{10} = 0.864876$

$e_{10} = 0.880792/0.0249022 = 34.730907$

$b = 1/18.183749 = 0.054994$

$BR = 54.99$

Table 6.3 Stable estimates of birth rate, death rate, gross reproduction rate, and life expectancy at birth using regional model life tables and stable populations: India, female, 1911

Measure and model life table	Age segment used as estimating parameter						
	0–5	0–10	0–15	0–20	0–25	0–30	0–35
BR							
West	43.44	52.11	47.88	42.00	43.17	46.19	50.67
South	44.12	55.68	53.70	48.23	50.61	55.73	62.25
East	50.51	64.39	60.19	51.60	53.64	58.51	64.71
North	40.63	49.32	47.43	42.90	44.72	48.38	53.46
DR							
West	38.18	46.85	42.62	36.74	37.91	40.93	45.41
South	38.86	50.42	48.44	42.97	45.35	50.47	56.99
East	45.25	59.33	54.93	46.34	48.38	53.25	59.45
North	35.37	44.06	42.17	37.64	39.46	43.12	48.20
GRR ($\overline{M}$ = 27)							
West	2.672	3.185	2.933	2.588	2.656	2.832	3.099
South	2.810	3.536	3.409	3.065	3.213	3.539	3.955
East	3.116	3.957	3.694	3.181	3.303	3.593	3.964
North	2.562	3.091	2.975	2.698	2.809	3.033	3.350
e_0							
West	26.57	21.98	24.01	27.46	26.73	24.88	22.58
South	26.32	20.66	21.47	23.99	22.78	20.64	17.98
East	22.86	17.10	18.88	22.35	21.52	19.56	17.05
North	28.53	23.31	24.27	26.95	25.80	23.79	21.45

A large discrepancy from earlier estimates by itself may not be a convincing argument against the South or East model life tables. The point is that it is highly improbable that the birth rate in India was 55 (or above) in 1911. The birth rate in the decade 1951–1961 was about 40 according to currently available (1971) estimates and around 44 according to our estimates. If the birth rate were around 55 in the decade 1901–1911 and 44 in the decade 1951–1961, the age distribution in 1961 would have been older than in 1911. But instead of getting older, the 1961 age distribution has become a little younger than in earlier years. Therefore the birth rate in 1911 must have been lower than 55. An alternative possibility is that the birth rate was still around 50 in the decade 1951–1961, in which case the death rate would have to be above 30 for these rates to be consistent with observed population growth. This latter alternative is extremely unlikely.

The distinctive features of the South and East life tables are high infant mortality, low young and adult mortality, and increasingly high mortality at ages above 50 [42]. But infant mortality in India with a given life expectancy seems to be much lower than in the East or South life tables. Some recent surveys that are believed to have been more intensively and carefully conducted than most of the past surveys yield estimates supporting our contention. The Khanna study [55, 56] in 11 Punjab villages (1956–1969) reveals an infant mortality rate of 161.7 during the period 1956–1959. The Poonamallu survey (1951–1952), confined to a rural area in Tamil Nadu, gave an estimated infant mortality rate of 140.73 per 1,000 live births [87].

The U.N. Mysore study, based on a much bigger sample, provided an estimate of 168.1 and 110.9 for rural plains and urban areas in the State of Karnataka in the year 1952 [95]. The pooled estimate for the combined rural and urban areas would be around 154. The corresponding life expectancies were not given. Our estimates of life expectancy in the zones of India for the decade 1951–1961 range from 35 to 39 years. It is highly probable that the true life expectancy in the various zones was below 40 years. Corresponding to a female e_0 of 40 years, the female infant mortality rate would be 200.96, 144.04, 254.50, and 194.08 for West, North, East, and South life tables respectively.

The sample registration system initiated in 1964, which largely avoids the pitfalls of the basic registration system, provides a pooled estimate: an infant mortality rate in India of about 136.8 (male and female together) along with an estimated e_0 of 47.3 for the period 1968–1972 [84]. For a female e_0 of 47.5 the female infant mortality rate is 174.26, 126.57, 183.65, and 154.58 for the West, North, East, and South life tables respectively [42]. The estimates provided in these surveys are not sacrosanct. But collectively they may be taken as an indication that for a given e_0 the infant mortality rate in India is nearer to that in the West than in the other model life tables. Besides, child mortality and young adult mortality in India are not so low as one would expect at comparative levels of e_0. Among women, the incidence of puerperal mortality is high; and among both men and women, young adult mortality is higher than in East life tables.

Comparative q_x values

Another kind of indirect evidence is provided by a comparison of the q_x values in the Indian census life tables and the different families of model life tables at the same level of mortality. While making this comparison one must bear in mind the severe limitations from which Indian census life tables suffer [25, 109]. Life tables for India were prepared by comparing the age distributions at two consecutive censuses and obtaining the census survival ratios for different age groups. The age data had to be subjected to a drastic smoothing operation before the P_x values could be estimated. Such a smoothing operation might have ironed out many real peaks and troughs in the Indian age distribution, rendered the smoothed age distribution largely fictitious, and led to an element of arbitrariness in the Indian life tables.*

A study of the interpolated q_x values for the male and female population in Indian life tables and the West, North, East, and South model life tables for the same level of mortality reveals that with a given value of e_{10}, the q_x values in Indian tables match better with those in the West and North tables than those in the East and South. Comparison of the deviations of model q_x values is facilitated if the 14 deviations are summarized in a single index. It is suggested that the root-mean-square deviation of the model q_x values $[(q_x)m]$ from the corresponding Indian q_x values $[(q_x)i]$ may be used as such an index (Table 6.4). The root-mean-square deviations have been worked out for each family of the model life tables for the years 1951 and 1961. For the other three census years they have been calculated only for the West and North and U.N. model life tables for the male population and the West and U.N. tables for the female population.

The values of e_{10} in India for census years 1901, 1911, and 1931 were found to be considerably lower than the lowest values of e_{10} (at mortality level 1) indicated in the South and East tables for the male population and the South, East, and North tables for the female population. Consequently, model life tables corresponding to e_{10} in Indian life tables for 1901, 1911, and 1931 could not be identified.

In spite of the limitations of Indian census life tables, it is significant that the deviations of model q_x values from Indian q_x values are smaller for the West tables than for others. It adds support to our hypothesis that the West tables conform better to the Indian mortality pattern than do the other three families. Moreover, the bottom rows of Table 6.4 show that the root-mean-square deviations for the U.N. tables and the West tables are nearly equal. One may infer that the U.N. tables are as good as the West tables for estimating vital rates from Indian age distributions.

---

* It is not suggested that valid life tables cannot be constructed from age data. In countries like South Korea where age data are fairly reliable, valid life tables can be derived.

The U.N. model life tables

An important consideration in favor of the West model life tables was that the regional model life tables were—but the U.N. tables [90, 104] were not—differentiated with respect to distinctive patterns of mortality observed in various groups of countries. As many as 130 life tables were used in the preparation of the West tables, and all of them had been constructed from actual mortality data. But the U.N. tables were based not only on life tables constructed from actual mortality data but also on those constructed by comparing age distributions at different times. As a matter of fact, among the 158 life tables used by the United Nations there were four Indian life tables relating to the census decades 1891–1901, 1901–1911, 1921–1931, and 1941–1951. This imparts an element of unreality to the U.N. model life tables and partly explains why the deviations of q_x values in the U.N. tables from Indian q_x values were small at low levels of life expectancy. Of three life tables with a value of e_{10} around 30 years, two were Indian life tables. The other two Indian life tables used by the U.N. had a value of e_{10} around 35 years. Thus the Indian q_x values used as input variables in building the regressions must have greatly influenced

Table 6.4 Root-mean-square deviations of q_x values in model life tables from q_x values in Indian census life tables with same e_{10}: male and female, 1901–1961

Model life table	Root-mean-square deviation				
	1901	1911	1931	1951	1961
WEST					
Male	28.53	40.94	21.32	12.94	25.62
Female	23.29	32.48	53.82	25.62	42.64
NORTH					
Male	44.42	64.35[a]	40.61	23.19	33.77
Female	b	b	b	25.00	50.11
EAST					
Male	b	b	b	30.38	34.64
Female	b	b	b	72.48	72.29
SOUTH					
Male	b	b	b	39.84	43.41
Female	b	b	b	67.89	76.84
U.N.					
Male	25.87	30.18	14.23	12.36	26.42
Female	12.86	4.44	23.46	19.76	41.64

a North table values for 1911 have been extrapolated.

b Parameters for model life tables could not be obtained by extrapolation.

the estimated q_x values in the U.N. model life tables, particularly at low levels of life expectancy.

A brief reference may also be made here to the three sets of model life tables presented in the U.N. Population Studies No. 39, published in 1968. These three sets have been designated the downward-deviating model life tables, the intermediate series model life tables, and the upward-deviating model life tables [104:77—115]. The intermediate series model life tables are identical with the initial set of model tables prepared by the United Nations in 1955. The differentiation of upward-deviating and downward-deviating series was made on the basis of the results obtained in a factor-analytical study of the 158 life tables used by the United Nations in 1955 [71:139—168].

Our preference for the West model life tables is not based on methodological differences in the preparation of the regional tables or the U.N. tables, but on the stronger data base of the regional tables. Whatever the merit of the factor-analytical study, the data base of the 1968 U.N. tables was weaker than that of West tables.

Using a period growth rate for estimation

The question is: Which growth rate is to be used for estimating fertility and mortality—the growth rate based on twenty-year periods, that based on ten-year periods, or the instantaneous growth rate prevailing at a given time? Logically, the growth rate and the age distribution should relate to the same time. Therefore the relevant growth rate to be used is the instantaneous growth rate.

We have worked out the period average growth rates and instantaneous growth rates in simulated projections under assumptions of constant fertility and changing mortality broadly similar to conditions in India in the respective phases. Table 6.5 shows the differences between the instantaneous growth rates and average annual growth rates based on ten-year and twenty-year periods in hypothetical populations projected with three alternative levels of fertility (constant GRR = 3.100, 3.200, and 3.400) and under the assumption of mortality conditions resembling those in India during the period 1881—1921.* Table 6.5 read jointly with Table 5.3 shows that the fluctuations in the ten-year growth rates before 1921 are similar in the simulated projections and actual Indian conditions. Moreover, the peaks and troughs in the ten-year growth rates occur in the same manner in the simulated projec-

---

* The assumed values of e_0 for time points equivalent to 1891, 1896, 1901, 1906, 1911, 1916, and 1921 are 21.45, 21.45, 18.00, 22.00, 22.50, 22.50, and 17.36 respectively.

Table 6.5 Instantaneous and average growth rates in simulated projections assuming fluctuations in mortality similar to those in India, 1881–1921

Type of growth rate and period	Annual growth rate per person		
	GRR = 3.100	GRR = 3.200	GRR = 3.400
Instantaneous, 1901	−0.00033	−0.00398	−0.00182
Average, 1891–1901	−0.00166	0.00136	0.00352
Average, 1881–1901	0.00048	0.00258	0.00474
Instantaneous, 1911	0.00369	0.00501	0.00732
Average, 1901–1911	0.00292	0.00267	0.000
Average, 1891–1911	0.00063	0.00202	0.00420
Instantaneous, 1921	−0.00188	−0.00634	−0.00425
Average, 1911–1921	−0.00222	0.00212	0.00429
Average, 1901–1921	0.00034	0.00240	0.00458

tions as in the Indian conditions and are similarly ironed out when the rates of natural increase are calculated on the basis of twenty-year periods.

Instantaneous growth rates and ten-year growth rates are also worked out for simulated projections under assumptions of a monotonic decline in mortality and constant fertility (Table 6.6). The time path of mortality changes is different under different assumptions. In a period of declining mortality, it is the different time paths of mortality changes rather than differences in the level of fertility that cause the discrepancies between instantaneous growth rates and period average growth rates. We think that the possible differences between the instantaneous and period average growth rates in the actual Indian

Table 6.6 Instantaneous and average growth rates in simulated projections assuming GRR = 3.200 and a monotonic decline in mortality

Type of growth rate and period	Annual growth rate per person			
	Mortality assumption A	Mortality assumption B	Mortality assumption C	Mortality assumption D
Instantaneous, 1931	0.01103	0.01585	0.01457	0.01314
Average, 1921–1931	0.00797	0.01107	0.01079	0.00967
Instantaneous, 1941	0.00873	0.01471	0.01361	0.01484
Average, 1931–1941	0.00926	0.01543	0.01290	0.01350
Instantaneous, 1951	0.01035	0.01827	0.01513	0.02042
Average, 1941–1951	0.00910	0.01677	0.01380	0.01724
Instantaneous, 1961	0.02222	0.02205	0.02360	0.02802
Average, 1951–1961	0.01610	0.02026	0.01915	0.02404

NOTE: For the time path of mortality changes under the various assumptions see Table 6.9.

conditions are covered within the range of such differences in the simulated projections. Table 6.6 indicates that the discrepancies are larger for 1931 and 1961 than for 1941 and 1951. This is evidently due to the fact that recovery from the high mortality conditions of pre-1920 years was fast in the decade 1921–1931 and that the decade 1951–1961 witnessed a sharp acceleration in the rate of mortality decline.

Estimates of fertility and mortality have been derived from the same age distribution using successively the average annual growth rates based on ten-year periods and twenty-year periods. It is noteworthy that the estimates based on twenty-year growth rates are more in conformity with similar estimates derived for other years than those estimated on the basis of ten-year growth rates. The age distribution in India is not the result of the transient conditions of a decade: it has been shaped by the long-term conditions of fertility and mortality. The use of a negative or near-zero growth rate as an estimating parameter in conjunction with an age distribution that bears the mark of a long-term positive growth rate leads to estimates of birth rates and death rates that are fantastically high. Hence, from the standpoints of both logic and expediency, it is better to use the growth rates based on twenty-year periods than those based on ten-year periods.*

R elasticity of the estimates

Despite attempts to make correct estimates of the rate of natural increase, there exists the possibility of errors in such estimates. The errors arise mainly out of three factors: differential undercount of population in different censuses; overestimation or underestimation of net migrational growth; and use of an average growth rate over a period in place of an instantaneous growth rate.

As regards the differential undercount, if the degree of omission is the same in two consecutive censuses, the growth rate remains unaffected. It is only to the extent of a differential undercount in two consecutive censuses that the growth rate is underestimated or overestimated. To suggest a ceiling as the maximum possible error on this ground would be highly speculative. As experience accumulated over the years and awareness of census operations developed, the degree of undercount expectedly diminished. It is believed that between two consecutive censuses a 2 or 3 percent differential undercount may be a reasonable estimate of the possible error. For the country as a whole,

---

* The snag, however, is that the longer the period for which the average annual rates are calculated, the greater the possible error in the computed rate of natural increase—owing to the differential undercount in different censuses.

the error in estimates of net migration is negligible. For the zones, the contribution of migration was within the range of 2 percent for all census years up to 1941. In the next two decades migration contributed from +1 to +2 percent of the total population in the Central and Southern Zones. In the Eastern, Western, and Northern Zones, the net contribution of migration was larger, but in no case did it exceed +5 percent. Assuming a maximum possible error of 50 percent in the estimated contribution of migration, the error in estimated growth rate would be within a range of 1.25 percent per year. Errors arising out of a wrong count of total population and wrong estimation of migrational growth may not occur in the same direction and hence may not have cumulative effects. Even if they did, the maximum possible error in the estimated annual growth rate would be +0.225 percent for India and all zones up to 1941, +0.300 percent for India and the Central and Southern Zones for 1951 and 1961, and +0.425 percent for the other zones for 1951 and 1961. It is therefore necessary to examine to what extent the derived estimates of vital rates are affected by variations in growth rate used as an estimating parameter.

When the age distribution is given, the higher the given value of R, the higher the estimated value of e_0 and the lower the estimate of birth rate, death rate, and GRR. Conversely, the lower the given value of R, the lower the estimate of e_0 and the higher the estimates of birth rate, death rate, and GRR. For the purpose of illustration, we have taken the female age distribution of India for 1961 and have derived 18 sets of estimates of the vital rates with 18 hypothetical growth rates as estimating parameters. The growth rates (r) have been so chosen that they deviate from the observed growth rate by an amount equal to ±0.00050, ±0.00100, ±0.00150, ±0.00200, ±0.00250, ±0.00300, ±0.00350, ±0.00400, and ±0.00450. Table 6.7 provides five sets of estimates corresponding to five values of r: 0.01396, 0.01596, 0.01796, 0.01996, and 0.02296. Two generalizations follow: (1) as r increases, the estimated birth rate decreases by about 1,000r; (2) as r increases, the estimated death rate decreases by about 2,000r.

Linear regressions have been fitted with y for the estimated vital rate and x for the input value of R (= 1,000r); the number of observations in each case is 18. By differentiating the regression function ($y = a + bx$), we have a measure of the R elasticity of the estimated vital rates. Therefore

$$\frac{dy}{dx} = b$$

Table 6.7 Stable estimates of birth rate, gross reproduction rate, death rate, and life expectancy at birth derived from female age distribution of India (1961) with different assumed growth rates

Assumed growth rate	Age segment						
	0–5	0–10	0–15	0–20	0–25	0–30	0–35
BR							
0.01396	46.81	60.98	53.46	46.08	45.94	47.79	48.40
0.01596	45.37	57.99	50.74	43.82	43.80	45.81	46.56
0.01796	43.62	55.15	48.41	41.99	42.11	43.80	44.89
0.01996	42.08	52.51	45.94	40.09	40.30	42.20	43.14
0.02296	39.85	48.89	42.85	37.50	37.88	39.95	41.04
GRR ($\bar{M}$ = 27)							
0.01396	2.922	3.815	3.332	2.877	2.868	2.982	3.021
0.01596	2.846	3.644	3.180	2.756	2.755	2.873	2.831
0.01796	2.752	3.843	3.052	2.652	2.659	2.763	2.831
0.01996	2.666	3.329	2.908	2.544	2.557	2.674	2.732
0.02296	2.550	3.126	2.738	2.403	2.427	2.557	2.625
DR							
0.01396	32.85	47.02	39.50	32.12	31.98	33.82	34.44
0.01596	29.41	42.03	34.78	27.86	27.84	29.85	30.60
0.01796	25.41	37.19	30.45	24.03	24.15	25.84	26.93
0.01996	22.12	32.55	25.98	20.13	20.34	22.24	23.18
0.02296	16.89	25.93	19.89	14.54	14.92	16.99	18.08
e_0							
0.01396	30.98	23.05	26.96	31.53	31.64	30.24	29.81
0.01596	33.89	25.61	29.79	35.16	35.17	33.51	32.87
0.01796	37.48	28.54	33.20	39.24	39.11	37.48	36.28
0.01996	44.44	31.80	37.26	43.93	43.66	41.29	40.18
0.02296	48.46	37.54	44.24	52.25	51.61	48.30	46.69

The regression coefficient itself is a measure of the R elasticity of the estimated values. Table 6.8 sets out the fitted values of a and b and the respective correlation coefficients for the four estimated vital rates. Figure 6.1 depicts the regressions graphically. Note that the correlation coefficients are close to −1.0 or +1.0, indicating that the relationships are truly functional. That they come so near their theoretical limits testifies to the validity of the estimation process as well as to the reliability and internal consistency of the OPR stable population tables used in the present study.

Note also that the R elasticity of the estimated birth rates varies from −0.8 to −1.3 for the different age sectors and that of the estimated death rates ranges from −1.8 to −2.2. Similarly, R elasticity for GRR and e_0 lies within a range of −0.5 to −0.7 and +1.6 to +2.3 respectively. The implication is that, given the range of uncertainty in

Table 6.8 Parameters of regression equation $y = a + bx$ and values of correlation coefficient (r_{xy}) between growth rate (x) used as estimating parameter and derived estimates of birth rate, gross reproduction rate, and life expectancy at birth

Age segment used for estimates	r_{xy}	a	b
y = birth rate			
0–5	−0.9996	58.0048	−0.7950
0–10	−0.9991	79.4392	−1.3426
0–15	−0.9989	69.5561	−1.1756
0–20	−0.9978	58.7998	−0.9333
0–25	−0.9961	57.2831	−0.8458
0–30	−0.9890	59.3090	−0.8545
0–35	−0.9984	59.4187	−0.8072
y = GRR $(\overline{M} = 27)$			
0–5	−0.9992	3.5264	−0.0428
0–10	−0.9925	4.8679	−0.0769
0–15	−0.9990	4.2392	−0.0662
0–20	−0.9978	3.5827	−0.0517
0–25	−0.9989	3.5205	−0.0478
0–30	−0.9904	3.6272	−0.0474
0–35	−0.9975	3.6078	−0.0432
$y = e_0$			
0–5	0.9913	2.4571	1.9801
0–10	0.9972	0.0724	1.6032
0–15	0.9835	0.6906	1.3520
0–20	0.9957	−1.2296	2.2892
0–25	0.9891	0.9179	2.1663
0–30	0.9973	1.6728	2.0024
0–35	0.9977	3.3018	1.8585

the computed values of R, the estimates of birth rate and gross reproduction rate are likely to be nearer their true values than those for death rates or expectation of life at birth.

The need for correction

Correction of the stable estimates for changes in mortality is necessary because a history of mortality changes produces an age distribution somewhat different from that produced by a regime of unchanging mortality—assuming the current rates of mortality to be the same in both cases. These differences are responsible for an error in estimates of vital rates derived from age distribution [38]. The magnitude of the error depends on the extent to which the changes in mortality pull away the resulting quasi-stable age distribution from the stable one. It is therefore useful to examine to what extent the quasi-stable age dis-

Figure 6.1 Regression of stable estimates on values of 1000 *r* as an estimating parameter with age segment 0–30

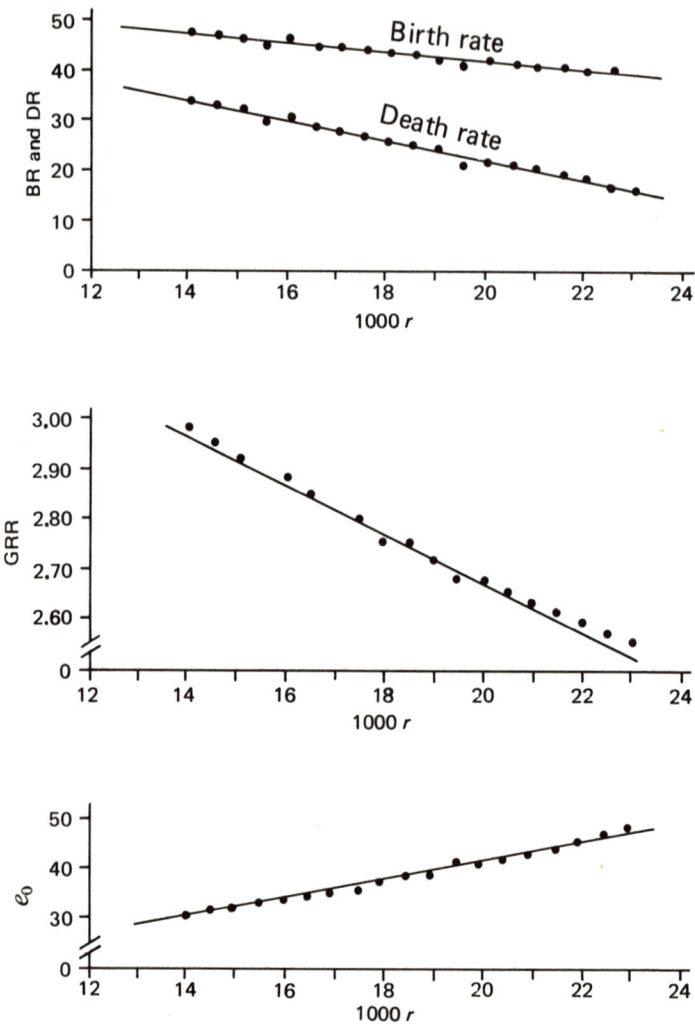

tribution of India deviates from the corresponding stable age distribution implied by prevailing levels of fertility and mortality.

To obtain a measure of this deviation, we generated hypothetical quasi-stable age distributions by assuming constant fertility and changing mortality similar to those in India. We then compared the simulated quasi-stable age distributions with the stable age distributions implied by the same level of fertility and the ruling level of mortality at the moment. The probable level of mortality in India in a particular year is obtained from the stable estimates of e_0 derived from the female age distribution of India for that year.

Since the exact time pattern of change in the values of e_0 in India is not known, we have used four sets of assumptions about changes in mortality to obtain values of e_0 (Table 6.9). These values of e_0 accord with the stable estimates derived from the age distribution and growth rate in India and its zones for the respective periods. Moreover, they are corroborated by whatever historical information on mortality changes we have from various sources. It is expected that the actual levels of mortality in India and its zones are covered within the range of mortality levels indicated by these alternatives.

Whereas the quasi-stable age distributions $[cqs(a)]$ have been obtained from the simulated projections, the corresponding stable age distributions $[cs(a)]$ have been obtained by interpolation from the West set of stable populations prepared by the Office of Population Research. Along with the respective constant values of GRR, the estimated current values of e_0 for 1911, 1921, 1931, 1941, 1951, and 1961 have been used for such interpolation. The ratios $cqs(a)/cs(a)$ for the sets of corresponding quasi-stable and stable populations under the

Table 6.9 Values of e_0 under various mortality assumptions: 1911–1961

| Time (t) | Equivalent year | Values of e_0 under mortality assumptions | | | |
		A	B	C	D
0	1911	22.00	27.50	23.00	22.12
5	1916	16.63	20.00	16.63	22.93
10	1921	19.08	20.00	20.00	23.74
15	1926	25.50	27.50	28.00	26.36
20	1931	27.00	30.00	30.00	28.97
25	1936	27.00	32.00	30.00	30.24
30	1941	27.00	32.00	31.50	31.52
35	1946	27.00	35.00	31.50	34.30
40	1951	27.00	35.00	31.50	37.09
45	1956	32.00	37.50	35.50	42.50
50	1961	38.00	38.50	40.00	47.91

various assumptions of mortality changes and fertility levels are set out in Table 6.10 and depicted in Figure 6.2.

All these ratios are equal to 1.0 in the initial year (t_0) equivalent to 1911 in India—up to which year mortality conditions are assumed to have been constant. Once mortality starts changing, the ratios depart from 1.0—an indication of the discrepancy between quasi-stable and stable age distributions. At time t_{10} (equivalent to the year 1921) the ratios for age sectors 0–5 and 0–10 drop below 1.0—a consequence of the so-called left-arm effect of rising mortality. As time advances, the ratios for the different time points and different age segments move to and fro and up and down. Note that the ratios for t_{10} as well as t_{20} through t_{60} are different from those indicated by Coale. The reason for this difference is that the impact of the rising death rates in the decade $t_0 - t_{10}$ is felt on the projected age distributions. Besides, Coale assumes a uniform rate of increase in e_0 over time [38:182–187]. In our projections the rate of increase in e_0 per unit of time varies from decade to decade.*

Methods for correction

Coale and Demeny observed empirically that the bias in the estimates derived from a quasi-stable age distribution is not sensitive to fertility levels and is approximately a linear function of the rate of mortality decline. That is, the faster the rate the larger the deviations from stable age distribution.

Coale and Demeny developed the concept of K and defined it as the rate of annual increase in fertility equivalent in its effect on the age distribution to the given annual change in mortality. K is approximately given by the expression

$$K = \frac{1}{t} \log_e \left[\frac{\ell_5(t)}{\ell_5(0)} \times \frac{{}_5P_{25}(t)}{{}_5P_{25}(0)} \right]$$

It follows that for different values of K, the factors for correcting the

---

* Such exercises were repeated with the same values of e_0 but with GRR = 3.2 and 3.4. The results are not reproduced here. But it was observed that the ratios $cqs(a)/cs(a)$ do not differ significantly between different levels of fertility, the course of changes in mortality being given. The ratios do differ significantly between different assumptions regarding changes in mortality, the level of fertility being given.

Table 6.10 Ratios $cqs(a)/cs(a)$ with GRR (29) = 3.000 and mortality assumptions A, B, C, D

Age segment t =	0	10	20	30	40	50
MORTALITY ASSUMPTION A						
e_0 =	22.00	19.08	27.00	27.00	27.00	38.00
0–5	1.000	0.980	1.017	0.965	0.974	0.993
0–10	1.000	0.982	0.994	0.982	0.970	0.969
0–15	1.000	1.002	0.958	0.997	0.973	0.949
0–20	1.000	1.014	0.944	0.993	0.983	0.941
0–25	1.000	1.018	0.951	0.975	0.994	0.944
0–30	1.000	1.018	0.961	0.967	0.994	0.954
0–35	1.000	1.017	0.970	0.970	0.984	0.966
0–40	1.000	1.014	0.977	0.976	0.980	0.973
MORTALITY ASSUMPTION B						
e_0 =	27.50	20.00	30.00	32.00	35.00	38.50
0–5	1.000	0.998	1.027	0.978	0.966	0.995
0–10	1.000	1.016	0.994	0.994	0.962	0.986
0–15	1.000	1.042	0.957	1.000	0.967	0.977
0–20	1.000	1.052	0.950	0.988	0.975	0.972
0–25	1.000	1.052	0.962	0.969	0.982	0.973
0–30	1.000	1.047	0.973	0.964	0.979	0.978
0–35	1.000	1.040	0.982	0.971	0.970	0.984
0–40	1.000	1.032	0.988	0.978	0.970	0.983
MORTALITY ASSUMPTION C						
e_0 =	23.00	20.00	30.00	31.50	31.50	40.00
0–5	1.000	0.974	1.018	0.953	0.969	1.010
0–10	1.000	0.976	0.993	0.969	0.965	0.993
0–15	1.000	0.997	0.953	0.985	0.968	0.975
0–20	1.000	1.011	0.936	0.982	0.977	0.967
0–25	1.000	1.016	0.943	0.964	0.987	0.966
0–30	1.000	1.017	0.954	0.955	0.965	0.972
0–35	1.000	1.016	0.964	0.960	0.978	0.980
0–40	1.000	1.014	0.972	0.967	0.973	0.984
MORTALITY ASSUMPTION D[a]						
e_0 =	22.12	23.74	28.97	31.52	37.09	47.91
0–5	1.004	1.002	0.990	0.974	0.973	0.977
0–10	1.009	0.994	0.979	0.976	0.965	0.967
0–15	1.013	0.990	0.970	0.977	0.961	0.958
0–20	1.013	0.992	0.965	0.974	0.962	0.952
0–25	1.012	0.994	0.964	0.970	0.965	0.952
0–30	1.010	0.996	0.968	0.969	0.967	0.956
0–35	1.009	0.998	0.974	0.970	0.968	0.961
0–40	1.007	0.999	0.980	0.974	0.970	0.966

a e_0 is assumed to have been 23.64 ten years before t_0 and to have subsequently declined to 22.12 at t_0.

Figure 6.2 *cqs(a)/cs(a)* for GRR = 3.0 and mortality assumptions A, B, C, D

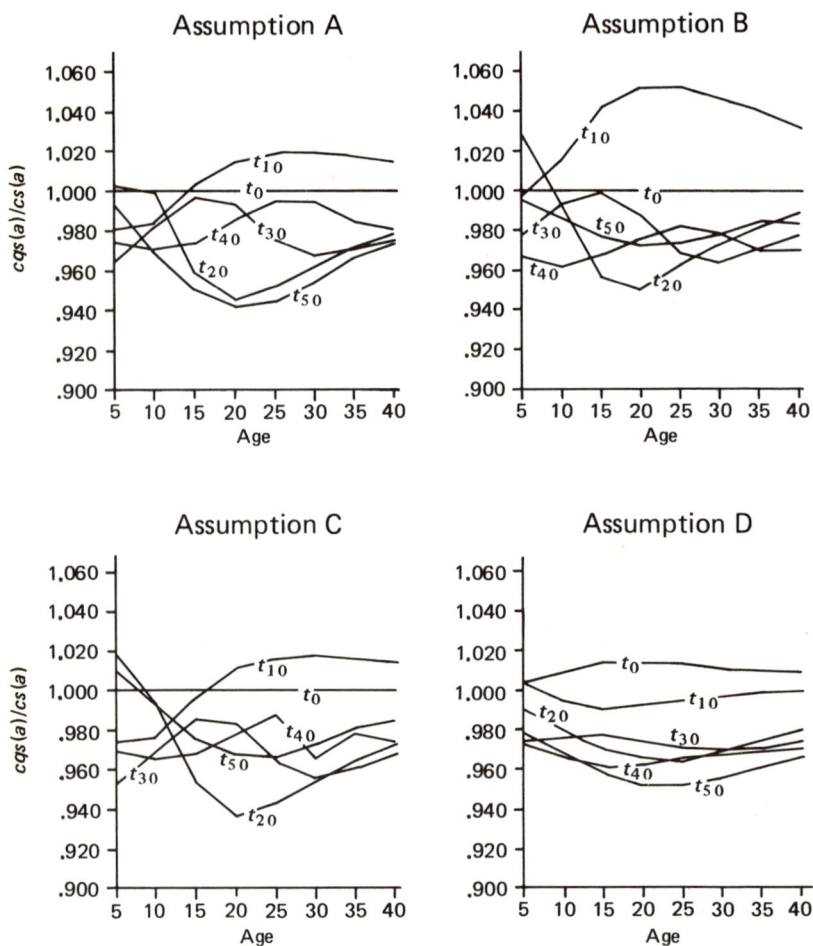

stable estimates would be different. The value of K in any given case may be obtained according to the following relationship:

$$K = 17.8 \times \frac{\Delta r}{\Delta t}$$

where Δr is the increase in growth rate of a population at a given time since the beginning of the destabilization process and Δt is the number of years between the beginning of mortality decline and the given time.

Coale and Demeny provided a set of factors for correcting the stable estimates derived from a quasi-stable population corresponding to a value of $K = 0.01$. Since the bias due to quasi stability is linearly related to the rate of decline in mortality, one could use these correcting factors in any given case after scaling them up or down according to the actual value of K.

The implicit assumptions in this method are that mortality remained unchanged till 1921 and then kept on declining at a uniform rate. These assumptions are not true for India, however. We have therefore tried to extend Coale and Demeny's method of correction by taking into account the historical changes in Indian mortality since 1911 and developing a new set of correction factors accordingly. We have also suggested the manner of adjusting them for any given quasi-stable population. Our basic correction factors relate to India and are specific for age sectors from which the stable estimates are derived. They are to be scaled up or down by a factor equal to $\Delta_i r(t)/0.01$ to yield the adjusted correction factor for a given age sector (i) according to the formula

$$(CF)_i = (CF)_{ib} \times \Delta_i r(t)$$

where $r(t)$ = growth rate of given population at time t

$\Delta_i r(t)$ = difference in growth rate of given population at time t and $(t - 5_i)$ years

i = age sector for which a particular correction factor is relevant (i may assume seven values $1, 2, \ldots, 7$ corresponding to age sectors $0-5, 0-10, \ldots, 0-35$)

$(CF)_{ib}$ = correction factor for age sector (i) derived from standard quasi-stable population

$(CF)_i$ = needed correction factor for age sector (i)

The sources of error likely to be introduced in the calculation of these factors are as follows: (1) the estimated rates of natural increase for India have their own uncertainties, particularly in the years prior to 1901; (2) the calculation of such rates for midcensus periods is based on the assumption of a uniform rate of change in mortality over the decade, which in reality might not have been the case.

Coale and Demeny's method of correction is more appropriate for age distributions having a history of monotonic decline in mortality. For age distributions with a history of fluctuating mortality as in India, our method seems to be more appropriate for correcting estimates relating to time points near the date when mortality decline started. For time points 40 or 50 years after the onset of mortality decline, the two methods yield similar results. Nevertheless there remains the need for a more general method of correcting stable estimates for past changes in mortality.

7

Quasi-stable estimates
of fertility and mortality

Chapter 6 discussed the method of preparing quasi-stable estimates of fertility and mortality. This chapter presents the estimates and examines their internal consistency. But before we discuss the estimated rates, a word on the estimates of GRR is in order.

Mean of the female fertility schedule

Estimates of GRR are not fully defined unless the respective means of fertility schedule ($\bar{M}$) going with such estimates are indicated. To obtain values of $\bar{M}$ for the female population in India and its zones, we have elaborately processed the census data on marital status by age in a manner similar to that adopted for processing the age-sex composition (see Chapter 2). This gave us the proportion of currently married women in the various age groups for the seven censuses 1901 through 1961 (Table 7.1). The other ingredient for calculating $\bar{M}$ is the data on marital fertility by age. In the absence of such data in the required form, we used the National Sample Survey (NSS) data (14th round—rural) [65] on age-specific fertility rates. The underlying marital fertility rates have been abstracted from the specific marital status observed in the samples in the various states and territories in the respective zones. Assuming that the schedule of marital fertility rates in the respective zones remained constant during the period 1901–1961, we

Table 7.1 Proportion of currently married women among all women by age group: India and zones, 1901–1961

Zone and age group	1901	1911	1921	1931	1941	1951	1961
INDIA							
15–19	0.8015	0.8179	0.7762	0.8698	0.7181	0.6945	0.6962
20–24	0.8830	0.9018	0.8740	0.9156	0.9094	0.9160	0.9183
25–29	0.8593	0.8816	0.8532	0.8963	0.9027	0.9032	0.9424
30–34	0.7879	0.8137	0.7885	0.8551	0.8547	0.8768	0.9149
35–39	0.7175	0.7423	0.7196	0.7565	0.7639	0.8276	0.8708
40–44	0.5766	0.5970	0.5924	0.7035	0.6707	0.7386	0.7771
45–49	0.5190	0.5218	0.5199	0.5715	0.5371	0.6747	0.6977
EASTERN							
15–19	0.8568	0.8338	0.7402	0.8549	0.7575	0.7214	0.7343
20–24	0.8854	0.8906	0.8239	0.8735	0.9032	0.8962	0.9122
25–29	0.8474	0.8562	0.7951	0.8695	0.8910	0.8942	0.9336
30–34	0.7595	0.7765	0.7364	0.7832	0.8338	0.8690	0.9075
35–39	0.6708	0.6905	0.6545	0.6714	0.7436	0.8323	0.8576
40–44	0.5240	0.5514	0.5385	0.5797	0.6421	0.7462	0.7689
45–49	0.4495	0.4760	0.4639	0.4332	0.5136	0.7176	0.6792
CENTRAL							
15–19	0.8393	0.8817	0.8584	0.8935	0.8209	0.8073	0.8358
20–24	0.8897	0.9209	0.9100	0.9270	0.9479	0.9295	0.9623
25–29	0.8725	0.9021	0.8920	0.8899	0.9192	0.9209	0.9659
30–34	0.8060	0.8376	0.8258	0.8496	0.8659	0.8985	0.9424
35–39	0.7461	0.7816	0.7711	0.7328	0.8407	0.9181	0.9073
40–44	0.6068	0.6216	0.6270	0.6493	0.7264	0.8303	0.8205
45–49	0.5719	0.5632	0.5612	0.4804	0.5909	0.7071	0.7518
SOUTHERN							
15–19	0.7079	0.7279	0.7002	0.7471	0.6048	0.5735	0.5693
20–24	0.8703	0.8802	0.8643	0.8670	0.8682	0.8827	0.8762
25–29	0.8473	0.8704	0.8523	0.8391	0.8694	0.8867	0.9181
30–34	0.7780	0.8036	0.7793	0.8078	0.8213	0.8514	0.8815
35–39	0.7104	0.7342	0.7141	0.6617	0.7217	0.7992	0.8329
40–44	0.5649	0.5944	0.5861	0.6076	0.6284	0.6919	0.7211
45–49	0.4991	0.5098	0.5157	0.4436	0.4937	0.6245	0.6391
WESTERN							
15–19	0.7951	0.8561	0.8304	0.8591	0.7316	0.7051	0.6687
20–24	0.8737	0.9128	0.8898	0.9257	0.9173	0.9709	0.9208
25–29	0.8517	0.8922	0.8658	0.9250	0.9074	0.9118	0.9449
30–34	0.7866	0.8279	0.7967	0.8148	0.8573	0.8864	0.9186
35–39	0.7105	0.7517	0.7207	0.7397	0.7587	0.8172	0.8738
40–44	0.5729	0.6001	0.5909	0.6101	0.6550	0.7272	0.7776
45–49	0.5051	0.5155	0.5065	0.4756	0.5060	0.6117	0.6898
NORTHERN							
15–19	0.7804	0.8232	0.8278	0.8488	0.7240	0.6836	0.6629
20–24	0.8953	0.9224	0.9247	0.9554	0.9339	0.9655	0.9363
25–29	0.8876	0.9074	0.8977	0.8921	0.9310	0.9234	0.9702
30–34	0.8268	0.8447	0.8208	0.8639	0.8945	0.9034	0.9491
35–39	0.7776	0.7871	0.7731	0.7469	0.8170	0.8662	0.9154
40–44	0.6289	0.6322	0.6376	0.6427	0.7421	0.7895	0.8345
45–49	0.5962	0.5777	0.5835	0.5175	0.6035	0.7614	0.7810

have superimposed such rates on the proportion of currently married women to yield the means of the fertility schedule relating to India and its zones for the respective census years (Table 7.2). Note that $\bar{M}$ lies mostly between 27 and 29 years. It has been appropriately used for interpolating the precise value of GRR from pairs of such values of GRR estimated from the tables of stable population corresponding to values of $\bar{M}$ equal to 27 and 29 years. In a few cases, when the observed $\bar{M}$ was below 27 years or above 29 years, extrapolation was necessary for obtaining the required GRR value.

The variation in $\bar{M}$ over time is broadly similar for India and its zones. It remains almost unchanged or shows a slight up and down movement during the period 1901–1931. (The slightly anomalous movements in 1931 may perhaps be explained by the vagaries of the unsmoothing process. See the discussions relating to unsmoothing of age data for all women in Chapter 2.) During the period 1931–1961, $\bar{M}$ shows a slowly rising trend. The relative stability during the period 1901–1931 may be due to the near equality of the proportions of currently married women. Although age at marriage during this period increased [15], such increases affected mainly girls below age 15, so that the proportion of currently married women aged 15–19 did not substantially decline. It was after 1931 that the proportion of currently married women demonstrably declined for age group 15–19.

The increase in $\bar{M}$ during the period 1931–1961 is a consequence of the two kinds of changes in the marital pattern. As the proportion of currently married women aged 15–19 decreased, fewer births occurred to younger women. Moreover, the increase in the proportion of currently married women at higher ages resulted in a larger number of births to women in higher age groups. A relatively larger number of births occurring to women at ages above the mean helps to push up the mean. With the marital fertility schedules as given and the observed changes in marital status in the various age groups, the net effect was a small increase in $\bar{M}$.

Table 7.2 Mean age of fertility schedule: India and zones, 1901–1961

Zone	1901	1911	1921	1931	1941	1951	1961
India	27.53	27.56	27.61	27.63	27.90	28.19	28.24
Eastern	26.88	27.00	27.17	26.97	27.41	27.87	27.89
Central	27.96	27.94	27.97	27.82	28.23	28.58	28.50
Southern	25.83	25.87	25.89	25.72	26.24	26.53	26.66
Western	27.31	27.28	27.26	27.21	27.58	27.77	28.09
Northern	28.04	27.93	27.90	27.75	28.35	28.62	28.86

Though the amount of increase is small, the upward trends in the different zones are similar. That the same type of variation occurs in all zones and in each census decade is significant. The somewhat anomalous movement of $\bar{M}$ during 1921–1931 is explained by the uncertainties involved in the unsmoothing of the 1931 age data, and by the large number of young girls herded into the married state immediately before the enactment of the Child Marriage Restraint Act by parents eager to escape the provisions of the Act [57:651–653].

Quasi-stable estimates of female birth rate and GRR

For each of the decades 1891–1901 through 1951–1961, seven estimates were made from the seven age sectors 0–5, 0–10, 0–15, 0–20, 0–25, 0–30, and 0–35 for India and its zones. Figures 7.1, 7.2, and 7.3 depict the course of the estimated female birth rates over the successive age sectors.

The variation in estimated rates observed in Table 6.1 is fairly wide, owing to errors in age data (see Chapter 6). The problem now is to identify as precisely as possible, under the circumstances, the location of the true rate within the range of this variation. The table reveals an underlying similarity and consistency in the pattern of variation of the estimated rates for the different zones in different years. This gives us a clue in the search for the true rate. Suppose we draw a straight line parallel to the x axis at an altitude roughly representing the average of the estimates made from age sectors 0–10 and 0–15. Let us draw another straight line parallel to this at a rate of two fewer births per 1,000. These two lines contain between them by far the greater part of the locus of the seven estimated rates. This happens with all the decades. We infer that the true rate lies somewhere between the two levels indicated by the two lines.* Table 7.3 sets out the upper and lower estimates of the female birth rate for India and its zones. Following the same procedure, we have made corresponding estimates of the female gross reproduction rate (Table 7.4). The following features of the estimated rates emerge from the tables:

1. With a few exceptions, the estimated birth rates for different years seem to be consistent among themselves for India as well as for each zone.

---

* The two-point spread is somewhat arbitrary. But it is based on an examination of the movement of the rates over the age sectors for seven successive decades. Estimates with a four- or five-point spread would be less likely to go wrong, but the usefulness of the estimates would correspondingly diminish. Note also that a two-point spread in the gross reproduction rate is wider than a two-point spread in the birth rate.

Figure 7.1 Corrected estimates of female birth rate: India and Eastern Zone, 1901–1961

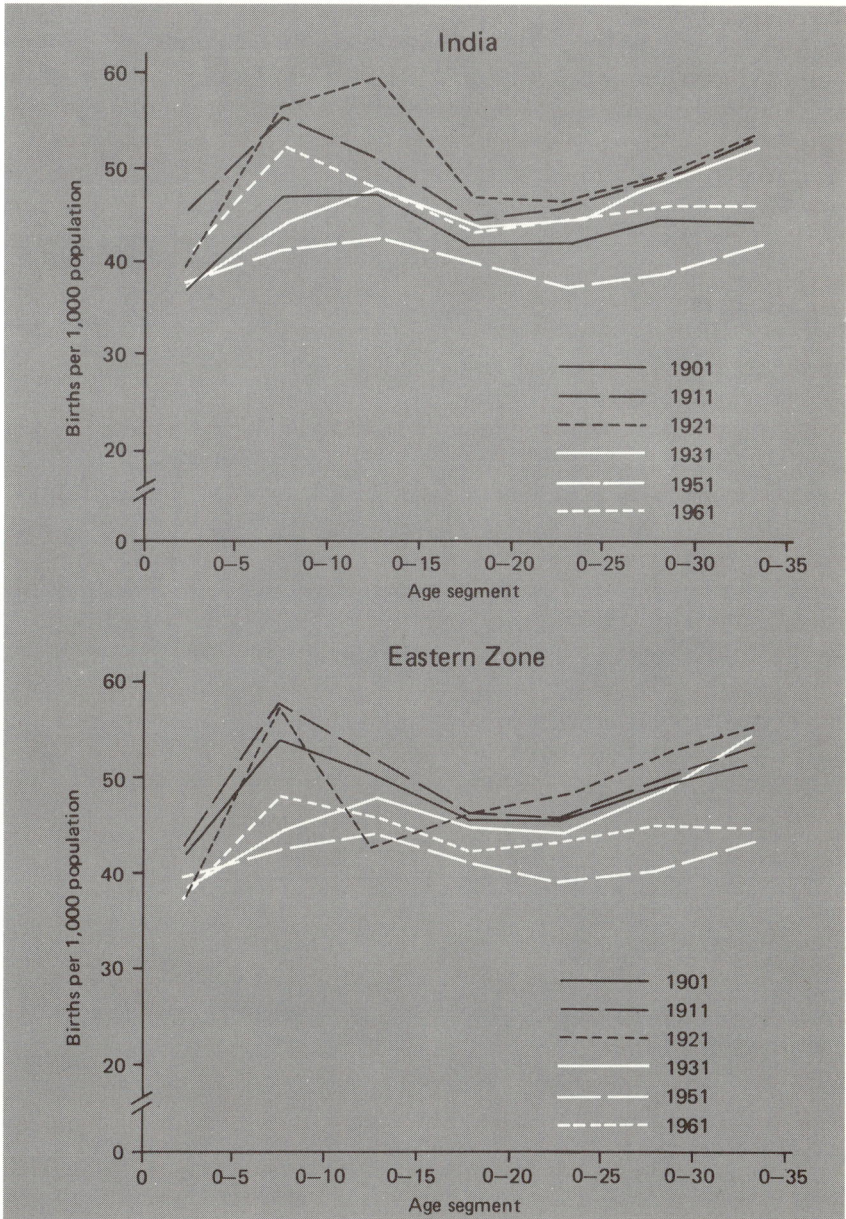

Figure 7.2 Corrected estimates of female birth rate: Central and Southern Zones, 1901–1961

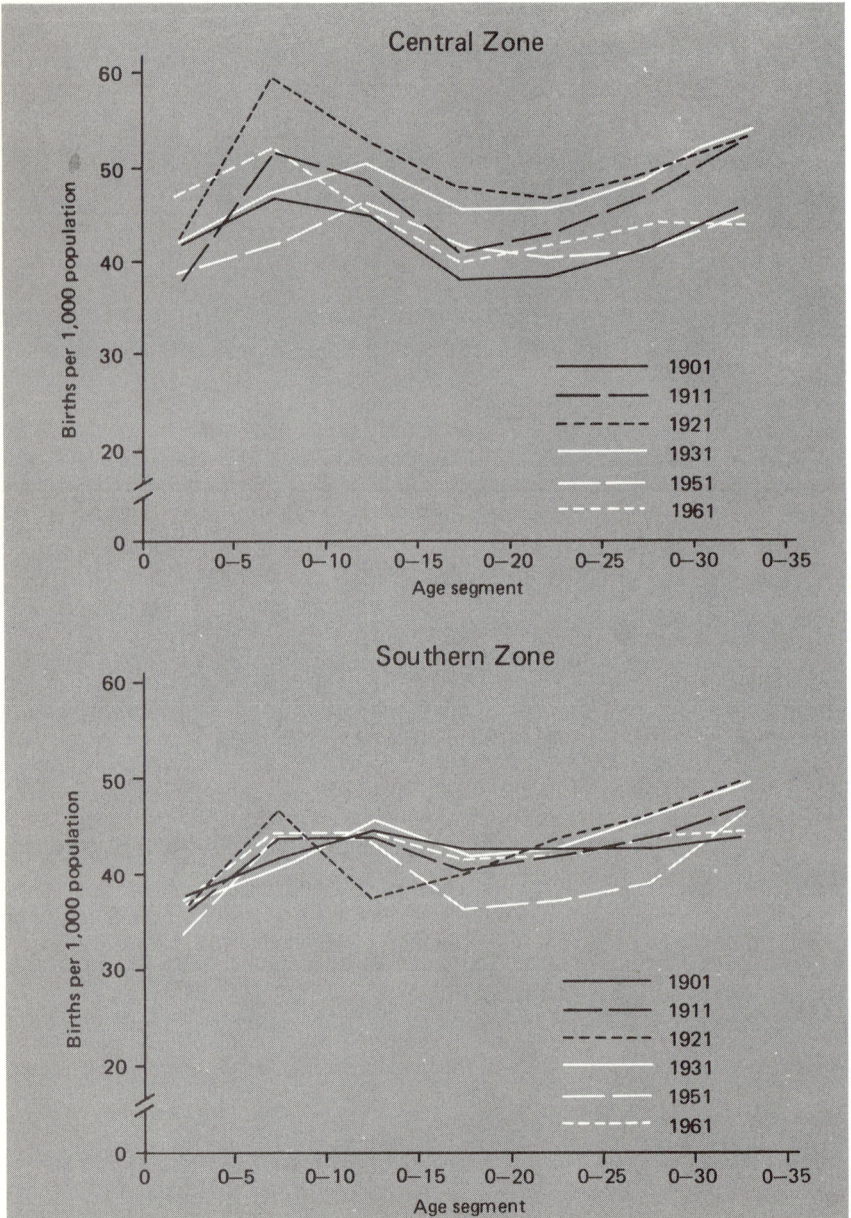

Figure 7.3 Corrected estimates of female birth rate: Western and Northern Zones, 1901—1961

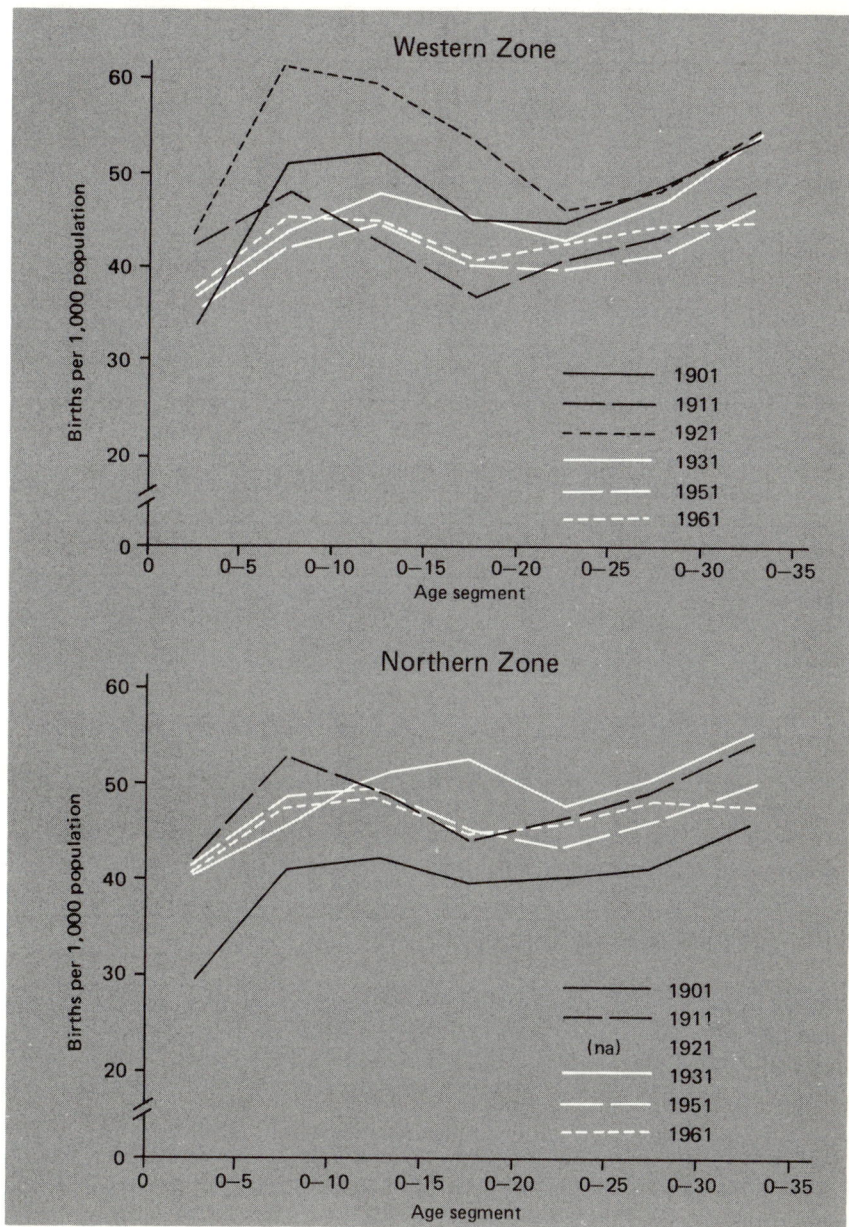

Table 7.3 Lower and upper estimates of female birth rate: India and zones,
1901–1961

Zone	1891–1901	1901–1911	1911–1921	1921–1931	1931–1941	1941–1951	1951–1961
India	46 48	47 49	47 49	46 48	44 46	43 45	44 46
Eastern	49 51	48 50	48 50	47 49	45 47	44 46	45 47
Central	45 47	46 48	48 50	47 49	45 47	44 46	44 46
Southern	43 45	44 46	44 46	43 45	43 45	42 44	41 43
Western	47 49	48 50	46 48	46 48	44 46	43 45	43 45
Northern	47 49	49 51	48 50	48 50	48 50	46 48	46 48

Table 7.4 Lower and upper estimates of female gross reproduction rate for
respective values of $\overline{M}$: India and zones, 1901–1961

Zone	1891–1901	1901–1911	1911–1921	1921–1931	1931–1941	1941–1951	1951–1961
India	2.8 3.0	2.9 3.0	2.8 3.0	3.0 3.1	2.9 3.1	2.8 3.0	2.9 3.1
Eastern	3.0 3.2	2.8 3.0	2.9 3.1	3.0 3.2	2.9 3.1	2.7 2.8	2.9 3.0
Central	2.8 3.0	2.9 3.1	3.0 3.2	3.0 3.2	2.9 3.1	2.8 3.0	2.9 3.0
Southern	2.6 2.7	2.7 2.8	2.6 2.8	2.7 2.9	2.7 2.8	2.8 2.9	2.7 2.8
Western	2.9 3.1	2.7 2.9	2.8 2.9	2.7 2.9	2.8 2.9	2.9 3.0	2.8 2.9
Northern	2.8 3.0	3.0 3.2	3.0 3.2	2.9 3.0	2.9 3.0	2.9 3.0	3.0 3.1

NOTE: Values of $\overline{M}$ are given in Table 7.2.

2. Again with only a few exceptions, the interzonal differences in birth and gross
reproduction rates, though small, are similar and persistent over the period.
(See also Table 7.7.)

3. Estimates of birth rate and gross reproduction rate for a given year and given
area are in keeping with the theoretical relationship between these two variables.

4. With minor exceptions, the ranking of the zones by level of birth rate and gross
reproduction rate is the same. The exceptions are a consequence of differences
in the age composition of the population.

5. In areas where the estimated gross reproduction rate is high, the mean of the fertility schedule is also high. If the values of the gross reproduction rate are interpolated or extrapolated for a uniform mean, then the differences between the estimated gross reproduction rates for different zones will be somewhat narrowed.

Estimates of female death rate and life expectancy

Two methods may be adopted to estimate the death rate. One may derive seven stable estimates corresponding to seven age sectors in the same manner as with the birth rate, correct them for past changes in mortality, and finally select from among the seven corrected estimates a lower and an upper value. Or one may take the lower and upper estimates of birth rate from Table 7.3, compare them with the respective rates of natural increase set out in Table 5.3, and derive the corresponding death rates.

We have chosen the second method. The first would yield independent estimates of the death rate and hence might be considered preferable. Actual computation reveals, however, that the estimates prepared through the first method tally well with those made through the second (Table 7.5).

The estimated death rates reveal the following features:

1. Those for 1901–1911 represent the pre-1921 quasi-stable situation. During this period mortality seems to have been higher in the Eastern, Western, and Northern Zones than in the Central or Southern.

2. In the decade 1911–1921, as we have already noted, there was a sharp rise in the death rates in India and all its zones except the Northern. In the Northern Zone, death rates had been much higher in the two earlier decades than

Table 7.5 Lower and upper estimates of female death rate: India and zones, 1901–1961

Zone	1891–1901	1901–1911	1911–1921	1921–1931	1931–1941	1941–1951	1951–1961
India	44	42	47	37	32	30	26
	46	44	49	39	34	32	28
Eastern	44	43	49	37	34	32	24
	46	45	51	39	36	34	26
Central	42	43	49	40	32	34	27
	44	45	51	42	34	36	29
Southern	36	36	42	32	31	27	25
	38	38	44	34	33	29	27
Western	47	40	48	33	31	28	23
	49	42	50	35	33	30	25
Northern	55	53	48	36	32	30	24
	57	55	50	38	34	32	26

in the other zones. Moreover, the spurt in mortality witnessed in the rest of the country during 1911–1921 was not observed in the Northern Zone, although the absolute level of mortality was the same as in the country as a whole. Note that high death rates persisted in the Northern Zone for three consecutive decades, leading to a negative rate of natural increase for the entire period.

3. The high death rates in the Western Zone in the decades 1891–1901 and 1911–1921 indicate that such a situation possibly existed there too over the whole period except for an interlude in the decade 1901–1911.

4. Since 1921, death rates have kept on declining in all the zones. The decline has been greater in the Eastern, Northern, and Western Zones than in the Southern and Central.

5. Since 1951, death rates seem to be lowest in the Western Zone and highest in the Central.

The method of estimating e_0 has been slightly modified. Instead of using the growth rate and the age distribution we have used the growth rate and the estimated death rate as parameters to derive estimates of e_0 from the tables of stable populations (Table 7.6). Note that such stable estimates of e_0 are different from the stable estimates corresponding to seven age segments. This method gives a single estimate instead of seven different estimates. As with the birth rate and GRR, we obtained stable estimates from projected quasi-stable populations (all the parameters of which are available) and compared them with the true values of e_0 in the simulated projection. The stable estimates were found to be close to their true values, and the size of any possible correction factor would therefore be small. Under these circumstances, we decided to use these estimates without further correction.

Table 7.6 Stable estimates of female life expectancy at birth: India and zones, 1901–1961

Zone	1891–1901	1901–1911	1911–1921	1921–1931	1931–1941	1941–1951	1951–1961
India	22.50	23.90	21.70	28.46	31.86	33.34	38.63
	21.00	22.96	20.00	27.15	30.30	31.68	36.73
Eastern	23.51	23.88	22.27	27.46	30.11	31.16	38.97
	21.59	22.86	21.41	26.31	28.75	29.66	36.97
Central	24.40	23.31	19.69	26.09	31.40	29.97	36.07
	23.34	22.29	18.74	24.91	29.88	28.60	33.25
Southern	28.47	28.56	26.48	31.27	31.96	36.54	37.62
	27.11	27.20	25.24	29.72	30.38	34.62	35.63
Western	21.58	25.91	23.82	30.57	32.42	35.48	41.01
	20.69	24.77	22.76	29.19	30.89	33.70	38.81
Northern	23.30	21.04	21.28	28.55	28.18	33.63	39.10
	22.89	20.16	20.39	27.26	26.95	32.01	37.11

The estimates of birth rate, GRR, and death rate for India and its zones are strikingly higher, and the estimates of e_0 (Table 7.6) strikingly lower, than those prepared by conventional methods. On the other hand, the present estimates are in close agreement with those prepared recently by Saxena, Visaria, and others through the quasi-stable population method as adopted by us [86, 100, 110]. A comparative study of our own estimates and other available estimates will be made later (see Chapter 9). It is important to note here that the level of fertility in India used to be underestimated with conventional methods. It is only in recent years that we have been obtaining higher and more realistic estimates, mostly through the application of non-conventional techniques. The present estimates, therefore, corroborate and reinforce those made in recent years.

An examination of the rows in Table 7.7 relating to the birth rate reveals that the different zones are ranked similarly in successive census years. We have worked out a combined rank for all the years for

Table 7.7 Ranking of zones according to estimated birth rate, gross reproduction rate, death rate, and life expectancy at birth: female, 1901–1961

Zone	1901	1911	1921	1931	1941	1951	1961	Mean rank value	Combined rank
BR
Northern	2.5	1	2	1	1	1	1	1.35	1
Eastern	1	2.5	2	2.5	2.5	2.5	2	2.14	2
Central	4	4	2	2.5	2.5	2.5	3	2.93	3
Western	2.5	2.5	4	4	4	4	4	3.57	4
Southern	5	5	5	5	5	5	5	5.00	5
GRR
Northern	3.5	1	1.5	3	2	1.5	1	1.93	1
Eastern	1	3	3	1.5	2	5	2.5	2.57	3
Central	3.5	2	1.5	1.5	2	3.5	2.5	2.36	2
Western	2	4.5	4	4.5	4	1.5	4	3.50	4
Southern	5	4.5	5	4.5	5	3.5	5	4.64	5
DR
Northern	1	1	3.5	3	2.5	3	3.5	2.50	3
Eastern	3	2.5	1.5	2	1	2	3.5	2.21	2
Central	4	2.5	1.5	1	2.5	1	1	1.93	1
Western	2	4	3.5	4	4.5	5	5	4.00	4
Southern	5	5	5	5	4.5	5	2	4.36	5
e_0
Northern	4	5	4	3	5	3	2	3.71	5
Eastern	3	3	3	4	4	4	3	3.43	4
Central	2	4	5	3	5	5	5	3.43	3
Western	5	2	2	2	1	2	1	2.14	2
Southern	1	1	1	1	2	1	4	1.57	1

each zone on the basis of a simple arithmetic mean of the rank values for different years. The relative position of the different zones is reflected in the combined ranks.

With respect to life expectancy and the death rate, the similarity of ranking from year to year is less pronounced than for the fertility measures and the deviations from the combined ranks are larger, particularly in 1941, 1951, and 1961. This discrepancy in the picture revealed by the birth rate and GRR on one side and the death rate and e_0 on the other is due to the fact that fertility has remained substantially unchanged over the whole period, whereas mortality started declining after 1921 and the rate of decline accelerated in the decade 1951–1961. The uneven rate of mortality decline in the different zones caused variations in their relative ranks during the process of decline.

Estimates for the male population

For the purpose of studying the consistency between the estimates for the two sexes, we have derived quasi-stable estimates from the male age distribution by repeating each step adopted for deriving the female estimates. Tables 7.8, 7.9, 7.10, and 7.11 set out the estimated birth rates, gross reproduction rates, death rates, and life expectancy for the male population. The pattern of variation in the male estimates over time and space is similar to that observed in the estimates for females. The high death rates and low life expectancy in the decades 1891–

Table 7.8 Lower and upper estimates of male birth rate: India and zones, 1901–1961

Zone	1891–1901	1901–1911	1911–1921	1921–1931	1931–1941	1941–1951	1951–1961
India	48	48	49	46	44	42	43
	50	50	51	48	46	44	45
Eastern	51	49	50	46	45	42	44
	53	51	52	48	47	44	46
Central	46	50	48	46	43	40	43
	48	52	50	48	45	42	45
Southern	45	46	42	44	44	37	42
	47	48	44	46	46	39	44
Western	50	49	48	46	42	43	42
	52	51	50	48	44	45	44
Northern	45	46	46	45	44	43	42
	47	48	48	47	46	45	44

Table 7.9 Lower and upper estimates of male gross reproduction rate: India and zones, 1901–1961

Zone	1901	1911	1921	1931	1941	1951	1961
India	3.2	3.3	3.2	3.3	3.0	2.7	3.0
	3.4	3.5	3.4	3.5	3.2	3.0	3.2
Eastern	3.4	3.5	3.4	3.3	2.8	2.7	2.9
	3.6	3.7	3.6	3.5	3.0	2.9	3.1
Central	3.2	3.4	3.2	3.4	3.0	2.8	3.0
	3.4	3.6	3.4	3.6	3.2	3.0	3.2
Southern	3.1	2.9	2.8	3.0	2.9	2.6	2.8
	3.3	3.1	3.0	3.2	3.1	2.8	3.0
Western	3.2	a	3.4	3.1	3.1	2.8	3.0
	3.4	a	3.6	3.3	3.3	3.0	3.2
Northern	3.0	a	a	3.1	3.1	3.1	3.0
	3.2	a	a	3.3	3.3	3.3	3.2

a   Estimate could not be constructed because of negative rate of natural increase.

1901 and 1911–1921 are in keeping with recorded history of famines, plagues, and influenza epidemics in India during those two decades. The particularly high death rates in the Western Zone in the decade 1891–1901 and in the Northern Zone in the decades 1891–1901, 1901–1911, and 1911–1921 are also supported by evidence cited earlier (see Chapter 5).

Table 7.10 Lower and upper estimates of male death rate: India and zones, 1901–1961

Zone	1901	1911	1921	1931	1941	1951	1961
India	49	42	49	35	31	29	24
	51	44	51	37	33	31	26
Eastern	49	42	49	34	32	29	25
	51	44	51	36	34	31	27
Central	49	46	50	38	30	30	25
	51	48	52	40	32	32	27
Southern	38	36	39	33	32	22	25
	40	38	41	35	34	24	27
Western	63	40	49	33	29	29	22
	65	42	51	35	31	31	22
Northern	53	47	46	34	28	28	20
	55	49	48	36	30	30	22

Table 7.11 Stable estimates of male life expectancy at birth: India and zones, 1901–1961

Zone	1901	1911	1921	1931	1941	1951	1961
India	20.46	24.37	20.45	28.75	33.97	35.82	38.89
	19.71	23.33	19.71	27.42	32.20	33.92	36.84
Eastern	22.12	24.33	20.49	29.50	31.40	35.49	37.76
	21.36	23.31	19.76	28.14	29.89	33.83	35.84
Central	20.28	22.44	20.06	27.08	35.57	35.06	37.73
	19.50	21.58	19.30	25.87	33.69	33.16	35.79
Southern	27.11	27.88	25.59	30.62	31.74	41.54	37.51
	25.89	26.66	24.44	29.18	30.18	37.97	35.56
Western	a	a	20.57	30.62	33.90	33.58	41.76
	a	a	19.80	29.22	32.16	31.90	39.48
Northern	17.88	a	a	29.66	34.49	34.75	43.57
	17.02	a	a	28.29	32.77	33.01	41.16

a Estimate could not be constructed because of highly negative rate of natural increase.

Consistency of estimated birth rates for males and females

The method of testing the consistency between male and female birth rates is based on a widely observed phenomenon that the sex ratio at birth in different countries and periods varies within narrow limits [68]. If the quasi-stable estimates derived from the male and female age distributions fit within these limits, the presumption is that the estimates are consistent from this point of view. The sex ratio at birth in almost all non-African populations varies from 105 to 107 boys for 100 girls. For African populations the ratio varies from 102 to 104 [5]. Assuming that the Indian populations resemble non-African populations in this respect, and allowing for sampling and nonsampling errors, let us put the probable sex ratio at birth between 103 and 109. In that case, the ratio between the female birth rate and the male birth rate in the Indian populations should lie between certain determined limits depending on the sex ratio in the population. Let FBR = female birth rate, MBR = male birth rate, FP = female population, MP = male population, FB = number of female births, and MB = number of male births. Then

$$\frac{FBR}{MBR} = \frac{FB/FP}{MB/MP}$$

$$= \frac{FB}{MB} \times \frac{MP}{FP}$$

= (female ratio at birth) ×
(male ratio in population)

With the limits of the male ratio at birth as indicated above and the male ratio in the population as indicated in Table 7.12, the expected limits of the values of FBR/MBR for India and its zones are as set out in Table 7.13.

Table 7.14 presents the observed values of the ratio FBR/MBR obtained by relating the lower estimates of female birth rate to the lower estimates of male birth rate (Tables 7.3 and 7.8). Comparing Table 7.13 with Table 7.14, we find that in each zone the observed values of this ratio are within the limits of the expected values of FBR/MBR in at least five of the seven census years. Discrepancy occurs in two years in the Eastern, Southern, Western, and Northern Zones and in one year in the Central Zone. In India as a whole, there is no single case of discrepancy [81].

When the observed value of the ratio FBR/MBR is below the expected range, the indication is that either the estimate of the female

Table 7.12 Sex ratio for India and zones: 1901—1961

Year	India	Eastern	Central	Southern	Western	Northern
1901	102.83	99.01	105.19	99.41	103.05	114.58
1911	103.68	99.88	106.97	99.23	104.20	117.02
1921	104.60	101.46	107.85	99.78	105.48	117.24
1931	105.16	103.42	108.22	100.01	105.67	115.94
1941	105.73	105.20	108.05	100.77	105.71	114.80
1951	105.60	105.84	107.97	100.54	105.88	113.20
1961	106.20	105.93	108.46	101.43	106.65	113.56

Table 7.13 Expected values of FBR/MBR on assumption of sex ratio at birth between 1.03 and 1.09: India and zones, 1901—1961

Zone	1891—1901	1901—1911	1911—1921	1921—1931	1931—1941	1941—1951	1951—1961
India	0.9984	1.0066	1.0156	1.0210	1.0265	1.0253	1.0311
	0.9434	0.9512	0.9596	0.9647	0.9610	0.9688	0.9743
Eastern	0.9613	0.9697	0.9851	1.0041	1.0214	1.0276	1.0285
	0.9083	0.9163	0.9308	0.9488	0.9651	0.9710	0.9718
Central	1.0213	1.0386	1.0471	1.0507	1.0491	1.0483	1.0530
	0.9650	0.9813	0.9894	0.9928	0.9913	0.9905	0.9950
Southern	0.9652	0.9634	0.9688	0.9710	0.9784	0.9761	0.9848
	0.9120	0.9103	0.9154	0.9175	0.9245	0.9224	0.9305
Western	1.0005	1.0117	1.0241	1.0260	1.0263	1.0280	1.0355
	0.9454	0.9559	0.9677	0.9694	0.9698	0.9713	0.9784
Northern	1.1125	1.1361	1.1383	1.1257	1.1146	1.0991	1.1026
	1.0512	1.0735	1.0756	1.0636	1.0532	1.0385	1.0418

Table 7.14 Observed values of FBR/MBR in quasi-stable estimates: India and zones, 1901–1961

Zone	1891–1901	1901–1911	1911–1921	1921–1931	1931–1941	1941–1951	1951–1961
India	0.9583	0.9792	0.9592	1.0000	1.0000	1.0238	1.0233
Eastern	0.9608	0.9796	0.9600	1.0217	1.0000	1.0476	1.0227
Central	0.9783	0.9200	1.0000	1.0217	1.0465	1.1000	1.0233
Southern	0.9556	0.9565	1.0476	0.9773	0.9773	1.1351	0.9762
Western	0.9400	0.9796	0.9583	1.0000	1.0476	1.0000	1.0238
Northern	1.0444	1.0652	1.0435	1.0667	1.0909	1.0698	1.0952

birth rate is too low or that of the male birth rate is too high. When the observed value of FBR/MBR lies above the expected range, the indication is that either the female estimate is too high or the male estimate is too low. Thus the direction in which the estimates need to be modified is suggested in the observed ratios.

For the purpose of calculating the observed value of FBR/MBR we have related the two lower estimates for the female and male birth rates (Tables 7.3 and 7.8). Almost the same values would have been obtained if we had related the two upper estimates. The assumption implicit in thus combining the two lower or the two upper estimates is that if we accept the lower estimate for the female population, we should accept the lower estimate for the male population also. Actually, in any given case it is possible for the true rate for the female population to be closer to the lower estimate and the true rate for the male population to be closer to the upper estimate. The observed values of FBR/MBR would be lower in such cases than those indicated in Table 7.14. Similarly, if the true rate for the female population was closer to the upper estimate and that for the male population was closer to the lower, the observed ratio FBR/MBR would be higher than that indicated (in Table 7.14). If we recognize the possibility of such combinations of the true rates, the few cases in which the observed value of FBR/MBR lies beyond the range of the expected values will be explained away.

Consistency between female birth rate and GRR

Another method of internal checking may be suggested: checking female GRR against the female birth rate via the age pattern of marital fertility rates and the observed age distribution and marital pattern. The steps in this checking process are as follows:

1. Combine the marital fertility rates and proportion of currently married women in the seven reproductive age groups obtained earlier to construct a basic fertility schedule with total fertility equal to unity $[f_i^b(t)]$.

2. Combine the basic fertility schedule with the female age distribution to obtain a basic birth rate $[B^b(t)]$.

3. Divide the estimated quasi-stable birth rate by the basic birth rate and thus obtain a scalar that is an estimate of total fertility $[L(t)]$.

4. Multiply the scalar by the female ratio at birth to obtain an estimate of the synthetic GRR and compare this with the quasi-stable estimate of GRR.

The method of calculation may be symbolically stated as follows. Let

$$f_i^M = \text{marital fertility rate from NSS data for age interval } (i)$$

$$m_i(t) = \text{proportion married in age interval } (i) \text{ in year } (t)$$

$$f_i^b(t) = \text{basic fertility rate for age interval } (i) \text{ in year } (t)$$

$$B^b(t) = \text{basic birth rate in year } (t)$$

Then

$$f_i^b(t) = \frac{f_i^M m_i(t)}{\sum_1^7 f_i^M m_i(t)}$$

$$B^b(t) = \sum_1^7 c_i(t) f_i^b(t)$$

Let us designate the scalar as $L(t)$, the synthetic gross reproduction rate as $\text{GRR}^s(t)$, and quasi-stable estimate of the birth rate as $B^{QS}(t)$. Then

$$L(t) = \frac{B^{QS}(t)}{B^b(t)}$$

As we can easily see, $L(t)$ is nothing but an estimate of total fertility synthetically constructed with the given marital fertility schedule, the given proportions of currently married women in the seven age intervals, and the given age distribution. Also,

$$\text{GRR}^s(t) = \frac{100}{206} L(t)$$

Table 7.15 Synthetic values of female gross reproduction rate obtained by relating basic birth rate to quasi-stable estimate of birth rate: India and zones: 1901–1961

Zone	1901	1911	1921	1931	1941	1951	1961
India	2.718	2.745	2.752	2.725	2.714	2.661	2.784
	2.836	2.862	2.870	2.843	2.837	2.784	2.910
Eastern	2.884	2.823	2.797	2.684	2.722	2.739	2.853
	3.001	2.941	2.913	2.799	2.843	2.864	2.980
Central	2.632	2.668	2.924	2.811	2.813	2.744	2.809
	2.749	2.784	3.046	2.931	2.938	2.868	2.936
Southern	2.609	2.555	2.574	2.459	2.622	2.481	2.491
	2.730	3.672	2.690	2.572	2.744	2.599	2.612
Western	2.658	2.705	2.851	2.733	2.631	2.606	2.673
	2.771	2.818	2.975	2.851	2.751	2.727	2.797
Northern	2.766	2.852	3.090	2.967	3.174	2.945	3.012
	2.883	2.968	3.218	3.090	3.306	3.073	3.143

Table 7.15 sets out the values of the synthetic GRR. Comparing the values in this table with those in Table 7.4, we find a close proximity of the two sets. Tables 7.3, 7.4, and 7.15, read jointly, lead to the following inferences:

1. For any given year, the estimated birth rates and gross reproduction rates are consistent among themselves and both are consistent with the observed age composition and marital pattern in that year.

2. The variation in estimated rates over time is in keeping with whatever changes occurred in the age distribution and marital pattern.

3. In India as a whole as well as in each of its zones, the female birth rate recorded a slight decline while the female GRR remained stable or perhaps increased slightly.

A summing up

We may now sum up the whole situation in the following manner. Estimates of the four measures—birth rate, GRR, death rate, and e_0—have been presented for the male and female populations for India and each of its five zones for seven census decades. Altogether we get 336 values as the respective estimates ($2 \times 4 \times 6 \times 7 = 336$) of the four measures. These 336 values are consistent with the observed age distribution and marital pattern of the population. Estimates of the same parameter for different times and different zones are consistent among themselves. Moreover, estimates of the different parameters for the *same time* and *same zone* are internally consistent. Female birth rates are compatible with female gross reproduction rates. Male birth rates are consistent with female birth rates. Birth rates, death rates, and growth rates for both male and female populations are consistent among themselves. There is nothing to show that the estimates of e_0 and GRR for the male and female populations are not compatible with each other. These 336 parameters thus constitute a logically interrelated system, free from internal contradiction, moving together or not moving at all, but always behaving according to some well-established law. Each corroborates and strengthens the other. It is therefore believed that they reflect with a high degree of accuracy the demographic situation of the country during the period.

8

Derivation of fertility and mortality by the forward projection method

Estimates of the birth rate, death rate, GRR, and e_0 derived through the quasi-stable population model were presented in Chapter 7. This chapter demonstrates how the reconstructed age distribution can be used to derive estimates of fertility and mortality through the forward projection method (FPM) and compares the two sets of estimates prepared by means of the two methods.

The method

The steps involved in the FPM may be briefly stated as follows [6, 88]:

1. Calculate the ten-year cohort survival rates from a set of model life tables at mortality levels conjectured to encompass the probable range of the mortality levels of the given population.

2. With the ten-year cohort survival rates thus obtained, project the population in a census year (say 1901) in each age group from $[x - (x + 5)]$ to $[(x + 10) - (x + 15)]$ ten years later, successive values of x being 0, 5, 10, . . . , 70+.

3. Obtain the aggregate projected population aged x and over for values of x equal to 10, 15, 20, . . . , 50 successively.

4. Compare the reverse-cumulated census population of 1911 aged x and over with the projected and reverse-cumulated population thus obtained for each

of the age segments (e.g., 10+, 15+, 20+, . . . , 50+) under different assumptions of mortality level. The choice of mortality levels should be so designed that the reverse-cumulated 1911 census population lies between the relevant pairs of projected population at two consecutive mortality levels.

5. Interpolate the value of e_5 corresponding to the reverse-cumulated census population of 1911 and obtain nine estimates of e_5 corresponding to age segments 10+, 15+, 20+, . . . , 50+.

6. Select the median value of e_5 from among these estimates, which is the probable estimate e_5 for the decade 1901–1911.

7. To obtain the age-specific mortality rates corresponding to this value of e_5 interpolate between the two consecutive mortality levels—one lower and the other higher than the level indicated by this value of e_5.

8. Multiply the age-specific mortality rates by the mean population for the decade for each five-year age group and add the products to obtain the total number of deaths (D) in the decade.

9. Obtain the number of births (B) in the decade as follows:

$$B = D + P(1911) - P(1901)$$

10. Choose a suitable basic fertility schedule (extracted from NSS data or some other reliable source) with total fertility equal to unity and combine it with the mean female population in various age groups to get a hypothetical number of births $[B(0)]$.

11. Then the estimates are given as follows:

$$DR = \frac{\text{no. of deaths } (D)}{\frac{1}{2}\,[P(1901) + P(1911)]} \times 1{,}000$$

$$BR = \frac{\text{no. of births } (B)}{\frac{1}{2}\,[P(1901) + P(1911)]} \times 1{,}000$$

$$TFR = \frac{B}{B(0)}$$

$$GRR = 0.4854\,(TFR)$$

An illustrative estimation of mortality

In this section the FPM is used to estimate life expectancy at age 5 and the death rate for the male population of India, 1901–1911. Worksheet 8.1 sets out the survivors of the 1901 population in 1911 in age segments 10+, 15+, 20+, . . . , 50+ and also the reverse-cumulated census population for 1911 for the same age segments. Note that the cumulated census population (1911) aged 10 and above lies between the two projected 10+ populations under assumed mortality levels 3 and 4; the cumulated 15+ population (1911 census) lies between the two projected 15+ populations under assumed mortality

Worksheet 8.1 Estimates of survivors of 1901 census population in 1911 compared with 1911 census population: India, male

Age sector	Assumed mortality level							1911 census population
	1	2	3	4	5	6	7	
10+	81,759,116	83,767,265	85,589,627	87,258,648	88,796,939	90,221,609	91,548,969	85,822,125
15+	71,696,732	73,362,309	74,881,521	76,278,659	77,572,255	78,775,342	79,898,790	72,177,324
20+	58,174,709	59,494,590	61,085,527	62,363,944	63,547,951	64,650,582	65,681,183	62,810,058
25+	45,933,163	47,303,534	48,556,838	49,711,389	50,779,977	51,777,040	52,707,706	52,638,215
30+	38,016,905	39,257,844	40,393,137	41,439,195	42,408,806	43,313,554	44,158,566	42,166,780
35+	31,037,080	32,138,789	33,147,034	34,076,485	34,939,062	35,743,738	36,496,509	32,717,877
40+	23,526,910	24,453,084	25,300,341	26,032,382	26,809,186	27,487,787	28,123,212	25,088,973
45+	16,585,232	17,318,895	17,989,605	18,610,124	19,187,615	19,727,232	20,233,064	17,525,924
50+	11,890,799	12,472,075	13,003,154	13,495,454	13,953,452	14,382,304	14,784,755	12,994,495

NOTE: The assumed P_x values are taken from Coale and Demeny's West model life table [42:2–11].

levels 1 and 2; and so on. The values of e_5 are interpolated on the basis of the observed number of persons (1911 census) in each age segment and the corresponding projected number at two consecutive mortality levels (see Worksheet 8.2). The median value for e_5 is 38.95 years, and the corresponding M_x values are given in Worksheet 8.3. The estimated death rate and birth rate are 41.81 and 47.81 respectively.

A few points regarding the estimation procedure may be raised here. First, the variation in the values of e_5 estimated from various age segments is due to misreporting of age. If the extent of misreporting is large, the range of variation will be wide and the median e_5 will lose all significance. It is difficult to suggest a standard measure of variability for separating good estimates from bad. The narrower the range of variation in the interpolated values of e_5, the more reliable is the estimate of median e_5.

In some pre-1921 decades, the level of mortality indicated by a comparison of the reverse-cumulated projected population and the census population was below the lowest level of mortality for which tabulated values of P_x, M_x, or e_5 are available in the West model life tables. In such cases we noted the number of age segments out of nine that would give an estimate of e_5 below 35.786 years—the value corresponding to the lowest mortality level (mortality level 1) in the West tables. If the number of such age segments were four or less, the median mortality level would lie above level 1 and there would be no problem of interpolating the needed values of e_5 and M_x. But if there were more than four age segments for which the extrapolated e_5 would be less than 35.786 years, and it would be necessary to obtain the median e_5 itself by extrapolation from a mortality level below level 1, no estimate was prepared. The number of such cases was, however, small.

Worksheet 8.2 Estimated values of e_5 corresponding to reverse-cumulated population of 1911 census for different age sectors

Age sector	Mortality levels used for interpolation	Interpolated value of e_5
10+	3 and 4	39.19
15+	1 and 2	36.25
20+	3 and 4	40.46
25+	6 and 7	44.93
30+	4 and 5	41.67
35+	2 and 3	37.83
40+	2 and 3	38.58
45+	2 and 3	37.88
50+	2 and 3	38.95

Worksheet 8.3   Estimating the number of male deaths: India, 1901−1911

Age group	Mean decadal population	M_x interpolated on basis of median e_5	Number of deaths
0−4	14,432,304.5	0.164350	2,371,948
5−9	15,564,354.5	0.011588	180,366
10−14	13,460,199.0	0.008253	114,389
15−19	9,492,143.5	0.011247	109,009
20−24	9,186,890.5	0.016125	148,138
25−29	10,084,743.0	0.018149	183,023
30−34	9,469,850.0	0.021094	201,864
35−39	7,020,973.0	0.024810	174,188
40−44	7,442,399.0	0.030047	223,624
45−49	4,356,501.5	0.034732	151,310
50−54	5,672,496.0	0.043974	223,056
55−59	2,047,237.0	0.053381	109,283
60+	5,392,014.5	0.104673	564,399
All age groups	113,722,106.0		4,754,597

NOTE: Number of deaths (D) = 4,754,597

Number of births (B) = $P(1911) - P(1901) + D$

Death rate (DR) = $\dfrac{2(D)}{P(1901) + P(1911)} \times 1{,}000 = 41.81$

when R = rate of population increase per 1,000 per year

Birth rate (BR) = $R + DR = 6.00 + 41.81 = 47.81$

Application of the FPM requires that the population at the beginning and at the end of the decade relate to the identical territory. The
reconstructed age composition for India and its zones (Basic Table 1)
for any given year includes the population of those states and territories for which age data were available for that year. In order that the
inclusion of new areas in the latter decade not vitiate the estimate of
e_5, care was taken to limit the computation to the same set of areas
for the entire period of 80 years. Therefore we excluded the population of certain states and territories from that of the respective zones
(Table 8.1). Because the excluded population constitutes only a small
fraction of the total population, estimates derived from the population
of the uniform set of states and territories may be considered valid for
India and its zones.

This method also requires that the given population be closed to
migration. For the country as a whole, this assumption is very nearly
true. Moreover, the volume of long-distance migration being small, estimates for the zones are only marginally affected by whatever migration might have occurred to and from the zones. The situation is dif-

Table 8.1 Areas and populations excluded for derivation of FPM estimates

State or territory excluded	Total population in 1961 (1000's)	Population in excluded areas as percentage of zonal population
EASTERN ZONE		
Tripura	1,142	
Nagaland	369	
North-East Frontier Agency	337	
Subtotal	1,848	1.63
CENTRAL ZONE	0	0.00
SOUTHERN ZONE		
Laccadive, Minicoy, Amindivi Islands	24	
Pondicherry	369	
Subtotal	393	0.36
WESTERN ZONE		
Dadra and Nagar Haveli	58	0.09
NORTHERN ZONE		
Chandigar	99	
Jammu and Kashmir	3,561	
Rajasthan	20,155	
Subtotal	23,815	49.71
Goa, Daman, Diu	627	
Total	26,741	6.10

ferent for individual states and territories. The amount of migration—both gross and net—for states like West Bengal, Maharashtra, and Assam is not negligible, and estimates based on the FPM may be distorted. Therefore such estimates have been prepared and presented only for the country and its zones.

Estimates of mortality for India and zones

Table 8.2 presents estimates of the crude death rate and life expectancy at age 5 derived through the FPM for India and its zones for the decades 1881—1891 through 1951—1961. Estimates for the decades 1881—1891 and 1891—1901 are liable to large errors because of the possibility of a greater degree of error in the first three censuses. So far as the decade 1911—1921 is concerned, an estimate of e_5 could be prepared for only two zones: Southern (male and female) and Northern (male only). In other zones, the mortality level dropped considerably below level 1 and no estimates were prepared. The estimated values of e_5 and death rate for all other decades would reveal both

Table 8.2 FPM estimates of death rate and life expectancy at age 5: India and zones, 1881–1891 to 1951–1961

Decade	Male						Female					
	India	Eastern Zone	Central Zone	Southern Zone	Western Zone	Northern Zone	India	Eastern Zone	Central Zone	Southern Zone	Western Zone	Northern Zone
CRUDE DEATH RATE												
1881–1891	39.81	47.83	41.06	35.92	28.24	47.65	40.02	42.83	39.46	37.66	32.46	44.31
1891–1901	47.93	a	a	30.89	a	32.73	46.85	a	a	32.73	a	a
1901–1911	41.81	46.46	47.88	32.72	34.92	a	46.04	47.20	a	35.55	40.93	43.07
1911–1921	48.44	a	a	42.29	a	36.70	48.93	a	41.39	47.64	a	a
1921–1931	35.37	40.23	36.24	33.22	34.90	29.68	40.85	41.25	29.60	40.52	38.59	40.67
1931–1941	26.05	27.65	27.60	26.48	27.31	18.02	30.15	29.89	29.95	32.81	29.37	24.24
1941–1951	29.78	27.90	36.40	19.95	25.46	29.75	32.90	32.35	39.95	23.59	30.94	41.34
1951–1961	25.86	22.54	25.75	26.60	23.58	16.68	29.22	27.44	29.07	33.72	25.63	25.20
LIFE EXPECTANCY AT AGE 5												
1881–1891	40.00	37.44	39.33	41.64	45.22	37.42	42.27	39.40	40.53	41.05	43.81	a
1891–1901	37.11	a	a	44.40	a	43.08	37.45	a	a	43.72	a	41.92
1901–1911	38.95	37.37	36.79	43.25	41.48	a	37.46	37.18	a	41.85	39.22	a
1911–1921	36.54	a	a	39.10	a	41.28	32.94	a	a	36.75	a	37.79
1921–1931	41.34	36.78	40.00	42.80	41.81	44.88	39.18	38.64	39.03	39.33	40.41	39.92
1931–1941	46.65	45.24	45.70	46.67	46.09	53.38	44.65	44.57	45.20	42.98	45.27	48.91
1941–1951	44.75	45.74	41.46	51.17	47.16	46.00	43.23	43.69	40.03	48.55	44.32	40.13
1951–1961	47.36	49.51	47.35	46.82	48.57	55.23	45.62	52.35	45.77	42.66	47.77	48.60

a Estimate not constructed because out of the nine estimates of e_5 made from the nine age sectors, more than four were below the lowest value of e_5 in West model life tables.

agreement with and discrepancy from the estimates derived through the quasi-stable population method.

The monotonic decline in the death rate since 1921 is established in both sets of estimates. The death rates estimated through the FPM are close to the estimates derived through the quasi-stable population model (see Tables 7.5 and 7.10). Even when there are discrepancies between the respective estimates, such discrepancies have good explanations: they occur chiefly in the estimated rates for the decades 1931–1941 and 1941–1951 and mainly in the Eastern and Northern Zones. Reference has already been made in Chapter 5 to the overenumeration in 1941 in the states of West Bengal (Eastern Zone) and Punjab (Northern Zone). As a consequence of that overenumeration, the death rate for 1931–1941 was underestimated and that for 1941–1951 was overestimated. Thus two things are clear: first, the estimates derived through the quasi-stable population model and the FPM are consistent; second, the reconstructed age composition is consistent with the probable trends of vital rates, GRR, and life expectancy.

Limitations of the FPM

One important limitation of the FPM is that the estimates yielded by this method are highly sensitive to errors in the counts of total population in two consecutive censuses. If there is a relative overcount in the latter census, the estimated e_5 is too high and the estimated death rate is too low (e.g., 1931–1941). If there is a relative undercount in the latter census, the estimated e_5 is too low and the estimated death rate is too high (e.g., 1941–1951). In this respect, the limitation of the FPM is similar in nature to, but greater in degree than, that of the quasi-stable population model.

Assuming a given rate of increase in population, an underestimation of the death rate leads to an underestimation of the birth rate also. But since there has been a relative overcount in the latter census, the rate of increase in population has already been somewhat overestimated. Whether the overestimation in the rate of natural increase is less than, equal to, or greater than the underestimation in the death rate is difficult to say. And therefore it is difficult to say to what extent the birth rate is underestimated. But it may be safe to infer that in case of a relative overcount in the latter census, the discrepancy between the estimated birth rate and the true birth rate is less than that between the estimated death rate and the true death rate. The reverse is true regarding a relative undercount in the latter census.

Demographers have already noted that estimates made through the

FPM are relatively insensitive to errors in age reporting, because the projected populations are cumulated over a wide age span [99]. Underenumeration in the age group 0–4 leads to underestimation in the mean decadal population in this age group and hence in the estimated number of deaths during the decade. On the other hand, the estimated e_5 may be too low if the undercount in the earlier census in age group 0–4 is compensated by an overcount in age group 5–9. Although the projected population in age group 10–14 will be too small, the projected population in age group 15–19 will be too large. And since the survival ratios P_{0-4} are very much lower than P_{5-9}, the net effect will be an overestimation of the reverse-cumulated population in age sector 10+–and hence an underestimation in the values of e_5 and an overestimation in those of M_x. This overestimation in the M_x values may offset the underestimation in the mean decadal population in the 0–4 age group. Thus there are mutually compensating errors in the estimation of the number of deaths. Even if there is some net underestimation in the number of deaths, it is likely to be quantitatively small.

Migration may lead to a distortion in the estimated value of e_5 in three different ways. First, a net positive migration may lead to overestimation of the survival rate and hence underestimation of the death rate. Second, a net negative migration may lead to opposite effects: underestimation of the survival rate and hence overestimation of the death rate. Third, even if adjustments are made for the effects of migration on the size of the population, the age-distributional effects of migration persist.

Sensitivity of the estimates to differences in the age pattern of mortality

Until now, we have tacitly assumed that the West model life tables are most relevant for India, and hence all estimates have been constructed through them. Since nobody knows for certain which mortality pattern best fits Indian conditions, it would be useful to examine the sensitivity of the estimates to differences in the age pattern of mortality. Table 8.3 sets out the estimated death rates and e_5 for India by using the five sets of model life tables referred to in Chapter 7. Note that the estimates of e_5 are close for all mortality patterns. The reason is obvious. The mortality patterns are differentiated mainly on the basis of mortality rates below age 5. Since mortality below age 5 has only marginal influence on the estimation of median e_5, the estimates of e_5 are largely insensitive to differences in the age pattern of mortality. But in the estimation of death rate, M_x values below age 5 have an

Table 8.3 Estimates of death rate and life expectancy at age 5 with five sets of model life tables: India, 1881–1891 to 1951–1961

Decade	Male					Female				
	West	North	South	East	U.N.	West	North	South	East	U.N.
DEATH RATE										
1881–1891	39.81	43.73	a	a	35.79	40.03	40.42	46.72	49.82	35.74
1891–1901	47.93	49.91	a	a	41.11	46.86	47.81	a	a	39.85
1901–1911	41.81	45.68	a	a	37.06	46.04	a	a	a	39.66
1911–1921	48.44	a	a	a	41.68	43.43	a	a	a	45.97
1921–1931	35.37	39.54	a	52.37	33.10	40.85	43.66	a	a	35.52
1931–1941	26.05	28.76	32.50	34.65	25.85	30.15	31.82	37.82	35.98	27.89
1941–1951	29.78	33.17	39.17	41.08	28.85	32.90	34.18	39.79	40.16	29.98
1951–1961	25.86	28.42	33.43	34.28	25.85	29.22	31.49	35.86	35.67	27.34
LIFE EXPECTANCY AT AGE 5										
1881–1891	40.00	36.92	a	a	39.80	40.27	38.94	39.84	40.72	40.14
1891–1901	37.11	34.62	a	a	37.16	37.45	35.66	a	a	37.68
1901–1911	38.95	35.85	a	a	38.87	37.46	a	a	a	37.51
1911–1921	36.74	a	a	a	36.78	32.94	a	a	a	34.62
1921–1931	41.34	38.10	a	40.71	40.85	29.18	36.80	a	a	39.45
1931–1941	46.65	44.09	45.25	46.33	46.16	44.65	42.90	43.06	45.20	44.75
1941–1951	44.76	41.72	42.39	44.33	44.32	43.22	41.65	42.21	43.47	43.35
1951–1961	47.36	44.93	45.51	47.11	46.84	45.62	43.56	44.56	45.76	45.60

a   Estimate not made because mortality level was so low that the value of e_5 or death rate could not be extrapolated.

important part to play. Therefore the estimated death rates are sensitive to differences in the age pattern of mortality.

Pursuing an argument analogous to that stated in Chapter 6, we observe that the East and South model life tables yield extremely high death rates, which would imply correspondingly high birth rates. If the death rate were to be 34 in the decade 1951–1961, the birth rate would have to be at least 53–which is unlikely. If the East and South tables are eliminated, the choice lies between the West, North, and U.N. model life tables.

Examination of sensitivity using hypothetical populations

We may further examine this problem of sensitivity of the estimates to the mortality pattern with the help of some hypothetical populations whose death rates are exactly known. The hypothetical populations chosen for the purpose are the ones projected by Demeny [49]. The projections assume the continuance of high fertility [GRR(29) = 3.00] and rapidly declining death rates. These assumptions are relevant for India, and thus the projected populations may be used for comparative purposes. The projected populations at different times are given by Demeny in percentages, so that the total is always equal to 100. We have converted the projected percentage distribution into so many quasi-stable populations in absolute number by multiplying them by the respective indexes of growth. The projections are given at intervals of five years: $t = 0, 5, 10, 15$, and so on. In order that the interval between successive time points be equal to ten years, we have taken the projected populations into two sets in the following manner:

$$\text{Set I: } t = 0, 10, 20, 30$$

$$\text{Set II: } t = 5, 15, 25, 35$$

Notwithstanding the broad comparability noted above, there are some differences between the assumptions underlying Demeny's projections and the conditions in India. Demeny generated the projections using the East model life tables. Our assumption is that the pattern of mortality in India is close to the West tables. Moreover, the rate of mortality decline in Demeny's projections is much faster than it has been in India. As our purpose is only to test the sensitivity of the estimated e_5 and death rate to the assumed mortality pattern, the results of the analysis are instructive in spite of these differences.

Table 8.4 sets out the FPM estimates of the crude death rate and e_5 for Demeny's projected population with five different sets of model life tables. The true rates have also been given. The true rates in

Table 8.4 FPM estimates of death rate and life expectancy at age 5 with five sets of model life tables for Demeny's projected population

Hypothetical decade	True rate	Rate estimated from model life tables				
		East	South	North	West	U.N.
CRUDE DEATH RATE						
0–10	42.64	44.27	40.47	34.85	31.92	30.93
5–15	35.41	34.91	36.50	31.35	29.42	27.92
10–20	29.81	28.67	28.64	24.87	22.52	23.52
15–25	24.93	24.25	26.45	22.70	20.88	21.31
20–30	20.72	17.58	19.45	17.06	17.07	17.31
25–35	17.09	15.96	18.47	15.68	14.05	15.67
EXPECTATION OF LIFE AT AGE 5						
0–10	43.37	44.56	43.30	42.30	45.06	44.68
5–15	46.39	46.70	44.96	44.36	46.42	46.18
10–20	49.32	50.87	49.77	48.84	51.16	50.61
15–25	52.16	52.81	61.41	50.85	52.60	52.15
20–30	54.88	57.02	56.20	55.18	55.39	57.16
25–35	57.54	58.83	67.91	57.23	58.69	57.13

SOURCE: [49:530].

Demeny's tables are instantaneous rates. We have estimated the mean decadal rates by taking the arithmetic average of the instantaneous rates at two time points ten years apart.

As expected, the death rates and e_5 estimated through the East or South tables are close to the true values. The sensitivity of the estimates to differences in age pattern of mortality is well illustrated in Table 8.4. At low levels of mortality, i.e., when life expectancy is low, the East tables provide an estimated death rate of 44.27, while the West tables yield an estimate of 31.92. The U.N. model life table provides an estimate of 30.93. The differences are indeed striking. When life expectancy increases, differences in the estimated death rates diminish. We may infer that even if the age pattern of mortality in India does not conform to the West tables, the estimated death rates for the decades 1941–1951 or 1951–1961 are likely to be deviant from the true rates by a small margin. The deviation in earlier decades, however, may have been considerable. It may also be inferred that whether the Indian age pattern of mortality is similar to that in the West or North or U.N. model life tables, the estimated rates are not significantly sensitive to such differences. So long as the probability of the East and South pattern of mortality being closer to Indian conditions can be eliminated, the estimates drawn through the FPM may be taken to be tolerably good.

9

Final estimates and comparisons

Until now we have presented all our estimates separately for male and female populations. In this chapter, we intend to prepare estimates for both sexes and institute some comparisons—first, between our estimates and other available estimates for the Indian population; and second, between Indian fertility and mortality as estimated by us and fertility and mortality of some foreign countries.

Joint estimates

Joint estimates have been prepared for the birth rate, death rate, and expectation of life at birth. Table 9.1 presents the joint estimates; Figure 9.1 depicts them graphically. The story told is clear and unambiguous. At the end of the last century, both the birth rate and the death rate in India were about 48 with a near-zero rate of natural increase. During the next two decades, the birth rate remained at about the same high level, but the death rate declined in the first decade (1901–1911) and increased in the second (1911–1921). Thereafter the birth rate recorded only a marginal increase and remained high. The death rate decreased substantially and monotonically, leading to an accelerated rate of growth in population. This was the overall picture in the country, although there were variations from zone to zone. All these facts are generally known, and earlier estimates have already

Table 9.1 Estimates of joint birth rate, death rate, and life expectancy: India and zones, 1901–1961

Zone	1901	1911	1921	1931	1941	1951	1961
BR							
India	47–49	48–50	48–50	46–48	44–46	42–44	43–45
Eastern	50–52	48–50	49–51	46–48	45–47	43–45	44–46
Central	46–48	48–50	48–50	46–48	44–46	42–44	43–45
Southern	44–46	45–47	43–45	43–45	44–46	40–42	42–44
Western	49–51	49–51	47–49	46–48	43–45	43–45	42–44
Northern	46–48	47–49	47–49	46–48	46–48	44–46	44–46
DR							
India	47–49	42–44	48–50	36–38	32–34	30–32	25–27
Eastern	45–47	43–45	49–51	35–37	33–35	31–33	25–27
Central	46–48	45–47	50–52	39–41	31–31	32–34	26–28
Southern	37–39	36–38	41–43	33–35	32–34	24–26	25–27
Western	55–57	40–42	49–51	33–35	30–32	29–31	22–24
Northern	54–56	50–52	47–49	35–37	30–32	29–31	22–24
e_0							
India	21.48	23.65	21.07	28.61	32.94	34.61	38.28
Eastern	22.82	24.10	21.37	28.50	30.77	35.44	38.37
Central	22.29	22.86	19.88	26.60	33.57	32.61	36.92
Southern	27.79	28.22	26.04	30.94	31.85	39.05	37.56
Western	a	a	22.15	30.60	33.18	34.50	41.42
Northern	20.41	a	a	29.15	31.55	34.22	41.49

a   Joint estimate could not be prepared because male estimate was not available.

revealed such a picture. Although our estimates do not add much to a general understanding of the situation, with respect to the precise rates and their regional variations there are certain differences between them and those made earlier. It is therefore useful to compare our estimates with others derived from registration data, from survey data, and from census data. Numerous estimates belonging to each of these categories are available. We have chosen one or two typical sets from each category.

Estimates based on the sample registration system

The deficiency of registration data in India is well known: estimates of birth and death rates obtained from the registration system are far below the true rates. Therefore attempts have been made not only to improve the vital registration system but also to arrive at better estimates of birth and death rates through what has been called the sample registration system [67, 84]. Using data collected from about 1,500 sampling areas (units) containing a population of 1.9 million,

Figure 9.1 Male, female, and joint birth rates, death rates, and life expectancy: India and zones, 1901–1961

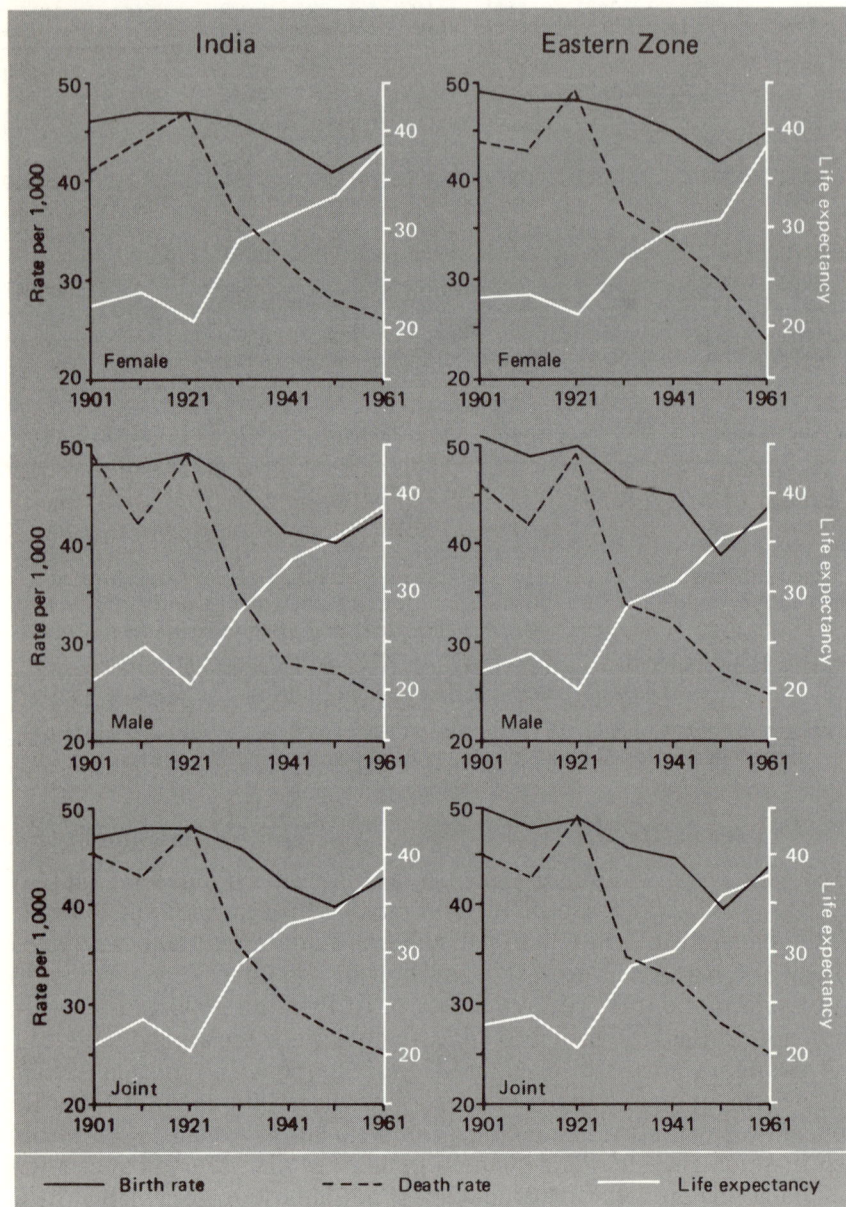

Figure 9.1 *(continued)*

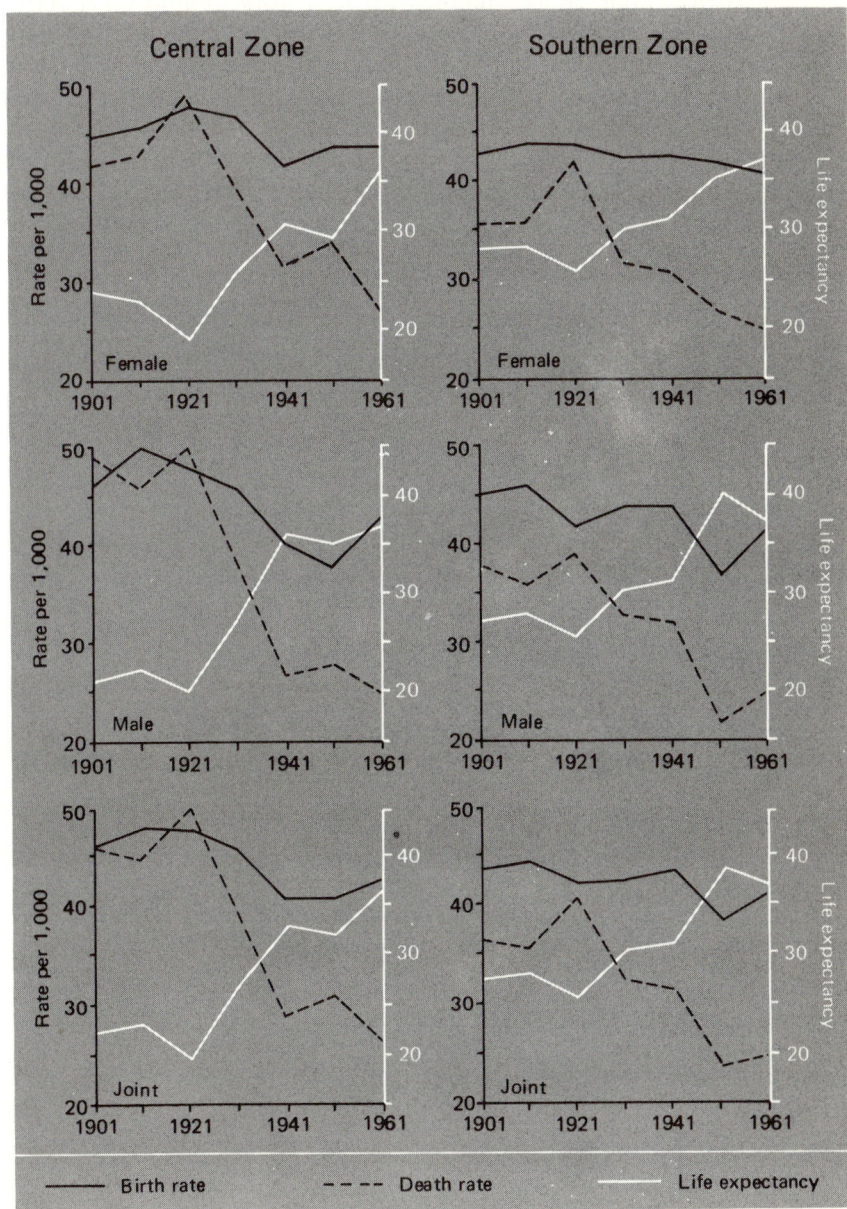

Figure 9.1 *(continued)*

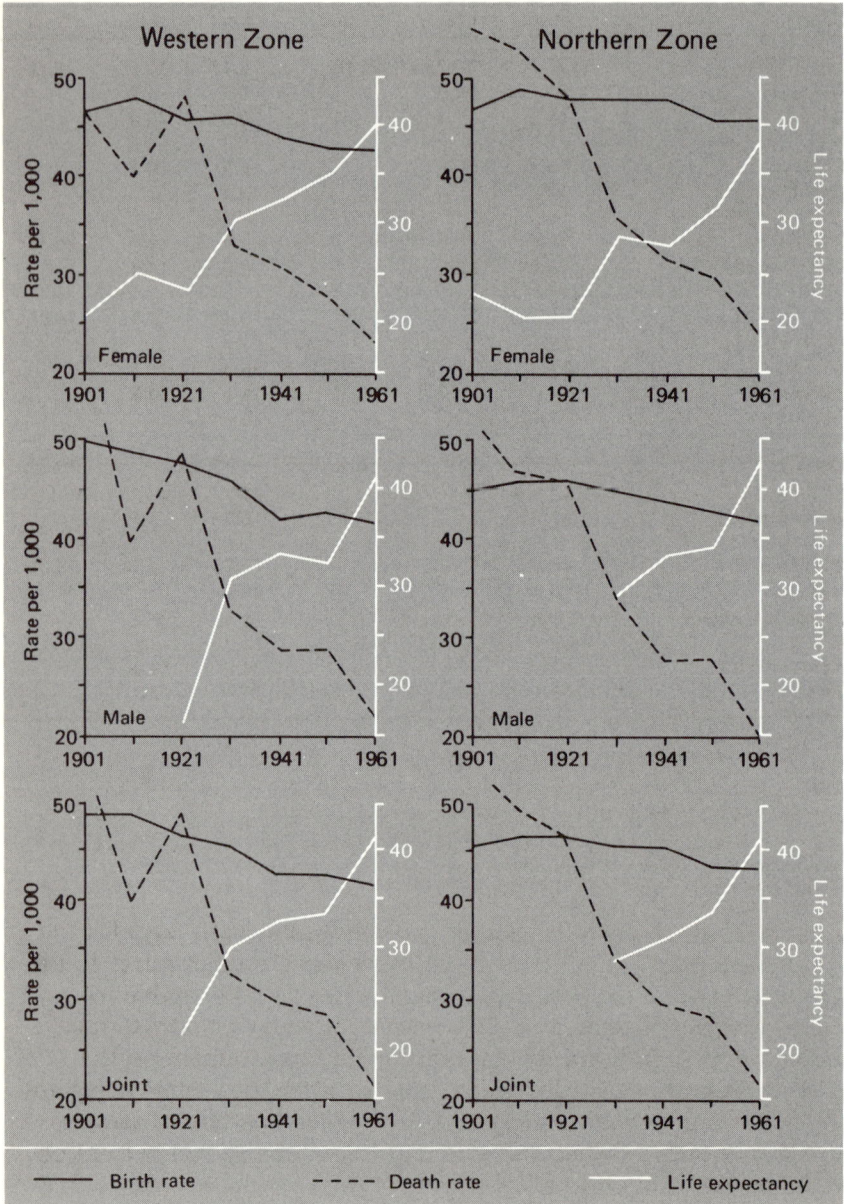

Western Zone   Northern Zone

Table 9.2 Estimates of birth rate and death rate based on sample registration system: India, 1969

Zone	Birth rate			Death rate		
	Rural	Urban	Total	Rural	Urban	Total
EASTERN	36.16	30.72	35.46	15.17	10.46	14.56
Manipur		24.2			4.7	
Assam	45.5	31.1		20.0	10.6	
Bihar	35.0			14.9		
Orissa	39.3	30.8		15.5	10.7	
West Bengal	32.2			13.4		
CENTRAL	45.6	35.9	44.31	25.6	14.4	24.11
Uttar Pradesh	45.6	35.9		25.6	14.4	
SOUTHERN	33.94	28.9	32.88	15.89	9.5	14.55
Andhra Pradesh	35.4			17.2		
Kerala	31.1			9.0		
Mysore	34.0	28.9		15.4	9.5	
Tamil Nadu	33.8			18.7		
WESTERN	36.19		36.19	17.32		17.32
Gujarat	42.3			20.7		
Maharashtra	32.9			15.5		
NORTHERN	40.0	32.33	38.34	17.63	10.34	16.05
Haryana	39.7			11.7		
Jammu and Kashmir	39.5	28.5		14.4	7.4	
Punjab	33.6	28.2		11.6	9.8	
Rajasthan	44.0	37.7		24.0	13.6	
Delhi	42.4	33.0		14.7	7.5	

SOURCE: [84].

Ramabhadran constructed estimates of birth and death rates for the different states of India (Table 9.2). Since our estimates relate to the zones, and not to the states, they are not strictly comparable to Ramabhadran's. Nonetheless, it is important to note that although the sample registration estimates are a great improvement on the earlier estimates made through the basic registration system, they are still below our estimates. Moreover, the regional pattern of sample registration rates is somewhat different from the regional pattern observed in our estimates.

Estimates based on survey data

Of the many surveys conducted by various organizations and insti-
tutes* during the last 20 years we have selected the National Sample
Survey (NSS) for purposes of comparison [66].

The NSS started collecting fertility data from the 2nd round in
1952, but the inquiry into current fertility and mortality was started
on a comprehensive scale in the 14th round (1958–1959) in rural
areas. It was continued in rural areas in the 15th round (1959–1960),
in urban areas in the 16th round (1960–1961), and in both areas in
the 17th and 18th rounds (1963–1964). Tables 9.3 and 9.4 summa-
rize the results [65].

Table 9.3　Estimates of birth rate, death rate, and growth rate in rural areas of
India from two interpenetrating samples: NSS 14th, 15th, and 18th
rounds

NSS round and sample	BR	DR	GR
14th round (July 1958–June 1959)			
1	38.50	19.47	19.03
2	38.02	18.58	19.44
Combined	38.26	19.02	19.24
15th round (July 1959–June 1960)			
1	39.58	14.87	24.71
2	38.28	15.29	23.00
Combined	38.93	15.08	23.85
18th round (Feb. 1963–Jan. 1964)			
1[a]	37.49	12.40	25.09
2[a]	37.64	12.39	25.25
Combined	37.57	12.39	25.18

a　Half-sample.
SOURCE: [66:9].

The NSS estimates of birth and death rates are significantly lower
than ours. The real differences in the level of fertility are larger than
indicated in the estimated birth and death rates. Whereas the NSS estimates relate to rural areas only, ours relate to urban and rural areas
jointly. Rural birth rates have been known to be higher than urban

---

* To mention only a few: All India Institute of Hygiene and Public Health
(Calcutta), Gokhale Institute of Politics and Economics (Poona), International
Institute of Population Studies (Bombay), Institute of Economic Growth
(Delhi), Demographic Research Center (Trivandrum), the various universities,
and the health departments of state governments.

Table 9.4 Estimates of birth rate, death rate, and growth rate in rural areas of India: NSS 13th and 14th rounds

Zone	13th round BR	14th round BR	DR	GR	Index of BR 13th round	14th round
India	35.16	38.26	19.02	19.24	100.0	100.0
Eastern	32.96	34.11	16.02	18.09	93.7	82.6
Central	42.36	44.11	27.78	16.33	120.5	116.2
Southern	28.07	34.30	13.97	20.33	79.8	87.9
Western	32.81	38.94	17.87	21.07	93.3	101.2
Northern	37.08	40.60	15.77	24.83	105.5	111.0

SOURCE: [64:12–14, 104].

birth rates. This may be due not to differences in marital fertility rates (about which our information is scanty) but to differences in age composition and marital pattern in rural and urban areas.

We believe that the NSS estimates of the birth rate are low and that our own are nearer the true rates. If the true level of fertility were as indicated in the NSS birth rates and general fertility rates (whatever the mortality level might have been), India would have a considerably older population than has been observed in the census age returns. If the estimated GRR in India in 1961 was 2.4 or 2.5, the GRR in 1901, 1911, or 1921 could not have been much higher. There is no evidence in Indian age distributions of any significant decline in fertility (see Chapter 4). Even granting that age returns in India contain various types of bias and distortion, it is highly probable that the effects of a decline in fertility would have been visible in age segments 0–10 or 0–30 or 0–35. It is noteworthy that although changes in mortality affect the age distribution to a much lesser extent than do changes in fertility, the effects of mortality decline during the period 1921–1961 are distinctly visible in the age distribution.

Let us assume for argument's sake that all the census age returns are biased in a certain direction, that the proportions of population in age sectors 0–10, 0–30, and 0–35 are all overstated in the census age returns, and that the real proportions are less than those indicated in the census data. This is extremely unlikely, but even if we make this assumption, the question is whether the observed growth rate of India's population is consistent with a GRR of 2.5. The answer probably is no. A GRR of 2.5 can yield a growth rate of 5.0 per 1,000 only if the expectation of life at birth is about 30 years. During the decade 1901–1911, the annual growth rate for the male and female populations was 6.0 and 5.2 respectively. Indian life tables give male e_0 for 1901–1911 as 22.59 and female e_0 as 23.31. It has been shown in Chapter 6 that Indian life tables overestimated the values of e_0 in earlier decades particularly. If the decline in mortality in subsequent decades is accepted as a historical fact, the value of e_0 for the female population in India during the decade 1901–1911 could not have been anywhere near 30 years. The same argument holds true for each of the other decades. With a GRR of 2.5, life expectancy for the female population in the decade 1921–1931 should have been around 35 years. Such high values of e_0 in the respective decades are highly improbable.

Besides differences in the level of fertility, there are also discrepancies in the regional pattern of birth rates revealed in the NSS and our own estimates. The NSS estimates indicate a lower level of fertility in the Eastern Zone than in other zones. Our finding is that the Northern and Eastern Zones have the highest and next to highest level of fertility. The fact that fertility is the dominant determinant of age composition—and that differences between age distributions in different zones reflect the regional pattern of fertility differences revealed in our estimates—lends credence to our estimates.

Estimates based on census data

Estimates based on census data may be classified into those derived from survey data collected by the Indian census organization and those derived from the usual census data on total population, age composition, and so forth. Let us first consider rates derived from survey data collected by the census. Since 1921 the Indian census organization has conducted fertility inquiries on a sample basis along with the normal census operations. Such surveys were held in 1921, 1931, 1941 [95],* 1951, and 1961.† The data collected in these surveys relate to the reproductive histories of the sample women in rural areas. The existence of a varying but unknown degree of response error in such data on reproductive history severely limits the value of these studies—particularly because the information was presented in such a manner that it is hardly possible to make even a rough guess of the extent of recall lapse, response error, and investigator bias [95]. Besides, the surveys in 1921 [14] and 1931 [15] were different in nature and limited in scope. For whatever historical interest there might be in the findings of these surveys, one may refer to the respective census reports.

---

* The 1941 fertility inquiry was held only in some states, and fertility data are available for only a small fraction of the total population [17].

† In 1961 fertility data were collected, but the results were not published—perhaps because they were judged unusable.

Table 9.5 Upper estimates of birth rate for selected areas of India: 1951 census fertility inquiry

Area	BR
Travancore-Cochin	36.8
East Madhya Pradesh	46.4
North-West Madhya Pradesh	41.7
South-West Madhya Pradesh	43.5
West Bengal (six districts)	35.5
West Bengal (four districts)	37.4

Fertility* data collected in the 1951 census were processed for three states [22]. Logistic graduation was applied to the data on the number of children ever born, and specific fertility rates were obtained on that basis (Table 9.5). These estimates were made after so much statistical manipulation of the raw data that there appears to be an element of unreality in them. We may, however, look at the estimates for whatever they are worth. The estimated birth rate for Madhya Pradesh does not seem to be unlikely, but the estimates for Travancore-Cochin and particularly for West Bengal seem to be too low.

Among the estimates made from normal census data, mention may first be made of those prepared by Jain, who applied the so-called differencing method and the reverse survival method to 1951 census data [22]. We may examine these estimates a little more closely.

The essence of the differencing method consists of comparing the total populations enumerated in two consecutive censuses and making a broad estimate of the mean decennial growth rate and the mean decennial death rate. The sum of the death rate and the growth rate equals the birth rate. The estimates of birth and death rates obtained by this method are given in Table 9.6.

There is an important similarity between the differencing method and our own. In both, the decennial growth rate is determined first and then the vital rates are estimated. The difference between the methods lies in two aspects. First, in the differencing method the death rate is estimated first, and the birth rate is obtained by adding the growth rate and the death rate. In our method, the level of mortality is first estimated, then the birth and death rates are obtained by interpolation from tables of stable populations. Second, in our method we use the age segments as estimating parameters. In the differencing

---

* The registrar general of India preferred the term *maternity* instead of *fertility*.

Table 9.6 Estimates of birth rate and death rate by zone obtained by differencing method, reverse-survival method, and registration: Indian census actuary, 1951

Zone	Differencing method		Reverse-survival BR	Registered BR
	BR	DR		
INDIA	39.9	27.4	39.2	27.5
EASTERN	38.5	28.3	41.3	22.0
Bihar	39.0	26.6	42.2	21.9
Orissa	37.2	29.9	39.3	28.2
West Bengal	35.4	28.6	37.4	20.5
Assam + Manipur	46.7	31.8	50.4	16.8
CENTRAL	41.0	30.8	39.8	27.9
Uttar Pradesh	38.6	27.2	37.1	24.8
Madhya Pradesh	46.1	38.5	45.1	37.0
Madhya Bharat + Vindhya Pradesh + Bhopal	44.2	35.8	44.3	u
SOUTHERN	37.5	23.3	38.1	27.7
Madras	35.7	22.8	34.7	30.8
Mysore	36.9	18.9	38.7	16.2
Travancore-Cochin	37.4	18.0	39.8	20.3
Coorg	38.7	18.6	38.7	17.2
Hyderabad	43.1	29.5	47.2	u
WESTERN	41.1	24.9	41.9	32.9
Bombay	41.0	24.9	41.8	32.9
Saurasthra (Kutch)	42.2	24.9	42.4	u
NORTHERN	41.9	27.5	42.7	37.9
Rajasthan	42.5	27.2	47.9	u
Punjab	41.2	26.3	37.6	39.5
Pepsu	41.5	31.3	36.6	u
Ajmer	45.0	38.0	46.8	28.9
Delhi	41.2	26.3	45.3	29.9

u—unavailable.
SOURCE: [22:136–37].

method the total population in one census and the population in the age sector "10 and above" in the next census are used for estimating death rates. The weakest point in this method is the uncertain nature of the effect of migration as well as the much too bold assumption that the ratio of all deaths to deaths at ages "5 and over" is the same for registered deaths and actual deaths. The variation in this ratio between 1.40386 and 1.84835 in different states of India in Jain's own estimates is itself strong evidence against the validity of the method.

The arguments stated above acquire added force when it is recalled that for a number of states the death rates computed on the basis of the differencing method are lower than the registered death rates [22].

The reverse survival method is well known and hardly needs explanation. If the number of persons at age x is N_x, ℓ_0 is the radix, and L_x is the number of persons living between age x and $x + 1$, then the number of births corresponding to the cohort N_x is

$$\frac{\ell_0}{L_x} (N_x)$$

This is a handy method and has been widely used for estimating birth rates. But it does have severe limitations. The Indian life tables have been constructed by comparing the populations of two consecutive censuses. The Q_x values for ages 10 to 70 have been obtained from actual age data (though after drastic smoothing), but those for ages below 10 (as well as above 70) have been obtained by extrapolation. This imparts an element of unreality to the life tables.

Using the life tables prepared by the Indian census actuaries, Kingsley Davis constructed estimates of birth and death rates in India through the reverse survival method (Table 9.7). It is interesting that Davis's estimates are close to our own for the respective decades. This may be fortuitous. His estimates relate to India including the territories now in Pakistan and Bangladesh. We have already seen that the age distribution in the Northern and Eastern Zones is somewhat younger than in the rest of India and hence the birth rates are a little higher in the territories comprising Pakistan and Bangladesh.

Of late some demographers have prepared estimates of fertility and mortality by using the census age data and applying the quasi-stable population model—in the same manner as we have done. Mention may

Table 9.7 Birth rates and death rates estimated by Davis: India, 1881–1891 to 1931–1941

Decade	BR	DR
1881–1891	49	41.3
1891–1901	46	44.4
1901–1911	48	42.6
1911–1921	49	48.6
1921–1931	46	36.3
1931–1941	45	31.2

SOURCE: [47:36].

be made of Saxena [86] and Visaria [110] in this connection. We may quote from Saxena's paper as summarized in the proceedings of the World Population Conference [100:204]:

An application of the stable population theory reveals that the birth rate in India during the years 1901–1921 was 53 per 1,000. In 1931 it was 45 per 1,000 and during the period 1941–1961, it was about 43 per 1,000 population. Estimated life-expectancies at birth are 20, 22, 19, 28, 35, 35, and 37 years for females and 20, 22, 18, 29, 35, 35, and 42 years for males in 1901, 1911, 1921, 1931, 1941, 1951, and 1961 respectively.

As these rates are based on the assumption that age distribution under perfect stability is exactly identical to that under quasi-stability, these estimates require a correction. The corrected birth rates in 1941 work out at 47 and during 1951–1961 at 46. The corrected estimates of expectation of life for females are 28, 33, and 37 years in 1941, 1951, and 1961 respectively. The corresponding estimates for the males are 29, 34, and 42 years.

Visaria constructed estimates for the country as a whole for two decades, 1941–1951 and 1951–1961 (Table 9.8).

The estimates constructed by Visaria, Saxena, and ourselves are close to each other—which is only to be expected, because the method of estimation is the same. The only difference is that we used the age data as reconstructed in this study and prepared elaborate estimates for all the zones and for each of the seven census decades. Moreover, we preferred to present the estimates within a range whereas Visaria and Saxena presented exact estimates. However, the outstanding feature is that all three sets of estimates tell the same story: The estimates hitherto prepared by conventional methods were too low and failed to explain the dynamics of population growth and the statics of the age structure in India during the sixty-year period.

Table 9.8 Birth rates, death rates, life expectancy, and gross reproduction rates estimated by Visaria: India, 1941–1961

Rate	1941–1951[a]		1951–1961	
	Male	Female	Male	Female
BR	42.11	42.99	40.98	45.75
DR	29.62	30.39	21.45	26.81
e_0	33.33	32.83	41.86	36.44
e_5	45.55	45.20	50.67	47.51
GRR		2.75		2.99

a Stable estimates corresponding to age sector 0–15.
SOURCE: [110:91–116].

Comparison with some advanced countries

Table 9.9 sets out the birth rate, death rate, gross reproduction rate, life expectancy at birth, and summary measures of the age distribution for France, Sweden, Great Britain, and the United States; it also puts side by side the estimated values of the same parameters for India in 1901, 1941, and 1961. The persistence of a high birth rate and gross reproduction rate in India stands in glaring contrast to the low level and further decline of these rates in the four advanced countries—particularly during the period 1901–1941. The two postwar decades saw a slight reversal of the declining trend and a temporary upswing in birth rates in the advanced countries, but still the disparities between India and these countries remains large. The Indian birth rate is three times that of Sweden, two and a half times that of France or Great Britain, and about double that of the United States.

The contrast in death rates and life expectancy is less pronounced, because India did achieve a considerable decline in mortality and an increase in life expectancy during this period. The gains in life expectancy and decline in the death rate were larger in the advanced countries than in India in absolute terms. But since mortality conditions had considerably improved in the advanced countries even before 1901, the relative position of India improved slightly during the period 1901–1961.

The contrast in age structure between India and the other countries is a logical consequence of changes in birth rates and death rates. The persistence of a young age distribution in India is remarkable. The already old age distribution in the advanced countries has become still older.

From the standpoint of economic development India is often called a developing rather than an underdeveloped country. From the standpoint of demographic evolution, the epithet "developing" can hardly be claimed for India. India continues to be demographically underdeveloped.

Table 9.9 Demographic parameters for four industrialized countries and India:

Parameter	1901					1941
	France	Sweden	United Kingdom	United States[a]	India	France[b]
BR						
Both sexes	21.86	26.79	28.51	23.42	48.00	15.53
Male	22.65	28.20	30.05	23.62	49.00	16.49
Female	21.09	25.43	27.06	23.22	47.00	14.64
DR						
Both sexes	20.63	16.19	16.91	12.49	47.00	15.73
Male	21.74	16.63	18.11	12.91	49.00	17.21
Female	19.57	15.78	15.79	12.04	45.00	14.37
GRR (female)	1.39	1.94	1.69	1.64	2.90	1.02
e_0						
Male	45.02	51.53	45.40	54.49	19.50	56.27
Female	48.53	54.26	49.39	56.41	21.00	62.14
POPULATION (%)						
Male						
under 15	26.55	33.79	33.43	31.49	38.66	25.79
15–60	61.72	55.37	59.76	60.96	56.77	60.72
60+	11.72	10.84	6.82	7.55	4.57	13.49
Female						
under 15	25.70	31.24	31.38	32.04	37.42	23.45
15–60	61.14	55.89	60.60	60.49	56.98	60.42
60+	13.15	12.87	8.02	7.46	5.60	16.13

a   U.S. figures are for 1919–1921.

b   France figures are for 1934–1938.

1901, 1941, and 1961

				1961				
Sweden	United Kingdom	United States	India	France	Sweden	United Kingdom	United States	India
15.76	14.95	18.07	45.00	18.07	14.02	17.58	23.65	44.00
16.32	17.24	18.54	45.00	19.03	14.48	18.70	24.59	44.00
15.20	13.11	17.60	45.00	17.17	13.56	16.53	22.74	45.00
11.14	13.54	10.64	32.00	11.32	9.82	11.81	9.39	26.00
11.22	15.69	11.87	32.00	11.91	10.36	12.46	10.85	25.00
11.06	11.81	9.41	33.00	10.76	9.26	11.20	7.97	27.00
0.93	0.85	1.13	2.90	1.37	1.08	1.35	1.80	2.90
65.62	58.54	61.14	33.00	67.46	71.54	68.10	66.84	39.00
68.42	64.63	65.58	30.00	74.23	75.22	73.97	73.40	37.00
21.09	25.13	25.47	39.27	27.72	23.04	24.28	32.17	40.93
66.07	59.88	64.10	55.28	58.46	61.17	61.33	55.43	53.60
12.84	14.98	10.42	5.45	13.81	15.79	14.39	12.40	5.47
19.97	19.58	24.76	39.02	25.21	21.74	21.66	30.19	41.16
65.46	65.04	64.58	55.04	54.83	60.13	58.36	55.72	53.03
14.58	15.38	10.66	5.94	19.96	18.12	19.98	14.08	5.81

SOURCES: France, Sweden, United Kingdom, United States: [70:324, 332, 326, 90, 491, 501, 506, 103, 525, 530, 536, 107, 142, 147, 152, 74]. India: Chapter 7 and basic tables.

Appendix:
the 1971 age distribution

This study was completed before age data from the 1971 census were available. Toward the end of 1972 the 1 percent sample tabulations of the 1971 census age data were published in mimeographed form [33]. Table A.1 shows the age distribution for the total, rural, and urban populations of India in 1971 based on the 1 percent sample tabulations. The sample tabulations do not provide data at the subnational level, however.

The census paper on the economic characteristics of the population [34] provides a classification of workers and nonworkers by sex in eight broad age groups: 0–14, 15–19, 20–24, 25–29, 30–39, 40–49, 50–59, and 60+. The last columns of Basic Tables 1, 2, 3, and 4 present the age composition in the eight age groups for India and its zones, states, and territories for 1971 in absolute numbers. Basic Tables 5, 6, 7, and 8 reduce it to percentage distribution.

Note that the broad age profile in India remained substantially similar in 1971 to that of earlier decades, though marginal changes occurred during the decade 1961–1971. The proportion of the total population in age interval 0–14 increased somewhat, except in the Southern Zone where the proportion among males remained unchanged (Table A.2).

By superimposing the proportions in age groups 0–4, 5–9, and

Table A.1 Percentage age distribution of total, rural, and urban population: India, 1971

Age group	Male			Female		
	Total	Rural	Urban	Total	Rural	Urban
0—4	14.11	14.60	12.26	14.68	14.93	13.64
5—9	15.04	15.58	12.98	15.10	15.34	14.10
10—14	12.71	12.85	12.19	12.10	11.96	12.72
15—19	8.96	8.64	10.18	8.49	8.14	9.96
20—24	7.60	7.02	9.84	8.23	7.93	9.53
25—29	7.10	6.81	8.21	7.82	7.72	8.26
30—34	6.43	6.23	7.17	6.84	6.85	6.78
35—39	6.07	5.95	6.51	5.97	5.94	6.09
40—44	5.33	5.26	5.63	5.05	5.10	4.84
45—49	4.38	4.35	4.49	3.95	4.01	3.69
50—54	3.93	4.00	3.66	3.58	3.65	3.25
55—59	2.38	2.45	2.09	2.21	2.27	1.95
60+	5.96	6.26	4.79	5.98	6.16	5.19
All age groups	100.00	100.00	100.00	100.00	100.00	100.00

SOURCE: [34:125—27].

10—14 obtained from the sample population on the proportion in the broad age interval 0—14 in the total population, we obtained the proportions in age groups 0—4, 5—9, and 10—14 for India as a whole (Table A.3). Note that the proportion in age group 0—4 decreased marginally and that in age group 5—9 increased marginally. Only in age group 10—14 did the proportion increase decisively. To our thinking, the decrease in the proportion of age group 0—4 indicates a slight decline in fertility starting from about the middle of the decade.

If the process of secular decline in mortality which started earlier and accelerated in the decade 1951—1961 is assumed to have con-

Table A.2 Percentage of population below age 15: India and zones, 1961 and 1971

Zone	Male		Female	
	1961	1971	1961	1971
India	40.93	41.88	41.16	42.20
Eastern Zone	41.34	42.62	41.97	43.53
Central Zone	40.74	42.58	40.44	42.28
Southern Zone	40.02	40.00	39.93	40.10
Western Zone	41.24	41.71	41.63	42.19
Northern Zone	42.10	42.91	43.24	43.55

SOURCES: [30:20—21] ; [34:125—27].

Table A.3 Percentage of population in age groups 0–4, 5–9, and 10–14, based on 1 percent sample: India, 1961 and 1971

Age group	Male		Female	
	1961	1971	1961	1971
0–4	14.68	14.12	15.47	14.79
5–9	14.63	15.05	14.86	15.22
10–14	11.62	12.71	10.83	12.19
Total 0–14	40.93	41.88	41.16	42.20

SOURCES: [30:20–21]; [34:125–27].

tinued in the decade 1961–1971, the proportion in age group 0–4 should have increased in 1971. That the proportion actually *decreased* may have resulted from three different circumstances: a rise in mortality in the period 1966–1971; a deterioration in census enumeration in 1971, resulting in a greater undercount in age group 0–4; or a decline in the number of births during the period 1966–1971.

There is no evidence of a rise in mortality in either the earlier or the later half of the decade. On the other hand, the small increase in the proportion of population in age group 5–9 might indicate a continuation of the declining trend in mortality accompanied by unchanged fertility in the earlier half of the decade. The significant increase in the proportion of age group 10–14 is due to the relatively larger number of children enumerated in age group 0–4 in 1961, which in turn is explained by the accelerated decline in mortality among children born in the years 1956–1961.

The hypothesis that a deterioration in the quality of census operations resulted in a greater undercount of children in 1971 than in 1961 does not seem tenable. In 1971 there was no particular motivation among the people to deflate their numbers and no organizational factors in the census that might have led to increased undercounting.

A disaggregation of 1971 age data into rural and urban might also lend support to the hypothesis of a marginal decline in fertility. Table A.4 presents the comparative shifts in the proportion of rural and urban population in the younger age groups during the decade 1961–1971.

The rural age distribution in 1971 is somewhat younger than the urban age distribution—a feature also observed in 1951 and 1961. The difference between the rural and urban age distributions is larger for the male than for the female population, possibly because of the greater incidence of migration among females and the age-sex selec-

Table A.4 Percentage age distribution of rural and urban population, based on 1 percent sample: India, 1961 and 1971

	Male		Female	
Age group	Rural	Urban	Rural	Urban
YEAR 1961				
0–4	15.10	12.87	15.63	14.71
5–9	14.98	13.15	14.90	14.66
10–14	11.71	11.26	10.26	11.66
15–59	52.50	58.30	52.86	53.86
60+	5.71	4.42	5.95	5.11
Total	100.00	100.00	100.00	100.00
YEAR 1971				
0–4	14.60	12.26	14.93	13.64
5–9	15.58	12.98	14.34	14.10
10–14	12.85	12.19	11.96	12.72
15–59	50.71	57.78	51.61	54.35
60+	6.26	4.79	6.16	5.19
Total	100.00	100.00	100.00	100.00

SOURCES: [30:20–21]; [34:125–27].

tivity of rural-to-urban migration in India. The crucial fact, however, is that between 1961 and 1971 a greater reduction occurred in the 0–4 age group among the urban population than among the rural population. The inference is that the hypothesized decline in the birth rate was greater in urban areas than in rural areas. Such an inference is consistent with the widely observed phenomenon that urban people tend to accept family planning practices earlier than rural people.

Quasi-stable estimates of fertility and mortality have been constructed from the 1971 age distribution according to the methods discussed in Chapter 6. Since complete census data were not available, the following approximations have been made:

1. The population is assumed to be closed.

2. The mean of the female fertility schedule is assumed to be the same as in 1961.

3. Correction factors for changes in mortality relevant to 1961 have been used to correct the stable estimates for the decade 1961–1971.

Table A.5 sets out the quasi-stable estimates of birth rate, death rate, gross reproduction rate, and expectation of life at birth. In spite of all the limitations of data, the estimates appear to be consistent with those for earlier years (see Chapter 7). The slight decline in female birth rate and GRR hypothesized earlier seems to be corroborated by these estimates. The steep decline in male death rate and rise

Table A.5 Quasi-stable estimates of birth rate, death rate, gross reproduction rate, and life expectancy at birth: India, 1961–1971

Estimate	BR[a]	DR	GRR	e_0[b]
FEMALE				
Lower	42	21	2.7[c]	42.92
Upper	44	23	2.9[c]	40.50
MALE				
Lower	39	17		47.50
Upper	41	19		45.11
BOTH SEXES				
Lower	41	19		45.29
Upper	43	21		42.89

a   Correction factors for changes in mortality assumed to be same as for year 1961.

b   Note that lower estimates of e_0 are associated with upper estimates of birth rate, death rate, and GRR.

c   Female $\overline{M}$ = 28.24 years.

in male life expectancy are also noticeable. However, such a large difference between male and female life expectancies does not seem to be likely. When complete data from the 1971 census are available, these estimates may need to be modified.

The female and male birth rates seem to be consistent. The sex ratio at birth in 1971 was 1.0754. If sex ratio at birth is assumed to be between 1.03 and 1.09, the expected values of FBR/MBR should be between 0.9866 and 1.0441 (see Table 7.13). If the values of FBR/MBR are computed by relating the upper estimates of the female population to those for males (or the lower estimates of the female population to those for males), the expected values of FBR/MBR would lie outside this range. But if we compare the lower estimates of the female population with the upper estimates of the male population, then the resultant values of FBR/MBR would lie within the expected range.

In summary, the limited data available until now do not permit us to draw firm inferences regarding the 1971 census age composition. But the preceding estimates seem to give a broad view of fertility and mortality trends in India in the decade 1961–1971. The joint birth rate is of the order of 41 to 43, the joint death rate is of the order of 19 to 21, and the joint expectation of life is about 43 to 45 years. A small but perceptible decrease in the birth rate and female GRR and a somewhat greater decrease in the death rate along with a significant increase in the expectation of life at birth seem to have occurred during the decade. And, in spite of a slight fall in the proportion of the population in age group 0–4, the process of rejuvenation in the age structure continued.

References

No attempt has been made to provide an extensive bibliography on the subject treated. Only those references have been cited that were sources of data or ideas presented in this study.

1. Agarwal, S.P. Interrelationship between Population and Manpower Problems in the Context of Socio-Economic Development of the ECAFE Region. In *Interrelation between Population and Manpower Problems.* Bangkok: U.N. Economic Commission for Asia and the Far East, 1972.

2. Agarwala, S.N. *Corrected Age Data of the 1931 Indian Census.* Delhi: Asia Publishing House, Institute of Economic Growth, 1967.

3. Bower, W.G., and T. Aldrich Finegan. *The Economics of Labor Force Participation.* Princeton: Princeton University Press, 1969.

4. Brass, W. The Graduation of Fertility Distribution by Polynomial Functions. *Population Studies* 14(2), 1960.

5. Brass, W., et al. *The Demography of Tropical Africa.* Princeton: Princeton University Press, 1969.

6. Carrier, Norman, and John Hobcroft. *Demographic Estimates for Developing Societies.* London: Population Investigation Committee, London School of Economics, 1971.

7. Census of Bengal, *Report on the Census of Bengal, 1872.* Calcutta, 1873.

8. Census of India, *Bibliography of Census Publications in India,* Office of the Registrar General, India. New Delhi, 1972.

9. Census of India 1871–72, *Memorandum on the Census of British India of 1871–72.* Calcutta, 1873.

10. Census of India, 1881, vol. 1.

11. Census of India, 1891, vol. 1.

12. Census of India, 1901, vol. 1, pt. 1.

13. Census of India, 1911, vol. 1, pt. 1.

14. Census of India, 1921, vol. 1, pt. 1.

15. Census of India, 1931, vol. 1, pt. 1.

16. Census of India, 1931, vol. 5, pt. 1.

17. Census of India, 1941, vol. 1 (India report).

18. Census of India, 1941, Paper 1 of 1948 (age tables for West Bengal on Y-sample), foreword.

19. Census of India, 1941, vol. 17 (Baroda).

20. Census of India, Paper 3 of 1954 (1951 age tables).

21. Census of India, 1951, vol. 1, pt. 2A.

22. Census of India, 1951, vol. 1, pt. 1B.

23. Census of India, 1951, vol. 6, pt. 1A.

24. Census of India, Paper 5 of 1953.

25. Census of India, Paper 2 of 1954 (life tables–1951).

26. Census of India, Paper 4 of 1954 (displaced persons).

27. Census of India, Paper 1 of 1957 (general population tables and summary figures by districts of reorganized states).

28. Census of India, 1961, Paper 2 of 1963 (age tables).

29. Census of India, 1961, vol. 1, pt. 2A(i).

30. Census of India, 1961, vol. 1, pt. 2C(i).

31. Census of India, 1961, vol. 1, pt. 2C(iii) (migration tables).

32. Census of India, 1971, Series 1, Paper 1 of 1972.

33. Chandrasekhara, A. *Census of India, 1971: All-India Census Tables* (estimated from 1 percent sample data), Series 1, India, pt. 2, Special. New Delhi, 1972.

34. Chandrasekhara, A. *Census of India, 1971: Economic Characteristics of Population* (selected tables), Series 1, India, Paper 3 of 1972. New Delhi, 1972.

35. Chandrasekharan, C., and M.G. George. Mechanism Underlying the Differences in Fertility Patterns of Bengalee Women from Three Socio-economic Groups. *Milbank Memorial Fund Quarterly* 40(1), 1962.

36. Clark, Colin. *Population Growth and Land Use.* New York: Macmillan, 1967.

37. Coale, Ansley J. The Effects of Changes in Mortality and Fertility on Age-Composition. *Milbank Memorial Fund Quarterly* 34, January 1956.

38. Coale, Ansley J. Estimates of Various Demographic Measures Through the Quasi-Stable Age-Distribution. In *Emerging Techniques in Population Research.* New York: Milbank Memorial Fund, 1963.

39. Coale, Ansley J. How a Population Ages or Grows Younger. In *Population: The Vital Revolution,* ed. Ronald Freedman. New York: Doubleday, 1964.

40. Coale, Ansley J. *The Growth and Structure of Human Populations: A Mathematical Investigation.* Princeton: Princeton University Press, 1972.

41. Coale, Ansley J. The Determination of Vital Rates in the Absence of Registration Data. *Milbank Memorial Fund Quarterly* 49(4), pt. 2, October 1971.

42. Coale, Ansley J., and Paul Demeny. *Regional Life Tables and Stable Populations,* pt. 2. Princeton: Princeton University Press, 1966.

43. Coale, Ansley J., and Edgar M. Hoover. *Population Growth and Economic Development in Low Income Countries.* Princeton: Princeton University Press, 1958.

44. Colecraft, E.A. Social and Economic Aspects of the Problem. In *Population Growth and Economic Development in Africa.* London: Heinemann, 1972.

45. Commission on Population Growth and the American Future. *Population and the American Future.* Washington: U.S. Government Printing Office, 1972.

46.   Das Gupta, Ajit. An Empirical Approach to the Measurement of Under-employment. *Bulletin of the International Statistical Institute,* 32nd session, vol. 38, bk. 2. Tokyo, 1960.

47.   Davis, Kingsley. *The Population of India and Pakistan.* Princeton: Princeton University Press, 1951.

48.   Davis, Kingsley. Cities and Mortality. In *Proceedings of the International Population Conference,* vol. 3. Liege, 1973.

49.   Demeny, Paul. Estimates of Vital Rates for Populations in the Process of Destabilization. *Demography* 2, 1965.

50.   Demeny, Paul. Investment Allocation and Population Growth. *Demography* 2, 1965.

51.   Durand, John B. Population Growth and Changing Structure of Economic Activity. In *Interrelation between Population and Manpower Problems.* Bangkok: U.N. Economic Commission for Asia and the Far East, 1972.

52.   Easterlin, Richard A. Effects of Population Growth on the Economic Development of Developing Countries. American Academy of Political and Social Science *Annals* 369, January 1967.

53.   Enke, Stephen. The Economic Aspects of Slowing Population Growth. *Economic Journal* 76(301), March 1966.

54.   Gini, Corrado. Note in *Economic Journal,* March 1921.

55.   Gordon, J.E.; Sohan Singh; and J.B. Wyon. Demographic Characteristics of Deaths in Eleven Punjab Villages. *Indian Journal of Medical Research* 51(2), March 1963.

56.   Gordon, J.E.; Sohan Singh; and J.B. Wyon. A Field Study of Deaths and Causes of Death in Rural Populations of the Punjab, India. *American Journal of Medical Sciences* 241(3), March 1961.

57.   Government of India, Child Marriage Restraint Act. In *India Code,* vol. 3, pt. 4. New Delhi, 1929.

58.   Government of India Planning Commission. *Approach to the Fifth Five Year Plan: 1974–79.* New Delhi, 1973.

59.   Hainsworth, G.B. The Lorenz Curve as a General Tool of Economic Analysis. *Economic Record* 40, 1964.

60.   Hainsworth, G.B. Measures of Imbalance in International Trade Payments. *Sankhya: The Indian Journal of Statistics* 29, series B, pt. 1 and 2. Calcutta, June 1967.

61. Harbison, Frederick H., and Charles A. Myers. *Education, Manpower and Economic Growth.* New York: McGraw-Hill, 1964.

62. Hodge, G., and J.D. Paris. Population Growth and Regional Development: Implications for Educational Planning. In *Demography and Educational Planning,* ed. Betty McLeod. Toronto: Ontario Institute for Studies in Education, 1970.

63. Hoover, Edgar M., and Mark Perlman. Measuring the Effects of Population Control on Economic Development. *Pakistan Development Review* 6(4), 1966.

64. Government of India, Cabinet Secretariat. The National Sample Survey, 14th Round, no. 48, *Preliminary Estimates of Birth and Death Rates and of the Rate of Growth of Population.* Delhi, 1961.

65. Indian Statistical Institute, National Sample Survey, 14th Round—Rural, July 1958—June 1959, no. 76, *Fertility and Mortality Rates in India.* Cabinet Secretariat, Government of India, 1963.

66. Indian Statistical Institute, National Sample Survey, 18th Round, mimeographed report, *Preliminary Estimates of Birth and Death Rates and the Rate of Growth of Population.* Calcutta, 1965.

67. Jain, S.P. The Indian Programme for Improving Basic Registration. In *Papers Contributed by Indian Authors to the World Population Conference, Belgrade, Yugoslavia.* New Delhi: Office of the Registrar General, 1965.

68. Karmel, P.H. The Relations between Male and Female Reproduction Rates. *Population Studies* 1, 1947.

69. Keyfitz, Nathan. *Introduction to the Mathematics of Population.* Reading, Mass.: Addison-Wesley, 1968.

70. Keyfitz, Nathan, and Wilhelm Flieger. *World Population: An Analysis of Vital Data.* Chicago: University of Chicago Press, 1968.

71. Kurup, R.S. A Revision of Model Life Tables. In *Papers Contributed by Indian Authors to the World Population Conference, Belgrade, Yugoslavia.* New Delhi: Office of the Registrar General, 1965.

72. Kuznets, Simon. Population Change and Aggregate Output. In *Demographic and Economic Change in Developed Countries.* New York: National Bureau of Economic Research, 1960.

73. Lal, Brijesh B. Length of Life in India. *Sample Registration Bulletin* 8(1). Registrar General, New Delhi, April 1974.

74. Lee, Everett, et al. *Population Redistribution and Economic Growth in the*

United States: 1870–1950, pt. 1. Philadelphia: American Philosophical Society, 1967.

75.   Lopez, Alvaro. *Problems in Stable Population Theory.* Princeton: Office of Population Research, Princeton University, 1961.

76.   Lorenz, M.C. Methods of Measuring the Concentration of Wealth. *Publications of the American Statistical Association,* vol. 9, new series, 1905.

77.   Lorimer, F. Dynamics of Age-Structure in a Population with Initially High Fertility and Mortality. *Population Bulletin of the United Nations,* 1951.

78.   Lotka, A.J. On the True Rate of Natural Increase (appendix). *Journal of the American Statistical Association* 20(150), new series, September 1962.

79.   Meade, J.E. *The Growing Economy.* London: Allen & Unwin, 1968.

80.   Mitra, S. The Pattern of Age-specific Fertility Rates. *Demography* 4(2), 1967.

81.   Mukherjee, S.B. Inconsistency between Male and Female Reproduction Rates. *Bulletin of the Calcutta Statistical Association,* Department of Statistics, Calcutta University, 1957.

82.   Notestein, F.W. Mortality, Fertility, Size, Age Distribution and the Growth Rate. In *Demographic and Economic Change in Developed Countries.* New York: National Bureau of Economic Research, 1960.

83.   Okazaki, Y. Population Change and Development in Man Power, Labour Force, Employment and Income. In *Population Aspects of Social Development.* Bangkok: ECAFE, 1972.

84.   Ramabhadran, V.K. Experience and Problems in the Creation of the Sample Registration System in India. Paper presented at the International Symposium on Statistical Problems in Population Research, Honolulu, 1971.

85.   Risley, H.H., and E.A. Gait. *Census of India, 1901 Report,* vol. 1, pt. 1, 1903.

86.   Saxena, G.P. Estimates of Fertility and Mortality in India from 1901 to 1961. In *Papers Contributed by Indian Authors to the World Population Conference, Belgrade, Yugoslavia.* New Delhi: Office of the Registrar General, 1965.

87.   Sharma, H.M. *Enquiry into Infant Mortality in Poonamallee Health Unit Area.* Mimeographed, Madras, 1955.

88.   Shryock, Henry S., et al. *The Methods and Materials of Demography.* Washington: Bureau of the Census, 1971.

89. United Nations Population Division, Department of Social Affairs. The Causes of the Aging of Populations: Declining Mortality or Declining Fertility? *Population Bulletin of the United Nations* 4, 1954.

90. United Nations Population Division, Department of Social Affairs. *Age and Sex Patterns of Mortality: Model Life Tables for Underdeveloped Countries.* New York: United Nations, 1955.

91. United Nations Population Division, Department of Social Affairs. *Methods of Appraisal of Quality of Basic Data for Population Studies,* no. 23, manual 2. New York: United Nations, 1955.

92. United Nations Population Division, Department of Social Affairs. *The Aging of Populations and Its Economic and Social Implications.* Population Studies no. 26. New York: United Nations, 1956.

93. United Nations Population Division, Department of Social Affairs. *Recent Trends in Fertility in Industrialized Countries.* Population Studies no. 27. New York: United Nations, 1958.

94. United Nations Population Division, Department of Social Affairs. *The Aging of Populations and Its Consequences in Industrialized Countries.* Population Studies no. 27. New York: United Nations, 1958.

95. United Nations Population Division, Department of Social Affairs. *The Mysore Population Studies.* Population Studies no. 34, ST/SOA/Series A/34. New York: United Nations, 1961.

96. United Nations Economic Commission for Africa. *Principles of Applications of Demographic Data and Analysis to Development Planning in Reference to Africa.* E/CN, 14/Pop/3. Addis Ababa: United Nations, 1964.

97. United Nations Economic Commission for Africa. *Technical Paper on Non-sampling Errors and Biases in Retrospective Demographic Enquiries.* E/CE, 14/CAS, 4/vs/3. Addis Ababa: United Nations, 1964.

98. United Nations Department of Economic and Social Affairs. *General Principles for National Programmes of Population Projections as Aids to Development Planning.* New York: United Nations, 1965.

99. United Nations Department of Economic and Social Affairs. *Methods of Estimating Basic Demographic Measures from Incomplete Data.* New York: United Nations, 1967.

100. United Nations Department of Economic and Social Affairs. Estimates of Birth Rate and Expectation of Life in India on the Basis of Quasi-stability. In *Proceedings of the World Population Conference, Belgrade, 1965,* vol. 1. New York: United Nations, 1967.

101. United Nations Department of Economic and Social Affairs. *Methods of Estimating Housing Needs.* New York: United Nations, 1967.

102. United Nations Department of Economic and Social Affairs. Papers on Demographic Aspects of Savings, Investments, Technological Development and Industrialization. In *Proceedings of the World Population Conference, Belgrade, 1965,* vol. 4. New York: United Nations, 1967.

103. United Nations Department of Economic and Social Affairs. Papers on Demographic Aspects of Economic Growth. In *Proceedings of the World Population Conference, Belgrade, 1965,* vol. 4. New York: United Nations, 1967.

104. United Nations Department of Economic and Social Affairs. *The Concept of a Stable Population: Application to the Study of Population of Countries with Incomplete Demographic Statistics.* New York: United Nations, 1968.

105. United Nations Department of Economic and Social Affairs. *Population Aspects of Social Development.* Asian Population Studies, series 11. Bangkok: United Nations, 1972.

106. United Nations Department of Economic and Social Affairs. *Report of the Inter-regional Seminar on Application of Demographic Data and Studies to Development Planning, Kiev, 1964.* E/Cn, 9/223. New York: United Nations, 1969.

107. United Nations World Health Organization. *National Health Planning in Developing Countries.* Geneva, 1967.

108. United States Department of Labor. *The Forecasting of Manpower Requirements.* Washington, 1963.

109. Vaidyanathan, L.S. Actuarial Report on Age Returns and Life Tables for India and for Provinces. *Census of India 1931,* vol. 1, pt. 1.

110. Visaria, P.M. Mortality and Fertility in India: 1951–1961. *Milbank Memorial Fund Quarterly,* January 1961.

111. Yntema, L. *Mathematical Models of Demographic Analysis.* Leiden: Green & Zoon, 1952.

112. Zachariah, K.C. *Historical Study of Internal Migration in India.* Bombay: Demographic Research Institute, 1960.

References for basic tables

All references relate to Census of India reports for respective years and administrative divisions. In some cases complete references are not available.

Andaman and Nicobar Islands

1881, Andamans.
1901, Andaman and Nicobar Islands, vol. 3, p. 298.
1911, Andaman and Nicobar Islands, vol. 2, pt. 2, pp. 131–137.
1921, Andaman and Nicobar Islands, vol. 2, pt. 2, pp. 57–64.
1931, Andaman and Nicobar Islands, vol. 2, pt. 2, pp. 105–108.
1941, Andaman and Nicobar Islands, vol. 13.
1951, Andaman and Nicobar Islands, vol. 17, pt. 2, pp. 43–45.
1961, India, vol. 1, pt. 2C(i), pp. 454–455.

Andhra Pradesh

1881, Hyderabad, vol. 1.
1881, Madras, vol. 2, table 7.
1891, Hyderabad, vol. 23.
1891, Madras, vol. 14, pp. 26–57.
1901, Hyderabad, vol. 22-A, pt. 2, pp. 57–128.
1901, Madras, vol. 15-A, pt. 2, pp. 57–76.
1911, Hyderabad, vol. 19, pt. 2, pp. 37–62.

Andhra Pradesh *(continued)*

1911, Madras, vol. 12, pt. 2, pp. 28–59.
1921, Hyderabad, vol. 21, pt. 2, pp. 25–52.
1921, Madras, vol. 13, pt. 2, pp. 32–59.
1931, Hyderabad, vol. 22, pt. 2, pp. 41–82.
1931, Madras, vol. 14, pt. 2, pp. 44–71.
1941, Hyderabad, vol. 21, pt. 2.
1941, Madras, vol. 2.
1941 age tables (Madras) on Y samples, paper 8, 1951, pp. 4–14, 24–38.
1951, Hyderabad, vol. 9, pt. 2, pp. 89–98.
1951, Madras, vol. 3, pt. 2, pp. 72–96.
1961, India, vol. 1, pt. 2C(i), pp. 424–425.

Assam

1881, Assam, appendix B, table 7, pp. 2–3.
1891, Assam, vol. 2, pp. 44–50.
1901, Assam, vol. 4-A, pt. 2, pp. 10–33.
1911, Assam, vol. 3, pt. 2, pp. 15–33.
1921, Assam, vol. 3, pt. 2, pp. 16–36.
1931, Assam, vol. 3, pt. 2, pp. 36–62.
1941, Assam, vol. 9.
1941 age tables on Y samples, paper 1, 1949, pp. 2–8, 14–26.
1951, Assam, vol. 12, pt. 2B, pp. 251–306.
1961, Assam, vol. 3, pt. 2C, pp. 46–59.

Bihar

1881, Bengal, vol. 2, pp. 59–157.
1891, Bengal, vol. 4, pt. 2, pp. 113–250.
1901, Bengal, vol. 6-A, pt. 2, pp. 25–53.
1911, Bengal Bihar, Orissa, and Sikkim, vol. 5, pt. 3, pp. 27–39.
1921, Bihar and Orissa, vol. 7, pt. 2, pp. 27–44.
1931, Bihar and Orissa, vol. 7, pt. 2, pp. 29–46.
1941, Bihar, vol. 7, pt. 2, pp. 126–127.
1941 age tables on Y samples, paper 5, 1950, pp. 2–9, 17–25.
1951, Bihar, vol. 5, pt. 2A, pp. 245–284.
1961, India, vol. 1, pt. 2C(i), pp. 428–429.

Delhi

1881–1921, Delhi: same as Haryana.
1931, Delhi, vol. 16, pt. 2, pp. 51–71.
1941, Delhi, vol. 16, pp. 92–95.
1951, Delhi, vol. 8, pt. 2.
1961, India, vol. 1, pt. 2C(i), pp. 456–457.

Gujarat

1881, Bombay, vol. 2, pp. 25–34, 116–125.
1891, Bombay, vol. 8, pt. 2, pp. 47–84, xxxi–lvi.
1901, Bombay, vol. 9-A, pt. 2, pp. 53–96.
1911, Bombay, vol. 7, pt. 2, pp. 63–98.
1921, Bombay, vol. 8, pt. 2, pp. 62–98.
1931, Bombay, vol. 8, pt. 2, pp. 93–133.
1941, Bombay, vol. 3, pp. 127–137.
1941 age tables (Bombay) on Y samples, paper 10, 1951, pp. 1–31.
1951, Bombay, vol. 4, pt. 2B, pp. 417–454.
1961, India, vol. 1, pt. 2C(i), pp. 430–431.

Haryana

1881, Punjab, vol. 2, table 7.
1891, Punjab, vol. 20, pt. 2, pp. 46–87.
1901, Punjab, vol. 18-A, pt. 2, table 7, pp. i–xxx.
1911, Punjab, vol. 14, pt. 2, pp. 46–99.
1921, Punjab, vol. 15, pt. 2, pp. 34–91.
1931, Punjab, vol. 17, pt. 2, pp. 69–123.
1941, Punjab, vol. 6, pp. 66–69.
1941 age tables (Punjab) on Y samples, paper 7, 1951, pp. 4–9, 16–23.
1951, Punjab, Pepsu, and Himachal Pradesh, vol. 8, pt. 2A, pp. 179–269.
1961, Punjab, vol. 13, pt. 2C(i), pp. 182–220.

Himachal Pradesh

1881–1951, Himachal Pradesh: same as Haryana.
1961, India, vol. 1, pt. 2C(i), pp. 458–459.

Jammu and Kashmir

1891, Kashmir, vol. 28.
1901, Kashmir, vol. 23-A, pt. 2, pp. 37–47.
1911, Kashmir, vol. 20, pt. 2, pp. 31–48.
1921, Kashmir, vol. 22, pt. 2, pp. 19–44.
1931, Jammu and Kashmir, vol. 24, pt. 2, pp. 31–74.
1941, Kashmir, vol. 22, pt. 2, pp. 137–181.
1951, Kashmir: not available.
1961, India, vol. 1, pt. 2C(i), pp. 432–433.

Kerala

1881, Madras, vol. 2.
1891, Cochin, vol. 2, pp. 17–33.
1891, Travancore, vol. 2, pp. 12–47.
1901, Cochin, vol. 20-A, pt. 2, pp. 10–18.

Kerala *(continued)*

1901, Travancore, vol. 26-A, pt. 2, pp. 25–65.
1911, Cochin, vol. 18, pt. 2, tables 7, 15.
1911, Travancore, vol. 23, pt. 2, pp. 17–30.
1921, Cochin, vol. 19, pt. 2, table 7, p. xvi.
1921, Travancore, vol. 25, pt. 2, pp. 13–22.
1931, Cochin, vol. 21, pt. 2, table 7, p. xvii.
1931, Travancore, vol. 28, pt. 2, pp. 25–30.
1941, Cochin, vol. 19, pt. 2.
1941, Travancore, vol. 25, pt. 2, pp. 39–84.
1951, Travancore-Cochin, vol. 13, pt. 2, pp. 177–189.
1961, India, vol. 1, pt. 2C(i), pp. 434–435.

Laccadive, Minicoy, and Amindivi Islands

1881–1951, Laccadive, Minicoy, and Amindivi Islands: not available.
1961, India, vol. 1, pt. 2C(i), pp. 460–461.

Madhya Pradesh

1881, Central India, table 7.
1891, Central India, vol. 12, pt. 2, pp. 10–43.
1901, Central India, vol. 13-A, pt. 2, pp. 57–128.
1911, Central Provinces and Berar, vol. 10, pt. 2, pp. 36–51.
1921, Central India Agency, vol. 20, pt. 2.
1921, Central Provinces and Berar, vol. 11, pt. 2, pp. 38–57.
1931, Central India Agency, vol. 20, pt. 2, pp. 44–81.
1931, Central Provinces and Berar, vol. 12, pt. 2, pp. 51–78.
1941, Central India, vol. 18, pt. 2.
1941, Central Provinces and Berar, vol. 8, pt. 2.
1941 age tables on Y samples, paper 9, 1951, pp. 4–39.
1951, Madhya Pradesh, vol. 7, pt. 2C, pp. 125–170.
1951, Madhya Bharat and Bhopal, vol. 15, pt. 2, pp. 181–213.
1961, India, vol. 1, pt. 2C(i), pp. 436–437.

Maharashtra

1881, Bombay Presidency, vol. 2, pp. 25–34, 116–125.
1881, Central Provinces, vol. 2, pp. 60–75.
1881, Hyderabad, vol. 1.
1891, Bombay, vol. 8, pt. 2, pp. 47–84, xxxi–lvi.
1891, Central Provinces, vol. 12, pt. 2, pp. 10–43.
1891, Hyderabad, vol. 23, pt. 2.
1901, Bombay, vol. 9-A, pt. 2, pp. 53–96.
1901, Central Provinces, vol. 13-A, pt. 2, pp. 57–128.
1901, Hyderabad, vol. 22-A, pt. 2, pp. 30–64.

Maharashtra *(continued)*

1911, Bombay, vol. 7, pt. 2, pp. 63–98.
1911, Central Provinces, vol. 10, pt. 2, pp. 36–51.
1911, Hyderabad, vol. 19, pt. 2, pp. 37–62.
1921, Bombay, vol. 8, pt. 2, pp. 62–98.
1921, Central Provinces, vol. 11, pt. 2, pp. 38–57.
1921, Hyderabad, vol. 21, pt. 2, pp. 25–52.
1931, Bombay, vol. 8, pt. 2, pp. 93–133.
1931, Central Provinces, vol. 12, pt. 2, pp. 51–78.
1931, Hyderabad, vol. 22, pt. 2, pp. 41–82.
1941, Bombay, vol. 3, pt. 2, pp. 127–137.
1941, Central Provinces, vol. 8, pt. 2.
1941, Hyderabad, vol. 21, pt. 2.
1941 age tables (Bombay) on Y samples, paper 10, 1951, pp. 2–31.
1941 age tables (Madhya Pradesh) on Y samples, paper 9, 1951, pp. 4–39.
1951, Bombay, Saurashtra, and Kutch, vol. 4, pt. 2B, pp. 417–454.
1951, Hyderabad, vol. 9, pt. 2B, pp. 89–98.
1951, Middle Provinces, vol. 15, pt. 2.
1961, India, vol. 1, pt. 2C(i), pp. 440–441.

Manipur

1881, Assam, vol. 2, p. 146.
1891–1931, Manipur: same as Assam.
1941, Assam, vol. 9.
1951, Assam, Manipur, and Tripura, vol. 12, pt. 2, pp. 302–303.
1961, India, vol. 1, pt. 2C(i), pp. 462–463.

Meghalaya

1881–1951, Meghalaya: same as Assam.
1961, Assam, vol. 3, pt. 2C(i), pp. 56–57.

Mysore

1881, Mysore, vol. 5, pp. 10–20.
1891, Mysore, vol. 25, pt. 2.
1901, Mysore, vol. 24-A, pt. 2, table 7.
1911, Mysore, vol. 21, pt. 2, pp. 25–50.
1921, Mysore, vol. 23, pt. 2, pp. 27–50.
1931, Mysore, vol. 21, pt. 2, pp. 33–68.
1941, Mysore, vol. 23, pt. 2, pp. 47–83.
1951, Mysore, vol. 14, pt. 2, pp. 237–270.
1961, India, vol. 1, pt. 2C(i), pp. 442–443.

Orissa

1881–1931, Orissa: same as Bihar.
1941, Orissa, vol. 11, pp. 45–51.
1941 age tables on Y samples, paper 4, 1949, pp. 4–8, 14–20.
1951, Orissa, vol. 11, pt. 2, pp. 247–273.
1961, India, vol. 1, pt. 2C(i), pp. 444–445.

Punjab

1881–1931, Punjab: same as Haryana.
1941, Punjab, vol. 6, pt. 2, pp. 36–39.
1941 age tables on Y samples, paper 7, 1951, pp. 4–9, 16–23.
1951, Punjab, Pepsu, and Himachal Pradesh, vol. 8, pt. 2, pp. 179–269.
1961, Punjab, vol. 8, pt. 2C(i), pp. 182–220.

Rajasthan

1881, Ajmer-Merwara.
1881, Rajputana.
1891, Ajmer-Merwara.
1891, Rajputana, vol. 26, pt. 2, p. xxxi.
1901, Ajmer-Merwara, vol. 2-A, pt. 2, pp. 25–50.
1901, Rajputana, vol. 25-A, pt. 2, pp. 36–108.
1911, Rajputana and Ajmer-Merwara, vol. 22, pt. 2, pp. 25–67.
1921, Rajputana and Ajmer-Merwara, vol. 24, pt. 2, pp. 29–58.
1931, Rajputana and Ajmer-Merwara, vol. 26.
1931, Rajputana Agency, vol. 27, pt. 2, pp. 36–61.
1941, Ajmer-Merwara, vol. 24, pt. 2.
1941, Rajputana.
1951, Rajasthan and Ajmer, vol. 10, pt. 2, pp. 197–245.
1961, India, vol. 1, pt. 2C, pp. 448–449.

Tamil Nadu

1881, Madras, vol. 2, table 7.
1891, Madras, vol. 14, pt. 2, pp. 25–103.
1901, Madras, vol. 15-A, pt. 2, pp. 29–67.
1911, Madras, vol. 12, pt. 2, pp. 28–57.
1921, Madras, vol. 13, pt. 2, pp. 31–57.
1931, Madras, vol. 14, pt. 2, pp. 43–97.
1941, Madras, vol. 2.
1951, Madras, vol. 3, pt. 2, pp. 73–96.
1961, India, vol. 1, pt. 2C(i), pp. 438–439.

Tripura

1881–1941, Tripura: same as West Bengal.
1951, Assam, Manipur, and Tripura, vol. 12, pt. 2, pp. 304–305.
1961, India, vol. 1, pt. 2C(i), pp. 464–465.

Uttar Pradesh

1881, North-West Provinces and Oudh, vol. 2, table 7.
1891, North-West Provinces and Oudh, vol. 17, pt. 2, pp. 1–13.
1901, North-West Provinces and Oudh, vol. 16, pt. 2, pp. 41–73.
1911, United Provinces of Agra and Oudh, vol. 15, pt. 2, pp. 53–91.
1921, United Provinces of Agra and Oudh, vol. 16, pt. 2, pp. 55–93.
1931, United Provinces of Agra and Oudh, vol. 18, pt. 2, pp. 109–169.
1941, United Provinces, vol. 5.
1951, Uttar Pradesh, vol. 2, pt. 2.
1961, India, vol. 1, pt. 2C(i), pp. 450–451.

West Bengal

1881, Bengal, vol. 2, pp. 59–157.
1891, Bengal, vol. 4, pt. 2, pp. 113–250.
1901, Bengal, vol. 6-A, pt. 2, pp. 30–53.
1911, Bengal, Bihar, and Orissa, vol. 5, pt. 2, pp. 28–53.
1921, Bengal, vol. 5, pt. 2, pp. 31–68.
1931, Bengal and Sikkim, vol. 5, pt. 2, pp. 35–59.
1941, Bengal, vol. 4, pt. 2, pp. 109–120.
1941 age tables on Y samples, paper 1, 1948, pp. 1–29.
1951, West Bengal, Sikkim, and Chandernagore, vol. 6, pt. 2, pp. 313–395.
1961, India, vol. 1, pt. 2C(i), pp. 452–453.